ROB ROY
MACGREGOR

W.H. Murray, the distinguished writer and mountain-eer, was born in Liverpool in 1913 and educated at Glasgow Academy. He was employed by the Union Bank of Scotland and it was during the thirties that he discovered his love for the Scottish mountains.

In the Second World War, Murray served as a Captain in the Highland Light Infantry before being captured. It was during his imprisonment that he first began to write, but his manuscript was confiscated by the Germans. After the war he decided to write for a living and it was the book he had started while in prisoner of war camp that became his first published work – *Mountaineering in Scotland* (1947) was hailed as a masterpiece.

In the immediate post-war years he also took a leading part in a number of expeditions to the Himalayas and his pioneering work in this region prepared the way for Hilary's conquest of Everest in 1953.

Murray has gone on to write over twenty books in a number of fields including mountaineering, history and fiction. They include his *Companion Guide to the West Highlands* (1968), *The Islands of Western Scotland* (1973) and *Rob Roy MacGregor* (1982). His awards include the Mungo Park Medal for Himalayan exploration; the Literary Award of the U.S.A. Education Board; the O.B.E.; an Honorary Doctorate from Stirling University and a D.Litt from Strathclyde University.

He lives with his wife, Anne, in Argyll.

D0055149

ROB ROY'S SIGNATURE

At Portnellan 24th   Yours as formerly
June 1711   Ro: Campbell

Rob Roy signs as Ro: Campbell because his own name
had been proscribed

W H Murray

Rob Roy
MacGregor

His life and times

Canongate

First published in Great Britain in 1982 by
Richard Drew Publishing Ltd.
First published by Canongate Press Ltd. in 1993.
This editon published in 1995 by Canongate Books Ltd, 14 High
Street, Edinburgh EH1 1TE.

The publishers acknowledge the financial assistance of the
Scottish Arts Council in the publication of this volume.

British Library Cataloguing-in-Publication Data
A catalogue record for this book is available on request from
The British Library.

ISBN 0 86241 5381

Typeset by Palimpsest Book Production Limited,
Polmont, Stirlingshire
Printed and bound by W.S.O.Y., Porvoo, Finland

Contents

Acknowledgments

In writing this book I have received help and advice from many people. Among those to whom I feel greatly indebted are:
James D. Galbraith, Assistant Keeper at the Scottish Record Office, for advice on sources; Dr Barbara L. H. Horn at the Scottish Record Office for her kindness in making transcripts of Rob Roy's letters; J. K. Bates, Deputy Keeper of the National Register of Archives, and Dr Frances J. Shaw, for advice and help in getting access to various estate papers; Sir Gregor MacGregor of MacGregor and the archivists of Glasgow University for access to Clan Gregor Papers; Murdo MacDonald, archivist for Argyll and Bute District Council for advice on Argyll Papers; Sir Donald Cameron of Lochiel for his help in tracing a letter written in 1716 by John Cameron, Younger of Lochiel (about Rob Roy at the battle of Sheriffmuir); Alexander Fenton, Keeper of the National Museum of Antiquities, for advice on eighteenth-century buildings; Lachlan Mackinnon, Broadford, Skye, for a Gaelic translation; the Reverend Ian Muirhead, chairman of the Church of Scotland Historical Society, and Professor William H. C. Frend of Glasgow University, for advice on ecclesiastical history; and to R. E. Hutchison, Keeper of the Scottish National Portrait Gallery, for advice on portraits.

My thanks for permission to reproduce oil paintings go to the Duke of Atholl for the portrait of John, the first Duke of Atholl; to the Earl of Mar and Kellie for John, the sixth Earl of Mar (eleventh in the original creation); to the owner of the portrait (in a private collection) of James, the first Duke of Montrose; to the Scottish National Portrait Gallery for John, the second Duke of Argyll and for John, the first Earl of Breadalbane; to Edinburgh City Libraries for the drawing of the Tolbooth; to Glasgow Museums and Art Galleries for the pistols of Thomas Cadell; to the Mitchell Library, Glasgow, for the scenes of Glasgow, of Dunkeld and of Dumbarton; and to Donald Bennet and Tom Weir for scenic photographs.

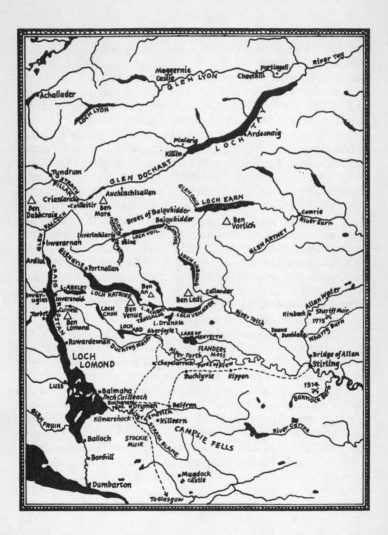

Foreword

ROB ROY MACGREGOR has been as elusive to biographers as he was in his own day to more dangerous pursuers. To the people of his time, his name and figure were so well known that no one thought of writing down a physical description, not even in proclamations of reward for arrest, whether issued to officers of the law by the Lord Advocate at Edinburgh, or to the press by the duke of Montrose, or in public posters from King George at St James's Palace. Nor is there direct record of his first eighteen years of life. The later, factual record of his adult life and character became buried long and deep in great chestsful of estate papers, which over the centuries had fallen into disorder. Rob Roy's life was there – a needle in a haystack problem, gradually opening to solution in recent years when archivists of the Public Record Offices, of universities, and of local authorities, were given the chance to bring order out of the chaos.

The personal record has needed interpretation from the social and political records of the Highlands. These reveal so much of his people's way of life, and even of the skills Rob Roy had developed under training, that an accurate account can be given of the kind of early life he lived, and be known as one from which his personal experience could have differed little. The lack of this account has led in the past to misapprehension of his character and motives. The two records, personal and social, have thus allowed me to track Rob Roy down to his own country and people, to establish his position there and in Scotland, to display his extraordinary virtues, misdeeds, failures, and aspirations, and to say in what way he came by them, and how they developed or why fell away.

I have been able to give Rob Roy's personal appearance and character in some detail, for these were passed on orally to writers of last century by men who had briefly met him in early years, but the man in his intimate life remains elusive still. We can imagine but not fully know. Those who could have told did not – 'everyone' knew Rob Roy.

It may seem surprising that his notoriety should have changed to lasting celebrity. After two hundred and fifty years there is no sign of its dying away. His statue by the Queen's Sculptor was recently unveiled at Stirling. My search into the reason has been rewarding, the more so because the early written 'Lives' fell far short of the truth.

Fictitious or mistaken as published stories were, they did hold truth enough to support common belief and draw a respect for the man even from enemies. His acts of rough justice had been free of the terrorist's cruelty so familiar to us today. People of his own country could identify with his aim. His character and lifestyle captured public imagination, especially after the publication by Daniel Defoe of his *Highland Rogue* in 1723.

The rulers and leaders of Britain, south of the Highland Line, had been unaware that men of their country could live like North American Indians in a primitive accord with nature. They had forgotten their roots in a too long and envious contemplation of Europe's social sophistication. This to them was the time of the *Grand Monarque* in France, and Scotland's 'Auld Alliance' still loosely held. Most Scots of family knew Paris better than London. Louis XIV, the sun of Europe's social world, had built his palace of Versailles with the fabulous *Galerie des Glaces*, salons, and staterooms overlooking a park with an orangery, flashing fountains, and a Grand Canal covered with Venetian gondolas. Through the tapestried apartments, courtiers on high red heels strutted with the support of beribboned canes. Gorgeous as their silk and lace and huge powdered wigs might be, their ladies surpassed them. Silks and satins were ballooned like para-chutes around their hips and towers of powdered hair crowned their heads. All over Europe, including Britain, Louis' splendour had aroused emulation in miniature by princes and nobles rich enough to afford it. Hard-headed politicians admired his policy of bribery, which he had elevated to a state system that could often gain his ends more economically than war and repression. This double decadence, material and moral, had invaded every country including Scotland, until nowhere was there righteous leadership. Even the Stewart kings were on his payroll. The iniquitous social system entailed suppression of the lower orders, yet did allow the flowering of the arts. Among the European masters were: in literature, Addison and Swift; in science, Newton and Boyle; in music, Bach and Handel; in painting, Watteau and Hogarth; in architecture, Wren and Vanbrugh. Against that backdrop of flourishing arts and fantastic luxury, Rob Roy's life startled his countrymen by its incongruity, its alarming closeness to their own doorsteps, and its robust vigour combining so oddly with kindness.

This had topical concern for his fellow Scots and Englishmen. A civilization that unites vigour with gentleness in other than fine arts is a hard thing indeed to achieve, as the people had been learning at first hand from the cruelties of religious and civil rulers who preceded and followed the 'Glorious Revolution'. The Stewart dynasty had been toppled. New ways of government were on trial. Scotsmen had been persuaded (in part by Queen Anne's bribes dispensed after the example of Louis) to give up their independent Parliament. The national figure cut by Rob Roy became one among other warnings of danger ahead. The political aspirations of Gaeldom were not those of the Lowlands, or of the Edinburgh and London Parliaments in which the common people had no voice. Violent expression was inevitable, failing reforms in law and franchise.

That Rob's fame endured beyond his time had nothing to do with his politics, and little to do with Walter Scott's use of his name to title a good novel, but everything to do with his force of character. Rob had figured in Scott's story incidentally and been grossly libelled, although still with the grain of truth that won esteem. His life's lasting value came of his fight to keep personal integrity through long trial. He was not like Job a man of piety. But he did have an uncommon regard for his fellow men and the Highland way of life. Perhaps in the courts of Heaven the 'Adversary' had repeated against Rob the old charge made against privileged men, that he loved because he prospered. The test was made. Adversities were heaped up until he could know temptation in anguish and yet, by a simple betrayal of trust, end all ills. The predicament is universal to man, and the way it is met of perennial interest. The strengths of mind, will, and heart required to confront it were in Rob, and I should have liked to believe that the public discerned this behind the romantic narratives of Defoe, Macleay, Scott, and Millar. Instead, I think the people of the Lowland South ranked him with his buccaneering contemporary Edward Teach (Blackbeard of the Spanish Main), or, in more recent times, perhaps with Al Capone. It is a vagary of the human mind to exalt chosen villains above their infamy. The honour thus paid to Rob Roy was for once the man's due, although not until this century, and only since mid-century, has it become possible to win the true facts from original sources.

To get the truth, or as near to it as possible, I have searched out Rob's life in the estate papers of Argyll, Atholl, Breadalbane, Buchanan, MacGregor, Montrose, and others; in the records of the Privy Council, Estates of Parliament, and local government; in the historical MSS held by the Scottish Record Office, War Office, and the National Library; and in the social histories of the seventeenth and eighteenth centuries. The *Bibliography* gives a full list. The apparent anomalies in his character and acts, which had baffled early writers, now become explicable; his basic integrity emerges battered but unbroken, and a life that outwardly failed can be seen as the triumph it was.

In righting the wrong done to Rob Roy's name by Scott, and by the historians whom he and others followed, I have found Rob Roy to be of stronger character than the early writers had imagined. Their works on Rob Roy require so much correction and refutation that few readers would wish to plough a way through the quagmire. I have spared them an exposition of past errors save on a very few points of importance to character, and instead have given my sources.

A reader new to the social life of the Highlands of 1700 may receive an impression of economic poverty greater than it was, unless he appreciates the difference in the value of money then and now. No accurate comparison of prices and earnings can be made. Fuel was not bought, it came free from the peat-banks. Cattle, the staple of trade and wealth, were abundant but of very much smaller weight than today's. Clothes were mostly handwoven at home from home-grown wool and flax. All manner of domestic items were home-made, ranging from ploughs to houses. Wages were paid partly in kind, and rents almost wholly in kind. The merk mentioned in the text was a silver coin worth 13/$\frac{1}{3}$d sterling. The pound Scots equalled 1s. 8d. sterling. As a merely approximate indication of the value of money in 1700, I compared the prices of fifteen products in common use (given below) with their prices in a Highland village in 1982. These revealed an average price increase of nearly 170 times.

1700

oatmeal	6/8d	a boll =	$\frac{3}{4}$p a pound
flour	6/8d	a stone =	$2\frac{1}{2}$p a pound
butter	3/4d	a stone =	$1\frac{1}{4}$p a pound
cheese	1/8d	a stone=	$\frac{1}{2}$p a pound
sugar	1/-	a pound =	5p a pound
chicken $2\frac{1}{2}$lb	$2\frac{1}{2}$d	a bird =	1p
salmon	1d	a pound =	$\frac{1}{2}$p
mutton	1d	a pound =	$\frac{1}{2}$p
beef	1d	a pound =	$\frac{1}{2}$p
claret	1/4d	a bottle =	$6\frac{1}{2}$p
ale	$\frac{1}{2}$d	a pint =	$\frac{1}{4}$p
whisky	6d	a bottle =	$2\frac{1}{2}$p
shirt	6d	=	$2\frac{1}{2}$p
shoes	2/-	a pair =	10p
plaid	11/3d	=	56p

$89\frac{3}{4}$p

The Houses of Glenstrae, Glenlyon and Glenorchy

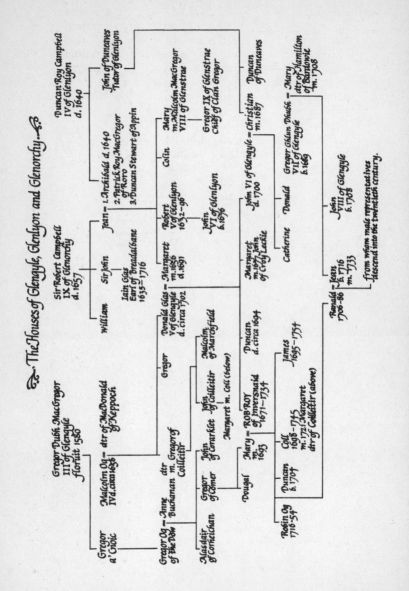

CHAPTER ONE

~

THE HOMELAND

Birth and Baptism

ROB ROY MACGREGOR was born at the head of Loch Katrine in February 1671, third son of Donald Glas, a chief of Clan Gregor, and his wife Margaret Campbell. The month of birth is known only from the record of baptism on March 7, for no Highland baby was left unbaptized for more than two or three weeks. The clergy insisted on haste and the people complied, for they (Protestants and Catholics alike) shared the common fear that if a baby died, as two-thirds of the new-born did,[1] he could not be called to Heaven if unchristened.

The Register of Baptisms of Buchanan (then called Inchcailleach) has this entry: 'On the 7 day of March 1671, Donald M'Gregor in Glengyle, ps of Calendar, upon testificat from ye minister yrof. Margaret Campbell son baptised called Robert. Witness, Mr Wm. Anderson, minister, and John MacGregor.'

Christenings took place in parishioners' homes, not in church. Although Donald's house stood in Callander parish, this christening was by the minister of Inchcailleach, to whose kirk Donald belonged. Most of the land he ruled lay in that parish, and all of it, including his farm in Glen Gyle, fell under the titular superiority of the chief of Buchanan. Donald and his clan were Protestants. The two parish churches were nominally of the Presbyterian Church, yet both ministers were of Episcopalian sympathy,[2] and later were Jacobites. They were able to retain their livings for two reasons. It was usual for Highlanders to accept their minister's view of the rival systems, which differed not at all in the verities of the faith, only in rules of which they were careless; and Episcopacy was favoured by king and Parliament (Charles II had to be publicly Protestant while secretly Catholic).

Rob Roy's descent was from both the Clan Gregor and Clan Campbell chieftains of Glengyle and Glenlyon, each branching from its own Glenorchy stock.[3] His mother, Margaret, now aged about thirty-five, had been brought up with her elder brother Robert, the fifth chieftain of Glenlyon, at Meggernie

1

Castle. Whether or not she inherited her Breadalbane family's good looks (her brother in youth had been called an Adonis),[4] she passed on to her youngest son their fair complexion and the name of her Campbell grandfather, Sir Robert, the ninth chief of Glenorchy. Since Clan Gregor had a strong settlement in Glen Lyon at Roro, men of the four other branches were frequent visitors; hence Margaret's sister Mary married Malcolm MacGregor, chief of the senior Glenstrae line and therefore of the whole clan, while Margaret in 1656 married Donald Glas, fifth chieftain of the youngest line named (from its founder) Clan Dughaill Ciar.

Donald had been named Glas, or pale, from the natural pallor of his skin. His people had occupied the land east of upper Loch Lomond and Glen Falloch since 1533, and held it *coir a' chlaidhheamh*, by right of the sword. Although charterless, Donald was acknowledged MacGregor of Glengyle in all legal and state papers. These titled him lieutenant-colonel from his command of a regiment of foot in the army of Charles II following the Restoration of 1660. He had taken this commission to get pay and training at a time when his clan was impoverished from more than a century's harassment by neighbours. As chieftain of a clan's branch, he was poor in land and cattle relative to those more powerful chiefs proper, who early in the century journeyed out of their castles with a 'tail' of up to twenty office-bearers. He lived close to his people and worked his own ground as they did, but for all this could command several gillies (young clansmen) to do his bidding, and could raise some three hundred fighting men at short notice, or nearly double that given time. His clansmen paid him rent in kind and services, as might be agreed between them; he in turn seeing to their defence, cattle-trade, domestic and land problems, and leadership in arms, including cattle raids far afield.

He and Margaret already had three children, all now in their early teens. Their eldest, Iain, would be at university (or recently down from it) for that was the rule for chiefs' eldest sons aged twelve to fourteen. His brother Duncan and sister Margaret were just a little younger. Iain, called John in all papers of the time, would not as a minor be the John MacGregor who witnessed the baptism. That would almost certainly be John in Corarklet, the eldest son of Donald's near neighbour, friend, and cousin, Gregor Og in the Dow of Glengyle.[5] His was the second family of the clan.

Donald's house, where he himself had been born, was the

biggest of Glengyle and a *tigh geal* or white house, so named because the outer stone-work was mortared, giving it a lighter appearance than dry-stone. It stood two or three hundred yards above the river Gyle's north bank. When he stood by the door on that christening day, he looked out across broad fields, nearly always in early March blanketed in snow, where a couple of garrons (Highland ponies) might be standing forlornly, nostrils smoking in the morning air. Half a mile beyond them, he would see the clan's birlinns (galleys) moored or beached alongside the stone jetty at the head of Loch Katrine. Early on a winter's morning, if there was no heavy cloud about, there would always come a sudden brightening of the sky seven miles east, where the rising sun struck the snow-cap of Ben Venue. All Strath Gartney below, including this nearer half of Loch Katrine, then lay gripped in ice-blue shadow.

The house measured at least seventy feet by fifteen internally.[6] Floors throughout were of stamped earth. The eastern quarter was a byre, sheltering in winter a few cows, goats, hens, and geese. The house proper, partitioned from the byre by thick pine-boards, was divided in three by stout wicker-work partitions raised to wall-height, but not to the roof, which had no loft. Hens perched on the top boards unless chased. Facing the door was a storeroom full of barrels, tubs, churns, quern, skins, chests, sacks of grain, earthenware pots, weapons, and weaving loom. To its right lay the bedroom, to its left the common room, lit early morning and night by tallow candles. A big iron pot hung on a chain from a roof beam over the central hearth, which vented smoke through a hole in the thatch. The blackened roof-tree and rafters were oak. The only furniture was a table, shelves, a few benches and stools, several chests, and straw mattresses, boxed. The uncurtained windows were glazed in their upper halves, shuttered in the lower. The gentlemen of a clan all had books, and one of Donald's shelves would bear a dozen to twenty in French, Latin, and English. A big Bible would be prominent among them, that too in English, for the first Gaelic translation was only now being edited by the Reverend Robert Kirk of Balquhidder.[7] It was customary for a man of Donald's position to read his family a verse or two from the scriptures daily, both for devotional reasons and to exercise his children in a needed tongue.

Baptisms, like weddings and funerals, were memorable social occasions in the Highlands. Most of the guests would walk in from ten miles around, but many would sail up Loch Katrine or Loch Lomond, unless the lochs were frozen, as they were for long periods every winter – the weather then was much harder than now.[8] The people, carrying food for the day, would thus arrive widely dispersed, enter the house to ask blessings on it, then receive token refreshments and go outside to mix with friends and neighbours.

Where a chief was host, the christening ceremony was followed by whisky and ale for hundreds, food for all who wanted, and a ceilidh at night. Unless old or infirm, all clan families would be represented, and of these there were a hundred and fifty at Craigrostan alone[9] (by Loch Lomondside at the townships of Inversnaid, Culness, Pollochro, Stucnaroy, Rowchois, Doune and others). There were thrice that number along the shores of Loch Katrine as far as the Trossachs and Brig o' Turk, and by Loch Ard, Loch Chon, Glen Dubh and Comer. That was still not counting the folk of Glen Gyle, or the long Balquhidder glen to the north-east, or the outposts in Glen Falloch. Guests from long distance would find floor-space at night in every available house. Rob's name that day was to be made known to many hundreds. It was to be known to a nation before he died.

The boy in his cradle by the fireside must have looked an unlikely candidate for notoriety. Like any other baby when the dawn fires were stoked, he had certainly squalled incessantly, eyes stung by smoke and his face licked by the passing collies. He had his mother's bright red hair, eye-catching even by candle-light, a halo destined to darken with the years, as hers had too, but meantime to be enjoyed, her boy's peculiar glory and constant reminder of her lost youth. If she already called him 'Rab ruadh' (anglicised by the world to Rob Roy) she would breathe it as an inward whisper, for ill-luck was held to attend open declaration before the sprinkling of water.

Margaret's dress was that of her people, which varied little from one glen to another save in minor detail. From shoulder to heel she wore a white plaid, sparsely criss-crossed with thin stripes of red, blue, and black.[10] The plaid was pleated and worn as an overdress, under which, and with sleeves displayed outside it, she wore a bodice, probably not the popular scarlet, which would have clashed with her hair, but more likely yellow or green. The bodice flowed full at the arm, but came tight at the gold lace of the wrists. The plaid was secured by a high leather belt inlaid with silver. Its plaited end, set with semi-precious stones, hung eighteen inches in front. Her plaid was fastened at the breast with a big brooch, either of silver or hammered brass, deeply engraved with interlaced rosettes and wild mammals. Her tanned hide brogues, cut to the shape of the feet, were no different from her menfolk's – thin soles, no heels, and uppers punched to let out water, for rivers rarely had bridges and the Highlands no roads. On her head she wore a white linen kerchief, folded to form the *corrachd tri-chearnach*, or three-cornered cap (symbolic of the Trinity) worn by all wives from the morning after marriage.[11]

Her boys were dressed like their father in the kilted plaid but without trews. Her girl, hair clasped in a maiden's snood, wore a sleeveless tartan smock and coloured blouse. All children went bare-foot even in winter, except for special occasions like today's, when the boys wore hose and brogues. Highland girls were no footgear.

On this cold March morning, with snow on the hills, Donald at forty was old enough to feel thankful for his close-fitting tartan trews, which held his legs in woollen warmth from foot to waist. His shirt was of white linen. Above it he wore a waistcoat of one colour, with another of tartan on top, but six inches longer with sleeves. Over all came his plaid of finely woven wool.[12] It was twelve to eighteen feet long and nearly five feet wide. To put it on, he would go outside, unless in wild weather, lay his broad leather belt on a bank by the house, shake out the plaid and fold it lengthwise on top of the belt, make several pleats at the near end of the cloth, then lie on top, buckle the belt, and so rise kilted. The long end of the plaid he drew loosely up his back and either for present warmth over both shoulders, or for free movement over the left shoulder and broadly across the chest, then around his back again to finish over the same shoulder, where he would pin it with a bodkin of deer's bone. The loops were thus left to hang at each hip, and the sword arm was left free. The tartan of reddish brown was a common one throughout the Highlands, since brown dyes were so easily had from bark. The particular sett or pattern of stripes was the choice of his wife Margaret who wove it, and not peculiar to Clan Gregor. Next month, when the snows had withdrawn to the tops, it would blend into hillsides of yellowed grass, browned heather, and dead bracken. His thick blue bonnet bore a sprig of Scots pine as badge of Clan Gregor, and for the day's occasion two eagle's feathers to mark his chieftainship.

No Highland chief receiving visitors felt properly dressed without his weapons. These, laid out for him on the common room bench, were a broadsword and belt, a foot-long dirk, and a pair of steel pistols with engraved butts. (When moving abroad he

would add to these a capacious calf's skin sporran, powder-horn
and shot, and a flintlock musket.) Girded with skin and steel,
Donald felt ready to face a christening.

When he glanced down at the cause of all this trouble, and saw
his son's innocent face, he may well have wondered how true it
could be that the boy had inherited original sin from Adam. His
minister reminded him so at each birth. If his boy died unbaptised,
he would suffer exclusion from the Kingdom of Heaven – not
be damned but subject to some milder kind of perdition. It
was hard to believe that God like man was uncompassionate:
to which the clergy answered, quoting St Augustine, that without
an inclination to evil a man could have no victory over sin, thus
no upbuilding of character. The *Treatise on Original Sin and
Confessions* stood with the Bible on most gentlemen's shelves.
Donald was able to appreciate that while baptism brought his
child the Holy Spirit's protection from Satan, that was only until
such time as he could think for himself. That is, if he were ever
to think on the subject at all – which Donald must have known
unlikely. If he felt a momentary twinge on the score of his own life,
it would certainly not include repentance for cattle raids, which
followed Highland custom. Men had to lift cattle according to
seasonal loss and need or else go under, or for sport in time
of plenty. Any cause of guilt came on the flood-tide of action,
when sudden greed moved a man to seize too much and leave his
victim destitute, or when sudden anger and fear spurred him to
kill, burn houses, hough cattle, fire barns. Men were mean, cruel,
bloody, and ferocious not just in the Highlands but everywhere,
and not least at every seat of government, whether in Edinburgh
or London. All fell short in compassion.

It is no idle speculation to wonder whether Donald thought
thus, and perhaps resolved to instil if he could compassion
in his youngest son; for instilled it was – strongly enough to
stand test. Compassion had to go too with a fighting spirit. If
he lacked that he'd be stamped down. No one knew it better
than a Gregarach father.

The people gathered. The boy was raised up, the dedication
made, and the oath sworn. Whatever hopeful words the Reverend William Anderson uttered that day, the good book had other
true things to say: 'I saw under the sun that the race is not to the
swift, nor the battle to the strong, neither yet bread to the wise,
nor yet riches to men of understanding, nor yet favour to men
of skill – but time and chance happeneth to them all.'

The Homeland

Rob Roy was lucky in the time of his birth. He had eighteen years of peace in which to grow. Clan wars had virtually ended by mid-century. Civil war had stopped with the restoration of Charles II, and even the Covenanters lay quiet for the present.

Glen Gyle formed the upper end of Strath Gartney. This great strath, nineteen miles long, split the Trossachs from lowland Callander to the hills at Loch Lomond's head. It was twisty, wooded, and more than two-thirds filled by the waters of Loch Venachar, Loch Achray, and Loch Katrine. The hills to either side rose close around the waters in broad ranges, split by a tangle of glens into forty tops, mostly rising above 2000 feet. They formed a ring of foothills to a still wider cirque of mountains, which lay farther out on a nine-mile radius from the Trossachs.

Apart from its foot-tracks, this whole Trossachs country was roadless, its intricate ways complicated for any visitor by wood and water, by bridgeless rivers and craggy hills. Yet the valleys were inhabited by several thousands of people.[13] The hills gave them shelter as a natural fortress enclosing good hill-pastures for large herds of cattle, and lower arable for oats and barley. Its heart was Loch Katrine.

There were three main gateways: the first from Callander or Aberfoyle by the pass of *Na Troiseachan*, the Cross-hills (anglicised to 'The Trossachs') – where a defile has been cut by the Achray Water; the second, the wooded Pass of Aberfoyle by the shore of Loch Ard; and the third to the north, where the pass of Balquhidder (pronounced Balwhidder) breached the outer mountain cirque.

These ways seem obvious on good maps, but in Rob Roy's day, when there were no Highland maps for travellers and all traffic went by boat, or on foot or pony-back, the Trossachs remained a wild fastness, unknown land except to its native people, and subject to false rumour of brigandage. Lowlanders had little incentive to approach the hills, much less travel into them. Scotland had no roads as now understood, or none that could take a stage coach. Coaches could use only town roads (and not even these north of the Tay, where the first was in 1725 at Inverness). All mail between towns went by foot-runners, even as far as Thurso from Edinburgh. Horses could travel no faster on the rough tracks – riders from Edinburgh to Moray took five days for 150 miles.[14] The Highland bridleways went by the drove roads, miry tracks over heather, bog, and river. The Trossachs for all its nearness to Glasgow remained for Lowlanders a mountainous backdrop scene, a foreign land where no English was spoken, to be approached by the venturesome few only for business reasons – men like factors from the fringing estates of Menteith, Atholl, or Breadalbane, itinerant pedlars, tailors, and cobblers, stocking-makers, gypsies, iron-smelters and their foresters, officers on reconnaissance or soldiers on duty. And these knew only the main glens.

Glen Gyle, where Rob was born and bred, was one of the least accessible valleys in all that country. The flanking hills rose to 2500 feet, but the Parlan pass, just a thousand feet above his house, gave a route of only five miles to Glen Falloch, where Inverarnan was the night stance, or resting place, for cattle herds driven from Argyll to the autumn tryst at Crieff. Smaller herds bound for the markets at Doune, Stirling, or Edinburgh crossed the Parlan pass to Glen Gyle and so by Loch Katrine's head to Aberfoyle. Seasonal traffic thus passed through the glens, which although now deserted were intensively cultivated.

The two principal families of Glengyle were those of Donald Glas and Gregor Og MacGregor, whose house faced Donald's across the glen. The two shared the same grandfather by descent from elder and younger sons. Donald's father, Malcolm Og the fourth chieftain, had been one of the heroes of his clan. The tale was still told at ceilidhs of his outmanœuvring the king's troops in 1610, when they came in force to extirpate Clan Gregor. His too was the first long-barrelled gun brought into the Trossachs – an event long remembered. On a hill by Loch Earn, he had shot one of the bloodhounds then much used in tracking his clansmen, and the hill to this day is named *Meall a' Mhadaidh*, the Hill of the Hound. In 1624, the earl of Moray had given Malcolm Og the farmland at Brig o' Turk, in reward for leading three hundred MacGregors to the Moray Firth, where they had driven Clan Chattan out of the earl's land of Petty.[15] Although Malcolm had died twenty years ago, his name lived, and still shed lustre on his sons and grandsons.

Gregor Og's house had been named the Dow, a corruption of Dubh, being a *tigh dubh* or black house, for its unmortared walls gave a darker appearance than Donald's *tigh geal*. Ten years ago, Gregor Og had acquired the lands of Stronachlachar, then of Comer, and finally of Corrie Arklet.[16] He had three sons: John had Corarklet, the farmland on the north side of Loch Arklet, which his father had bought just a year before from the chief of

Buchanan; Alexander, the youngest, was twenty and unmarried; and Gregor held Comer, a great green hollow on the north-east flank of Ben Lomond. Gregor's son Dougal was soon to have a sister christened Helen Mary, destined to marry Rob Roy.

Scattered around the glens and shores of the clan's land were numerous townships, or groups of houses whose tenants lived from the products of the land on which the houses stood. The groups varied in size from four to fifty houses. Few of these were stone-built. Most had turf walls and many turf roofs as well, so that in summer they looked like green hillocks. Poultry, sheep, and goats occasionally grazed over the roofs, and if the house were built against a steep bank, sometimes a cow too, for all were small and agile.[17]

Throughout the Highlands, stone houses were a rarity save at the Lowland fringes.[18] However built, none in the glens had chimneys. The rafters of stout branches were thatched with straw, bracken, rushes, turf, or heather (Glen Gyle had no heather), roped down to boulders along the wall-tops. The roofs' inner surfaces were darkened with peat-soot and leaked brown fluid in heavy rain – there was no furniture of a kind that could suffer harm. The walls being short, small windows were often placed deep in the thatch. They were unglazed and closed against wind or cold with a straw bung. Only the *duinevasal* or gentleman of a clan had glazed windows.

Stamped earth floors were universal. They became muddy in prolonged wet weather, and since the ground outside was then miry from the passage of cows, ponies, sheep, and goats, not to say fouled by their dung, all members of a family went about their daily work or play barelegged, skin being more readily washed than clothing. In every house from the chieftain's down to the townships' turf huts, the women fought an unflinching battle with dirt. Almost every day, summer or winter, some of them would be down at the Gyle Water with a big tubful of clothes. They rarely had soap unless they made it, and more often used a lye made from ashes. Skirts hoisted up to their knees, they washed their linen clean by long stamping in the tub. In hard frost their feet and legs became dull red with cold. To speed the job, two would often stamp in one tub with arms on each other's shoulders.

The furnishings of commoners' houses, whether in Highlands or Lowlands, differed little in the late seventeenth century. They were minimal. So too were crockery and cutlery. The plates and shallow drinking bowls (*cuach* in Gaelic, *quaich* in Scots) were wooden. A house had only one glass or pewter tankard for ale, whisky, and wine, which was handed round the company,[19] Spoons were horn or wood, and table cutlery rare. The house had cleavers and skinning knives, and the Highlanders dirks and hunting knives, but the people ate solid food from the fingers and picked the bones with their teeth. Stew pots were placed in the middle of the table and everyone helped himself with the spoon.[20] In the Highlands, sheets and towels were linen, which the people made at home, and the mattresses stuffed with straw. There were no clocks in the glens. People had the sun and stars above, and the habit of observation; they could judge time by the light and allow for cloud and season.

Donald, like other chieftains when at home and working his farm, dressed no differently from his clansmen. He held their respect by qualities of character, bearing, and leadership. Clan Gregor prized in its leading men above all else a clear head, courage, and personal vitality. On these their own safety depended.

Home and Family

Highland babies were fed from the breast till the end of their second year.[21] To the fore among Rob's early recollections of this world were most certainly winter cold and peat smoke, especially on dark mornings when the fire was built up and doors and windows had to be opened to icy draughts. He had to suffer the universal child-affliction, a perpetually running nose. Directly behind the house rose twin hills of 2400 feet, called the Meall and the Stob. The house had been built beside a burn running down between the two, and there Rob as a boy would be dragged by the hand for daily bathing. Adults as a general rule washed their faces only on Sundays, and always out of doors – in the Lowland countryside as well as the Highlands.[22]

Towards the end of his first year, when he was crawling, his mother would dress him in two shirts, linen and woollen, with nothing under them. In high winds and hard weather children were warmly wrapped in a plaid, but from the second year no cover was given to head or feet. Highland parents thought it unnecessary to coddle their children and bad to pay them too much attention. Out of doors they could run wild, but in cramped home quarters were disciplined.

The most comfortable times in winter were at evening and night, when the house was warmed up and the peats glowed red. The warm air from the hearth fire then held the smoke up to the roof, so that everyone sitting could be free of it.[23] Every kind of interesting activity was then under way: his mother and Duncan might be plaiting birch twigs for cordage, like halters and harness, or straw bands for horse-collars and cruppers; his sister, repairing a salmon net; Iain, fitting a new hemp or linen string to his bow, for the bow and arrow were still much used in hunting; his father, forever writing letters with his quill pen taken from the left wing of a goose (because the left quill curled outward), if not honing his dirk, broadsword, and the great blade of his fifteen-pound claymore, or his mother more enthrallingly might be making tallow candles.

The tallow was made from suet cut from the carcases of sheep and cows around Martinmas, when meat was salted down for the winter. Smelly fumes filled the house while the suet was melted down over the fire; then the tallow was poured into tin moulds through which flax wicks had been stretched tight. Tapers were made at the same time by dipping wicks of soft cord, or more often rush stalks. When the supply of tallow ran out, Margaret lit iron crusies. These had an open bath burning oil of any mammal fat, or fish, or butter or linseed, in which a pith wick floated, projecting over a lip at one side and giving off a smoky and smelly flame. Many poorer houses burnt nothing but rush lights, some no light at all apart from the hearth fire. All made occasional use of flaring pine splints, one of which if rich in turpentine could light up a room.[24]

A feature of every home was the mother's whirring spindle, which she fed with fleece or flax from a distaff. The teased out wool or tow between her fingers became drawn to a long thin yarn, and this for a brief space entranced the younger children – a magic she worked daily at all hours and nearly every night – until they took it for granted. (Spinning wheels were not used in the glens until next century.) Children had no toys other than gaily-coloured rag dolls. The games played by the family were dice, cards, and draughts.

Whatever the night's activities, if Donald were at home they were likely to be visited by neighbours near and afar, for every township had its problems and the men and women of the district had frequent need of a *ceilidh* (or conversation) with the chieftain. Often the room was packed. This indeed was the reason for the chieftain's bigger house. The community built the house to meet a need for all.

Rob fell asleep most nights to the hum of conversation coming clear over the tops of room-partitions. The sound was most soothing, peculiarly comforting in itself apart from the assurance that he and his family were surrounded by well-wishing friends. The knowledge of warm-heartedness sank deep into his mind and bound him to the people of his country. This was their life and his. Always a time would come when the talk gave way to stories and song, or to music on the chanter, pipes, and fiddle. A spontaneous demand would arise for poetry and the sagas of the race; no men were more respected than the bards, who retold the old tales and folklore. They would chant the longer ones in metre. These occasions were never formal. They arose in the course of the ceilidh, and were repeated in most houses of the community.

In summer, after the day's work and when supper had been eaten, the people would stroll round calling on each other, for no house was a place of private retreat. In one house or another a ceilidh would start and the rest followed. Since there were plenty of young around, dancing to the pipes would start up out of doors, where there was room. Dancing indoors in winter had to be limited to solo performances done to the fiddle, or in its frequent absence to *puirt-a-beul*, a mouth-music sung in rapid repetitive rhythm, sounding not unlike muted pipes. Its recurrent vowel sounds gave it a most lively quality. Rob like every other child grew up to the sound of music; it was part of everyone's life from cradle to grave, around the home and out in the summer fields; for there were labour songs for every mechanical action – rowing the galleys, grinding the corn by quern, spinning, reaping, milking and churning, waulking the cloth after weaving. Song was never so all-pervading in the Highlands as it was in the Hebrides, for the mainland had less peace, but the Trossachs was left unharried for more than half a century from 1660.

Rob heard the ceilidh at first only as background music, rising and falling like sea-rollers to the flowing tide of his sleep. As his mind sharpened and curiosity quickened, his want to hear and know more would be quickly met, for the young were not forgotten at ceilidhs. Games were played that gave mental exercise; each person in turn had to propound a riddle or repeat a proverb that had not been previously mentioned, or to compose impromptu a rhymed verse to which all were expected to add.

Nearly two-thirds of all Highlanders over the age of eight were illiterate in the seventeenth century,[25] but they had for that reason most retentive memories, and active minds that enjoyed stimulus. The term illiterate is here misleading, for the cultural expression of the Highlands and Islands was oral, faithfully transmitted from one generation to another as myths, romances, the Ossianic tales of Fionn and his son Ossian, and in new verse. The Edinburgh Privy Council in 1616 had banned the use of Gaelic in schools[26] – an act of mental darkness. A century later English was still not spoken north of the Highland Line. The chiefs, their children and near relatives all had English, which they spoke with a Gaelic, not a Lowland Scots, accent,[27] but few others in Highland counties had more than a smattering.

In mid century a Celtic renaissance had begun, when new bards like Mary MacLeod and Iain Lom MacDonald transformed Irish and Scots poetry with new rhythms and stressed metre. Their works were widely known and recited in Highland homes.

Eulogies and elegies had predominated in the earlier verse and not without point. Panegyrics on the chiefs and their martial deeds had often been censured by government and church for encouraging the heroics of war, but the bards also extolled courage, generosity, and wisdom, and in praising honour, fortitude, and kindness to the weak, had a moral force in country where the clergy were thin on the ground. Panegyrics were not just flattery of ruling families, but hopefully made to incite leaders to get or imitate virtues for the good of their clansmen. The elegies in turn justly reflected the lethal character of much Highland history and Clan Gregor's in particular. Mary MacLeod and bards who followed had lifted Celtic verse to a higher plane.

Rob Roy's earliest education was thus firmly grounded on the ceilidh, whatever later teachers might do to widen, enrich, or correct it. He learned respect for literature, whether Gaelic or English. Later in life he was one among a small number of eminent subscribers to the publication of Bishop Keith's *History of the Scottish Reformation*.[28] He met from his earliest years a rich variety of men and women able to express ideas freely and fluently.

He imbibed distrust of the Scots Parliament and privy Council virtually with his mother's milk, and heard the Stewart kings and their governments fiercely criticized by all. He learned endlessly about the intrigues and fortunes of the clan's powerful neighbours, who ringed them with potentially hostile forces: to the west across Loch Lomond, the Colquhouns of Luss and the Campbells of Argyll; north across Glen Dochart, the

Campbells of Breadalbane; to the east beyond Strathyre, the Murrays of Atholl and Drummonds of Strathearn; close to their south, the two Grahams of Menteith and Montrose, and the Stewart Earl of Moray. Still closer around them were ancient enemies, now friends: the Buchanans, from whom they held land; westward, the MacFarlanes between Loch Lomond and Loch Long; eastward the MacLarens, Stewarts, and MacIntyres of Balquhidder; and northward the MacNabs of Glen Dochart. An intimate knowledge of all these clans and their power-seeking princes – two dukes, two marquises, three earls, and a baronet, who at one time or another all held high office in the State, unless they were losing their heads to the Maiden (the Edinburgh guillotine), was essential to all sons of Donald Glas, who year by year supplemented all they heard in Glen Gyle with the latest news and speculations that flowed in from allies everywhere between Edinburgh and Lochaber. Rob might be too young to understand much of it at first, but he absorbed it all in time, and his life would one day hang on the accurate recall of these oral dossiers with their complex inter-relationships.

No less decisively for his future, he discovered the story of his clan.

CHAPTER TWO

THE CHILDREN OF THE MIST

Clan Alpin

E VERY FATHER of Clan Gregor was keenly aware how important it was to his sons' lives that they should know their own
roots and the stony ground from which they sprang. Much as
Rob might glean at the ceilidhs, Donald had to see to it that he
heard it in the round from his own lips. No men could be more
critical than the Gaels in assessing their own clan's policies and
leadership, so long as they were talking among themselves.

The tale came in four lessons. The first – the rise of the
Campbell dragon – began with a look at the MacGregor arms.
The crest showed a crowned lion's head within the peripheral
scroll *'S Rioghal mo Dhream*, My Blood is Royal, proclaiming
descent from the family of Kenneth MacAlpin, the first king of a
united Scotland in 843, and from twelve kings of Scots preceding
him back to the kings of Ireland. (The line of Clan Alpin can no
longer be traced back through the twelfth to the tenth centuries.
They were certainly one of the few clans of purely Celtic descent
in the male line.)

Their earliest known land was in Lorn, first in Glen Orchy
in the thirteenth century, from which they spread over Glen
Strae and Glen Lochy, all coursed by big salmon rivers running
south-west into the head of Loch Awe, where they were flanked
by the mountain ranges of Ben Cruachan and Beinn Laoigh, each
cast on a spacious scale. Their chief, Iain of Glenorchy, came
out against Edward of England when he claimed the crown in
1296, fell prisoner, and died without male issue. His nephew
Gregor succeeded, but a daughter by ill-fortune married into
the Campbell family, whose seat was then the castle of Innis
Chonnail, an island near the south end of Loch Awe. Through
her, the chiefs of Clan Campbell laid claim to the three glens.
Campbell chiefs, whatever their christened names, were called
in Argyll *MacCailein Mor*, Son of the Great Colin. Their land
policy was unlimited expansion.

Their claim on Clan Alpin was void under an ancient Celtic

rule and custom that clan land belonged to the clan, not to a person. The chief held a superiority of it, but only in the name of the clan, as its 'father'.[1]

The chief in all clans represented their common ancestry, his office being hereditary not to his person but to his ruling family, from whom successors were elected. Choice of the most able man available was thus ensured by excluding primogeniture as a principle of succession. The early clan system was aristocratic but not feudal. The people were free and could speak as equals to their chief, as children to father. He on inauguration was granted land and cattle for his maintenance. He held that land in trust, and ruled by dividing it among his near relatives, whose members in turn subdivided the arable by lot among the clansmen. Pasture was held in common.[2] The chief's job was to lead, and maintain the life and safety of all. His relatives' job was to bring out of the land a sufficient yield of crops, cattle, and well-fed fighting men. Leases were verbal and rents paid in kind – cattle, sheep, poultry, butter, cheese, barley, and oats. The rents were minimal until the fifteenth century, for the chiefs had small need, but thereafter were taken in full and sent to market, by boat wherever possible.

The Campbell's impudent claim was rightly rejected by the clansmen, who had elected as chief Iain's nephew Gregor. They re-named themselves Clan Gregor to emphasize that repudiation of Campbell. They continued to hold the glens by *coir a' cleadhaimh*, as they had in the past, until MacCailein Mor married the sister of Robert the Bruce. Thereafter the expansion of Campbell territory began to take on its sinister character.

MacCailein Mor became the godfather of a Scottish mafia, more efficient and powerful than the later Sicilian, for he enjoyed the king's confidence. In 1432, he obtained for his second son, Sir Colin, a charter of Glen Orchy. Colin built Kilchurn Castle at the head of Loch Awe, while his relatives began to colonize Clan Gregor's lands. In 1457, MacCailein Mor was raised to the earldom of Argyll. Seven years later, after successfully plotting the assassination of the Lord of Lorn, he won that title too.[3] Campbell headquarters were then moved to Inveraray on a bay of Loch Fyne. In 1499, Archibald, the second earl, kidnapped the four-year-old heiress of the thane of Cawdor. The girl, torn from her mother's arms at Kilravock Castle, was taken to Inveraray, and when fifteen made to marry the earl's son. The lands of Cawdor were thus acquired and the Campbell dragon grew its third head. All had this greed of property, which alone gave power.

The dragon refined its technique, turning from murder and rape to less open, more patient ways. The devices used to cheat men out of their homelands were the charter, the mortgage, the false promise, instigation to violence, false witness, the control of courts of justice, and Letters of Fire and Sword. The latter was the Privy Council's written authority to kill and burn, granted to men strong enough to harry an offending clan.

The charter was the most rewarding device. None of the Celtic clans had held land by charter in the first millennium AD. There had been no feudal kings to grant titles until David I, who had spent twenty years in the Norman court of England, came to the throne in 1124, and brought back with him a thousand Norman landseekers, to whom he distributed estates by dispossession of native owners. One such Norman had been Robert de Brus, who received Annandale. The eighth Robert, called 'the Bruce', and his successors to the crown, forced the principal chiefs to accept charters in their own names for their clans' lands. The clan system was thus undermined by introduction of the feudal principle. Under primogeniture, leadership was weakened by chance succession, interregnums, and minorities; the idea of trusteeship gave way to personal ownership of land; and the result was misgovernment, local and national. Feuds and clan wars degraded Highland life to that of the jungle in the sixteenth century. The clansmen loathed the feudal system with its division of people into classes (vassal-barons, tenants, and serfs) and some chiefs held out against it as long as they dared. They succumbed one by one to charter-acceptance rather than lose their clan's land to an overlord. After that their successors quickly thought of the land as their personal property.

Feudal overlords did not as a general rule seek to dispossess the native races, whose fighting men were needed as allies, and not wanted as ruinous enemies. The chiefs' baronial powers of life and death were confirmed. Throughout the Highlands, the clans held their lands in strength, with or without crown charters, and increasingly with them. Clan Gregor were left irreconcilable to that change, for they were never given the chance to have second thoughts. The dragon was in the gate.

A *house divided*

The Campbell's basic principle in their empire-building days, was the exploitation of their victims' twin weaknesses, pride and pugnacity. The method was to win a victim's confidence, play upon any cause of resentment against a third party, or supply one if lacking, incite him to a violent act, and then step in to keep the peace armed with Letters of Fire and Sword and a charter to the victim's land. The legal instruments required were easily won from troubled kings, grateful to any confidence-man who seemed willing to uphold the king's 'law', and who held the king's ear. The technique had its own refinements, and its sequence of events might need delays to cover the operator's tracks and to embroil the prey more deeply. Another prevalent weakness was shortage of money, which the Campbells could exploit by lending on mortgage and foreclosing at an opportune moment.

The task of ousting and destroying Clan Gregor could not be done in a day. The Gregarach (men of the clan) were numerous and vigorous. Soon to be known in Gaelic as *Clann a' Cheathaich*, the Children of the Mist, their pride and spirit were rooted in love of their land and a Celtic social life that gave immense cohesive strength. Their destruction had to be a long-term project. Based on Kilchurn Castle, the Campbells usurped the Glenorchy name and inched forward into the big glens. The chance to set the Gregarach by the ears and weaken them by division came early in the sixteenth century.

Gregor of Glenorchy's younger son, Dughall Ciar Mor (Big Brown Dougall), carried off and married Campbell of Glenorchy's daughter. He was famed for his strength and energy. The Campbells used him. They fostered his ambition, declaring him chief of Clan Gregor, knowing that he could not be accepted by the clan's main Glenorchy line. The Campbells admitted in their own records that the claim was 'not righteous',[4] but it sufficed for their purpose. The Gregarach took to the sword, at first against each other. Weakened by disunity, they had then to fight for their lands against Campbell evictions. In order to live, they had to plunder the farms taken from them, and so could be denounced by the Argyll mafia to the king and Privy Council as rievers, caterans, and thieves. The evicted men took shelter with any kinsman who still possessed land, and made desperate by affliction took land as best they could where it lay empty, or could bear some tenuous claim through marriage. The Gregarach thus spread over the districts of Rannoch and Breadalbane at Strathfillan, Glen Dochart, and Glen Lyon; and in the Trossachs country.

The Clan Dughaill Ciar, distinguished now as a junior branch of the main clan, moved into Glengyle and neighbouring straths and glens around 1533.⁵ In 1542 and 1558, the Children of the Mist overran Balquhidder. North of Glen Dochart their troubles continued, for Campbell of Glenorchy was still pushing east into Breadalbane and netting the Gregarach of Glen Lyon. The founder of the forthcoming Breadalbane family was Black Duncan, a knight standing high at the court of James VI. He obtained charters to oust Clan Gregor anew, and won other lands, like Fletcher's of Achallader on Rannoch Moor, by criminal fraud.⁶ The true owners could have no successful recourse to the courts at Edinburgh, since the office of Lord Justice General had been made hereditary to the earls of Argyll since 1528. Black Duncan built a fortress tower at Achallader to protect his Rannoch properties against rightful owners. He had others by Loch Tay.

The Campbells felt ready to deliver the *coup de grâce* to Clan Gregor.

Letters of Fire and Sword

By Act of the Privy Council at Stirling on 22 September 1563, Letters of Fire and Sword against the clan were granted to Sir John Campbell of Glenorchy and all nobles. The grants were repeated in 1588, 1590, and 1597, and were renewed at intervals over a hundred and thirty years. Their policy was genocide. The only monarch to call a halt to it was Mary Queen of Scots. Hers had been the original Letters. In 1566 she ordered that Clan Gregor be given land and stock at Loch Rannoch.⁷ When next year she lost her crown the oppression was reimposed. The details of the pursuit make ugly reading. Never before or since had such bloody persecution been applied so persistently to any race of people in Britain. An astounding feature is that the clan now held together, scattered as it was, as an identifiable unit able to act in concert and always dangerous. Injustice had made it so – and its desperate common lot. The chiefs' own folly contributed. This can best be seen not in repetitious forays, which had to range far and wide through surrounding counties to get in food and cattle, since their own had been carried off; nor in their quickness to give and take offence, exacerbated by long-lasting denigration of their people; nor yet their ferocity in attack and defence, for they had need to sell their lives dearly as a deterrent; but rather in the trust they continued to repose in the word of men of power.

The true Celts always had this ingrained confidence that a man's word was his bond. It was a legacy of their long history: their agreements in trade, land, and social life had always been verbal; no leases, contracts, or charters had normally been set on paper. Man's memory was sound. He put trust in the spoken word, which had to be honoured unflinchingly. The MacGregors had still not realized that in dealing with the new feudal princes, the landowners or 'charter men', only the written word now counted, and then only if free of legal loophole. Speech was for dissembly. The MacGregors' blindness to the new morality led to the double raid on Luss, the most notorious event in their history, deeply affecting the lives of Rob Roy and all Gregarach born in the seventeenth century.

The tragedy opened as a minor incident in the early winter of 1602. Two MacGregors, travelling from Glasgow to their home at Dunan near the head of Loch Rannoch, were benighted while passing through Colquhoun's land by Loch Lomond. Cold and hungry, they asked food and shelter at Luss and were refused. At this breach of Highland hospitality they took shelter in an empty hut, killed a sheep, and ate. Next day, Sir Alexander Colquhoun had them seized and executed, although they offered payment.[8] No proscription against Clan Gregor was at that time in force.

A report on the judicial murder went to the chief, Alasdair of Glenstrae, who lived on the north side of Loch Rannoch, where he held land under Menzies of Weem. He felt bound to act. It was a merit of the clan system that while every man gave his chief the respect due to a father by his family, and found there his first duty, the chief in turn was responsible for the life of every member. The mutual trust engendered was almost wholly good, but even Tacitus had noted a danger: 'The Celts adopted all enmities as well as friendships.' An injury to one was a hurt to all, and unless a chief understood how profoundly true that was it led him to feuding. The close-knit Clan Gregor were in present circumstances the least likely to let the Luss injury pass, and Colquhoun should have known it. Alasdair was a man of mettle and gave the punitive order.

On 7 December 1602, a MacGregor raiding party of eighty men came down Glen Finlas in the hills above Colquhoun's old castle of Rossdhu by Loch Lomond. They killed two men[9] and lifted three hundred cows and more than double that number of sheep, goats, and horses, which they drove into Argyll

(MacCailein Mor was at feud with Colquhoun), and reset the stock at Kinlochgoil, Ardkinglas, Strachur, and Appin. A stratagem for revenge occurred to Colquhoun. He led a large party of Luss 'widows', mounted on palfreys, before King James VI at Stirling. James was known to be squeamish at the sight of blood, so to gain the desired effect each sham widow carried her man's 'bludie sark' aloft on a spear-point. The shirts had been dipped in sheep's blood to give a uniform exhibition. Horrified by the sight, James responded by granting Colquhoun Letters of Fire and Sword.

The MacGregors were enraged by the deceit of the Stirling exhibition, by the exaggerated, one-sided report, and at royal condemnation without a hearing. Alasdair of Glenstrae now had MacCailein Mor's assurance of moral support and advice to take vengeance. Blinded by the moment's passion he failed to see that his clan were being hounded out against Campbell's enemy at the most ill-chosen moment. The king must feel it a personal affront. No one could profit except MacCailein Mor.

Alasdair of Glenstrae gathered three hundred men [10] and led them to Loch Longside, where he cut back south-east to the head of Glen Fruin, which ran down into Colquhoun's best farmland. Colquhoun had early warning and gathered in three hundred mounted men and five hundred foot. They met at the head of the glen on 7 February 1603. The MacGregors' courage in attacking such greatly superior force was justified by Alasdair's generalship. The Colquhoun force was routed. The Register of the Privy Council reported that eighty Colquhouns were cut down. Their chief escaped to his castle of Bannachra in the lower glen, while six hundred cows were lifted and still more sheep, goats, and horses. As before, these were reset in Argyll's land, by Loch Fyne and Loch Goil. An angry king gave his order to 'extirpate Clan Gregor and to ruit oot their posteritie and name'. On 3 April 1603, an Act of the Privy Council proscribed the use of the names Gregor or MacGregor, and prohibited those who had borne the names from carrying arms. The execution of the Act was entrusted to commissioners who were men of power, chiefly to Campbell in the west and Murray of Atholl in the east.

The hunt was on and prosecuted with extraordinary venom. Hounds were used to track the Gregarach and no mercy was shown. Warrants for their extermination were put on public sale as though they were game to be killed for sport. Their women were branded on the cheek, their homes burned, their livestock and possessions carried off, their families left destitute.

The men as always gave more than a good account of themselves and took heavy toll of pursuers. Their long training in living off the country, contriving ambush, using cover, and traversing hill-ground by night in all weather over great distances, made their planned extermination impossible and the effort costly in life lost. At the same time, the relentless pursuit over eight months reduced the clan's families to pitiable condition. Their deprivation of warmth and shelter and adequate food when winter came in caused more suffering than the chief could bear to watch. He determined to end it by surrendering his own person and kinsmen to MacCailein Mor. He had reason, he said, to anticipate mercy from the man who had given him secret encouragement for the Glen Fruin raid. He made one condition, that he and his kinsmen should be allowed exile in England. Argyll accepted and they gave themselves up. They were at once sent under guard across the Tweed at Berwick. Argyll's promise having been met if not honoured, the soldiers wheeled right about and brought the prisoners back to Edinburgh.[11] On 20 January 1604, they were taken before the Court of Justiciary, where the jurors included Colquhoun's men.[12] MacGregor was hanged at the Mercat Cross that same day, together with five of his kindred. The others were hanged in February and March. The records show that of the chief's immediate family, twenty-two were hanged, four beheaded, three murdered by arrows in the back, and five killed in battle.

Alasdair of Glenstrae put his dying statement on paper. He declared that Argyll had incited Clan Gregor to aggression against Luss and several other landed men who were his personal enemies. The original paper (in General Register House, Edinburgh) is lengthy.[13] An excerpt reads: I, Allester MacGrigour of Glen stra, Confesse heir before God . . . he (Argyll) moweit my brother and sum of my freindis to commit baith herschip and slauchter upoune the Laird of Luss . . . he did intyse me, with oft and sundrie messages, that he wald mak my peace and saif my lyfe and landis . . . .'

When Clan Gregor heard of their chief's betrayal by Campbell, and while the mock trial of their leaders in Edinburgh was still proceeding, the fiery cross went round. The clan spontaneously rose and took terrible vengeance on Sir Duncan Campbell of Glenorchy, whom they believed to be Argyll's prompter. The records of the Glenlyon Campbells declare that when the storm broke, 'Even Sir Duncan quailed. They laid waste Culdares and Duneaves in Fortingall, Crannuich in Breadalbane, Glenfalloch, and Bochastel in Menteith, and burnt his castle at Achallader.'

His loss in money was £66,666 Scots. The loss in men was not collated.[14]

The Clan Gregor then went to earth. Their chief's execution, the sudden accession of James VI to the English throne in March 1603, and his departure for London on 5 April, with all that the move entailed for Argyll and Atholl, took heat out of their pursuit. The clansmen watched and waited. They submitted to law in so far as they took the surnames of the clans on whose ground they happened to be living – Murray, Campbell, Drummond, Graham, Buchanan and others, while some went back to origins with the name MacAlpin – yet their family branches kept communications open and their unity in repair.

The Acts of the Privy Council and Parliament, and the king's letters, always referred to the MacGregors in words of vitupera-tion that read oddly in state papers – barbarous, wicked, inhuman, Godless, woulfis (wolves), notorious common malefactouris, and so forth – as if to justify government terrorism. All subjects were exhorted to 'slauchter and mutilate them and to raise fyre'. The king and Privy Council, and still more their Campbell adviser, continued in the brutal philosophy of unsure men: be seen to be strong, merciless, vicious, and success will be yours. They had learned nothing from their country's history, which had demonstrated so clearly and often that rebels, martyrs, assassins, and guerrillas are not born but made, driven to fierce ends by injustice or too prolonged cruelties. The men of government had been very busy sowing dragon's teeth. In depriving men of spirit of the necessary modicum of human dignity, in denying them even a right of reply in defence, they debased their lives while recharging them with rage.

The promised land

So far were the Gregarach from lying down to die as king and Campbell planned, that whoever attacked one of their number had still to reckon with vengeance taken. Since they had lost their lands and cattle, they had no choice but to take back from others the means of subsistence, theirs by human right. The alternative was to starve, and to their enemies' chagrin they declined to do it. Predatory forays were cleverly executed with little bloodshed, but inevitably there were exceptions to the rule. The Acts of proscription were five times renewed: in

1611 to forbid the sale of arms; in 1613 to forbid assembly in groups of more than four or the use of pointed knives to carve meat; in 1621 to renew the Acts against the risen generation; in 1627 to extend proscription to their children; and in 1633 by Charles I, when the clergy were forbidden to christen babies with the name Gregor, and fresh Letters of Fire and Sword declared that although the wicked and rebellious clan had been reduced by James, they had lately broken out again, committing open ravages in Angus, Clackmannan, the Lennox, the Mearns, Menteith, and the counties of Perth and Stirling. The centre of this activity was Glengyle and the Trossachs.

Since the execution of Alasdair of Glenstrae, the clan had no chief whom all would accept. Being those termed a 'broken' clan, its principal branches were led by their independent chieftains, who could no longer give their clansmen the protection and order enjoyed by men of other clans for their landholdings, stocks, crops, and domestic affairs. Yet they remained strong units, often able to cooperate. The most active and energetic branch was Clan Dughaill Ciar. Their powerful neighbours felt a growing desire to conciliate them, for their friendship would allow their own tenants more peace of mind, while as allies in war they certainly were prompt to act. An example was the earl of Moray's call on Glengyle to help him in 1624, when Malcolm Og had sped north with three hundred men to expel Clan Chattan. Two centuries of persecution had made Clan Gregor the toughest and most skilful guerrilla force ever to operate in Scotland.

From the outbreak of the civil war of 1638–51, Clan Gregor gave all its support to King Charles. They had little cause to love the Stewarts, whose proscriptions and Letters had shed the best of their blood over the last century. Historians of the time were astonished that the clan should now have been willing to shed it voluntarily. The reasons were good, and not those proclaimed by their bards – that the royal line of Gregor naturally fought for the royal house of the Scots. Nor did they oppose the Covenanters out of religious conviction. They came out for the king because Campbell led the Convenanters; therefore under the royal standard lay the only real hope of re-establishing the clan's name and fortune.

Their hopes came close to fruition in 1644–5, when James Graham, the Marquis of Montrose and the greatest general of his time, led the Highland army for the king. In a series of brilliant campaigns he defeated the Covenanters in six pitched battles fought in every quarter of the country. Clan Gregor played so conspicuous a part under their chief Patrick Roy of Glenstrae that Montrose's heart warmed to them. He promised in the king's name the restitution of Clan Gregor's lands. In June 1645, while at Cromar in Aberdeenshire, he put the promise in writing:

1645. June 7th
Whereas the Laird of MacGregor and his friends have declared themselfs faithfullie for his Majestie and doe follow us in his service These air therfor be power and warrand granted be his Majestie to us to certify and assure theme, that whatsoever lands and possessions belonged justlie, to the said Laird of McGregor and his predecessors in Glenlyon, Rannoch or Glenurchy, or whatsoever lands belonged justlie to his friends and their predecessors and ar now in the possession of Rebells and Enemys to his Majestie's service; They and ther Heirs shall have the same Disponed to them and confirmed be his Majestie under his hand and seal, when it shall please God to put an end to thes present troubles, Providing always that the said Laird of McGregor and his said freinds and their forsaids continow faithfull and constant in his Majestie's service, otherwise these presents shall be null.

Subscribed at Kinady in Cromar the seventh day of June One thousand sex hundreth fourtie fyve yeires.

Montrose

One week later, Charles was defeated at Naseby by Fairfax. In Scotland, it seemed as though his promise might still be honoured, for Montrose's greatest victory, at Kilsyth in August, left the country at his feet. The fighting seemed to be over for the season, and the plunder too, which Montrose forbade. Such large numbers of clansmen lived near subsistence level, without reserves, that the men had to get home to see the harvest in, or their families would suffer in winter. The Highland army melted away. That harvest need was always a weakness in the planning of long campaigns. Montrose had now to recruit in the Lowlands, but failed to raise sufficient men before David Leslie led a Covenanters' army north from England. In September, Leslie defeated Montrose at Philiphaugh neat Selkirk and the royal fortunes collapsed.

Clan Gregor's hope of restitution seesawed much in the next twenty years: to its lowest on Cromwell's rise, up to its peak when Charles was restored. The joy then was common to all Scotland.

A fountain of wine was rigged at the Cross of Edinburgh, where Clan Gregor had been outlawed and their chiefs hung, and there the new chiefs could drink with all others to Charles Stewart, whose promise they held. Their cup spilled over when Argyll was beheaded at the Mercat Cross for collaborating with Cromwell. His head was exposed at the west side of the Tolbooth, where the Covenanters had exposed Montrose's.

The lines that Montrose is said to have scratched on the window of his jail on his last night had expressed a philosophy shared with him by Clan Gregor:

> He either fears his fate too much,
> or his deserts are small,
> That puts it not unto the touch,
> To win or lose it all.

The proscription on Clan Gregor was annulled. The Clan was free. They waited now for the restitution of their lands. Charles in his reign of twenty-five years never once visited Scotland, and although reminded of the solemn pledge to Clan Gregor, chose to let it lie. The clan knew yet again the faithlessness of Stewart princes. The cause of it lay once more in the hills of Argyll. The man who stood to lose his lands to Clan Gregor was Margaret's cousin, Iain Glas, known down in the Lowlands as Sir John Campbell of Glenorchy, aged 26 in 1661, and soon to be earl of Breadalbane. Already renowned for his acumen, and described by a contemporary as 'a man of fair complexion, grave as a spaniard, as cunning as a fox, wise as a serpent but as slippery as an eel', he time and again throughout his life proved that assessment. He was a royalist, and foreseeing the possibility of the Restoration as soon as Cromwell died, had urged General Monk to recall Charles II. That might not have availed him much had not his new chief, Archibald Campbell, the ninth earl, been seen by the king's advisers as much too powerful for a subject strongly Protestant, and therefore a source of danger to the king. It seemed to them politic to retain the ambitious John of Glenorchy as a counter-poise to Argyll. And so it was agreed.

Clan Gregor's chance of regaining their ancient rights, the most basic rights of a Celtic people, had gone forever. They alone among the sixty principal families of the Highlands had no homelands.

CHAPTER THREE

―

THE BAREFOOT YEARS

1673–84

The moral environment

WHILE ROB ROY was a small boy his father was continually away from Glen Gyle in summer and early autumn, but although his brothers and sister were twelve to fourteen years older he suffered no lack of company. The now deserted glen and strath were then busy with life. Under twelve, the young were left to run gloriously free in dirty raggedness, the children of the *duinevasal* being indistinguishable from others except by command of English from early schooling.[1] As soon as a boy neared puberty his training to manhood began in earnest. He had to make a rapid advance to maturity, in the sense of accepted responsibility. Life was chancy in the Highlands. Land or stock was often in dispute, men bristled with weapons for defence of home and person, and the medical service was so bad that people were safer without. The average life expectancy was 26 ½ years, but this low figure was caused by heavy infant mortality.[2] The years of greatest danger were the first three. Thereafter people required for survival continued good health, good luck in avoiding accident, and alert self-possession. A man had to get control of tongue and temper. Granted all that, if he lived through infancy he could live to an old age. A father's first job was to see that his son had the primary equipment.

Donald Glas, born around 1631 from the marriage of Malcolm Og with a daughter of MacDonald of Keppoch, had been too young to adventure with his father and MacDonald uncles in the wars of Montrose. His early battle experience had been won against Cromwell's Roundheads in the 1650s.

In 1656, aged 25, he succeeded to the Glengyle chieftainship and married Margaret Campbell. When the monarchy was restored in 1660 he took commission in the army of Charles II, plainly to earn money, for the country was not at war. Surviving deeds show that by 1663 (aged 32) if not earlier, he had been promoted lieutenant-colonel. He appears to have relinquished this commission within eight years, for he accepted

27

one of a different kind from John Murray, the Earl of Atholl. Atholl presided over his own Court of Regality, whose fifteen 'assessors' formed a clan jury. He had by charter the power of pit and gallows, and was now also Lord Justice General of Scotland in place of Campbell of Argyll. On 11 August 1668, he commissioned Donald Glas for 'uplifting of all forfalters, fines, fugitives, from the Court of Justiciary held at Dunkeld'.[3] The apprehension of defaulters would require armed force and give lawful employment to a company of Glengyle MacGregors.

Donald's name is frequently mentioned thereafter in the Regality Books of Menteith, the Register of Sasines in Stirling, the Register of Deeds, the Proceedings of Estates of Parliament, and the Records of the Privy Council. These show that he was constantly travelling between Edinburgh, Glasgow, Perth, and Stirling, and to the glens of Atholl, Lochaber, Breadalbane, Badenoch and mid-Argyll, while raising money on loan for legitimate cattle trade and general farming. They disclose too that like almost every countryman of means from Cumberland to Caithness he enjoyed the profits of cattle rieving, and had to suffer its losses.

Donald's sons were bred to double standards in cattle-dealing from infancy. Rieving was a time-honoured custom in the Highland and Border counties; all classes were involved from noble lords to cottars. Throughout his boyhood, Rob Roy was indoctrinated with the current ethics, which while probably not discussed as such, since they were taken for granted, were vindicated by several concurrent arguments, which he would hear expressed over his formative years from many different lips: the drovers who crossed the Parlan pass; the family's friends and neighbours while planning or celebrating a *creach* or foray, or discussing the disposal of the *spreidh* or livestock plunder; the great tales of the ceilidhs recounting some legendary hership, or cattle-lifting raid; the fierce arguments or even fights put up by neighbouring or distant clansmen while negotiating with Donald the levy due to be paid in kind for driving a *spreidh* through Clan Gregor's land; and of course his parents' views on all this activity.

The vindications were:[4]

1 Cattle were native to Scotland, feeding on God's hill-pastures on which man had spent no labour, and like red deer man's common property or prey.

2 Gaeldom's finest epic in the Heroic cycle, sometimes heard in part at ceilidhs, was the *Tain Bo Chuailgne*, the Cattle Raid

of Cuchullin. This great romance made plain that a chief's traditional duty over the last 1600 years had been to keep up his people's stock, and to travel far in the venture. Western islesmen raided up to Orkney, and the clans of the southern Highlands went as far north as Moray and Ross. The epic spirit while declining was still alive, and young men were still eager to emulate their heroes. It was expected of every chief when he came of age, or as heir before his succession, that he should prove his ability by leading a *creach* – and leading with dexterity; it gave the evidence needed of vigour on all levels. For most clansmen it was an adventurous sport; from a chief's viewpoint it gave excellent field training in hard campaign conditions, tactical planning, and the use of ground, not only for war but in the similar skills employed when driving their own cattle to distant markets.

3 Harsh seasons with heavy loss of stock by starvation hit different districts year by year, and to tide communities over the bad spell, those who suffered most lifted stock from clans with a temporary abundance. The latter would take in turn when their own time of need came. This practice had such real value to clan life that Gaels otherwise law-abiding viewed cattle-raiding not as theft but as a robust form of social welfare, to which everyone contributed. The 'contributors' of the day were expected to try to prevent raiders succeeding, and if surprise failed some blood-letting might ensue and be thought reasonable if controlled, as it nearly always was. Raiders withdrew after the token blood-spilling, as if by convention. So well-honoured were such conventions that if the losers could subsequently track their cattle down they had them back, or else the chief at fault would replace them, recovering from his own men later. Again, if the losers could track a lifted herd into the land of another clan and the track there vanished, the chief of that clan had by law to trace the herd out of his land or make good to the owner.

The important point to appreciate in regard to Rob Roy, and Gaeldom, is that cattle-lifting was not equated with crime or dishonesty. Theft of other property was (excepting war-time plunder). The state papers of the period, written by civil servants ignorant of Highland life, were totally wrong in supposing the Highlands to be full of brigands waiting to rob travellers. To the contrary, travellers of the time record that highway robbery was unknown. They could pass through the length and breadth of the Highlands while carrying large sums of money without any apprehension of loss by the way, or of danger by night, and that among the Highlanders themselves personal robberies were a great rarity.[5] House theft was unheard of; people of the Highlands and their Lowland fringe, whether living in huts or mansions, neither bolted, barred, nor locked their doors.[6] In these respects, the Highlands were more law-abiding than the Lowland towns, whose people were unaware of the fact, knowing clansmen only by ill-repute as cattle-rievers, and therefore 'brigands'.

The public records of the time unwittingly applied Lowland moral standards to a specific aspect of Highland society governed by a different ethic, and so came out with a wrong conclusion. The Highland people were no less honest than others, and held more firmly to the moral code in matters of daily living. Cattle rieving was a thing apart. And those clans living close to the Highland Line, like the MacGregors and MacFarlanes, fell under temptation to raid the richer Lowlands, where farmers were incapable of tracking their beasts through the hills. The Highlanders' ethic to be roughly just should have been confined to their Highland ground; but they found it hard to recognize the extension as wrong, for they held in mind that the Lowlands had once been part of their ancestors' inheritance, and should have been theirs still;[7] and while this political cleavage between the two remained as pronounced as the geological, each in turn were rebels in the other's eyes against king or Parliament or Church, and so were reckoned fair game.

Rob Roy acquired his moral code by slow degrees over the first fourteen years, and although it was to be much amended later, the base was laid. The abiding principle is cast up from the records of detail: that right must be seen to be done, no man left destitute, the given word honoured, the strictest honour observed to all who have given implicit trust, and that a guest's confidence in his safety must never be betrayed by his host, or *vice versa*. There was more of a like kind, and each held as its kernel the simple ideal of trust honoured. That was the prevalent code of the common Highland people, instilled into children by parents, clergy, teachers, and ceilidh. Breaches of it were abhorred and damned. A simple ideal deeply interpreted and applied to all aspects of living would regenerate a people, and of course that happened no more in the Highlands than anywhere else. The ideal was applied 'with discretion'. Its interpretation went deeply into domestic life but stayed shallow for war and politics. The records of massacres reveal a ferocity apparently peculiar to Scots, until compared with the still worse records of other countries. Pitiless cruelty is specific to no nation but to the human race.

Spring

Rob Roy's days of innocence, in his Garden of Eden by Loch Katrine, were unmarred by cruelties, unless those of weather. The springs came late, for Scotland was suffering an oscillation of climate that had brought the greatest cold since the Ice Age.[8] It reached its worst between 1550 and 1700 with a vast expansion of Arctic pack ice. The sea-temperatures off Scotland in winter slumped to 3°C (5° below present). The eye-witness records were of hard long winters and hot summers, interspersed with frequent bitter summers when harvest failed, cattle died, and woods were destroyed on exposed land. The big inland lochs like Loch Lomond and Loch Katrine froze in mid-winter. The farmlands deteriorated with a drop in the former abundance of oats and barley. Early in the spring, when the winter saltings of meat and fish began to run out, the men of each house would take a knife and bowl and go out to bleed the cows, which had first to be thrown if not too weak to stand. It was common practice to augment the failing diet with black puddings of blood, oatmeal, and onions. If the harvest had been poor, the cattle were blooded again in autumn, and the blood boiled to provide a dried store.

The spring was called 'lifting time', for the cows through lack of winter feed were almost invariably too weak to rise and walk, and had to be manhandled out to pasture. They put on weight well thereafter. The well-attested succulence of summer beef and mutton was due to the increase of new flesh after the winter's reduction. All cattle were the black or brown, shaggy aboriginal breed known as kyloes. (The tawny-red Highland cattle are a nineteenth-century cross-breed.) They were very small beasts – some as little as 11–14 stone.[9] An average sized bullock of five years weighed only 30–36 stone avoirdupois, and a heifer 24–30 stone. They could be fattened to near forty stone. In short, they were a very different breed from cattle of later centuries, and ideal for long-distance droving over hill ground, where agility was essential.

Large flocks of sheep and goats were herded on the hills of Glengyle and the Highlands in general, although individual holdings were small. There was at this time a universal belief that sheep had to be folded in winter to survive blizzards and icy winds. Their weight was 25–30 lb, for this was the indigenous pink-nosed breed no bigger than a dog, with a meagre fleece but a fine wool of long white hair mixed with short down. They were valued at approximately three shillings each, and their mutton at a penny a pound, yet little was eaten despite unanimous agreement (among travellers) that the meat was sweet and delicious. The sheep were kept for their wool and the export trade, and for Lowland sale; the goats for their milk, cheese, meat and skins.

The Glengyle arable lands, apart from Donald's on the flat ground below his house, were worked by the people as run-rig, meaning land cultivated on adjoining strips, each holding allotted to one household by annual draw. The lots were unfenced and sometimes overrun by grazing animals. Close co-operation was needed between families for herding, and for guarding crops by roster. The arable land around Donald's house, and the Glengyle townships, was divided into infield and outfield. The hill pastures were held in common.

Every Highland farmer made his own plough.[10] He never worked cattle on ploughing. They were not strong enough. He used garrons, again of the aboriginal stock and so small that a rider's legs trailed on the ground unless he held them up. They were numerous, lightfooted, and strong, and far better able to look after themselves than cows. They were mostly white with ragged coats, and ran wild on the mountains until eight years old; yet they kept themselves full-bodied even through the winter. The result was that they had not lost their ideas of independence; each March Donald and his boys had to fetch in gillies to hunt down a team of three or four. They would go out with several dogs and try to corner each garron against a crag, or impound it in a bog, or else chase it among rocks and rough ground until it submitted from exhaustion.[11] All this was exacting work for a small boy like Rob, until he became fast on the hill over short distances. The horses when rounded up were never shod; they had no more need of shoes than cows in this roadless land.

Where the soil was deep enough to plough, on the long flats at the head of Loch Katrine, Donald in late March would yoke four garrons abreast and lead the middle pair by their halters, walking backwards to watch the plough-share and guide it away from big stones. Iain and Duncan in their mid-teens would guide the plough from the rear, and be ploughing by themselves soon after.[12]

Hill ground on the flanks of the glen was dug by teams of men with the *cas-chrom*, or 'crooked foot', which had a six-foot shaft of ash with a long head bent at an angle and tipped with iron. The people used ordinary spades on ground where soil or drainage were insufficient. They dug beds there called *feannagan* (lazybeds) by trenching to either side of a strip and throwing the earth between. They fertilized the beds by spreading the winter's accumulated dung from the byre, together with peat-ash from the hearth, and sooted thatch from the roof if a re-thatching had been done during the previous year. They would even spread a whole turf house when its day was done.[13]

Donald prepared his ground for sowing with a wooden harrow pulled by a garron. The only crops sown were barley and flax on the infield, and oats on the outfield. A grassy plot close by each house gave a bite for a cow and garron in summer, but grass was nowhere grown for cropping as hay before the seeds formed. Its value as winter fodder was not appreciated, although a field of long grass was usually left standing in autumn for the beasts to nose out from the winter snows. No potatoes were cultivated until seventy years later. The most important cereal was oats, famous for its quality and abundance. Whatever work Donald might have around Scotland, he would always be at home for the April sowing.[14]

The day of spring to which Rob must have looked forward each year was *La Buidhe Bealltuinn*, The Yellow Day of the Fires of Bel. On the first day of May, the old Celtic New Year, the young folk from the parishes of Callander, Buchanan, Balquhidder, and Aberfoyle, met on the summit of Ben Ledi to commemorate an old Druidic rite – the lighting of the *Bealltuin* fires. Bel (from *Be'uill*, Life of All) had been the early Celtic sun god. In former days, all the hearth fires in the Highlands and Islands were extinguished before midnight to symbolize the dying of the old year. New sacrificial fires were kindled on local hill-tops, and the hearth fires relit from the purifying hill-top flames. The ceremonies had included a feast and several rites, like driving cattle between two fires of Bel to free them of disease in the coming year – rites since modified to a simple bonfire, a token leap through the flames, and shared food.[15] The choice of Ben Ledi was determined by its conspicuous position, isolated between two lochs on the Lowland border, with splendid views far south and north. The hill had been named *Ben le Dia*, the Hill of God, loosely interpreted now as the Hill of Light.

Rob's sister Margaret and brother Iain were both married in 1677 when Rob was six. Margaret's groom was John Leckie of Croy Leckie.[16] His family was an old one with a small estate in the Blane valley near Killearn. The expense of the wedding would bear much less heavily on Glengyle's resources than one with a Highland family, which entailed feeding hundreds for a week at least. Iain's wedding was for Rob a much greater occasion.

Iain had been courting a daughter of Drummond of Comrie, and when nineteen 'begged his stock'. By clan custom, the sons of a family were not allowed to marry until they had obtained a bit of land, or some certain prospect of settlement on which to live.[17] Like every other young Highlander of good repute, Iain had to set himself up by moving around his friends and relatives and begging from each a sheep or a cow, or seed to sow his land, and the wood for his roof-tree. This customary begging, called *faighdhe* in Gaelic or 'thigging' in Lowland Scots, continued until all was promised. He built his house by Loch Katrine in the late summer of 1676, apparently at Portnellan, and married a year later.

The wedding at Comrie in Strathearn, the Drummonds' homeland, may have been Rob's first journey out of Trossachs country. Many chiefs of Strathearn, Atholl, and Gowrie would be there, and Rob had the chance to make friends among their young. The Drummond friendships were to last all his life, and to stand him in good stead when most in need.

On Highland wedding nights the guests took possession of the house and made merry till dawn with claret, whisky, and dancing, while bride and groom were banished to sleep on straw in a dark barn by themselves.[18] In the following days, immense quantities of food and drink were consumed, while dancing, games, and hunting continued by day, with feasting and ceilidhs by night. The games were those annually enjoyed in the clan lands, when gatherings were held in late summer: running, wrestling, jumping, putting heavy stones by sudden push from the shoulder, and tossing the caber (Gaelic *cabar*), a young pine-tree trunk up to twenty feet long, thrown as far as possible so that it turned over and fell in a straight line from the tosser. The games were interspersed with bagpiping and dancing. The hunting was for red and roe deer, grouse and blackcock, and all carnivores sighted. These were unlikely to include wolves, which had become rare enough for a killing to be news. Wild boar survived in Cowal, but not east of Loch Lomond. The birds shot included swans, geese, and ducks, and much else, but not birds of prey unless by pure luck, for they presented too distant a target. The Highlanders, unlike the nineteenth-century landowners, did not try to kill everything that moved. They culled for the pot, or protection of livestock, and threatened the survival of no bird species as they did the boar and wolf. The clumsy flintlocks allowed no quick or accurate fire. When shooting, they lay down or took stance behind a rock or bank, on which they rested their piece and took a long time taking aim.[19] Powder and ball were carefully conserved.

Summer

The summer days before children went to school were filled with the township work and the fun that went with it. As soon as the fields were sown in April, they had to help in herding the cattle and sheep off the unfenced arable land. The cattle were normally pastured on the hillsides or moorland close above, and were not moved higher till June. The collies did most of the work, being always alert for a swift excursion, but constant watch had to be kept, especially in May when the men were away at the peat-banks (over the top of Glen Gyle) almost daily for three weeks. About seventeen days' cutting gave a year's supply. Work at the banks was virtually a social occasion, with much talk and song on good days, and shared food. In that high setting of great mountainscapes threaded by lochs and rivers, the spring air could seem as heady as wine. On their days off from herding or schoolwork, the boys would go along with the working parties to stack the peats for drying. They were dry enough for burning within a month, but were rarely gathered in bulk before autumn.

Early in June came the flitting or 'trial', as the move to the summer shielings was variously called.[20] The shielings were the dry and grassy hollows of the hill corries around upper Glen Gyle, where the *sgitheil bothain* or shieling huts stood, walled and roofed with turf. Early on the day appointed, the townships were as busy as ant-heaps, with the women scuttling around collecting churns, three-legged stools, bowls, jugs, and tubs for the dairy work; pots and griddles for cooking; spades, ropes, axes, great bundles of dead bracken and straw for bedding, and sticks to repair the roofs and kindle fires in the bothans; sacks of meal and bags full of cheese and bannocks, and much else besides. Meanwhile, the men and dogs were out gathering in the ponies and herds of cattle and sheep. When everyone was ready, they would load the ponies' and their own backs with all the gear and set off – sheep first, cattle next, and then the ponies. The men behind carried heavier gear, while the women with lighter, often bulkier burdens, straggled in the rear.

The youngest children were carried up in creels slung across the ponies' backs. The task of the barefooted boys and girls was to race ahead and alongside the herds to keep them together and moving in the right direction, all this with much screeching and shouting, while the men, each concerned for his own beast, bellowed directions, curses, pleas, or whistled their dogs, trying to make themselves heard above the neighing, lowing, bleating, and barking, and the shrill cries of their own offspring. The women, free at last from too familiar hearths, and shedding all responsibility now to the men, were in high spirits, and walked with the skirts of their plaids and coloured petticoats tucked under a woollen waist-rope to allow their legs easier movement, and to leave their hands free to knit or spin.

Each spinner carried a hank of fleece twisted round her forearm. She teased out the fleece and spun it into yarn on the spindle-and-bobbin that hung from it. An occasional flick of the middle finger and thumb kept the spindle whirring. Their hands were never idle, nor were their tongues. Sometimes they broke into song, as if leaving their cares in the world below. Behind them as they climbed, Strath Gartney opened out far east towards a lilac haze hiding the Carse of Stirling. Closer in, Loch Katrine, shining between oak and birch woods, stretched in a great double curve to the distant crags of the Trossachs.

When the shielings were reached and the loads dropped, the bothies were repaired. The men closed any gaps in roofs and walls with fresh-dug divots. The women spread the straw for bedding, and collected peats from the banks, where they had been drying for a month. Fires were kindled and the food laid out. Only then would Donald call the men together and get them to separate the stock into groups, so that each man could be seen to have brought his souming, or head of sheep and cattle allowed him for the grazing available. After the stock had been turned loose, the people enjoyed a simple feast in the open air. Every woman brought cheese from her last year's produce, the bannocks were divided, and Donald said grace, not only for themselves, but their beasts as well.

The main party returned to the lower glen, leaving behind two strong girls at each bothy, and a few of the older children to serve as herders. Lambs and kids had to be guarded from foxes, eagles, and any far-travelled wolf. And here they stayed for the summer, making cheese and butter, often visited from below by their people bringing up provisions, or occasionally making brief excursions themselves to carry down produce. In late summer the beasts were taken down to the lower pastures, where the grass had grown in the interval, and then moved back again to graze the shielings before the October sales. The stock to be retained for winter was held up at the shielings until the first snow came on the hills; only then, or shortly after, did everyone come down finally to the townships.

However much Rob may have enjoyed this life high on the hillside when he came to take his turn at it, he would not be able to spend more than a few days, for he had school to attend and much to do below, especially since Iain had married. In May and June there were hull and rigging repairs to be done on the birlinns, both on Loch Katrine and Loch Lomond. This was a clan responsibility on which each man had to work by rota. The boys had to watch and learn. The birlinns were clinker-built of pine on oak, on an eighteen-foot keel, and wide in the beam. They were masted and rigged with square sails, hoisted only for a fair wind and distance – not war galleys built for speed, but barges for transport of grain, goods, livestock, and men in number. The crews when rowing sang an *iorram*, or slow rhythmical boat-song to synchronize the dip of the oars.

The people made their own tartan cloth for plaids, jackets, hose and petticoats. While most was women's work, every child had to help in collecting the plants needed for dyeing a tartan that would retain its colours unfaded by age.[21] The only plant dyes imported were saffron, which was preferred to native yellows for shirt-dyeing, and indigo and woad to supplement native blues. These came from Holland – Scotland's main foreign trade was with the Netherlands.

The raw wool was first steeped in human urine to remove grease, then washed and dried. After the yarn had been spun, it was dyed by simmering in pots for eight hours, each hank to one of the several colours required for weaving a tartan. When woven it was waulked (fulled) by washing it in the burn, and then laying it wet on a board or grass mat in the open air. Six or eight women would sit on either side on bundles of straw and push and tumble the cloth with their bare feet to soften and thicken it. The motions were made to the rhythm of a waulking song, which rose to a crescendo near the finish. The whole process was time-consuming, hence tartans of brown, blue, or green ground-colours were preferred for their easier dyeing with more difficult reds and yellows confined to narrow stripings. The setts were evolved by local tradition. There were no clan tartans until late in the following century.[22]

Linen for sheets and shirts was no less troublesome. Home-grown flax had to be soaked to loosen the fibre from the stalks, scutched to remove straw, cut to length and combed, and then spun. When home supplies failed, Irish tow was bought in Glasgow. The brown woven linen was bleached during the summer: boiled first, then exposed to sun and weather for weeks on end.[23]

Fishnets and line were made from the linen yarn to take salmon and powan in Loch Lomond, trout and char in Loch Katrine (which salmon failed to reach), salmon and trout in Loch Venachar, and pike in Loch Achray.[24] The weaving and line-making were women's work, and so too the cutting of grass, heather, bracken, and rushes used by the men for thatching and rope-making. The women distilled whisky from oats and barley, and brewed ale from heather and barley, and the men drank the proceeds. Called *uisge beatha*, the water of life, whisky was drunk in no great quantity. The men had a dram with their breakfast, which was the main meal of the day if they were to be out on the hill, took a ram's horn with them, and hoped for a noggin at night. The women were abstemious, but children from six to eight years were allowed a nip to keep out the cold.[25]

The ten-gallon copper stills cost nearly £2.10/- each, so not many households had one. The townships shared the expense and the product. The grain was first steeped for two days in water, spread on a hard floor to germinate, dried on mats over peat fires to halt germination, then mashed and brought with hot water to fermentation in tubs. This wash was fed into the still and boiled over a peat fire until the steam had passed through a worm condenser into a barrel. The first distillation was returned to the still at least once to become whisky; a third got rid of all impurities. The final product was colourless. In towns whisky could be bought at fourpence-halfpenny a bottle, and this was an exorbitant price when a labourer's wages were fourpence a day. So the common man distilled his own, and learning the time-labour value and nuisance of production, used moderation in daily consumption.[26] Festive nights were another matter.

The home-brewed ale had a strong peaty flavour, and was apt to cause a mild diarrhoea unless laced with whisky. It was drunk out of shallow wooden quaichs with two lugs, or else from a stoup (a pint pot). Ale sold at inns and change-houses was twopence a Scots pint (two English quarts).[27]

The itinerant tailors, shoemakers, pedlars, and the gaberlunzie men who wore the tin badge of the licensed begger, came into the Trossachs and Loch Lomondside only in summer. The pedlars were especially appreciated for the variety of hardware carried, and the small vanities like mirrors and brooches. All had small local employment, hence their need to move on like grazing goats, yet all were made welcome for the news they carried, and were eagerly given hospitality.[28] A pair of shoes could be bought in town for two shillings, or a plaid for eight shillings, but this again was far beyond the means of most clansmen. The travelling tradesmen worked at fourpence a day plus food if given material, but few clansmen could think of paying so much for his brogues. Hence a common sight in Glengyle was the deerskins and cowhides staked out on the ground to be scoured and dried. When cut and shaped to the foot they were called *brog*.[29] Their life being short, they were rarely worn by people in their own glens.[30] Brogues had the merit of lightness, allowing the clansmen to skip at speed over rock and heather, on which heavily booted southerners laboured.

The plaid was an indispensable garment in the seventeenth-century Highlands, where men were frequently wading deep in water and travelling long distances through days of rain. In such conditions breeches stuck to and galled the skin, or induced rheumatism and other ills by keeping the legs constantly wet and cold. The loose kilted plaid allowed quick drying, and could easily be stripped off and wrung. The long journeys between settlements and the detours to be made by a foot-traveller in times of flood, forced men often to lie out on the hills, when the plaid served as tent and sleeping bag combined. Without it they could not have lain out in foul weather. Highlanders were so accustomed to open-air sleep that they refused to use tents when provided by army ordnance. In battle, they threw the plaid off and fought in shirt-tails, which were long enough to be tied under the crutch.[31]

Mobility was further assisted by their marching diet. If the clansman had his bag of oatmeal, the only addition he required in a day's hard travel was water. He carried his daily ration and the shot for his gun in his sporran, which was then a capacious pouch of deer or calf's skin drawn tight at the top by thongs, and held close to the waist by a thick belt that could take weight, not a mere purse worn low as now on a light strap.[32] On such rations, Montrose's army had more than once moved sixty miles in a day and been battle-fit at the end.[33] Rob from his youth accepted such high standards of action as proven for old men (of twenty-five or more), and therefore unquestionably within his own abilities in his late teens. Meantime, of course, inspired by the great tales of his race, not to mention real need, he and his fellows set out to make themselves hardy.

The opportunities for summer recreation abounded. The young swam in the lochs and the deep pools of Gyle Water, for the hot summers encouraged it, and all knew that this was a skill they must get for crossing bridgeless rivers. They fished with hazel rods, guddled for trout under the stones and banks of Gyle Water, where the clear pools were shaded by a long stretch of old stunted alders, learned to row the smaller birlinns, and to sail the bigger when their elders had time. They played unorganized games: football, which they enjoyed the more since the Privy Council over the last two centuries had 'decreted and ordained that futeball be utterly cryit doun and nocht usit' because it led to riot; shinty or *camanachd*, played with wooden clubs and a wooden ball, a game which the Scots had brought from Ireland in the third century; and horse-racing after harvest, riding bareback and barefoot with grass bridles and whips. All the year long, at any hour of the day, they practised singlestick in preparation for the broadsword. And at all seasons they revelled in the evening ceilidhs.

Schooling

Rob Roy's part in the wide range of district life was interrupted by his schooling, which if elementary was certainly thorough. His surviving letters in English, an example of which appears on page 234, show an extensive vocabulary, with grammar and composition comparing well with those of the noble statesmen of his day, and beyond those of many present day school-leavers, yet this at a time when Gaelic was exclusively spoken north of the Highland Line, including the Trossachs.[34] There is no record of his formal education, nor evidence that he had French and Latin, although he probably did – they were normally included in the curriculum for a chieftain's son. His elder brother Iain would be sent to university, most likely Glasgow (the university has no records of its students enrolled prior to 1697). Male heirs by custom attended college at the age of eleven or twelve to fourteen. If Rob went too it would be during the period 1682–85.

Whatever the Church's failings – intolerance, for example – it did insist despite all discouragements from the landowners (who were required to provide the money) upon the right of every Scots child to be drilled in the three Rs. As early as 1616, the Privy Council had commanded every parish to establish a school – and required that chief's sons be sent. By the 1670s a thin network had spread across the Lowlands.[35] In the Highlands and Islands, established schools with special buildings were unknown except in Argyll and Inverness. But informal schools met in barns and outhouses, where the pupils squatted on the floor without paper, books, or desks. They had slates if they were lucky, and better still, eyes, ears, and memories. Better accommodation came slowly in the deep Lowland countryside, where landowners could be parted from their money only with difficulty, and more rapidly in the burghs.

The teachers, mostly young students, old men, or cripples, were paid a yearly salary of 100 to 200 merks – between £5 and £11 sterling – but where landowners refused to contribute they could have only a fraction of that. In the Highland interior up to 1690, teachers if not schools were privately available, but were paid only ten shillings a half year, and not employed in summer.[36] In any event, they could not live on their money-earnings and relied on pupils' parents for gifts of oatmeal, peats, straw (for roof and bed), butter, eggs, milk, and the like, without which they would have died of hunger and cold. In some parishes the ministers taught a few pupils, and men of property engaged masters for their own children. Probably Rob and one or two neighbouring children from Craigrostan, Comer, and Corrie Arklet, attended a school provided by their parents within walking distance of Glen Gyle, or else were sent to the nearest Lowland school and boarded out.

The few children lucky enough to have schooling began at the age of five, or at oldest seven if long distances had to be walked across moor and bog. The children of the poor, if they went at all, rarely stayed longer than three years; the parents did not feel more to be needed. The tacksmen's children normally continued five years.

The curriculum under Church rule was based on religious instructions on the catechism, scriptures, and prayers backed by frequent use of the tawse. The Church took a realistic view of the human child. He was taught reading from the Bible, writing, simple arithmetic, and if older and brighter, Latin grammar. Learning was greatly inhibited by the Privy Council's ban on Gaelic in official schools – Highland children failed to relate what they learned to daily life, in which English had no part. While young, they learned lessons parrot-like. When older, they spoke English better than Lowlanders, with the grammatical correctness given to a foreign tongue, but still with the Gaelic lilt.

Rob Roy would have six or seven years local schooling, not skimped. He was either a bright boy and learned fast, or was well taught, or learned much from parents and brothers, and read the books available at home. Most probably all of these. If he were sent to university that would be around 1683. The chairs were recruited from Episcopal ministers. The subjects taught in successive years by the 'regents' were ethics, Greek (Latin was left to the schools), logic, mathematics, physics, and philosophy.[37] An aim was to exercise the mind and develop thinking capacity, but the boys were far too young to reap the full advantage. Their minds had not been given time to seethe with the new ideas that could, were they older, be developed and exchanged so rewardingly in talk among themselves and with staff. That feature of university life had to wait for later centuries, when students enrolled were adolescent. While it must remain surmise that Rob attended a university, he did at least learn to express himself fluently with ideas properly ordered.

The illiteracy of the great majority of his fellows was small material handicap to the Highland people, for the opportunity of improving their lot by work did not exist save by good chance. The low level of literacy indicated no want of intelligence. Highlanders were no less agile in mind than now, indoor education being no substitute for experience of life, and better equipped with retentive memories since they lacked printed reminders. Where they did have the chance, their minds could blossom, and some of Rob's MacGregor relatives held the chairs of medicine and mathematics at the universities of Aberdeen, St Andrews, and Edinburgh.[38]

Lowland and English spectators of Rob Roy's Gaelic society disclose its grimmer aspect. They record that hens and goats wandered in and out of ill-lit huts with leaking roofs; that early on cold mornings people would emerge naked from huts to squat on the nearby bog; that all were shabbily dressed by day, and so on. While writers have marshalled the evidence to dispel romantic illusions, the truth about Highland life lies between the extremes of heaven and hell. The animals that wandered in and out of houses were liked for their company and warmth, if not the scent left behind; leaking roofs were no Highland prerogative; the sanitation was by far superior to that of Edinburgh, and graced with abundant space and air; good town dress has always been inappropriate, or absurd, for daily wear in a mountainous environment. In short, primitive as conditions were, they were so by modern standards. The people were bred to the life, enjoyed it in communities much more lively and interesting than any now to be found in the glens, and had greatly varied work. The Trossachs country today is a pale ghost of its former self. The assessment of former poverty by present standards is grossly misleading. In many respects the people lived fuller lives than now, and happier ones. In others, they suffered colder winters, bore starvation in bad years, and knew more nearly and often the griefs of bereavement. They tended to hibernate in winter, unless there were men of vigour in the household, as there were in Glen Gyle. In no age have vigorous minds been numbed by primitive living if granted a necessary minimum of warmth, food, and comfort. The Highland homes had more than that minimum, for due provision was made.

CHAPTER FOUR

---- ~ ----

PREPARATION
1681–84

Fᴿᴼᴹ ʜɪs fourteenth year, Rob Roy would have to take a much greater part in his people's daily work. His preparation for this and his training to arms fell within long-set custom. Each year at Glengyle, the call-to-arms drill and harvest time were followed by intensive cattle-work, and the barrelling of fish and meat to provide for the six months ahead.

The Fiery Cross had rarely been used in earnest since the Restoration of 1660; for that reason chieftains felt a need to give practice, and to inspect the clans' weapons against emergency. When used in crises, two stout sticks charred at their upper ends were tied to form a cross together with a rag dipped in goat's blood. The symbol of fire and sword was borne through every township and clachan of a clan's territory by relays of runners, on foot or pony-back or by galley as the land allowed. Each bearer as he passed held the cross aloft and according to need passed written orders or just shouted the name of the gathering place, of which Clan Dughaill Ciar had two: Lendrick by Loch Venachar and Arklet above Inversnaid.

The Fiery Cross could travel through the clan's territory in three hours, each settlement being responsible for alerting its own outliers. More than seven hundred families occupied the glens, which did not mean that one man from each could be expected to mobilize. The muster was cut to five hundred by illness, absence, and the presence in the glens, especially by Loch Voil in Balquhidder, of other clans' families. Mobilization was rapid, since each man had only to pick up his plaid, weapons, and a bag of oatmeal to be fully provisioned. The oatmeal mixed with water was eaten out of the cupped hand, failing a quaich.

The muster dropped to three hundred for a war campaign – Donald Glas did not have the full coercive powers of a chief ruling clan lands. Men came by consent. He could not only raise a large body of men but also rent and services from his sub-tenants, which went some way to compensate for the neglect of his own farm caused by much absence on clan business.

The weapon inspection or wapinschaw would most often be held at Lendrick and be followed by games. The chieftain had to know how effective any defence of his territory could be, what aid he could give to friends, king, or government if need were, and what were the deficiencies in weapons. The modern flintlocks came from London and Birmingham, the older matchlocks from France, Spain, Italy, or Germany. Guns were prized possessions; only a minority had them. Apart from the flintlocks bought by leading men, most were old weapons acquired as plunder in former wars. Pistols were made close by at Doune and Stirling.[1] The Doune pistols, made of steel by Thomas Cadell since 1646 and continued by his sons and former apprentices, had no equal in Britain for sureness, strength, or beauty of workmanship. The engraving and shape delighted the eye; hence they were much sought after by noblemen as presents to princes abroad, and sold for anything from three to twenty guineas a pair. Donald would most likely inherit a pair by the first Thomas Cadell. Many of his followers had pistols by other makers, like Alexander Campbell in Doune.

All had swords of varied kind – the long claymore, backswords, broadswords, and dirks. Targes (usually bought from Glasgow and Edinburgh) were in relatively short supply. Some carried small armpit knives, called *sgian ockle*. None at this period wore *sgian dubh*, or black stocking knives.

Clan Gregor could not be distinguished from others by tartan. The kilted plaids were most often brown, not the red tartan later ascribed to Clan Gregor. While the fashion of sett and colour varied from one glen to another, it tended to conform to a local tradition, so that the wearer's tartan might reveal his district to a much-travelled observer. Clan Gregor had been so disrupted and scattered that no tartans ascribable even to districts had emerged. The clans in war were distinguished one from another only by cap-badges: the MacGregors, a sprig of pine; the MacDonalds, a sprig of heather; the Campbells, fir club moss; the Camerons, crowberry; and so with all.

Important as the gathering might be, the more urgent daily practice for young men was in broadsword play. As boys of six they started with single sticks, and their fathers saw to it that practice was not random.[2] Like other leading men, Donald possessed the *claidheamh mor* or great two-handed sword, which had a double-edged blade four feet two inches long, and five feet over all. Some were five feet eight inches. He had carried this sword in the wars against Cromwell, and would wield it once more at Killiecrankie.[3] Since the Restoration, its place as a Highland weapon had been taken, and its name was later to be usurped, by the broadsword with basket hilt, 38 to 40 inches long, usually single-edged with a false back-edge, but sometimes double-edged. The steel blades of excellent temper were most often engraved *Ferrara*, after Andrea Ferrara, a sixteenth-century Italian swordsmith. His name had become the trademark of a type made for the Scots in Germany, and usually carrying the Solingen wolf-mark.[4]

The dirk or *biodaig* used for in-fighting had a broad blade of twelve to twenty inches, generally with a very thick back. Some were double-edged and others a triangular spike. The scabbard often held small skinning knives. Normally worn at the belt on the right-hand side, concealed by the plaid, the dirk in fighting was held in the left hand point down.

The targe or round shield was made of two layers of wood twenty inches in diameter. The hide cover was nailed in concentric circles. The centre bore a big metal boss and often a three-sided spike. In battle the targe was worn on the left forearm and held by a hand-grip. It was normally carried slung on the back.

These were no weapons for boys. Practice began with the ash stick, through which a peg had been driven below the handle. Rob was taught (most likely by the clan's fencing master) first to take position – body upright, the feet and legs positioned in different ways for best balance and speed of action. When that was mastered, he was taught the cuts made from seven angles, and seven guard positions below and above breast level. Only when these had been thoroughly learned would he be shown the three thrusts, made with a straight wrist from eye-, breast-, and hip-levels, and finally three 'engaging' guards.

The rest was a matter of steady practice. The cuts and guards had to be made each and all from the different positions using a naked blade to get the proper turns of wrist and blade-edge; therefore it was common practice to make a square target from old boards, on which the fourteen cuts and guards were engraved. Rob would have to face it daily, and practice each stroke and guard point until they became second nature.[5]

Donald must have had reason to be pleased with Rob, who early on would show his exceptionally fast reflexes and a promise of strength and quickness excelling his brothers'. After a few years' stick play, Rob would learn the finer points of the art, and Donald pass on battle experience – how against a mounted enemy you must gain his left side and slash the horse's nose, which sent it right about; while against a man with a rapier, cut diagonally up at his arm. Ash stick play was the common course for all boys. They fenced assiduously and grew accustomed to hard knocks. The Highland male did not use his fists in a fight – that was *Sasunnach* or English custom; nor the cudgel like the *Gall* or Lowlander. He used cold steel. Therefore he was trained from the start to as high skill as he could compass, and while taught to kill and mutilate was still more importantly taught how not to kill, for the custom in quarrel was to concede victory to the first man who drew blood. Sword-points were then dropped and honour was satisfied. The young had to be disciplined to accept the custom and that meant a real discipline of mind and temper, and effective skill with the weapon. Men were not murderous, and life seemed short enough when only one in three children lived to puberty.

Highlanders were less given to brawling among themselves than Lowlanders,[6] by reason both of penalties incurred and discipline instilled; once involved in quarrel the 'wild Highlanders', so called, could more often withdraw coolheadedly before duelling point was reached if they saw the odds against themselves to be too great. This could be (and sometimes was) mistaken by Lowlanders for cowardice when it was commonsense. Donald appears to have instilled most thoroughly into Rob this prudent self-possession in the use of his arms, for his adult life gave many outstanding examples of it, hard to understand in its apparently alternating bravery and discretion, if its source in early training is unknown.

Autumn

The gathering, followed by the games, was timed to the prior claims of the harvest – before it if the season were late, after it if early. Harvest was always a variable date entailing much debate and worry. The barley and oats ripened at the end of August if the summer had been fair, or up till mid-October if bad. But the latter-end was so often wet that the grain suffered if not reaped earlier, even if not fully ripened. When wet windy seasons came every three or four years the corn rotted in the ground. The west Highland people then suffered distress and famine of which Lowlanders had small conception.

While the corn still stood it was plucked for daily use, and if dry switched off the ear with a stick, winnowed, and parched in a pot over the fire while stirred with a wooden *speilag*. Every house had a quern, made of two stone slabs, the lower concave and the upper convex. Two women milled, one rotating the upper slab by its peg, while the other fed in the parched grain by a central hole. The unleavened bread of oatmeal or barley flour (called *bannach*) could be baked and eaten within two hours of reaping.[7]

When fully ripe the corn was reaped by sickle, but if unripened it was uprooted by hand to allow the grain to fill out after the corn had been stooked.[8] This work was for women and children. When dried out, the bound sheaves were carried to the houses and the stacks built close by, thatched, and roped with stone weights to stand to the storms of winter. Threshing and winnowing followed at more leisure, and flour could be milled in bulk at Inversnaid,[9] or the mill of Chon at Loch Ard.

While the women were harvesting, the men were on the hills, either hunting red deer or selecting cattle for the October sales. Some droving to Glasgow, Dumbarton, Crieff, and Stirling, began as early as June, but October when the cattle were in best condition was the time of the great tryst at Crieff. The cows then fetched fifteen shillings to one pound sterling. Donald was active each year assessing stock available from early May, travelling far afield[10] to meet dealers and entering into contracts for collection of small herds at a variety of small trysts like Killin, for driving to Crieff.

In September, every household began to take thought for the winter's 'mart' (from Martinmas in November), when fish and meat had to be salted down for winter provision. To this end Donald or Iain would make an annual excursion to Glasgow to buy salt in bulk, and, if the year had been good, to sell the clan's surplus of corn, butter, cheese, and poultry. Donald shipped all goods by galley down Loch Lomond, and then by the river Leven to the Clyde. The freight included his rents as chieftain, but sale was made of any community produce.

It was most likely on one of these autumn trips that Rob paid his first visit to Glasgow. The custom was to sail from Inversnaid to Balloch, where the crew took the boat on tow down the Leven, until they could sail around Dumbarton Rock and Castle into the Clyde. The broad estuary, everywhere dotted by white and brown sails, narrowed at Bowling, where they timed arrival to catch the flood tide. The crew then took to the oars, until they reached the outskirts of Glasgow and could tie up beside the Broomielaw croft, named from the broom along its banks. The depth at high water was only three feet, falling to one foot at low water, when the people began to wade freely across the shoals between the north and south banks – saving a walk of three-quarters of a mile up-river to Brig o' Clyde. At high water the Broomielaw became busy with barges and wherries from Port Glasgow (seventeen miles down river) unloading brandy, wine, and salt from France, and loading Clyde salmon for export. Most were away on the ebb.

When Rob went ashore, he would make his way east along the bank of the Skinners' Green, then up the Saltmarket to the Mercat Cross. First visitors were always astonished by the size and splendour of the buildings. There were four main streets, all cobbled, meeting at a spacious market square: the Saltmarket running up from the river; the High Street running uphill to the university college and to the bishop's castle and cathedral beyond; at right-angles to these, the Trongate striking west through orchards and fields past the steeple of St Mary's kirk; and eastwards, the Gallowgate. The streets seemed of extraordinary width. The houses to either side were faced with squared sandstone, which the masons had occasionally ornamented. Every window was glazed, and some had the stone above engraved with the initials of the owner and his wife. Their lower storeys were supported on huge square columns with arches opening into the shops, like piazzas runing between the houses and setting them off to best advantage. At the town's east side, a broad green plain fringed by tall trees stretched far up the river.[11]

Glasgow with ten thousand people was one of the ten largest towns in Britain – yet small compared to Edinburgh, which had thrice that number. To Rob it must have seemed immense, and given status by its cathedral, college, and tolbooth. Westwards, the town had rubble-stone houses faced with rough-cast. Each had access given by an enclosed wooden staircase, with portholes like a ship's at the landings. The windows here bore glass on the upper halves only, and half-shutters below. At the town's outer fringes were low, turf-faced houses not unlike those of Glen Gyle, but with chimney-tops of bottomless tubs. The return walk eastwards by way of St Tenew's Gate (now Argyle Street) led back to the Mercat Cross, where Rob may have stopped to assess the strength of the barred and steepled tolbooth, little dreaming that one day he would lie prisoner there, expecting to hear the date of his execution.

The beauty of Glasgow was praised by all contemporary travellers, but the more lasting impression made on the young Rob Roy would most certainly be the unfriendliness of its citizens. And for that there was reason. The Gael and the Lowlander had long since drawn apart, spoke different tongues, followed different ways, and had lost mutual understanding. Mistrust went so far that clansmen had a comon name for it – *Mi-run mor nan Gall*, the Lowlander's great hate.

Hostilities were set aside at the market. Glasgow's day opened when the six o'clock gun announced the post-runner's arrival from Edinburgh. The city was promptly astir as people flocked to the postmaster's shop. Other shops in the Trongate soon opened up. At the market square the scene of bustle bordered on chaos. Donald or his delegate would hire horses and carts to carry the clan's goods from the Broomielaw, and scores of other carts jammed the streets. Before his first visit, Rob could never have seen a wheeled cart – the only Lowland roads on which they could move were those from Glasgow to Stirling and Edinburgh. They were all small, with wheels eighteen inches high if new, made of boards clenched together without iron rim-hoops, and mounted on a revolving axle. Some were filled with grass brought in green by the country folk for sale to feed merchants' horses. Others were filled with peats, coal, and logs, but most with produce like Donald's.[12]

The bargainers were usually separated by the carts and had to shout above the din to make themselves heard. Expostulations, jokes, and witticisms in the Lowland Scots interlarded most dealings, and Rob through his schooling in correct English would at first not understand one half of it. When the clan's sales had been made, the Gregarach might spend another few days buying salt by the barrel (imported from Brittany and Spain), copper and iron nails, fish hooks, ammunition, oil, lime, claret, flax tow and linen shirts, alum, indigo, paper and ink, small gifts for the family, snuff and pipe tobacco, and little else besides.

After the autumn market much had still to be done before the Crieff tryst in the third week of October. From early October to Martinmas (11 November), salmon, trout, and char were taken from the lochs by rod and net and salted in the barrel. Fish were much more plentiful than now and one rod in a good year had been known to take twenty salmon in a day out of Loch Lomond, or a dozen out of Loch Venachar. Smaller fish were hung above the hearth-fires to be dried and smoked. Cows and sheep were killed and beef and mutton salted. Summer travellers often remarked that Highlanders ate little or no meat, unaware that the meat was eaten not then, while beasts were fattening, but in autumn and winter. The poorer people combined in groups to share and salt down a cow between them, but the poorest could not afford even that. Nothing usable of a beast was wasted. Haggises were made from the sheep's lungs, liver, and heart, which were mixed with oatmeal, suet, and chopped onion, stuffed into the sheep's stomach-bag, and boiled for three hours. Soap was made by boiling tallow with a lye of plant-ashes, lime, and water.

The last of the peats were carried down from the banks in creels, and in sledges drawn by garrons. A year's fuel was piled up in pyramids near the door of every house. The store room at Glengyle House filled up with grain-sacks and barrels, and tubs of cheese and butter. The deer hunts continued while the cattle and sheep and goats were gathered down from the higher pastures. Donald, Iain, Duncan and many other men were away to the cattle droving and trysts, or in bad years on rieving expeditions planned for the end of September. The young women up in the shielings were helped down with their gear. All were home again and families united in mid November, while the hills whitened under winter snow.

Winter

Winter was a bad time in the glens for the old and infirm or men of sluggish spirit. The cold and boredom no doubt made them quarrelsome, and if they had the means they drank too much. For the young and vigorous it had compensations. Spring, summer, and autumn, they spent almost every minute of their waking time out of doors, rain or shine, unless at school. In winter, the privileged few trudged to school in bare feet as usual, however deep the snow, provided the distance was only three or four miles. Each child carried a peat for the school fire. If it began to snow and blow, a gillie turned out to shepherd them. Only in storm might they stay at home.

In 1683 when his schooldays ended, Rob was at last wearing brogues and blue bonnet. The young had winter enthusiasms. Piping was one of them, for those of musical talent. All had much chance of winter shinty – the lads played for hours on end if the ground were clear – and occasional sledging and skating. As part of his training for leadership and use of country in cattle droving, Rob had to learn to navigate across misty hills by close, continuous observation of wind and sun directions, and to avoid the summits in cloud. He and his friends walked the hills until they knew intimately every glen, hill, and corrie of the Trossachs country at all seasons, and knew something of all people living there. By that time they must have been well accustomed to covering thirty miles in a summer's day across high land, or half that in winter. All youngsters had to learn to sleep on the hills rolled up in plaids, to carry their oatmeal like men, and think nothing of the distance, for their elders could travel twice as far.

The Highlanders of the day were prodigious walkers in their own country, for they were mountaineers in a sense not now known in Scotland. Being supremely fit by constant traverse of roadless country, they found passage across hills of two or three thousand feet no more tiring than walking on the flat. Lowland travellers of the time, even through the following century, record that in several weeks' journey they would never set eyes on another horseman.[13] The chiefs and gentry would ride a horse to save a day on long Lowland journeys, but few others took such trouble. Glasgow to Edinburgh or Glen Gyle was a good day's walk. Rob Roy was brought up in this tradition, so that although his country abounded in horses, they were used as pack animals, not commonly ridden. He was first and foremost a mountaineer in the original sense of that word, like his forefathers over a thousand years.

CHAPTER FIVE

~

YOUTH
1685–87

WHEN DONALD GLAS turned a speculative eye on his youngest son, now fourteen, and wondered what might become of him, he would see a great potential strength on two planes. The boy had a frame like his own – unusual breadth of shoulder, arms long for his height, a big rib-cage and strong legs – but not like his own sheathed in muscle. All clansmen were lean and flat-bellied – one could search the Highlands and Islands in vain for a fat man[1] – but boys were as spare as spring bullocks, ribs prominent, raw-boned all over, and the skin tight on the face, where Rob's physical likeness to his father ended. The boy's face was like his Campbell mother's, fair and freckled. The hair flamed on its stalk like a lit splinter. More importantly, the boy had a mind of his own, quick, keen and incisive. He would be a natural leader, especially if he learned to control his tongue.

Great events on local and national level had been brewing while Rob was growing through his boyhood, and were still fermenting. Unknown to him or Donald they would determine his future, in particular through that of another boy named James Graham, now five years old and growing up at Mugdock Castle, just twenty-five miles south. 'When the young bird stretches its head over the edge of the nest and sees under the blue sky an earth ablaze with light, it does not know that the hawk that will one day silence its song is at that moment breaking out of its shell .... When the boy looks down from the heights of his dreams on to an alluring world, then is put in movement the misfortune that will strike his forehead like a stone from a sling. For the chain of events reaches far back ....'[2]

Rob had been only seven when the MacGregors had first intimation that John, the chief of Buchanan, was in deep financial trouble. He was (on paper) the feudal superior for their lands. In 1678 he sold more land by Loch Arklet to Gregor Og (who was married to Anne Buchanan). Two years later he sold Buchanan Castle on the Endrick to James Graham, the third Marquis of Montrose. At this time William Graham, the third Earl of Menteith, had also become insolvent, and having no heirs gave Aberfoyle and Port of Menteith to James the head of his house. James now moved his seat from Mugdock to Buchanan. The Buchanans had held their lands for nearly five hundred years, but when John died in 1682 their remaining homeland had to be sold. Apart from Craigrostan along the north-west flank of Ben Lomond, which had been sold to Colquhoun of Luss, all the rest was bought by Montrose. He thus became the superior for a great part of Donald's land. His family crest was an eagle, wings spread and talons in its prey.

Rob's mother was much worried all this while by her Glenlyon family's finances. Her brother Robert was chieftain and now fifty. A mass of fair, curly hair had in youth capped his tall, beautifully proportioned body. His father had died when he was eight, and his mother had then married MacGregor of Roro. The boy had succeeded to large properties and heavy debts, grown up frustrated under a tutor, and taking to the bottle and cards had incurred gambling debts that pinched his family for necessities. He had not taken kindly to plain living. He had long since sold his forest lands to timber merchants, who had felled nearly ten thousand pines. In 1684 he had finally sold Glen Lyon, which was occupied by 3600 of his people, to John Lord Murray, retaining only his wife's lands around Chesthill in the lower glen.[3] Margaret was desolated at the news, in despair of her brother, and apprehensive of future shame.

Rob would see that while his father felt sympathy, it was not heartfelt towards Uncle Robert. Campbell misfortunes could hardly be expected to disturb the peace of a MacGregor's mind. Donald, like nearly every other clan leader, was enjoying the downfall of Campbell of Argyll, and the rise of Murray of Atholl, who was now Lord Justice General. Archibald, the ninth Earl of Argyll had lived under the king's disdain, which masked fear, ever since his father's head had been taken off by the Maiden. He was that rare thing, a man of principle. Charles II, obliged to accept his people's Protestant faith, had promoted the episcopal form of Church government, but denounced the Covenanters, who had bound themselves to defend the Presbyterian Church. He had evicted their ministers, inflicted the boot and other tortures, executed their leaders, and billeted troops on their followers to bring ruin. The king in consequence lived in dread of rebellion. Archibald had been consistent in opposing the king's oppressive measures. He spoke out against them at a time when most landed men changed their religious politics to get safety and office. His courage brought its nemesis.

In 1681 Argyll was accused of treason and imprisoned in Edinburgh Castle. That he had lasted so long he owed to the good word of Charles's natural son, the duke of Monmouth, of whom the king was extremely fond. Argyll's immunity had ended when James, the king's Roman Catholic brother, was made Commissioner for Scotland.

Argyll did not languish long in prison. He escaped disguised as his daughter's page, holding her skirt from the floor while she walked off from a visit. He fled to Holland. His behaviour earned the grudging respect of Clan Dughaill Ciar (who unlike many Highland clans were Protestants), and made it easier for Rob Roy to see MacCailein Mor in a new light.

While Argyll's fortunes plummeted, Iain Glas of Glenorchy's soared. He bought the lands and earldom of Caithness from their bankrupt owner, Sinclair, whose wife was Argyll's daughter, Lady Mary Campbell. The conveyance took effect in 1676 on Sinclair's death, when Iain Glas promptly married the widow in hope of ousting George, the heir male, who instead took possession by force of arms. Iain's fiery cross raised seven hundred men between the Tay and Orchy. He gave command to Robert of Glenlyon. Robert marched north and slaughtered the Sinclairs, but George escaped and took his just complaint to the king. Neither king nor Privy Council could stomach Glenorchy's claim to the earldom, so they compromised, and following their policy of loading him with honours to counterbalance Argyll, created him earl of Breadalbane and threw in six lesser titles. In 1685, when Charles II died and James VII succeeded, Breadalbane had become the king's most powerful Scottish subject.

Donald ever since the Restoration had found himself in a political cleft stick. He had been the king's man, held his commission, given his oath, been hopeful at first of a restitution of Clan Gregor lands, and then with growing dismay had to watch Breadalbane's rise, the death of his hope, and the ruthless suppression of Lowland Presbyterians. This latter ill was not one that he felt his own, or his people's. The Highland clans were part Catholic, part Protestant. Most of the latter were Episcopalian and none Covenanters. Highlanders worshipped with serious mind and walked great distances to attend kirk or chapel. Some knelt down at first sight of the church building. But whether the Church was run by elders and ministers in presbytery or by bishops in diocese was not to them of fundamental importance.

They could conform to new rules so long as there was no change in the essential element, the teaching of Christ. Unlike Lowlanders, they were free of bigotry on administrative and doctrinal niceties. Thus Donald found it best to continue his allegiance to the king and his Commissioner, and to remain allied to Atholl, who was at least a weighty counterpoise to Breadalbane on his north frontier and Montrose on his south. In so deciding, he was in general accord with the policy of the western clans, who were united in their fear of Campbell ambition. It cannot be over-emphasized how largely the politics of the clans were determined over the centuries by detestation of MacCailein Mor, as distinct from the Campbell people with whom relations were normal. They freely intermarried and traded.

The war between king and Covenanters broke out again in 1678-9. At the battle at Bothwell Brig, when the Covenanters were routed by the duke of Monmouth, the clansmen brought in by Atholl for the king would likely include a contingent under Donald Glas. Rob Roy was then eight, and could have only a vague, one-sided notion of the rights and wrongs. Through all these years of religio-political disputes, his father and other chiefs were following expedient policies, which Rob was brought up to honour. Always their first concern was their own or their people's land. Without that home base they could not live. The vexatious differences between Catholic, Episcopalian, and Presbyterian forms of religion were to them not even secondary matters. Loyalty to their king was secondary. Material profit from plunder came third; ecclesiastical matters last of all. This order of priority was a general rule proven by a thousand examples, although no such rule could cover all men or contingencies. Rob Roy was to be no common man, since he had a mind of his own, but was indoctrinated by the rule in adolescence without conscious effort by anyone.

He was fourteen when the first definite sign was given that his peace at Glen Gyle could not last. And that event was the succession of James VII.

James was a Roman Catholic. The alarm felt by Episcopalians and Presbyterians alike was justified as soon as his brother Charles II died in February 1685. The first year of his kingship became known as 'the Killing Time'. The Covenanters were hunted down; hundreds when caught had an ear lopped off and were transported as slaves to American plantations; most others were shot. Monmouth fled to Holland, from where Argyll persuaded him to invade. In early May, Argyll sailed with three ships to raise the west of Scotland, while Monmouth tried to raise the west of England. Argyll made for the Mull of Kintyre and marched north, gathering men,[4] but no other clan would rise. The navy closed in and Campbell fled.

Atholl had already been made Lieutenant of Argyll and now devastated all Campbell country (except Breadalbane), a work in which Donald Glas and the Gregarach shared, more especially in Kintyre and Lorn.[5] The Atholl invaders sacked Dunstaffnage Castle, Dunoon Castle, Carrick Castle on Loch Goil, Carnasserie, and numerous other strongholds. The plunder taken was valued at over £60,000 sterling. An undue proportion was driven on the hoof to Glengyle (Atholl rightly or wrongly felt cheated and bore a grudge).[6] The benefits gained and the comforts enjoyed by the poorer people of his glen from such plunder, the general rejoicing and the excitement of inspecting the new stock and goods, and unusual trophies, or much-needed weapons and tools, all were seen by Rob with little or no hint given of the suffering caused in getting them.

Archibald Campbell was taken by the Athollmen on 18 June at Inchinnan near Renfrew, and executed by the Maiden at Edinburgh. Monmouth's defeat at Sedgemoor and beheading at Tower Hill came later in the month. News more important to the MacGregors, if less dramatic, began to reach them by instalments soon after. The new earl of Argyll, Archibald aged 34, was trying to reverse his father's and grandfather's attainders by offering allegiance to James. But Iain Glas of Breadalbane, now a Privy Councillor, wanted no rival in Argyll. Archibald's overtures were repulsed and his thoughts turned more positively to William of Orange. William's mother was a daughter of Charles I, his wife was the eldest daughter of James VII, and he was a Protestant. The Protestants of both England and Scotland were beginning to think that the coldness of this Dutchman (he had been brought up surrounded by enemies) might be more sufferable than the religious iniquities of James Stewart. Archibald departed for the Hague.

The years of initiation

The Highlands were little troubled by Lowland afflictions. Life continued smoothly in Glen Gyle, apart from domestic griefs and incidents. Iain's wife, who had borne no children, died. Iain was arrested at Michaelmas after the Atholl raid by a merchant at Doune for a debt of £82 Scots, and held until his father could raise the specie.[7] (Lords and commons alike were often at their wits' end to get coin to pay their way. Hardly any were free of debt, not through lack of means but lack of cash – Scotland's money circulation was only £150,000[8].) Rob followed the round of the seasons, taking year by year a fuller part in the ploughing and sowing, hunting and boat-management, stock raising and droving, thatching and house-building – the latter always a community task. Once the materials were assembled, a stone or turf house could be run up in a day.[9] On all domestic jobs of the kind the men worked in their shirt-tails and waistcoats. The work was many-sided to a degree no longer known or imagined in Scotland – and time-consuming. Between early summer and winter they worked from dawn to dusk, but for Rob there were added interests and enlivening excursions.

He had now to make advances in weaponry and trackings skills. A man was thought fit to bear arms at sixteen, and training had to be taken for the day, lest he kill himself by folly. The change from ash-stick duelling to cold steel was a salutary experience for each lad, but after a day or two confidence temporarily lost returned. This was the real thing at last, and Rob excelled in the fast co-ordination of eye, hand and foot needed for high skill. He must have given it unremitting practice day by day, year by year, until the broad blade seemed a part of his body. That his training to arms was prolonged and disciplined was proven by later events; no man without it, whatever his natural talent, could live as he did in Highland country, where every man was armed and proficient, and remain unscratched. And no man without prolonged training of a natural talent could so use his weapons, as he did, that no man ever lost his life to them except in war. No man, finally, could achieve his consistent record of sparing his opponent without having generosity of mind and a habit of compassion. In these early days, when he was learning everything, his parents would seem to have given Rob a good home life.

Many days and nights together had to be spent on the hills hunting and tracking, which meant careful, close observation of all wildlife, weather, landforms, sun and stars, the conscious, constant use of eyes, ears, nose, and the sense of touch in response to wind shifts, until the four senses remained alert all day long, without conscious effort: recording, warning, informing, guiding, in ways now lost to man in the Highlands where by comparison he is now only half alive. No compasses were used for navigation in mist, nor watches for time. In traversing the hills and moors in mist, direction was held by the wind, and even the lightest air sufficed when men were sensitive to its touch on skin, and from the sun by gradations of light in the cloud, to which Lowlanders were blind. The flight of birds could bring news. The slow, heavy flight of a heron, reluctantly moving from one bay to another by Loch Katrine, differed subtly from its more purposeful search for a fishing ground, and gave early warning of man's hidden approach. High on the hills, the scuttle of ptarmigans, the quick twist of a hind's head, the line taken by a darting hare or suddenly moving goats or ponies, were seen at long distance by the sharp eyes of Rob and his clansmen; they knew in every detail the lie of the land and could judge the source of disturbance. Their sight had a keenness rarely matched now by men who read much. Their powers of observation by the four senses were trained by the necessities of a life lived at one with nature, free of the artificial aids that blunt them.

Every scene, therefore, was much more meaningful to Rob and his compatriots than to men of later times, or townsmen of their own day, and much richer, both in its seen context and by their ability to interpret. This fact of their life rewarded them with a deeper love of their Highland ground than Lowlanders could appreciate, or be expected to understand. They did not understand, for example, that to deprive such men of such land was to uproot them as a tree is uprooted. They might exist, but no longer feel alive.

Some of the side-effects of acutely seeing everything that grew, lived, and moved in the wildlands seem nowadays to be startling. One was men's tracking skill over grass and heather,[10] which once trodden retained its downpress for a long time before it rose enough to be undetectable by a trained eye. Stolen cattle could be tracked within days of their passing; even men who had taken refuge on the hills were occasionally followed and found by foot-trace.

Rob's introduction to cattle-raiding had certainly begun early, for he was expert before he was twenty. There was no rival to this field exercise as a training for honest droving, which demanded discipline, tactical skills in planning movement, and fore-knowledge of raiders' methods in order to forestall them. It was important training also for two allied forms of business contract, which brought Donald Glas and his men a useful annual income – droving to England, and Watch duties in exchange for black mail.

Droving to England was routed by laws through Border towns, where the cattle were subject to tax, even although they had been freed of customs on the English border since 1669. But there was a wide range of other routes through the Border hills. Men of wide-ranging abilities like Donald were wanted as drove-commanders by men of capital to buy cattle and drive the herds for sale to the trysts and to organize droves into England. Donald and his sons became trusted, held the certificates of respectability required by all drovers under the Privy Council order of 1671, knew every remote route through the hills, and in evading tolls had unerring dexterity.

Donald's income from the Watch was irregular in law rather than illegal, for it was sanctioned by government. The word mail meant rent. This black rent was paid largely in kind by farmers of the central and east Lowlands, Moray and the northern counties, to clan chieftains along their mountain fringes, for guarding the hill passes against cattle raiders. (From this practice derives the more sinister 'blackmail' of today's usage.) The protector contracted to make good any loss, gave regular receipts for the money paid, and did in fact honour his agreement. He appeared to think of it as an insurance contract, on which the premium varied around £4 Scots on each £100 of the land-owner's or farmer's rent. It was obviously open to abuse. An Act of Parliament (1601) had made extortion and payment of black mail (to other than an authorised Watch) illegal, but landowners felt free to come to mutual agreements with chieftains, who were never so unwise as to extort money by threat. They offered a service, which could not be refused. If accepted, depredations stopped; if not, they continued. In support of peace and good order, such agreements had the frequent blessing of government. In 1658 and subsequent dates, the Privy Council authorized the MacGregors of Glengyle to protect the cattle of the Lennox, appointing their chieftains to command a Watch with power of fire and sword, and enjoining the landowners of the counties of Dunbarton and Stirling to maintain the Watch.[11] These orders were corroborated by the Justices of the Peace at Quarter Sessions at Stirling. The appointment of a Watch was thus a government compromise with black mail, and gave the MacGregors employment, in which Rob took his share.

The raiders' fast routes of escape north from the Lennox, by the passes of Balmaha, Aberfoyle, the Trossachs, Leny, and Keltie Water, were too easily guarded to be usable, unless in concert with the MacGregors when they had called off a Watch for non-payment of black mail. In that event the raiders had to pay Donald Glas a 'collop', which, since it varied according to the value of the plunder, meant disagreement and rough dealing, sometimes only to be settled by the sword, though not by loss of life. The collop was one of the overhead expenses, payable on all clan territories traversed on the route home. It was part of the raiders' game to avoid that levy, by choice of route and good timing. In effect it was less the main passes that had to be watched for prevention than the hill ground between. The raiders travelled by night and spent the day with their herds in high corries (the hilltop hollows) far from any likely passage of man. Near dusk they would cross the watersheds and descend, seeking hidden ways by side-glens and woodlands. Experienced leaders had an immensely detailed knowledge of all the Highland ranges, their ground-cover, and the settlements in the glens, built up over years of alert-eyed travel; each raid came as a challenge to skill and sagacity, and to every physical faculty, therefore, gave keen enjoyment and deep satisfaction when it went well.

In such excursions, generations of need and training had made the MacGregors the most accomplished of all the clans, therefore none were so valued as preventers. They could not hope to patrol all their hill ground day and night, nor had they need. They had sufficient men able to read all the signs given by plant and animal life on their hillsides and moorlands. They had expert trackers. Raiders who thought to slip east by the Allan Water or west by the Gare Loch were rapidly overtaken. The Lennox farmers could testify that in return for their mail they were honestly served to their great gain, and the ironies of that did not escape them.

Rob Roy was trained in all these arts to a pitch equalled but not excelled in Highland history. That he was trained, and did not simply pick up the skills when later need arose, is self-evident; they can no more be 'picked up' than skill in pipes and pibroch. They can be acquired under good tutelage by long and thorough practice and by that alone, if the boy is intelligent. Rob's early excursions must have ranged across Scotland from the Border passes to the far north in years of tireless walking and climbing, through rain and shine, blizzards and night frosts, while living hard on sparse diet. He had to learn how to lead a raid; how to conduct ten to thirty men a full hundred miles each way measured as the crow flies, or thrice that across country; how to provision them on the way yet direct them in small groups on to diverging and converging routes, selected so that no advance warning might reach the victim or alert the clans occupying the land traversed; where to rendezvous for the final reconnaissance, how to plan the round-up, dispose his men, secure the withdrawal; where to put out scouts, and to zig-zag the final long retreat to hide trace and to fox collop-collectors. He had to learn in what places cattle were best reset (accepted by buyers who knew their origin) if they could otherwise be identifiable at Crieff tryst, and if too numerous for support on the home grazings. Reconnaissance and planning had to be done well in advance, and as little as possible left to chance. Good luck, some said, was essential: a flash flood at some bridgeless river could spell disaster on the first night's withdrawal. Donald would have none of that. He had instilled into Rob the idea that ill luck was self-earned, a euphemism for ill judgment. The flash flood should have been foretold by searching the skies. The chance passer who gave the alarm should not have been allowed to pass. The traced track that led to the raiders' capture should have been covered by earlier use of a river-bed, or a diversion on to a drove road. Donald's motto, which Rob inherited, was not his clan's. It was *Bi air t' aire* (Be watchful). Rob, naturally hotblooded, was trained early away from impetuous action to action by forethought. The results were all-important in later life.

The time of greatest raiding activity in Britain – for it extended well into northern England – was around the end of September during the Michaelmas moon, when the cattle were in prime condition. Like other neighbouring clans, the MacGregors and the MacFarlanes of Arrochar and Inveruglas would occasionally act in concert. Their old enmities had long since been laid aside. Their meeting place for discussion (and also for barter of goods) had in earlier years been Eilean a' Butha (Brownie's Isle) on upper Loch Lomond, where the MacFarlane's small castle, like their bigger one on Inveruglas Isle, had been ruined by Cromwell. In later years they met in the chief's house at Cladach Mor on the Tarbet shore.[12] Stone-built and thatched with bracken, it had three rooms under a loft of cleft oak-beams. The living room had a glazed window, a fire against the gable with a roof-vent, and a chimney-pot of clay plastered on a twig frame. The MacFarlanes were heirs male of the twelfth-century Celtic earls of the Lennox (displaced by the Darnley Stewarts) through their ancestor Parlan, commemorated by the mountain of that name at the head of Glen Gyle. By Rob's day they were commemorated more aptly by their pipe tune *Thogail nam Bo* (Lifting the Cattle) for such was their prowess that the Michaelmas moon was known as MacFarlane's Lantern. A verse for the tune goes thus in translation:

> We drive the cattle through the glens
> Through the corries, woods and bens
> Through the sleet or misty rain.
> When the moon is shining low
> By frozen loch and drifted snow
> Stealthily and bold we go
> Though small our hope of gain.

At the Cladach Mor, Donald and his lieutenants would sometimes meet the MacFarlanes' leaders to plan the exchange of separately lifted cattle, so that each could lift from nearer home than usual, yet enhance safety by selling far off from the source of plunder. Thus the MacFarlanes would engage to raid south-west into Cowal, while the MacGregors raided north-east into Strathearn. By careful timing, the two herds could be driven to arrive on the same day at Inverarnan in Glen Falloch, exchanged, and either driven straight to Crieff and Dumbarton or hidden for a spell at Loch Sloy, which lay in a glen behind Ben Vorlich (*Loch Sloidh!* was the MacFarlane's war-cry), and in the corrie of the Snaid Burn. The use of these holding places became essential when heavy rain brought up the rivers in spate (not even the Leven had a bridge to Dumbarton), or if the losers' scouts drew close.

Long before the time for initial action, the victims' territories would be thoroughly reconnoitred, and such careful note taken that each party could describe to the other the colour, markings, age, condition, and number of the cows to be lifted.[13] It must have given mutual pleasure to the MacFarlanes and MacGregors to work together. Each had a professional efficiency and a cool restraint, so that numbers taken were those agreed, neither ruinous to the victims nor excessive for quick handling and sale. Similar arrangements with the MacDonalds of Glencoe caused worry, for they were hotbloodedly apt to carry off more than could be safely handled because an opportunity offered, to the injury of all concerned.

Rob by his very nature must have revelled in these adventures: the stealth of movement by night, the suspense while waiting for the moon to rise over the resting herd, the confusion of the round-up, the anxieties of the drive, the tense, day-long watch from hidden corries lest they be traced, and the exultation of safe home-comings. He was learning all the time about men and their frailties, cattle and their needs, and the great diversity of his own country and its living conditions. While discovering much of himself and his fears, he would find to his surprise that he could do more than he dreamed, that he could push himself always further without reaching an end to bodily strength and stamina. Such testing delights any vigorous youth. Rob's confidence was growing year by year. On his sixteenth birthday his father would by custom present him formally with broadsword, dirk, targe, pistols and a gun. Rob had been freely using them all as he wished for training, but hitherto only on loan from store. Now they were his to wear and carry. One February morning, Donald gave the traditional blessing to the weapons and the boy. He would add the usual advice, to fear nothing and to spare man and beast, but perhaps kept his words terse, for no words now could undo what had long since been built into the boy from his parents' own bodies and lives, and the Glengyle community.

CHAPTER SIX

YOUTH
1688–89

The course shaped

Rob was no sooner bearing arms than Iain announced his engagement to Christian, the daughter of Campbell of Duneaves at the foot of Glen Lyon. Her father had been Glenlyon's tutor. They were married that year of 1687 at Fortingall. The wedding gave Rob the chance of meeting his notorious uncle, Robert Campbell, and his Glenlyon kinsmen. Knowing his mother's anxieties over her brother, he would see the reasons confirmed in the flesh. The face that once had a feminine delicacy had become hearty, the complexion florid from years of convivial living. It displayed the man's dichotomy of character; the force of personality that made the visible effects of an effete life seem the more pitiable, and the weakness overt in his readiness to accept the most easy solution to trouble. Determined men of no scruple would find in Robert a pliable tool, useful if stupid.

The talk of the men after the wedding was given them by a national crisis. King James's Declaration of Indulgence had been newly published. It granted Roman Catholics freedom of worship. James Drummond, the Earl of Perth, had turned Catholic and as Lord Chancellor had introduced the thumbscrew for the better conversion of Covenanters; Melfort and Moray had turned too and were Secretaries of State. The new Indulgence, coming on top of James's claim to the Dispensing Power, which declared that he had power to abolish laws as he pleased, would yet cause civil war. The Lowlands and England would not much longer bear tyranny in the guise of religious 'toleration'. Prominent men of the joint kingdom were already in touch with MacCailein Mor and William of Orange, to sound them out on the Stewart succession, supposing that James's second wife, Mary d'Este of Modena, produced a son and heir. His first wife Anne had borne only two daughters, of whom the elder, Mary, was heir to the English throne and married to William of Orange, thus giving him the double Stewart connection; the younger, Anne, had married George of Denmark; since both had been reared as Protestants, all was yet tolerably well for the succession in Sassenach eyes. But Mary of Modena was 29 and James notoriously virile . . . how should the clans react if . . . or if . . . ?

Rob would hear but probably not take note of his elders' talk with all their 'ifs' and 'ors'. He was much more drawn to Mary of Comer than Mary of Modena. She was fifteen and black-haired. He had been long accustomed to the sight of her uncombed and ragged around Ben Lomond, but here she was with her parents and brother Dougal, groomed and dressed for an occasion when the notion of mating was for once foremost in young men's minds. Rob was now bearing arms and more aware of awakening manhood. She appears from all evidence to have been a woman of spirit. At fifteen she would feel inhibited by the presence of her parents, yet from around this time her relationship with Rob changed. He had been for her a likeable boy, wild and unruly, therefore fun. Now his voice had broken. He had probably begun to shave, that being the fashion for gentry since the Restoration (most clansmen were content to trim their beards with scissors once a week for the Sabbath).[1] His frame was broadening and filling out. His eyes, quick as ever to smile, were now apt to be suddenly and steadily penetrating, as if reading something behind her own. No one is likely to have looked into her eyes like this before. If at first it frightened her, she was soon to yield and to like it. Her old taken-for-granted friend was a new thing, a man in the making. He had possibilities . . . and she must have wondered what they might be, for her.

Rob could meet Mary now only at long intervals. He had to go off with his father to learn the cattle trade. Every class in the country engaged in it, from the greatest chiefs to their smallest Highland tenant who could earn a shilling a day as a drover. The leading drovers, responsible for the route and safe delivery, earned considerably more than the lesser, and often received a commission on the sale, if profitable. A four-year-old cow in 1688 sold for fifteen shillings. The dealers, who found the means to buy the herds and pay the marketing costs, made the real money, but the hazards were great.

If the drive were a long one, say from Caithness to Carlisle, it would take a month, or half that from Muir of Ord to Crieff; in neither instance was this economic for a herd of under two hundred beasts, when a drover's wages had to be paid on each fifty head, with tolls, market fees, and customs dues. The profit on a drove came to only a few shillings a head, therefore large herds had to be collected, and were available if the dealer took to the field early in the summer, as Donald did.[2]

Before the summer's dealings began, Donald had to go to Edinburgh, Glasgow, or Perth, and obtain from a known merchant-house or goldsmith a letter of credit and whatever small cash sums were available for the trade. He won these credits on his reputation for honest dealing, backed by the surety of land-owning friends and kinsmen. No man of whatever rank could borrow without first finding cautioners.[3] His second step, in which Rob required training, was to travel north and west deep into the Highlands, assessing stock in the glens and upper grazings. Highland land tenure ensured a large population of small-holders all with grazing rights. Since cattle were almost the only form of realizable wealth, the hills were overstocked, and the reduction of herds by export became an autumn necessity. Donald had to come to terms with the breeders, who, living so far from markets and short of cash, were anxious to sell but ignorant of prevailing prices. They were easy prey for unscrupulous dealers, who felt they had every excuse for cutting their offers as low as they could.

Few dealers could afford scruples. Their profits had to be won out of the difference between the breeders' selling and Sassenachs' buying prices. These prices fluctuated annually according to national demand, the condition of the cattle, and hard bargaining. The dealers' risks were so many, especially if they lacked experience, character, or confidence, and the exertions they had to make so great, that their own anxieties left them no thought for the breeders'. Donald had the qualities needed to free him of such worries. He may have felt it a point of honour to offer small farmers as high a price as he safely could out of regard for their defenceless position and need, for that trait became his son's. Rob's generosity in such dealings is well attested.[4] It seems likely that part credit should go to his father's example.

Donald made payment partly in cash and mostly in promissory notes or bills of exchange payable in three months. The bills at once passed into local circulation. The agreements reached greatly varied. The cattle were usually bought in relatively small numbers on promise of delivery at an agreed time and tryst, where they would assemble as a herd of several hundred for the main drove south. The country was covered by a network of trysts and linking roads. Trysts functioned also as fairs or markets for harvest products, and for home-made woollen goods, hides, timber, and the wares of packsmen. The drove 'roads' were not man-made

but routes trodden by cattle, broadening and narrowing like a
river-bed as the cattle flowed along or were channelled.

The night stances lay ten miles apart. If the herd were a big one,
the drovers required a topsman to go ahead and reconnoitre the
fords for alternative routes if the rain were heavy, or scout for
raiders, or arrange grazing at the night-stance if other droves were
in occupation. This work would be done by Donald or one of
his sons. The drovers were his own gillies. At the stances they
slept out on the heather. They slept lightly, for the cows had to
be kept herded against marauders, yet sleep they did despite the
night frosts of late September and October. If the moon rose late
and near the full, the cattle would often begin to move of their own
accord, in search of a bite. The drovers' hearing was so acute that
they could pick out the movement of some straying beast at the
farthest edge of a resting herd.[5]

The drovers carried no pots and pans. They would go to any
house near the stance to boil water for their brochan; otherwise,
they would moisten the oats from burn water, and take a dram
from their ramshorn, which all carried. Leading drovers carried
snuff in a mull, or horn box. Some had chewing tobacco, bought
at two shillings a pound, and others carried a pipe stuck into a
flipe at the side of their bonnets. They had few comforts. Often as
not they were drenched by sheeting rain that could last for weeks,
and slept damp at night, even if they found shelter. Accepting
cold, wet, and shelterless conditions as normal, such men had a
great psychological advantage in war campaigns over southerners,
who bred to a softer life and climate were more quickly made
miserable.

The trysts attended by Donald and Rob ranged widely across
the country from the west coast to Aberdeenshire and Moray.
Until the following century, few Englishmen attended the sales.
Feeling unable to cope with that wild land, they left their Highland
trade in the hands of the Scots.

The trysts came to their climax at Crieff in the second week of
October. This small town lay on the Highland Line at a focal point
for passes converging on the rich Lowland plain of Strath Earn.
On the open ground for several miles around were assembled
many thousands of black cattle, providing at close quarters a
scene of such chaos and noise that a newcomer like Rob could
not at first understand how business came to be done, or accounts
settled. In his own lifetime, the number of cows sold were to reach
an annual thirty thousand; they were probably nearer twenty
thousand when he first accompanied his father. The landowner

was the Drummond earl of Perth, who controlled the event, levied twopence a head on the cattle, and kept order by means of a baron-baillie, whose tryst court held the ultimate deterrent, a gallows. Disputes were quickened yet kept brief by the hard fact that coming late in the year this was a buyer's market. The seller could not drive his cattle north, where no one would have them, while to go on south so late was most hazardous. He had to sell now and trust to competing demands.

The vast space taken up by the cattle was held in some order by the drovers and their collies, who continued to sleep overnight with their beasts on the usually wet ground. The chieftains and gentlemen were no better off, unless they had friends living nearby (as Donald and Rob had with the Drummonds of Comrie), or could billet themselves in a house if any room were left. Everyone went unshaven, unwashed, and dishevelled. They picked up dirt from the very whisking of the cows' tails, for all had to thread a way among the drove-groups to assess the beasts on offer. As the pressure for standing space built up, the cows bellowed and dropped their dung, the dogs barked, the drovers shouted their fury, fluently cursing any man who disturbed their beasts, and threatening with claymore any arriving drovers who might seem to be edging the herd off its stance; until it seemed that in all this confusion no one could possibly know what he was doing or wanted, far less fix a price. But they knew. There were lynx-eyes and sharp minds behind the bleary faces. That became clear at last when the tryst ground was opened for the sale.

A great central space was reserved for the exhibition of the separate droves. Since it could not be large enough to take them all at once, they took their turn over several days. Around the outer fringe were placed tents for the clinching of deals in whisky and money, and open fires where broth was boiled in gigantic iron pots for the drovers. Fiddlers, beggars, jugglers, thimble-riggers, and packsmen were all part of the throng, hoping for some share of the drovers' money. There were no auctioneers. Buyers made their own way among the herds of cows and sheep. Having already made a first estimate of the state of the market, they now made the drovers their offers. When argument ended and a bargain was struck, the buyer might hasten on to another purchase, but all bargains were at last concluded in one of the tents. When Rob squeezed in with his father he would see the price paid in bills, snuff exchanged, and much toddy drunk.

The atmosphere was heavy with pungent scents. Drovers and buyers were alike big stalwart men, hairy of face and thigh; their damp plaids reeked of peat-smoke, heather, bog-myrtle, cattle, dogs, tobacco, and sweat, all mixing with the steam of the whisky toddy. The talk was not only of bone and flesh, weight and pastures, prices and trysts. There was much exchange of political news, as always the king's folly in coercing Presbyterians, rumours of intrigue, and alignments of one Scottish house against another. The Lowlands and England seemed to be ripening for civil war. Come what may, the clans would stand firm for the king. And so on – the same vague talk that he had heard at Iain's wedding and often since, but now mingled with openly spoken fear of embroilment with England's too weighty majority.

If Rob were enthralled by the new things seen and heard on his first tour of the Highlands, he would enjoy no less the bliss of home-coming. In that sudden relaxation after nerve and muscle had been so long keyed up in effort, the hardships suffered were perhaps airily dismissed while he told eager listeners of the rich variety of people met, the unfailing welcome from townships anxious to get the news they carried, emergencies met and overcome, the excitements of the busy trysts, and the bargains struck and profits made. In the warmth of the moment, a boy might be excused for speaking as if he had done all himself – and later feel grateful to a father who uttered no sarcastic word. When he prospered in after-years, Rob made no boasts of his dealings. By that time he had learned a keen appreciation of the trade's uncertainties.

Biannual visits to Glasgow and Edinburgh, before and after the trysting months, were essential to raise credit or meet bills of exchange. Donald may have travelled on pony-back, with Rob and two gillies jogging alongside. Like all other visitors, they would time arrival to avoid the horrors of the night drum. When Edinburgh's clock struck ten, the people were allowed by beat of drum to throw their day's slops and excrement out of the windows on to the streets. Since there were thirty thousand people living within a square mile, all on the flanks of the long ridge that sloped down from the castle to Holyrood Palace, this avalanche from ten storeys high was too grim a penalty to be paid for late arrival, however much time it might save on the morrow.

Rob on his first visit may well have felt appalled by the vision summoned up. The pleasant surprise of the morning's arrival would seem all the greater. They approached across wide grasslands where cows and goats were grazing, to the edge of the Nor' Loch close under the castle rock. Women washed their clothes there by stamping in tubs, just as they did at home, beside a small burn that flowed through the meadows to the seas of the Firth of Forth. Three hundred feet above this green flatland, the Rock towered splendidly, wearing its castle like the old Scots crown. They skirted the Rock to its south side, where they could see ahead a high wall with battlements, which completely ringed the town. They passed through the mean suburb of Portsburgh to the West Port, one of six gates that were always shut at night, and so entered the Grassmarket. When they climbed up to the High Street, Rob would find no trace of the expected sludge. Scavengers daily swept all clean when the bell of St Giles tolled seven. Winds off the sea whistled through all the alleys and left the town fresh for another day.

Glasgow houses were more handsome and spaciously set, but in Edinburgh they rose like canyon walls to a height of seven, eight, or even twelve storeys. Much rebuilding had been done since the Restoration. Most of the old wooden frontages had gone, replaced now by harled stone. Except in the suburbs, the thatched roofs had been replaced by slate. The windows were glazed, at least along the High Street. The tenements, called Lands or Laundes, nearly all had their backs to the streets, and so were pierced by alleys leading into closes or courtyards at the front, where access to each storey went by outside staircases built either 'skale' or 'turnpike' (square or round). The ground floors were usually warehouses or shops with doors on to the street.

The town probably inspired in Rob something like awe, more especially around St Giles and Parliament Close. At the Mercat Cross his forebears had been put to the horn (outlawed by three blasts). At that same, north-east corner of the Kirk, the chief of Clan Gregor and all his kinsmen had been hanged in 1604 on a great black gallows-tree. At the north-west corner rose the huge pile of the Tolbooth jail, where so many of his name had awaited their end. Beyond these soared the Lands, and behind them, on the flanks of the High Street ridge, a dense pack of others, narrowly threaded by wynds and vennels (twisty or straight lanes).

Their lodging house had to be one of the best, for the second-best were infested with lice, bed-bugs, and itch-mites. First they had a struggle getting up the narrow stairs, which in the mornings were always congested with male and female carriers bearing water-casks to the houses from the public wells in the main street.[6] The rooms had wooden floors, but so caked with dirt that they might have been the earth floors of Glen Gyle, save that there floors were swept clean and here not.[7] The whole house stank. The bedrooms and kitchen, which opened off the

common room, each had a close-stool, or chamber pot set in a
wooden box, and the scents from that source were augmented
from windows opened to 'air the rooms', for the close was freely
used by passers-by, including the tenants, to relieve themselves at
all times of day. Rob would be thankful to get out into the streets
and breathe.

He accompanied his father on business visits, made to lodge
money and bills to meet the loans, interest, and bills now due,
and in order to get a first introduction to men who would one
day support his own investments in cattle. The establishment of
credit-worthiness could not begin too soon. The merchants and
landed gentry, in turn, were always on the look out for someone of
trust in Highland business. At 11.30 a.m. all repaired to the taverns
to drink their 'meridians' – a gill of brandy or tin of ale.[8] A dinner
of broth and salt beef was eaten at one o'clock. In the afternoon
and evening, the streets filled up with a display of life, fashion,
and business – there were well above a hundred noblemen living
in town, and still more rich commoners – the ladies in scarlet and
green silk plaids, the men in full-bottomed wigs; ministers around
St Giles in blue and grey coats, with three-cornered hats set on top
of fuzzed-up wigs, and gowned advocates gusting along to court at
Parliament Close. A few coaches made difficult way, for all traffic
was slowed down by the many sedan chairs carried by Highland
porters who spluttered Gaelic imprecations at all obstruction.
At the Cross, merchants were exchanging news and snuff and
goods. Lads of Rob's own age wore brown corduroy breeches and
double-breasted waistcoats under single-breasted jackets, both of
bright colour, blue, green, or scarlet, a shirt with black ribbon at
the neck, and stockings of worsted or blue cotton. Clumsy shoes,
made to fit either foot and secured with brass buckles, completed
their outfit.[9]

At dusk, Donald and Rob would make a round of the taverns
(to hear current affairs) until they became congested at eight
o'clock, when the town's shops closed. The next move was into
the coffee-houses to hear political news and the intrigues of the
Canongate. Coffee-houses had been open in Edinburgh for thirty
years past. They were clubs rather than cafés as now known, and
so notoriously places of political intrigue that Charles II had tried
to close them. His brother James had lifted the ban, perhaps
unwisely. In November 1687 they were humming with news
from London that the queen was pregnant. James had dissolved
Parliament and was introducing Catholics into all departments
of State. Halifax, Shrewsbury, and other Whig Lords had been

in touch with William of Orange, who had sent his envoy, Dykvelt, to London to make sure that their condemnation of the Declaration of Indulgence was soundly based and widely shared.

William had published a letter, under the name of his minister Fagel, condemning James's religious policies. William was angling for the throne. Things had gone so far that Louis XIV, alarmed lest his inveterate enemy should gain Scottish cannon-fodder for his wars against France, had warned James of his danger. But James as always was impatient of advice from anyone. Such was the talk of the coffee-houses, concluding with the great question, how would Scotland divide?

Clan chiefs and Lowland lairds were in town as usual, and nobles at the fringe of office. There was much to-and-froing between lodgings at the nine o'clock supper-time, the gentry visiting in sedan chairs if they had to penetrate the wynds. Since there was no street lighting each hired a caddie (pronounced cawdy), one of the numerous lads who hung around coffee-houses and all other public places to serve as guides or run errands. On the ten o'clock drum-beat the town resounded to the cries of 'Gardyloo!' as folk emptied pots and buckets. Then from the streets came the stench called the Flowers of Edinburgh, pouring in at the windows and close-mouths. Conversation stopped indoors while counter-measures were taken. Men tried to fumigate the rooms by scattering bits of lit paper across the floors and tables. When Donald and Rob returned to their lodging house, a caddie bearing a paper lantern would go ahead to cry 'Hud yur haunde!' in answer to any 'Gardyloo!' from above. They were free of the risk in the High Street if they kept to its curved back, for that was wide and few carriages then passed between the castle and palace.

The dirt and stink of town houses were far worse than those of the Highlands. Edinburgh houses could boast chimneys, which smoked less badly, yet with more space indoors they had less breathable air. They had convenient close-stools, but the natural sanitation of the Highland bog was healthier. Highland interiors smelt of sheep, cow, hen, and dog, but the inhabitants were less plagued by the 'itch', or nauseated by the human excrement that bred Edinburgh's diseases.

In snow-capped Glen Gyle that year, the Gregarach had penalties to pay for their healthier living conditions. Rob had known bad seasons before in his seventeen years, when harvests failed and his clan went hungry, but never one like 1688. It smote his own, the chieftain's family, no less than the most feckless of his clansmen, more especially in its after-effects. The New Year started ominously with hard frosts and heavy snowfalls prolonged into March and April. There was no spring. Late as the ploughing was, still no sowing could be done till late May, and then in sleety weather suddenly followed by hot sun and long drought. The beasts died for lack of grass and no crop grew.

The ground had to be resown with now scanty seed in hope of an Indian summer. Donald and Rob made a Highland tour to assess the cattle stock, and found everywhere the same conditions, more severe westward than eastward. Starvation faced their people.

CHAPTER SEVEN

THE RISING OF THE CLANS
1688–89

'The liberties of the English people'

DURING THAT grim summer of 1688, the political skies were clouded no less heavily. The storm signs appeared after 10 June, when Mary of Modena gave birth to a son, James Edward, who displaced his half-sister Mary in line of succession. The Catholics rejoiced with the king, but the Whig lords (Whig was the Scottish nickname for Presbyterians in the political field) sent Admiral Herbert to William of Orange, inviting Mary and him to 'secure the liberties of the English people'. They were not as yet offering the crown. In Edinburgh, the Privy Council as James's nominees rejected the Whig rebellion. Their policy drew credence from Lowland hesitations, for the invitation to William had been sent on purely English initiative, and more positive support from the Highlands, where the Auld Alliance (Franco-Scots) still held. Little as anyone liked James's rule, the Scots seemed to like still less the prospect of becoming drawn into William's wars against France.

Yet James in his folly refused Louis' offer of armed help. He would not, he said, use foreign troops against his own people. The Whigs suffered no such scruple. They were ready to welcome Dutch troops, if only these could be freed from the defence of Holland; and Louis, piqued at James's refusal, played into their hands. He turned his armies against the Rhineland, and William was able to move. In September, William sent a declaration to the Scottish people, promising just rule and a free Parliament, but laying no claim to the throne. No one should have known better than the Scots how light was a prince's word, but all Presbyterians could take comfort at the thought of a Protestant dominion. That they formed a Lowland majority became quickly evident when James in October called his Scottish forces south. The Privy Council sent him two divisions, one of horse under Graham of Claverhouse, and one of foot. No sooner were they over the Border than James's ill-wishers flocked into Edinburgh. The town mob rose and sacked Holyrood Chapel. In Ayrshire, where the Covenanters had suffered so much, the king's law no longer ran. The country had fallen overnight into disorder so great that William's supporters were seen by all to be the stronger party in the Lowlands.

The Scots army joined the royal army at Salisbury, unaware that John Churchill (later Marlborough) had organized the defection to William of English senior officers and whole regiments. The navy was likewise affected, and thus assured William sailed. James had stationed his fleet in the Thames, but a 'Protestant wind' held it in port while William landed fifteen thousand men unopposed at Tor Bay in Devon. He advanced to Exeter. Three weeks later, when battle seemed imminent, Churchill went over to the enemy. Numerous officers and some regiments went with him. The dismayed king fell back on London while news of fresh desertions reached him daily, including even his daughter Anne. His nerve broke. He fled in December to the castle of St Germain near Paris.

One of the few senior officers to stand fast for James, when most abandoned him, was John Graham of Claverhouse, whom James had created Viscount Dundee. Fourteen years earlier, while a young volunteer in the Dutch cavalry, he had by one of fate's ironies been raised from cornet to captain for saving William's life in battle, and transporting him to safety on the back of his horse.[1] With James gone, the temptation to join William must have been great. He was now forty, a privy councillor, and one of Scotland's most able men. William had need of such. Graham had a young and pregnant wife, Lady Jean Cochrane, at his home of Dudhope in Angus; if he accepted the 'Glorious Revolution', William might offer preferment. On the other hand, Graham had been notoriously active for James in holding down the Covenanters, who would now demand the abolition of episcopacy. The rejection of king and Church – acceptable to so many of his peers – could not be made by him without forfeiture of self-respect. That was decisive. He chose loyalty to the house of Stewart and trusted that a sufficient force of Scots would follow his lead.

All across Scotland, nobles and clan chiefs were facing similar problems, balancing personal advantage against principle, their own good against the nation's, certain only that no one liked William or admired James, and vainly trying to foretell the future. Breadalbane, the most powerful and astute of Highlanders, lay low at his castles of Finlarig and Kilchurn, declining to commit himself. His nephew, MacCailein Mor, had come over with William, and his likely elevation would rob Breadalbane of his great ambition, the Campbell leadership. But Breadalbane was no leader in war, and war was what a restoration of James would require. So he watched, and waited to see how the wind would blow, and the chief men of the land waited with him.

In Glen Gyle, Donald Glas had no doubt in mind. He was for the king. When he had taken his oath of allegiance he had meant it. That was bred in the bone. The news that came in from England, where William and Mary had accepted the crown in January, did nothing to lighten a dreadful winter. Neither Donald nor anyone else had been able to purchase grain in the early autumn. Rob knew real hunger, and probably never appreciated till later how his mother denied herself to give him the little he had, and to help his brother Iain, whose wife Christian had given birth to a daughter named Catherine.[2] The Highlanders' normal two meals a day had been reduced to one since November, and that grew weekly more scanty as the New Year advanced.[3] In the Hebrides, people were now dying of starvation; in the Highlands, famine prevailed in the west. Several days each week, the MacGregors were rationed to eat nothing at a meal but boiled goat's milk. The people grew gaunt, and while a few died directly of hunger, many suffered a lowered resistance that left them a prey in the spring to virus infections like influenza (known then only as bad colds), smallpox, and typhus.

Donald and Rob escaped serious ills, although it is not clear that others of the family were so lucky. Before the end of March, they were galvanized by the news that James had landed in Ireland on the 12th. He had recovered his spirit. The fight was on. But the clans would not rise without a national leader who commanded full confidence, and who that might be became plain within days of James's entering Dublin. He was *Iain Dubh nan Cath*, Black John of the Battles, the name by which John Graham, Viscount Dundee, was known to Highlanders for his black hair and wide battle-experience in France, the Low Countries, and Britain. He had the king's commission to raise the clans if necessary.

The Scottish crown could not be offered to William unless by an act of the Scots Parliament, which could not meet as such at the request of a foreign prince. William therefore called a Convention of Estates (the landowners who were members of Parliament) at Edinburgh on Thursday, 14 March 1689. Dundee rode in to attend. Most wisely, he came accompanied by a troop of forty horsemen, a devoted remnant of his division of cavalry, who had stayed with him as bodyguard since Salisbury.

Edinburgh buzzed with the news of James's arrival at Dublin two days before, and none of his known supporters were safe in the streets. By the weekend, Dundee knew that Convention would dethrone James and offer William and Mary the crown. Warned by friends that an attempt to assassinate him was imminent, he gathered his horsemen on Monday 18th and rode off to safety, hooves clattering and sparks flying on the cobbles of Leith Wynd.[4] He wheeled his troop round the Nor' Loch to the castle's west wall, dismounted, and climbed the castle rock to warn the duke of Gordon, who commanded the garrison, of events at Parliament House. He confirmed that Gordon would hold out for James, then headed north for home and his expectant wife.

While they waited together for the birth, messengers from the Convention appeared demanding his surrender. A few days later, on 30 March, news came that he had been proclaimed a rebel at Edinburgh, and at the cross of Dundee only two miles away. William's general, Mackay of Scourie, was already at Edinburgh gathering an army of English dragoons, the Scots Brigade from Holland, and militia raised by levy. He was preparing to move north through Fife.

Dundee coolly waited by his wife's side. His son was born on 9 April, but he stayed another week, continuing to give wife and son attention while he planned his campaign, received and despatched messengers, and organized an intelligence service. In mid April he moved a few miles out to his tower in Glen Ogilvie, where he raised the standard. The high quality of his intelligence unit became his campaign's outstanding feature. Hearing that Mackay's dragoons were riding fast through Fife to surprise him, he rode north for Inverness, recruiting as he went. At every move he was away just in time to escape Mackay's clutch.

General Hugh Mackay of Scourie, a veteran of the Dutch wars, had led William's advance into England, and now commanded in Scotland where the main threat to William lay. He pursued Dundee to Inverness, but arrived too late to prevent his enlisting Coll MacDonald of Keppoch, who was besieging Inverness with nine hundred men of clans Donald and Cameron. (The two had been students together at St Andrews University.) They arranged that the clans would gather in Lochaber in mid May. Keppoch returned west with his plunder, while Dundee led Mackay a merry dance through the counties of Aberdeen, Banff, Moray, and Nairn, moving with an ease reminiscent of his famous kinsman, the marquis of Montrose. He returned south to raid Perth for horses and to spend two nights with his wife, while Mackay floundered on the trail.

Reports of these events and the rumours of war penetrated

all parts of the Highlands with great rapidity. At Glen Gyle the ploughing and sowing had been hastened on through a blessedly mild spring.

Dalmucomar

One morning in May 1689, Donald Glas had word that his nephew, Gregor in Stucnaroy, the chief of Clan Gregor, required his presence. Stucnaroy was his farm in Craigrostan by Loch Lomondside, a mile and a half south of Inversnaid.[5] There is no written record of the meeting. Gregor was the ninth of the Glenstrae line, an only son, and at 28 still unmarried. He had received the king's letter calling out Clan Gregor.[6] The usurper William would be taking the coronation oath in London on 11 May, administered for Scotland by Campbell of Argyll. The clans would be led by *Iain Dubh nan Cath*. All were to gather by mid May in the Great Glen of Lochaber at 'Dalcomera' (a misnomer for Dalmucomar, literally 'the plain around the confluence' of the rivers Spean and Lochy). The need of the hour was to thwart MacCailein Mor and to reinstate King James.

Gregor's summons to Donald came of awareness of his own inadequacy. Donald Glas was the clan's most experienced leader. He, not Gregor, must act in the field. Donald accepted, and acted in the whole clan's name throughout the campaign. Later in the month, the king wrote again from Dublin Castle appointing Gregor to the colonelcy of a regiment, with power to commission all junior officers. There is no evidence that he ever took the field, whereas there is written record that Donald led the clan and signed in their name.[7]

Donald had to act with speed. Gregor wrote and signed letters; and these 'expresses' were despatched by runners to the chieftains of the cadet clans of Ladasach, Roro, Balhaldie, and Brackley. The fiery cross went out to the families of Clan Dughaill Ciar and Gregor's Glenstrae line. There was no hope of a big muster. So too with most other clans. The winter's severity had cut down the numbers of men available: they had another kind of fight on their hands, and the rallying fear of MacCailein Mor had weakened during his absence.

The various units of the clan marched north separately in their own time. Some failed to make Dalmucomar but joined the rising later. The Roro MacGregors joined in Atholl, which was much nearer their home in Glen Lyon, just missing Killiecrankie but in time for the battle of Dunkeld.

Donald Glas with his sons Rob and Duncan and his nephew Malcolm (his sister's son from Glen Falloch) and their followers, went over Rannoch Moor by the drove road. Fording the Orchy, they would spend their first night at Inveroran, lying out on the heather and perhaps hearing a wolf howling among the pines at the head of Loch Tulla. Next day they crossed the Black Mount and came down to Loch Leven between the cliffs of Glen Coe. There they met the Macdonald chieftain's eldest son John, and heard that his father Alasdair with his younger son Alasdair Og had already gone ahead and were banding with Keppoch. Donald too had left Iain at home. When chiefs took the field, it was their custom to bring younger sons and leave behind the heir to secure the home leadership. Rob's presence was obligatory.

They entered the Great Glen, passing Monk's fort at Inverlochy, which Sir Ewen Cameron had reduced to a ruin, passing under Ben Nevis, where snow and ice sparkled along the northern cliffs, and arrived at Dalmucomar on 18 May. Several thousand men had gathered on the grassland where the river Spean joins the river Lochy. The wide strath, fully open to the south, was filled with sun and the song of larks and cuckoos, but their song was drowned out at Dalmucomar by the Gatherings and Salutes of clan pipers. The throng was even noisier than a Crieff tryst, and more colourful, for the clans wore a multitude of tartans, their groupings identified only by their own banners and badges. Most wore the traditional saffron shirt, of which Camden said in describing a Highland army, 'They shine with yellow'.

The MacGregors of Balhaldie were there before them. Alasdair of Balhaldie was a bright young man, rich from trade in Stirling.[9] He had farmlands in Strath Allan, and three years ago had married Lochiel's daughter. Through this link, the whole MacGregor contingent, not being big enough to form a regiment, was placed under the red banner of the Camerons of Glendessary. Its presence and disposition were recorded by Dundee's standard-bearer, James Philip of Almerieclose.[10]

The atmosphere at Dalmucomar was a heady one. Rob had been long accustomed at home to hearing his father's shrewd judgments on kings and princes, chiefs and clans, their politics, and cynical manœuverings for advantage. Yet through all that open-eyed criticism there had run a conservative loyalty to the established rule of the kingdom. That could not have made sense to the boy, although his father obviously had fun out of life, knowing the rules of a game that stretched him. Dalmucomar quenched his doubt. Here were gathered several thousand of the Highlands' male youth, splendidly vigorous, some led by veterans fierier than themselves, others by chiefs as young as Rob, and all of famous name and high spirit. In such company, Rob was in his element. He would be welcomed with interest as the son of a redoubtable father, whom Dundee greeted with enthusiasm, the great chiefs with respect, and their followers with deference as the Gregarach's battle commander. He had reason to feel proud of his clan, small as their number was, and of his father.

Rob had also cause for excitement – the stir attending so many extraordinary personalities, the tough talk, the feats of strength and quickness, and the distinctiveness of dress and weapons. The men were heavily supplied from the clans' armouries. Apart from the arms common to all, many had Lochaber axes, broad-bladed spears, battle-axes, bows and arrows, two-handed claymores, steel helmets, leather cuirasses, and steel breastplates. A few like MacNaughton of Dunderave's son were suited in armour. Some of the legendary heroes of the wars of Montrose were here, and Rob was just eighteen. When the novelty of it all began to wear off, he would absorb the sentiment of his campfire companions at night and their fierce assurance in the training by day.

They were here from a powerful Jacobite sentiment; they hated MacCailein Mor to whom they had either lost or feared to lose their homelands; and they had full confidence in *Iain Dubh nan Cath*. That they had hope of plunder too was natural, and some like Keppoch talked of it overmuch to hide stronger feelings. The greater chiefs had already received from Hugh Mackay the offer of a bribe for their defection, and had either rejected it out of hand, or not replied, or in Lochiel's instance passed the letter unopened to Dundee. (It offered him titles, the governorship of Inverlochy, a colonelcy of a regiment, and money.)[11]

As Rob listened, the realization why he and all these other young Highlanders were here gradually dawned on him, and he made that plain later. They had not turned out to fight for James, or Bonnie Dundee, or the Church, or plunder. They had come out to fight for an established régime that offered no threat to Highland life, whereas the new régime would kill it. William and his Whig Parliaments at London and Edinburgh had no understanding of the Gael, and no liking. They held their way of life in contempt. The Stewarts, although anglicized, were less profoundly ignorant of their Celtic people, and deserted for the present by all save them, would if they kept the throne let Gaeldom live. Or so the clansmen trusted. In brief, they loved their own land and life. That was what they fought for. Other reasons offered were an accretion of jargon. Rob saw it clearly, for the same love was in him.

Rob's earlier acceptance of the Jacobite cause deepened to devotion at Dalmucomar. By comradeship too with so great a throng of men whom he admired, he grew affected by something of their Catholicism, which had after all been the faith of all their forefathers. Never thereafter could he feel religious prejudice. Perhaps it was here that he began to question his Protestant attachment, although not to real effect until much later.

The large and colourful army had gladdened Dundee's eye when he rode in, but not more than half would be committed to battle. Many were there for a useful and stirring social occasion, or were reserved for their home defence, or intended by chiefs to settle old scores against Whig clans before committal to war. The effective army placed at Dundee's disposal fluctuated over the next two months between one thousand seven hundred and three thousand of the Highlands' best fighting men, nearly all of three principal clans. Clan Donald made by far the biggest contribution. If the clans' response was smaller than it might normally have been, it was enough for Dundee's purpose.

He had good reason to be pleased with his army, and they with him. He looked the part for a start. He sat his horse well, back effortlessly straight, his normally pale, handsome face now browned by sun and wind and framed by a black wig that cascaded curls over his red-coated shoulders. His eyes were alert, his mouth decisive, and his whole air masterful. Yet he could smile and radiate an easy assurance rather than a tense fanaticism. The men felt that he knew what he was doing, would be unflappable, had commonsense, and could outplan Mackay of Scourie every time they met. He had already proved them right on these points and would so continue.

For their part, the chiefs pleased Dundee. He knew their fighting prowess and hard experience, and could recognize youthful spirit and fitness. He had no army that could be disciplined like a government's. The men could come and go as their chiefs pleased, and so he had the trouble of attaching them to himself as well as to James. This he could do. Every army, like any other big body of men, is subtly pervaded by the quality of its commander, even though the rank and file rarely glimpse him. His quality may filter down through the chain of command to some degree, but over and above that it asserts itself on the main body by intangible means, hardly explicable but certain in fact. Dundee made of the clans, and the rugged individualists who led them, a cohesive force with a high morale.

He knew the merits and faults of a Highland army – its singular mobility and impetuous courage, its loose discipline and careless preparation, and when the battle was done, its indiscipline in victory and proneness to disperse after plunder. For a long campaign, a great leader was needed to hold it together; if he could do that he could work miracles. In the little time allowed him, Dundee tried to cure at least some of the faults, and to instil the discipline. Clansmen, he knew, dreaded cavalry and tended to expend their fire too soon. They also exposed themselves to enemy fire too freely. So he taught them the best way to deal with a cavalry charge, to hold fire until the ball was sure of its mark, and equally on their own advance to hold their fire on the enemy's line until execution was assured.[12]

Near the end of May, Dundee led a mettlesome army east through Glen Spean into Badenoch. They had useful skirmishing for a month. He then disengaged the clans, appointing them to muster in late July for a march on Blair Atholl.

At Blair Atholl in Glen Garry stood Blair Castle, seventeen miles south-east of the Drumochter pass. It was the seat of John Murray, Marquis of Atholl, a life-long royalist, who had enjoyed a triumph over Campbell. He had ravished Argyll. Only Montrose shared such distinction. He was now close on sixty, but the steel of his nerve had gone. He wavered at the Revolution, would take no part in proclaiming William and Mary, but equally would not join Dundee. He shed his dilemma by departing for Bath, leaving the affairs of his great clan to be resolved by his two sons. John the elder supported the Revolution. James the younger declared for King James and gave assent to Dundee's order that Blair Castle be seized for the king. This was done before mid July. John, Lord Murray, besieged the castle and warned Mackay.

The clans reassembled in Badenoch around the 25th. They were joined by a company of Irish foot under Colonel Alexander Cannon. Apart from that reinforcement, the clans' muster was:[13] Clan Donald, 1600 men of Clanranald, Glengarry, Sleat, Keppoch, and Glencoe; Clan Cameron, 600 men of Lochaber led by Sir Ewen Cameron, the doyen of the chiefs at sixty, wise in judgment yet notoriously fierce in battle; and Clan Gillean, 500 islesmen of Mull, Coll, and Tiree, led by Sir John Maclean of Duart. These 2700 included some other clans like the MacGregors, Appin

Stewarts, MacNeils, and Grants, whose smaller units had been merged in the names of the larger.

Dundee now heard that Mackay had taken the bait. He was coming north through Perth. Dundee struck camp next morning and marched for Blair. He arrived at nightfall. Lord Murray had hurriedly withdrawn through the Killiecrankie pass, leaving a hundred men to hold it against pursuit – yet pursuit was the one thing he had no cause to fear. Dundee and the clans had come where they wanted to be. All waited for Mackay to rush into the web of the glens.

CHAPTER EIGHT

KILLIECRANKIE
1689–90

'All the world will be with us . . .'

SATURDAY, 27 July, was a day of prolonged nervous tension for Dundee's men at Blair Atholl. About ten o'clock in the morning they heard that Mackay had moved up from Dunkeld and must now be at Moulin, only seven miles away. His army of four thousand five hundred men would be at Blair shortly after noon, unless Dundee gave battle farther south. Dundee had already chosen the place. It was Raon Ruaridh, or Rory's Field, a farmland under corn, grass, and clover, three miles south-east between the river Garry and Creag Eallaich. Immediately beyond it, the Garry took a great bend under the craggy flank of Ben Vrackie, and there had sheared a mile-long ravine. It gave a pass through to the Tay, and a rough track wound among the woods and crags of its upper side. Mackay would have to spend a long time getting his men and gear through the pass, but could not be attacked there. It was held by Lord Murray's reluctant Athollmen.[1] The approach to it from Blair was flanked to the north by two rounded hills, the Hill of Lude and Creag Eallaich, the latter overlooking the mouth of the pass. Dundee had resolved to station his army on its lower slopes.

His first move was to send a small force down the Garry to prevent Lord Murray from moving back to Blair. He then led his army north-east up Glen Fender to make a five-mile, hidden detour around the Hill of Lude, and so down the Clunie Burn to eight hundred feet, where they traversed on to Creag Eallaich high above Urrard House. The short march of two hours brought everyone a sense of relief. They were in position half an hour after midday.

The greater part of a soldier's time is spent waiting for something to happen. He never positively forms the question, 'Will I be alive tonight?' Men before battle are protected by a fire-curtain, which the mind drops to cut off fearful imaginings. But they lurk in the background and try to filter through in disguise. Every sense is alert. The Garry was so richly wooded in oak, alder, birch, and pine, its rushing water so alive with light, the warm air humming with insects and scented by the clover of Raon Ruaridh – it held so firmly its atmosphere of an everlasting peace, that the idea of its bloody violation would seem to aware men grotesque. A sense of outrage could then slip through the curtain. War was lunacy. They should not be here. And that thought may have briefly visited Rob, new as he was to war, or even Dundee, who had been caught in this web of his own weaving. But Dundee had much to think about and Rob little. Hugh Mackay would at least be free of qualms, being on the march and duty-bound.

After its vain pursuit of Dundee, Mackay's army had fallen back to Edinburgh, only to turn right around on 22 July and march north again on the news of Blair Castle's capture. Mackay went through Perth, moving out on Friday 26th to camp at Dunkeld. At six this morning, when he began the final march to Blair Castle, he could take comfort from the thought that his army had a hard core of dragoons and the Scots Brigade. The militia so newly raised were bound to be soft, but would none the less be prickly. Mackay had issued his troops with bayonets. These by most happy chance had arrived at Edinburgh Castle from English ordnance at the time of his brief return to the capital. That surely was more than coincidence. Providence had smiled on his arms, and the God of Battles was for him. This would be the weapon's first appearance in Scotland and come as a grisly surprise to the charging clans. As he rode north by the banks of the Tummel under hot July sun, Mackay could imagine that steel hedge as impenetrable, and see the Highland army impaling itself.

At Creag Eallaich, the clans lay straggled across the hill-flank. Trickles of men were constantly making descents to the Allt Chluain for water. By Dundee's side were the chiefs and his second-in-command, Colonel Cannon. Around one o'clock, scouts ran in to report that nine regiments of enemy foot and two of horse were approaching the lower end of the pass. Dundee had his bugler sound an alert, and the clans began to move back to their stations. He had arrayed his men in eight battalions. The MacGregors stood left of centre with the Camerons.[2] To the left of their unit were the MacDonalds of Keppoch, Glencoe, and Sleat. To the right of centre were the MacDonalds of Glengarry and Clanranald, Cannon's Irish, and the Macleans. More scouts came in. Mackay was advancing into the pass.

The afternoon must have seemed to Rob interminable. He watched the pass in vain. The enemy had marched fourteen miles on a hot day. Perhaps they lingered, thankful for the shade of the trees. At last he had a glimpse of mounted red figures. They were fording the Allt Girnaig, which flowed into the Garry. They rode forward to Raon Ruaridh, and halted. They were scarlet-coated dragoons, hats rimmed with lace, their scarlet cloaks draped over their saddle-bows. They were joined by Mackay and his staff, followed by two hundred troops of Leven's Regiment, who moved forward on the track to Blair, where they sighted Dundee's detached force and halted. Only then did Mackay look up and see the clans above. He spurred back to the Girnaig with his officers and disappeared into the trees.[3]

After half an hour the enemy foot began to come forward, cautiously at first, then in steady flow. Four hours in all went by before the four thousand five hundred men were through and deployed for battle. Dundee all this while made no move. He wanted Mackay's whole force trapped, but would not attack while the sun shone directly into his men's eyes. Mackay brought his army up the hill beyond and above Urrard House to a rib of ground where he had the farm of Lettoch on his right. The clans were now within a musket shot along a higher ridge in front.[4] He extended his line a thousand yards along the hillside, perhaps to outflank the smaller Highland army when it came down, or to prevent its trying to outflank his own.

The Highland chiefs were realists. Mackay had nearly double their fire-power. Their leading ranks would be felled on the charge and Dundee would be irreplaceable. Lochiel and Glengarry implored him to direct the battle from the rear. Dundee seems not to have understood the fact of his own importance, or else to have scorned their hard-headed calculations. He was still waiting, intently watching Mackay's dispositions. The numerical odds were against the clans, but his men were fresh and rested, Mackay's relatively tired and extended only two deep – far too meagre a barrier to check the impetus of a Highland charge. He decided that Mackay was doomed, and gave last orders to the chiefs: the clan units in attack were each to stay compact but keep wide apart, even though outwinged by a quarter of a mile.

Another hour passed and Mackay grew impatient. To provoke Dundee, he opened desultory musket fire and bombarded with three cannons until their under-carriages broke. And still for another hour Dundee refused to be drawn. Rob felt the tension becoming unbearable, not only in himself but in all his fellows. Half an hour before sunset, at eight o'clock, Dundee turned abruptly and signed to his bugler, who blew the charge. Ignoring his chiefs' advice, Dundee spurred forward.

The clansmen threw off their plaids and with a roar charged down the slope in their yellow shirts, led at centre by Sir Ewen Cameron barefooted. They came down six or seven deep in a panic-causing, yelling avalanche with 'pipes blawand hiddeous'. They met a withering fire that felled six hundred of their leading men. Dundee, riding on Clanranald's flank to correct a rightward trend of attack, crossed the fire-path of Mackay's own regiment. A ball struck him in the left eye and carried him off his horse.[5]

He had trained his men well. With barely a check their great wave surged on to Mackay's line, and remembering to hold fire until within thirty yards, discharged their flintlocks with deadly effect. They threw down the guns. Targe on their left forearms, dirk in hand, they drew their broadswords. The flash of the blades lit the field. They ran on to a panicked enemy, for Mackay's new plug bayonets had to be screwed into the muzzle after firing the shot.[6] His men had thus been forced to fire too soon and were still fumbling with the screws when the Highlanders were on them. Blades whistling, dirks stabbing, pistols barking, the clans made carnage. Donald Glas, Alasdair Dubh of Glengarry, and several others who wielded the two-handed claymore – its last appearance on a battlefield[7] – did terrible execution. Eye-witnesses reported that Mackay's men 'were cut down through the skull and neck to the breasts, others had skulls cut off above the ears like nightcaps; some had bodies and cross belts cut through at a blow; pikes and small swords were cut like willows'.[8] Broadsword and dirk, if less spectacular, were faster.

In five minutes Mackay lost two thousand men. Survivors unable to escape through the throat of the pass, which had become choked with dying and fleeing men, and seeing no chance of surrender or hope of quarter, threw themselves into the Garry where most drowned. They were joined by their own dragoons, pushed over into the river by the weight of the Highland battalions.

Mackay was lucky enough to escape, but Dundee had taken a mortal wound. He died that night at Blair Castle and was buried in the yard of St Bride's Church at Old Blair. His last words spoken to Cluny were, 'All the world will be with us, blissed be God.' In truth, his death was to mean the death too of the Stewart dynasty. The great Highland nobles, Breadalbane, Atholl, Seaforth, and most others, would have moved in support had Dundee survived his victory. Breadalbane had already been intriguing with Dundee, and like many another royalist with cold feet, was ready to trim his sails to the wind. And the wind had

changed at sunset on the 27th. Hugh Mackay, utterly routed and
his army virtually destroyed, was left the *de facto* victor. His first
volley that brought down six hundred men achieved nothing. The
only shot in the battle that now counted was the one that found
Dundee.

The aftermath

Donald and Rob survived the battle unharmed. But never again
would Donald swing his great claymore. Next day Cannon took
command and marched the army to Dunkeld, where it was joined
by the Atholl clans – Murrays, Robertsons, Menzies, and Stewarts
– and by the MacGregors of Roro and others. Some of the clans
who had suffered heavy casualties returned home. Mackay and
his survivors had fled to Stirling, where they regrouped, but on
hearing of Dundee's death Mackay returned to Perth. He had
the effrontery to offer the clans terms of surrender. They laughed
that to scorn and Cannon led the main body north to Braemar
to recruit. He was joined by the Farquharsons, Macphersons,
Frasers, and Gordons, and now had an army of more than five
thousand men, an army stronger then ever but empty of head.
Cannon was no Graham. The man most fit to lead was Sir Ewen
Cameron, but one Highland chief would not serve under another.
It was during this waiting time, perhaps, that Mackay invented
his ring-bayonet, which would allow continued fire.

Cannon led his men back to Dunkeld in mid-August, and finding
the town and cathedral held by the Cameronians (named after a
Covenanter Richard Cameron, who had been killed by dragoons in
Ayrshire), most unwisely launched a full-scale attack. He soon lost
all control. The Highlanders were wholly inexperienced as street
fighters. The Cameronians repulsed them after four hours with
great loss. Cannon had no plan for immediate action, and the clans
having assessed him realized that harvest time was upon them.

Donald with other chiefs was called to Blair Castle by James,
Lord Murray, on 24 August. Events had taken a most ominous
turn, yet all was not yet lost. King James was still in the field
in Ireland. Help might come from Louis from France. So they
resolved to play for time and to sign a Bond of Association,
binding themselves in two ways: first, to meet in September and
to field an agreed quota of men; and secondly to bring aid to any
one of their number who might be attacked by the rebels. Donald

signed the bond for Clan Gregor, promising one hundred men.[9] The others signing were James, Lord Murray, Sir John Maclean, Sir Alexander Maclean, Sir Ewen Cameron, Donald MacDonald, Glengarry, Benbecula, Keppoch, Glencoe, Appin, Patrick Stewart, MacNeil of Barra, Robertson of Struan, Farquharson, and Mac Naughton. None would pledge more than two hundred men, from reluctance after heavy loss and in face of grim prospects. They had no general.

Donald and Rob had to go home without Duncan. He had been captured and was already lodged in the Edinburgh Tolbooth.[10] It was not known whether he was wounded, nor is there any record of where or how he was taken, but most likely in the battle of Dunkeld. Men were not then imprisoned by a sentence of court. Prisons were only for detention pending trial or its consequence in fines, stocks, pillory, scourging, banishment, torture, transportation, or death. How the new Edinburgh regime would deal with Duncan remained to be seen.

A more heartening event was the birth to Christian and Iain of their first son, Gregor. The christening should have been the occasion of great rejoicing, now muted. Donald's farm had suffered in his absence. The crops had failed again. He felt obliged to take his winter mart from the rebel Whigs of the Lennox. As enemies of his king they were fair game. He gathered his force in September and sailed down Loch Lomond to the Endrick Water. His first choice of prey was William Cochrane, the laird of Kilmaronock, who had withheld his annual mail of sixteen bolls of meal (value £5 sterling or under) due to Donald under contract for the Watch.[11] Perhaps Kilmaronock had put out guards, who spied Donald's galleys stealing between the islands under the Michaelmas moon, for a warning was sent to Drymen barracks. A company of Lord Kenmure's Regiment laid an ambush on the undulating, wooded farmland. Donald was taken in the very act of plunder.[12] They carried him off to Stirling Castle, where he was held three months until room could be found in the Edinburgh Tolbooth.

The Pyrrhic victory of Killiecrankie was followed so promptly by other reversals of fortune for Glengyle, that in the long term, rather than the short, they must have contributed to the cynicism that Rob Roy developed later in life towards Jacobite campaign plans.

Upon his brother Iain now fell the task of leading his clan. A first need was to console Margaret, bereft of husband and son, with a demonstration of family affection, with distraction from her own fears, and pride in her grandson. The leading men could give her assurance too that Kilmaronock would hardly be foolish enough to press charges against Donald, and that although Iain and Rob could not yet appear in Stirling, MacGregor of Balhaldie lived nearby and would send Donald food and visitors. Fortunately, the gathering of the clans arranged for September had been abandoned – the chiefs on returning home had been sobered by their losses and the arrears of work to be done in providing for winter.

Margaret's sorrows over Donald and Duncan were compounded with fearsome news from Glenlyon. Her brothers Robert and Colin had overnight been made destitute. The MacDonalds of Keppoch and Glencoe, on their way home from Atholl in October, had made one of their heaviest recorded raids on Breadalbane. They had shown none of the merciful restraint usual to clans raiding for winter mart. They had stripped the glen. They had taken 240 cows, 993 sheep, 36 horses, 133 goats, and everything of household furniture that could be carried.[13] Robert and his brother Colin of Cambuslay and their tenants had been left at the onset of winter with nothing to save them from starvation except the cereal crop, which this year had been poor. Since the earlier sale of his lands, Robert held nothing in the glen except the stone house and land of Chesthill (his wife's property), but his loss of nearly £3000 made a high proportion of the glen's total loss of £7540 Scots. Margaret's distress at his family's plight was perhaps mitigated by the thought that Breadalbane might help. He too had suffered. The MacDonalds had crossed the hills from Loch Lyon to Loch Tulla and sacked his tower and township at Achallader. They had done this by Cannon's order to deny its strength to Mackay, but were soon to pay a terrible penalty.

The winter was once again long and hard, causing much suffering in the glens. Driven by the inadequate mart, and alleged by enticement of Jacobite supporters in Glasgow, six hundred clansmen flocked down to the Lowlands between Glasgow and the Campsies, where they robbed farms and the post-runners up to the gates of the town itself. It was likely that Rob was there with other MacGregors.

In January 1690, Donald Glas was brought by troops into the Edinburgh Tolbooth.[14] There he joined Duncan. It was no happy reunion. The jail was crowded with Jacobites and its condition so insanitary that neither Donald nor Duncan ever again enjoyed good health. There was no ventilation or drainage. Every corner stank with excrement. Donald set about devising their release. William and Mary were now graciously pleased to extend the royal pardon to any gentlemen of the clans who would acknowledge them as rightful sovereigns. Donald would not do this for himself: he felt bound by oath to James. But Duncan was not bound and had taken the oath of allegiance in late August,[15] yet was still here, ailing from six months of foul air, straw-bedding contagious from the dirt and disease of previous occupants, damp cold, and deprivation of exercise.[16] On 15 March he was freed, but now with few years to live.

Iain and his friends of Clan Gregor had meanwhile persuaded the laird of Kilmaronock to withdraw charges. Iain would not crudely menace, but the laird on reflection would all too clearly realize that he would be wise to agree. Clan Gregor could take no reprisal while Donald was held alive and well. But if not so held, and should Kilmaronock fail to meet their restraint half way, his life would be plagued through all the foreseeable future with houghed and reft cattle, burnt barns, and worse. He must have sent a messenger to Edinburgh within the month, for Donald on 5 February was able to submit his petition to the lords of the Privy Council, declaring that in January he had been brought in to the Tolbooth 'where he has continued prisoner ever since, and nothing laid to his charge except that he was accessory to taking away the goods of the lands and tennents of Killmaronock. And seeing the Laird of Killmaronock not only does not insist against the petitioner, but is willing the Petitioner be set at liberty upon sufficient caution . . . .'[17] All to no avail. The lords of the Privy Council were not prepared to see a 'rebel' slip through their fingers so easily. The case against him was topped up with a charge of treason, worded as rebellion against his king. The specious charge wilted under scrutiny. As a commissioned officer he was under oath to King James. Wrong as the charge was, it gave the council excuse to hold him. And hold him they did, under the law's delays, for two years.

From February onwards James, based on Ireland, renewed his efforts to raise the Scottish Highlands. He sent Major-General Thomas Buchan on several secret visits to the chiefs, and to bring in supplies for a spring rising. Buchan came in again to the West Highlands with Cannon in April and raised the standard. Iain felt bound to honour his father's pledge and went north, with what reluctant men he could raise. Rob did not accompany them. Duncan had arrived home in poor shape (after 1694 no further mention of him is made in records that must have included his name had he lived). Rob could no longer be spared from Glengyle.

He stood second to the acting chieftain. His mother too was in need of care as her worries accumulated – Donald's plight, Duncan's illness, Iain's impending departure for war, and now her brother's latest folly, for Robert in March had been reduced to desperation by want and taken to raiding his own chief's lands of Strath Fillan. (Campbell of Glenfalloch finally stopped him by force.)

Only fifteen hundred men turned out for Buchan, who quickly proved himself incompetent. On 30 April he bivouacked with his army on the haughs of Cromdale, above the Spey near Grantown. He knew that Mackay had sent Sir Thomas Livingstone against him with a force to match his own, yet made no reconnaissance by patrol. The result was that Livingstone's dragoons rode down on the sleeping army at dawn on May Day. There was no battle at Cromdale – only a rout from which most escaped in their shirt tails, including Buchan and Cannon, while an unlucky four hundred were captured. Iain stayed on with the main force after it re-grouped, and joined a final conference of the chiefs at Tomintoul in mid June. The Cromdale affair had been too inglorious for any more recruitment under Buchan. The chiefs resolved to disband, but to keep in touch and refuse submission until James approved. They drew up a new Bond of Association, which all including Iain signed.[18] Next day the Highland army dispersed. Two weeks later, William defeated James at the battle of the Boyne.

CHAPTER NINE

KIPPEN
1690–91

The Whig coup d'état

WHEN IAIN arrived home at the end of June, he found Christian again pregnant. Their child would be born into a new Scottish era; indeed all were living in that now, but were too close to events to know it. The Revolution was permanent; the Jacobite cause lost; the Stewarts' claim to divine right over Church and State replaced by a people's right to make law, appoint kings, and choose their faith. 'The people', of course, were still the freeholders of land valued at a minimum rent of £400 Scots, and the peers by right of rank, these two alone being eligible for Parliament or franchise. Yet the Scottish Parliament in that year of 1690, in passing the Act to establish Presbyterianism, also abolished patronage in the appointment of ministers. Its powers had hitherto been negligible, being in the hands of a committee, the Lords of the Articles, whose membership was manipulated by the Privy Council, whose members were in turn chosen by the king. On the Revolution, the Lords of the Articles were abolished and the powers of the Privy Council restricted. Parliament even claimed now to control foreign policy and to compel royal assent to its domestic legislation. However that might be in practice, at least the claim had been formulated.

The Highland chiefs were aware that no such revolution could have been possible without the prior union of the crowns, which had provided otherwise ineffective Scots rebels against James with English leaders, arms, and enterprise. They were less aware that no revolution could have happened without a prior change in the political and economic role of Lowland Scots heritors. No longer feudal barons in the old style, owing vassalage, the landowners wanted above all a political climate that would nourish law and property.[1] They wanted profits out of their lands and so wanted civil order, peace, and the security of possession that Stewart rule had not allowed. Therefore they were Whigs. Their way had been made easy by the strength of popular religious feeling, which had over-ridden ancient loyalties. They had won. But the times appeared too unstable for Scots to recognize a turning point in their history – least of all the Clan Gregor. They were trapped by their sense of honour and tradition in loyalties and prejudices that could no longer be fruitful; worse, ill-fortune could now be their only product. Rob Roy saw or sensed this before most of his Highland compatriots – but too late to shape his course differently.

The Highland people had detested the union of the crowns for its subordination of Scottish to English interests, which the accession of William exacerbated. Preoccupied with wars in Flanders, he had damned the Scots for the nuisance they were, and had declined to come north to be crowned. Argyll being now restored to his titles and lands, made a Lord of the Treasury, and authorized to raise a regiment, was back in the midst of the clans, with the Old Stewart policy of using him to subject and tame his neighbours not only taken over by William but positively reinforced. The chiefs' sense of frustration was extreme, and would build up again and yet again to explosion point. In the aftermath of Killiecrankie they had to limit hostility to a refusal of allegiance. This disturbed William. The dissaffection of the Highlands might give Louis XIV a lodgment in his rear. Usually decisive, he wavered for a year between force and appeasement, while obliged by ignorance of the Highlands to listen to rival advisers and not feel able to judge.

Rob Roy must have felt rightly that his world was falling apart. The Stewart dynasty had for three hundred years (save the Commonwealth decade) given some framework to his people's history; if too few of its twelve sovereigns had been worthy, bearings could at least be taken from its familiar presence. Many Scots, both Highland and Lowland, now felt their people were adrift. To all came a sense of break with their past, welcomed with relief in some quarters, greeted with dismay in others. Clan Gregor was dismayed. Rob had felt so elated by the splendour of Dalmucomar, had become so fervent a Jacobite, and so proud of his modest part at Killiecrankie, that the death of Dundee, the folly of Dunkeld, the ignominy of Cromdale, the defeat of James at the Boyne, the imprisonment of his father and Duncan, all within the year, would have bewildered him and left him apathetic from shock. But not for long. He had the resilience of youth.

In Iain's absence he had given himself to the work of Glengyle. He had to see to the ploughing and sowing, order the peat-cutting, move the cattle up to the shielings, oversee the soumings and fitting-out of galleys, consult with the other heads of the clan's families, accept and give advice, make decisions for his clan, and the hundred and one other tasks that normally fell to a chieftain. He kept regular communication with his father through Archibald MacGregor of Kilmanan, who was heir (aged 31) to the chief of Clan Gregor. Kilmanan had a town house in Edinburgh, and was able to supply Donald with food, wine, visitors, and personal letters from his family. Rob had to give what comfort he could to his dispirited mother, whose health had been failing after successive bad winters. When Iain came home after Cromdale, Rob could not take up his cattle trading, for neither Iain nor he could appear in town to raise money. He abandoned the customary reconnaissance of Highland stock in favour of a Lowland reconnaissance. Cattle would have to be lifted there to get money for winter grain, salt, and other needful things.

This money shortage was everywhere prevalent, and Rob's reconnaissance revealed that Lowlanders were fearful of the consequence – another descent by raiding clans. The landowners of the Lennox had been alarmed by last November's incursion, and were now more than usually ready to pay for protection in kind. On hearing this, Iain planned to take his income there, and to take it within the law rather than risk joining his father in the Tolbooth. So he entered into a contract with Archibald MacGregor of Kilmanan (near Mugdock in Stirlingshire), to ask the Privy Council for the command of a Watch to protect the lands and cattle of the Lennox. Archibald (like Rob) was a first cousin to the chief, Gregor of the old Glenstrae line. His late wife had been Anna Cochrane, daughter of the minister of Strathblane, and he was a friend of Cochrane of Kilmaronock. His father, Captain Hugh MacGregor, had commanded Watches in former years.[2] Neither he nor Gregor had been out in the Rising. Therefore he was politically a most reputable associate for Iain, Rob, and the men of Glengyle, who would supply the skills, leadership, and force required. Their submission was backed by a petition from a dozen heritors of Dunbartonshire, led by Cochrane of Kilmaronock, who complained that their estates were harassed by broken men (outlaws) and asked for a Watch.[3] This having been lodged, the MacGregors would almost certainly go into business that autumn, pending the Council's decision.

There was still no prospect of Donald's release. His petition had been ignored. He had been held now for a full year without trial, and not until 22 December 1690, did the Privy Council minute their decision to prosecute, and issue 'warrant for processing Lt. Col. MacGregor for treason before the

Lords of Justiciary'. Margaret feared that she might never see Donald again.

The Privy Council, almost with the same breath used to threaten Donald, approved by Order in Council his son's petition, and sent it for promulgation to Stirling, where the Justices of the Peace at Quarter Sessions on 12 February 1691, made public announcement that John MacGregor of Glengyle and Archibald MacGregor in Kilmanan were appointed to command a Watch for the protection of heritors' estates in west Stirlingshire and east Dunbartonshire, and were for that purpose granted powers of the fire and sword by commission of their Majesties' Privy Council. The heritors concerned were enjoined to keep the Watch. That same month, Iain's wife bore him a second son, named Donald.

The prospective rise in his brother's status had not inhibited Rob's cattle-lifting activities in the previous autumn, except to direct them elsewhere than the Lennox, nor did these bar his sharing in the Watch. Although the command was in name of his brother and cousin, Iain had other, time-consuming duties, and Archibald was a sleeping partner, so that acting command of the Watch fell often to Rob. It appears that his Watch was efficient, and action taken with an aplomb and good judgment that earned the respect of the men of the Lennox and of neighbouring clans. His straight-dealing was matched by his tracking skill, which became sufficiently well-known for Breadalbane to call on his services.

The MacRaes of Kintail had raided Finlarig at the head of Loch Tay and carried off fifteen head of cattle. Trivial as the material loss might be to Breadalbane, this singeing of his beard within his stronghold could not be endured. He engaged Rob to recover the *spreidh*.

Rob arrived at Finlarig Castle with a dozen men. Handicapped as he must have been by the raiders' two days' start, he found and followed their trail through the Mamlorn forest, north over the Rannoch hills, and deep into the mountains of Badenoch held by Clan MacPherson. This was hostile country. Rob Roy guessed that the rievers were heading for the upper waters of the Spey, and feared that he must be on Keppoch's trail, but so faint had the trail become that by dusk of the second day he despaired of tracing it farther. His party bivouacked in a narrow glen. At nightfall, a flicker of firelight appeared higher up. Rob reconnoitred and discovered a band of gypsies, who told him that higher still he would find a band of Highlanders. A careful approach disclosed the MacRaes. Rob surprised them at dawn.

Blood was drawn on both sides, but the MacRaes were put to flight and Breadalbane's cows retaken. The fame of the exploit – a *tour de force* in tracking –⁴ spread over the southern Highlands, with the result that more lairds of the Lennox and Menteith put themselves under MacGregor protection. Rob Roy was thus able to increase his followers without causing alarm to neighbours. The good repute he thus won bore fruit in future years, when Kilmanan, Graham of Montrose, Breadalbane, and many other landowners, were to grant him land or entrust to him large sums of money.

While Rob's stock was rising in the country, that of his Glenlyon uncle was falling fast. Robert Campbell's need was greater than his nephew's, but his clumsy raids on Strath Fillan had no one's sympathy when they proved abortive. He had then been obliged to borrow money from Lord Murray to tide him over the winter. When he failed to repay in the spring, Murray put him to the horn. Breadalbane, exasperated, refused to intervene. He had written a year earlier to Campbell of Carwhin, remarking of Glenlyon, 'He is an object of compassion when I see him, but when he is out of my sight I could wish he had never been born.' Murray was preparing to hound him on to the hills when the debt was paid by his son-in-law, Campbell of Ardeonaig. Glenlyon felt sufficiently chastened to make a real effort to pull himself together. In his fifty-ninth year he took the first, resolute step of his life. He applied in April for a commission in Argyll's regiment, and received command of a company at Stirling, with the rank of captain at £146 a year.⁵

The political thunder-clouds that had threatened Donald Glas so long at last began to show signs of breaking up. The winds that blew them apart, just sufficiently to let a shaft of sunlight reach the Edinburgh Tolbooth, came in successive puffs.

Sir John Dalrymple, the Master of Stair, had been appointed joint Secretary of State in January 1691. An impatient lawyer, he favoured force against the clans, and was restrained only by the king's need of men and money for war with France. At his suggestion William, in April, instructed Breadalbane to meet the chiefs, reason with them, and offer bribes under the name of indemnities. They would be expected in exchange to lay down their arms and take allegiance. The issue was of great importance to Stair and the English statesmen who were aiming at a union of Parliaments. As a first step to that end, pacification of the Highlands was indispensable. William's advisers doubted that persuasion was possible; his army commanders were wholly sceptical. Stair's choice of Breadalbane as intermediary was good. He would know how to talk to clan chiefs, and his ambitions gave him powerful motive to achieve success.

In Donald's absence the MacGregors were not called to the meeting, which was held at the township of Achaladair, on Rannoch Moor, during the last week of June. Iain and Rob had the details of it soon after. Glencoe, Glengarry, Lochiel, Keppoch, Appin, Duart, and others were there, with Sir George Barclay and Major-General Buchan representing King James. Breadalbane talked with them for the better part of a week, at the end of which Buchan and Barclay signed an armistice to hold until I October. They did so under a secret provision that the truce would end if invasion by James became possible, or even if he disapproved of the treaty, and that if William were to reject the truce Breadalbane would join the rising. No bribes were paid, but promise of them given.

Breadalbane's minor triumph in moderating the chiefs' hostility, and gaining time for the government, astounded the sceptics. The treasonable provision leaked out, but William accepted that to gain the treaty Breadalbane had been obliged to make empty promises. He set aside its limitations by proclaiming on 17 August that he would pardon and indemnify all who had borne arms against him if they took an oath of allegiance before 1 January 1692. Until then they would be left unharried; after that, pursued with armed force. When the proclamation was posted at the market crosses of Scotland, the chiefs sent two messengers to St Germain, asking James to declare his will. They could not break with him unless he freed them, and time for decision was short.

Hopes of Donald's release were high in Glengyle by the end of August. Under the government's present policy of persuasion, no action had been taken to prosecute for treason, nor could it be till the end of the year. Iain and Rob were able to visit him at the Tolbooth. Now far into his second year's imprisonment, he was failing in health if not in spirit. He refused to consider allegiance to William. There is no record that his sons urged him to it, but if they did, telling him of their mother's need and illness, he would have pleaded that she be patient just a little longer. James would surely free the clan chiefs of their oaths when he heard, and then he could come home to his people with untarnished honour. Word must come any day now from St Germain.

But word did not come. James delayed, hoping that Louis might yet commit his army to the long-cherished plan of invasion, for which he was now preparing a fleet. Iain and Rob returned to

Glen Gyle in dismay. The bloom of robust life had withered from their father's face. His strong body seemed to have shrunk. There was still fire in his eye, and if only he would take the oath at once he might not be too late.

Margaret died at harvest time. She was 54 or thereby. Donald's heart broke on receiving the news. Shortly afterwards, he took the oath of allegiance and the Privy Council responded: '*Acta* . . . The said Lords of their Majesties Privy Council . . . give ordour and warrand to the Magistrates of Edinburgh and Keeper of the Tolbuith thereof to sett the petitioner at liberty furth of the Tolbuith . . . He and Robert, and John McGrigouris his sones, and Malcolme his brother son[6] shall live peacably . . . not converss or correspond with any rebells nor joyne robbers . . . and shall appear when called upon before the Privy Council under penalty 10,000 merks.'

They did not in fact then release him, but tried first to recover from him the costs of imprisonment.

Rob's desolation was deepened by his father's absence. To his parents he owed twenty years of happy and well-ordered life, which had allowed the family to ride the waves of seasonal hunger and plenty. They had enjoyed together the richness of their Highland society. Their lives had been enlivened by a continual succession of shared adventures. They had striven to the utmost for good or ill ends. They had lived – and lived as a unit. His mother's death was felt by Rob as a mutilation of his own life and his father's, but his grief for his parents turned to rage that September of 1691. His mother was scarce buried when government troops by court order seized his father's rents on their way to market – this to meet prison expenses, charged at sixpence a night.[7]

A loss of winter subsistence by act of nature he could accept, though it had helped to kill his mother, but not total loss by man's confiscation, least of all by Lowland Whigs. These Lowland heritors had little notion what hunger meant in a Highland winter; they had no right to administer justice when careless of the suffering caused to innocent people. This thought crystalized in his mind, and remained with him all his life. He would take back what his clan had lost, and take it from a Lowland Whig.

The term 'Whig' to Rob Roy and his fellow Highlanders expressed also a diabolic materialism, separate from its political connotation. Mrs Anne Grant of Laggan summed up the over-tones of the term: 'Whig was an appellation of comprehensive reproach . . . it was used to designate a character made up of negatives: one who had neither an ear for music, nor taste for poetry; no pride of ancestry; no heart for attachment; no soul for honour. One who merely studied comfort and conveniency, and was more anxious for the absence of positive evil than the presence of relative good. A Whig, in short, was what all highlanders cordially hated – a cold, selfish, formal character.'[8]

The hership of Kippen

Rob conceived a hership, or great raid, for Michaelmas. Iain as commander of the Watch could take no part. Rob as his active deputy received full intelligence of autumn cattle movements through the Lennox and Menteith. He heard that Sir Alexander Livingston of Bedlormie in West Lothian, who held land in Menteith, had ordered a valuable herd of cattle to be driven to Stirling by way of Balfron and Kippen. The Livingstons were an ancient family, earls of Linlithgow and Callander. A daughter of the house had been one of Mary Queen of Scots' Four Maries, celebrated in ballad. Sir Alexander had himself taken James VII's bounty as keeper of Linlithgow Palace. He had professed devotion to the Stewarts when they were in power, only to turn his coat when they lost it. He was a rebel in Jacobite eyes, had paid no mail to the Watch, and was ripe for plucking.

Apologists have declared that Rob had applied to King James and been granted a warrant to plunder the rebel Whigs.[9] No evidence for that has come to light, and if Rob did receive such authority it would come from Barclay or Buchan. It was improbable that he felt need of it. He was twenty, a chieftain's son whom time might call to leadership of Clan Dughaill Ciar. He had already given proofs of his powers, and this new opportunity seemed fated by the urgent need to provide for his people, and to foil injustice. His father had paid a bitter penalty for that incautious raid on Kilmaronock. Rob took care to make no mistake this time.

He summoned the young men of Glengyle, Craigrostan, Arklet, Strath Gartney, and upper Balquhidder to gather at Lendrick meadow fully armed at the end of September. On the day of Livingston's drive, he had them out at first light, fording the Black Water on to the Menteith Hills, then over the pass to the clachan of Aberfoyle. On the way down they would stop as always at the Witch's Stone, a big boulder close above the clachan. By immemorial custom, every man had to make an offering by casting a stone into the hollow round the boulder. They crossed the sluggish Forth to the old stone circle of the sun god, which they called 'the clachan', then forded Kelty Water on to the wide marshes and meadows of Flanders Moss (then unreclaimed). Their passage froze bitterns[10] and flushed ducks, which whirled away over sheltering trees. Pink-footed geese, newly arrived from the Arctic, took flight with shrill, indignant cries, descending elsewhere in a spiral whiffle that could be distinctly heard in the still morning air. Around half past nine they arrived at Buchlyvie on the drove road to Stirling. The township of low thatched houses straggled along the bridle-path midway between Kippen, some two miles nearer Stirling, and Balfron, two miles south towards the Campsie Fells. The township was empty of men, who were out on the fields. The people had heard nothing yet of Livingston's cattle, so Rob dispersed his men through the alleys, where they could wait and not be seen.

The field workers began to come in when they saw that a large body of clansmen had halted. When they came close, and saw them armed to the teeth, loitering at the doors and corners, talking to the women, but taciturn about their intentions, they took alarm, and fearing the worst sent men out to Balfron and Kippen, calling for help to repel rievers. By noon, Rob saw that more and more men were coming into Buchlyvie from the south armed with cudgels. As the day wore on, the local men's confidence grew with their numbers. They took on a menacing look, and called on the MacGregors to get out. Rob remembered two things, that he was not here to fight the countrymen, and his father's counsel not to stand on dignity, or hold ground, or risk bloodshed, where no vital need or loyalty was involved. His scouts had still no news of the herd. Therefore he led his men out to the open heathland of Kippen Muir, meaning if necessary to bivouac there overnight, and meanwhile to benefit from the wide field of view.

Unfortunately, the Buchlyvie men sent to arouse Kippen had spread an exaggerated tale of danger to local townships. The Kippen men had taken time to gather and arm themselves with agricultural weapons: toothed sickles, flails, cudgels, and one or two straight-handled scythes.[11] In the later afternoon, they advanced along the higher ground of the muir, placing the MacGregors between two hostile forces. Rob tried to spare them the penalty of that over-boldness. His well-armed men could make short work of them. He wanted no one accidentally killed. So he held in his men and made short avoiding moves until evening.

About five o'clock, when the sun was sinking towards the Luss hills, Livingston's drove was sighted. Rob had no sooner given the word for descent than the Kippen band ran down to block his advance. A fight could no longer be avoided. Using only the flat of their broadswords – their usual way of beating off Lowland cudgellers – the MacGregors strove in vain to break through the Kippen rank. Even a few well-handled scythes, when dispersed along ranked sicklers and cudgellers, could be nasty weapons. The Kippen men made the mistake of trying to press home their advantage. The MacGregors at once changed to cut and thrust. In a few moments it was all over and the Kippen men had fled. The MacGregors ran down on the herd. The drover, brave but foolish, made a defence and was struck down.

Rob Roy split his force in two. One drove the *spreidh* north towards the Aberfoyle pass by Loch Ard; the other he led to Kippen. The skirmish had angered him. Wounds had been given and taken unnecessarily and the drover killed in hot blood. He went not to quarrel with them further, but to make protest and read them a lesson. He came into Kippen at sunset and found it deserted. The panic of the battlefield had spread to the village. Rob's anger changed to exasperation. If there was not a Kippen man with the spirit to stand and talk, or defend their old people and stock, let them pay. He took cattle from every byre to make a second herd, and this he drove north over the Moss to Callander, then by Glen Artney to Crieff.

A proportion of both herds was no doubt kept in the Trossachs country for wintering. The Livingston herd, a most valuable one, could not be sold at Crieff or Dumbarton, and was reset at the heads of Loch Long, Loch Goil, and Loch Fyne, under long-standing MacGregor custom in difficulties of the kind.[12] No figure has ever been quoted for the head of cattle taken; it was big enough for the 'herdship of Kippen' to be known in the Lowlands and Glasgow a century later.[13] It made a deep impression on the public mind as a bold isolated act, and on Whig ministers of the Crown, for the Highland Line was supposed to be under the army's control.

Rob Roy's name was now on everyone's lips in the western Lowlands and Highlands, and denounced in the Lothians by Livingston. That might well have compromised Donald's release, but Iain and Archibald of Kilmanan, and perhaps Breadalbane, had made the Privy Council aware of Margaret's death, which their minutes recorded. They chose to act on the king's current policy of reconciling the chiefs, bearing in mind that the prisoner was related by blood and marriage to chiefs of Clans Donald and

Campbell. The Records of the Privy Council for 1 October 1691, had this note attached: 'Act of liberation Lieutenant Colonel MacGregor – takes the oath of allegiance – any little means he had, spent – his wife lately died, he liberated without payment of house or servants dues.'

Donald made a slow journey back to Glengyle. He came on horseback, for he could no longer walk any distance, and his heart was heavy. There was no Margaret waiting for him. They had been married for thirty-five years. She had borne him many children, and he had not been at her side when she died. With the loss of wife and health together he lost too his will to live, and never again took active part in his clan's trade and forays.

CHAPTER TEN

MACGREGOR OF INVERSNAID
1692–1701

Glencoe

ON 21 DECEMBER 1691, Duncan Menzies of Forneth rode into Edinburgh from Paris, exhausted from eight days in the saddle and one at sea. He bore from King James a written release of his Highland subjects from their oath of allegiance. James had not signed till the 12th. Only ten days were now left before William's Indemnity expired, and he had warned that a crushing blow would be struck at any who had not taken the oath by New Year's Day. Donald must now have felt great relief that his earlier act had been justified. Most of the Jacobite clans heard the news by Christmas or shortly after, which left all but a few chiefs time to reach their county sheriffs. Alasdair MacIain of the Glencoe MacDonalds was not one of the lucky ones. His clan was singled out for slaughter.

The news of the massacre of Glen Coe on 13 February reached Glen Gyle several days after the event by way of the Stewarts of Appin, who had given refuge to survivors. The tale was heard by Rob, and all else of Highland descent, with stunned incredulity, not at the massacre as such – not even the butchery in a winter's blizzard, for Clan Gregor had worse experience of man's inhumanity than Clan Donald or any other – but at the peculiar circumstance: the treacherous abuse of the victims' hospitality as the chosen means for surprising them in their beds before dawn. In the Highlanders' moral code, hospitality given or taken was sacrosanct; its breach a blasphemy of the most heinous kind. The detestation of murder under trust was expressed in Scots law by the punishment decreed in statute: preliminary hanging, live disembowelling, beheading, and quartering. There was never doubt in the Highlands that Stair and Breadalbane were the men responsible. Stair as Secretary of State had given the army its orders. King William had signed the paper and Breadalbane had almost certainly urged that an example be made of Glencoe, but neither had chosen the means. Breadalbane might conceive treachery and massacre, but not this kind; William had been cold enough to sign the order, but he was ignorant. The job was Stair's. Dalrymple of Stair's infamy crystallized by degrees over the years. More immediate odium attached to the Highland commander of the Glencoe detachment from Argyll's Regiment of Foot. His company had been quartered on the MacDonalds, when under orders from his superior officer at Fort William he had fallen on his hosts. Some days after the first news of the massacre the name of that commander became known. He was Margaret's brother, Captain Robert Campbell of Glenlyon. He was Rob's uncle. And Breadalbane was Margaret's first cousin. Rob must have wondered if he could ever again lift his head for the shame of it. He could be thankful that his mother would never know.

Rob, and his father, and Iain, and many others of Clan Gregor had good friends in Glen Coe. Rob's cousin Sarah (Margaret's niece) was Alasdair Og's wife, and she had been her uncle Robert's hostess over the days before the massacre. They were anxious for news of their kindred's fate, bitter at the government's return to cold-blooded planning of mass-murder, and angry at a Whig rule as bloody as the Stewarts' and less scrupulous. Rob felt confirmed in his Jacobitism, contemptuous of his country's rulers, and cynical about the hypocrisy of Presbyterians allegedly Christian. He felt and was rebellious. He wanted to fight these Whigs and get Scotland free of them.

His mood could find no political expression. The very last of the Jacobite hopes for James VII expired in May. Louis XIV, who had resolved at last to espouse James's cause, planned to invade with twenty thousand French and Irish troops. They were assembled for embarkation at La Hogue on the Normandy coast. The Brest fleet of 44 of the line was sailing up-Channel to protect the crossing when it met the combined English and Dutch fleets of 99 warships. They engaged on 19 May. The battle continued on and off for four days, at the end of which all but twenty of the French fleet were driven ashore and a round dozen burned at La Hogue before James's eyes. He had no one left to fight his battles. In Scotland, almost all chiefs had submitted to William, and the Cap La Hogue disaster brought in the rest.

Mary of Comer

Rob returned to his preoccupation with cattle. He had two lines of business, the Lowland Watch and droving. His rebellious mood had to find what satisfaction it could in seasonal rieving. As acting commander of the Watch, he was in honour bound to spare his trusting neighbours to south and north, and so took his prey eastward in the Murray lands of Strathearn. The marquis of Atholl held dominion over two hundred thousand acres, but Rob Roy appears from the Atholl Papers to have raided only the Tullibardine lands of his eldest son John, who had declared for William before Killiecrankie. Relying overmuch on his skills in planning and movement, Rob over the next three years repeated his Atholl raids too frequently. This was an error of youthful confidence and Jacobite zeal; impolitic too, since John was heir and his clan ranked in power with Clan Campbell. When Murray finally discovered the name of his predator, his lasting enmity was earned.

Rob meantime tightened the grip of the Watch company by enforcing contributions. The efficiency of the Watch had brought a marked decline in raids by more northerly clans. Landholders were no longer feeling a need to pay mail to the MacGregors. Their cancellation of contracts was short-sighted. The MacGregors saw no wisdom in awaiting the inevitable return of northerly rivals, and began lifting the cattle themselves. Landowners found that to pay black mail to the Watch was the lesser evil. Iain, Rob, and Archibald of Kilmanan had an easy conscience, for their acceptance of Whig mail seemed a virtue (of forbearance) when its collection gave less profit than rieving. But they preferred the Watch for its safety.

The Watch and the Atholl excursions were for Rob occasional activities that left him time for normal cattle trading. According to traditional reports, he is said at this time to have rented a large tract of Balquhidder as a grazing.[1] But these almost certainly relate to eight years later. The fact is that at the age of 21 he had no land of his own, and was living with his father at Glengyle House. But Rob had long since fallen in love with Mary of Comer, who was now living at Loch Arklet. By 1692 they were betrothed and Rob was begging his stock. It seems likely at this time that Iain and his family moved back to Glengyle House, the better to take the burden of acting chieftainship, and that Rob took their house at Portnellan – he headed letters from there.

He and Mary were married at the New Year. The Register of Buchanan Parish has the entry for 1 January 1693: 'Robert MacGregor and Marie MacGregor in this parish gave in their names to be proclaimed in order of marriage. Married at Coreklet.'

By a law of 1690, all weddings had to be in church, but the gentry refused to go. The buildings were too dirty for wedding-dress finery – even Sunday services were commonly held outside in the kirkyard if weather permitted – and so, with the minister's connivance, the groom paid a small fine and the weddings were held in the bride's house.[2]

Helen Mary MacGregor came of a good family. Her father, Gregor, had farmed the east side of Ben Lomond, while her uncles John and Alasdair farmed the north side at Loch Arklet. Since she lived with her uncle Alasdair at Corheichen, her father had presumably died. No record has been found of her birth, which may have happened at Comer around 1670 to 1672. The verbal reports of Mary, made by people who knew her to writers of the late eighteenth and early nineteenth centuries, are contradictory. She was described to the young Walter Scott as of fiery temper, yet 'princely' in manner when dispensing hospitality. Her spoken English had a graceful, declamatory style, since she had to render it out of her native Gaelic. Scott remarks that 'she seems to have deserved the character given to her for stirring up blood and strife'. Her black eyes shone as brightly as her black hair. She had pride, spirit, and a vengeful heart towards Lowlanders.

Others who knew and liked her say that Scott's informants did her injustice, that she was gentle, never meddled in Rob's political plottings, and that while the abuse she was to suffer from Whig enemies might have changed anyone's nature, she inclined to forgiveness, and won the love, pity, and respect of all in her country.[3]

Where opinions so different are sincerely held, the truth is likely to lie between the two, embraced in some fuller version. However loving and gentle Mary may have been, she had a spirited personality, for there is written evidence that when Rob was otherwise engaged she on occasion went out herself to collect the black mail due from landowners.[4] Rob had not married a quiet mouse of a woman, and must have paid the penalty in many a stormy scene, for which he and others no doubt gave her good cause. In love and hate, for which fuel was not short, she seems to have raised the same head of steam as he, and been able to vent it in furious action. Yet they stood together forty years, anchored by their roots in their land. They had been given time to grow the roots deep and strong.

Kilmanan

They had been married only a month when their fortune took a spiral turn upward. In February, Rob's first cousin Gregor, chief of Clan Gregor, died unmarried aged 32. He had made an ineffective chief. The *de facto* leader had been Donald Glas, but the *de jure* succession now fell to a more unfortunate heir, Archibald of Kilmanan, the tenth and last of the Captains of Glenstrae. He was cousin to Gregor through his father (whereas Rob and Iain were cousins through their mother), and although only 34 had tried to drown himself in drink after a sequence of bereavements: father, wife, and brother. On Gregor's death he made a last effort to pull clear of depression. He realized his responsibilities, and resolved to act like a chief. He joined Iain and Christian at Strucnaroy, and brought with him his two teenage sons, the elder named Hugh.[5]

Iain and Christian had sent out gillies to all branches of Clan Gregor and the Breadalbane clans. On Kilmanan's arrival, the decision was taken to bury Gregor on Inch Cailleach with his forefathers. Iain and Rob made all arrangements. This was to be the last occasion on which a chief was buried on the island, for the church was no longer in use, having been abandoned by the people of Buchanan since 1643.[6] They had found it too troublesome to make frequent crossings in stormy weather, and preferred to use a church close to the north-west side of Buchanan House. (The parish in course of time was thus renamed.)

On the first night of the wake, all relatives able to make the journey gathered with friends at Stucnaroy to keep the chief mourners company. They entered the house in relays to be offered a light snack of bread and cheese with ale and whisky, and these services were repeated at intervals when each new guest arrived.[7] The corpse, wrapped in its winding sheet of white linen and raised on benches (wooden coffins were rarely used in the Highlands until next century), lay at one end of the room; at the other stood kegs of oatmeal-whisky from which the women served. No expressions of grief were uttered. All was done in silence, except when grace was said by Kilmanan at each and every service of food, until he and Christian led the company in dancing that lasted till morning.

They formed a ring, and to the chant of laments danced where they stood in slow time. The wake and dancing continued each night until burial. The custom was observed at wakes everywhere in the Highlands except by people in the poorest circumstances.[8] On the third night, the corpse was placed on a bier and carried next morning to Inversnaid, where it rested overnight. A small fleet of galleys had assembled there during the day, and some had been engaged in transporting mourners arriving on the west side of Loch Lomond to their accommodation along the shore of Craigrostan. Every bit of floor-space in every house had been spread with dry bracken for the guests' bedding. A few important men were lodged at Glengyle House and Corarklet, but many had to lie out on the braesides on frosted ground.

Early in the morning, when the chief mourners had gathered at Inversnaid, a black banner was run up to the mast-head of the funeral galley. A score of women, who had been mustered above the shore, moaned and wailed while the bier was lifted abroad. Gregor's piper took position beside his dead chief, whose bier had been placed at the bow, face open to the sky. Archibald, wearing for the first time three eagles' feathers in his bonnet, then embarked with his sons, with Iain and Rob Roy, and the several chieftains of Clan Gregor and their families. As soon as they cast off, the moaners fell silent and the piper sounded the first notes of a coronach. The oarsmen pulled away. The other galleys came in to the beach in turn to pick up their complement and follow; meanwhile, the funeral galley was describing a *deasil*, a circle rowed three times sunwise. This symbol of eternity, blessing, and dedication, in the ideal form of the Celtic sun-god, had come down to them from their ancestors of two thousand years.

Proceeding as one flotilla, the boats were rowed thirteen miles south towards Inch Cailleach. To the men in the following galleys, and the women and children listening and watching by the oakwoods, the pipes sounded as the very voice of their people and homeland. The summits of Ben Vorlich, Ben Oss, and Ben Dubhcraig floated like icebergs of the sky, adrift on the clouds that engulfed the head of the loch. Ben Lomond towered close by over its Ptarmigan shoulder, given added height by the darker narrows beneath. Where the loch widened southward around a dozen scattered islands, its surface lay smooth as pewter in every shade of grey and white. The pipe music that indoors could sound harshly loud or shrill became muted across long waters and great space, more perfectly in harmony with wild land than the song of any other instrument.

After the flotilla had passed under Ben Lomond, other boats put out from communities along the shore and joined at the rear. When the first coronach ended, no other was taken up and all aboard remained silent, so that not a sound could be heard save the lap of water and dip of oars.

The oakwoods of Inch Cailleach came into sight at noon. A new lament then swelled out from the funeral galley, and as if at this signal another small flotilla put out from Balmaha, its boats gathering like a flock of ducks well off the north end of the island to give the main fleet open passage. The pipes fell silent for the last run in. The bell of the old parish kirk began the slow death-toll. The ministers of the two parishes, Inchcailleach and Callander, played no official part, for no religious service had been allowed at Scottish funerals since 1689, and the rule continued until late in the following century. Gregor's kindred carried his body ashore, where they set it down on a mound and made the triple deasil. Not till then, for lack of space, were the rest of the boats allowed to land. When all were ashore and marshalled, the bier was raised, the piper struck up his third and last coronach, the voices joined in full-throated, and led by the chiefs, the whole great cortège moved uphill at slow pace to the graveyard.

Such was the last high ceremony on Inch Cailleach.[9] Nothing in Gregor's life had become him like his leaving it. Others would be brought here to lie beside him, but never again with the ancient Celtic observancies, the gathering of the whole clan, and the muster of galleys.

The clan feasted that night beside bonfires at the head of Loch Arklet. Archibald met the chieftains of his clan, and among them Iain's young brother, Rob. Archibald had never been more than a sleeping partner in the Watch, lending only his name, but he knew Rob Roy well by repute, and from time to time must have wondered how that red-headed boy he had last seen six years ago at Iain's wedding had come so soon to be thought a man of mark. Even Breadalbane had spoken of him at table at Holyrood, and approvingly, if only to irritate Lord Murray. He saw Rob now as a young man among the many of his own country. In that company of chieftains and their gentlemen he appears to have taken Archibald's eye and won his quick esteem. Yet the two were poles apart in known character. Perhaps there lay the reason. Archibald would see in Rob the same hint of explosive inner energy that he might see in a bud about to burst on a chestnut tree. The contrast of a rampant life with his own near deadness could be heart-piercing. In him, all the surge of life had been wasted. But why see it wasted in others?

Archibald's interest in Rob thus took a practical turn. The lad was 22 and could hardly contain his energies of body and mind. He sparked. If time and chance allowed, he would achieve some great thing. Archibald began to look for a way to help – a gesture, say, from one beyond regeneration, a token of faith if not for himself. And the way was to come all too swiftly, on the collapse of his new-born hopes for his sons.

Archibald's elevation to chiefship did restore for a few months his lost sense of purpose. Although his own barony of Kilmanan lay near Mugdock in Graham country, some of his clan occupied the hill-lands of Ben Lomond, named Craigrostan, owned by Colquhoun of Luss, who had bought the ground from Buchanan. Archibald resolved to dignify his clan with legal ownership and bought the land from Colquhoun.[10] The conveyance, which was not recorded in the Register of Deeds until 6 September 1697, reads: '1693, May 27. Contract between Sir Humphrey Colquhoun of Luss knight and baronet and Archibald McGrigor of Kilmanan, in which Sir Humphrey for sum of 6500 merks and 240lb Scots at Mertenmass yearly in name of feu-ferme duty to be paid by said Archibald, sauld and disponed the ten pound land old extent of Craigrostan, comprehending various Lands in the parish of Inshealleache, viz. Rouskeneishe, Knockyle, Rouchoishe, Stuknaroy, Clackbuy, Innersnaid, Polinchra, Myln of Craigrostan, myln lands multure, and seequells thereof . . . .'[11]

No sooner had the conveyance been made than the younger of his two sons died. The elder, Hugh, had no interest in the property or chiefship and renounced both.[12] From this time their father was a dead man in all but official record. Before he sank into alcoholism, Archibald made up his mind that Rob and Mary should have Craigrostan. He was related to both their families and had come deeply to like and respect this young man, endowed with the qualities that he lacked himself – immense vigour, toughness of character, and self-respect. But that was not the kernel of Archibald's promptings. He had no illusions on human frailty. He had seen in Rob a man to be trusted in crisis, and the ground for trust was that something deeper than he would in crisis rise up and take over command. He, not Kilmanan, should have inherited chiefship. Rob's father Donald Glas was now too old, Iain his brother lacked stamina and personality, but Rob was born to lead. The chiefship after Kilmanan would pass by blood and birth rights to Iain Og of the line of Duncan Ladasach. This Iain Og was twenty-five, a Jacobite like all Gregarach, but a prudent lad, said to be busy amassing a fortune, which he would risk for no cause. If Rob could not aspire to chiefship, he should have Craigrostan, and uniting the Gregarach there with those of Glengyle, Arklet, and Loch Katrine, make Clan Dughaill Ciar much the strongest branch.

Knowing the vagaries of marriage, Archibald proceeded cautiously. He made at first a verbal pledge of land at Inversnaid, sufficient to allow Rob to make plans, and to begin building a new house at Inversnaid, where the Snaid Burn joined Arklet Water.

While Rob in August was putting the roof on his house, Clan Gregor heard that the long-lapsed penal laws against them had been unjustly and most unexpectedly renewed. The chiefs who had taken the oath had been pardoned, even the MacDonalds of Glencoe had been allowed to return home. The king's Highland policy was pacification. Yet on 15 June, Parliament had passed *An Act for the Justiciary in the Highlands*, which in its closing chapter 61 re-enacted in a brief clause the penal statutes against Clan Gregor. No reason was given; nor had there been any act of rebellion by the clan since Cromdale in 1690. The small clause seemed positioned to escape observation by members of Parliament. Its inclusion may well have been due to the malice of some legal drafters, such as those who only a year before had submitted to the Privy Council a list of oath-taking chiefs, from which Glencoe's name had been unjustly deleted, thus ensuring the massacre. Its inclusion may equally well have been Stair's work, for he was still in office. Whatever its source, the clause was law, and although the government did not follow it up with any physical persecution, the name MacGregor was again proscribed.

The MacGregors' anger was such as to render them speechless. There is no record of protest. Young Rob had lived free all his life and this needless proscription must have enraged him. Never before had he felt so helpless to redress a wrong. Mary seems to have felt no less frustrated, and her life-long dislike of Lowland Whigs may have taken its rise about now; only they would conceive such a law and enforce it. Rob's growing contempt of formal law took new strength, and his will to disregard it, new fire. He had to comply with it on the point of name, since he had to travel and trade throughout the kingdom, but that only fuelled the fire with humiliation. By taking the name of his mother's clan, he at least had further assurance of goodwill from Breadalbane, if not Argyll. Archibald took the name of Graham, as did Mary's family; Ian Og that of Murray, and so each according to territorial and family affiliations. They continued to use their real names in private papers.

Rob and Mary had been married a year when Archibald gave them written promise of Inversnaid. In a deed of 4 January 1694, he 'impignorated to Robt. McGregor, brother to John McGregor in Glengyle, and Mary McGregor his spouse, the three pound land old extent of Inversnait in the parish of InchCalzeach'.

The deed came as a firm pledge, although it gave no title to the property, as though Archibald were awaiting to see how the marriage shaped.

MacGregor of Craigrostan

During their first years the course of true love, if such it was, ran smoothly, apart from misadventures into which any Highland youth of Rob's clan status might fall, while short of experience. He now had to work harder, for Mary was pregnant. He had stock to build up, and a commercial reputation to establish so that money could be raised for droving. His Watch company earnings were insufficient for that good end. His land at Inversnaid supported numerous sub-tenants, but their rents were small and his only real advantage there was in services rendered. Thus, in January 1695, Rob mortgaged his land to Mary's brother Dougal in security for a loan. This had to be done on his behalf by Archibald – and to bring him to it was no easy task, for he was again at the bottle. (Earlier that winter he had murdered his own servant in a drunken fit, but as chief was not to be charged.)[13] The deed of 23 January was witnessed by John of Corarklet (Dougal's uncle) and by Rob Roy, without mention of the sum loaned. That it went for investment in cattle is most likely, for money was still scarce. The Bank of Scotland was founded later in the year, but without benefit to cattle dealers until next century.[14]

Rob's stock may have suffered a bad winter, for he supplemented Dougal's loan by resuming his raids into Atholl in May. This was the 'once too often' tempting of providence. John of Tullibardine now knew, and his arm was long. He wrote to his factor: 'May 21, 1695 . . . It was late when I writ last Saturday to my father . . . it was not concerning aney of Broadalbane's men but about one Rob: Cample a son of that Livt. Coll McGregor who cheated my father, and he & his family have continued to doe all they could against me . . . I have sent a party to apprehend that Rob: Campbel. I have not yett hard wt they have done. I believe Bread: indeed is his friend because he has taken that name & his lp has espoused his interest when he was persued before the justiciary court, wherfor I wish none of his lps frends at Dunkeld may gett notice . . . .'¹⁵

In short, Rob's excursions into Atholl had been exposed before his last raid. He had escaped justice at Dunkeld through the goodwill and power of Breadalbane, who had forgotten neither his past services nor that Rob was the son of his cousin Margaret, nor his anger at Lord Murray's filching Glen Lyon (he had allegedly taken his bare fists to Murray at Holyrood). It was he, not Argyll as early writers have it, who gave Rob Roy protection prior to 1715, and the fact is important to the proper assessment of Rob's later acts and character.

Rob soon saw the folly of these repetitive raids. He had no trouble in evading the posse, for he had many good friends in Strathearn – Drummonds, MacGregors, and Campbells – who gave timely warning, but if ever he was to drive an honest trade he had to make peace with the Murrays. There was only one why to do it now, and that was to submit to Lord Murray under the sponsorship of men of sufficient name to give his lordship confidence. It was Highland custom that when a chieftain or other gentleman felt that he had suffered another's just pursuit to a point no longer tolerable, he could go to the other and by full and frank submission receive pardon. This total trust in the other's mercy won a customary reward. Some fearsome exceptions to the rule could quoted, but a general rule it was.¹⁶ Rob would certainly take his father's advice on the means of achieving the desirable end, and Donald Glas persuaded two famous men of Clan Donald to act as surety: Glengarry and Alasdair Og of Glencoe. They all three went to Blair Atholl in June, where the submission was made and accepted. A bond was drawn up and signed. It reads (after a preamble):'I the said Robert Roy Campbell as principal and Alexr McDonnel, Laird of Glengarrie, and Alexander McDonald, brother german to John McDonald of Glencoe, as cautioners for me, Be ther presents hereby bind & oblidge us con^tie & sa^llie [conjointly and severally] our aires executors & successourts, That the S^d Robert Roy Campbell shall hereafter & in all time coming, not only behave himselfe as a loyall & dutifull subject under this present government but also as one honest, faithfull

& obedient servant to the noble Lord and shall present himselfe to his Lop when ever required & shall live honestly, peaceably & quietly in all time coming, and that under the penalty ane thousand pounds Scotts money, to be payed to his Lop by us in case of failzie. . . .'[17]

The bond was signed by Rob Roy, Glengarry, and Alasdair Og before three witnesses, one of whom was the notorious Simon Fraser of Beaufort, later twelfth Lord Lovat. Rob's formal humiliation had satisfied Murray, but no one except his lawyers could have taken the legal jargon seriously. They were all 'hard cases'. A year later, Simon Fraser (aged 29) kidnapped Murray's sister. His men cut off her stays with their dirks while bagpipers drowned her shrieks. He married her by force after the rape.[18] (She was rescued by three of her brothers, who led six hundred Athollmen north and devastated the Lovat country.) Rob Roy at least did keep his bond in sparing the Atholl lands and the 'present government'. He broke it by departing from peaceful ways 'in all time coming'. The most he could manage there was six months.

The Atholl Bond brought Mary a short-lived relief from anxiety. She gave birth about mid-summer to her first son James. All seemed to her well with Scotland. The king had even appointed a Commission to inquire into the Glencoe massacre. And she was too young to know the truth of Commissions. Their neighbouring landowners were beginning to talk of a Darien Scheme, which the Scottish Parliament had approved. They said it would make the country rich, almost overnight, by trade with Panama and Asia. The Craigrostan harvest had been good and Rob was settling down to the development of his cattlestock and droving. That same autumn of 1695, when he was away in Glasgow to buy Martinmas stores, Mary was stricken to hear that he had been caught off guard, arrested, and thrown into the Tolbooth. No record of the charge has survived – most probably the hership of Kippen. Mary was distraught. His father had been held two years for a lesser raid. Rob was more likely to suffer execution. If Mary was suppressing that thought, Rob was not. The Tolbooth bells sounding every hour told him how short was the time left. The magistrates had found him guilty. They were waiting only for the Privy Council's orders on his disposal, he fearing the worst and they hoping for it.

On 19 December, the Privy Council ordered 'Robert McGregor prisoner in Glasgow to be sent along with some others to Flanders'. His uncle Robert of Glenlyon was to die there the following year, but the king's insatiable need of cannon-fodder had for the present saved Rob Roy. The extra time required for assembling the draft was enough to let Rob and his friends arrange an escape. In the Lowland towns other than Edinburgh, the keepers and jailers (who could not be dignified with the title of 'prison officers') were usually of recent Highland origin; they could so often be persuaded to connive at the escape of Highland prisoners, especially of men of their own or allied clans, that the frequency of jail-breaking had grown notorious.[19] If a clan chief wanted the escape, and a magistrate or keeper came of the right blood, then it could be contrived. In Glasgow, where Highland stock was richly represented at all levels, Rob's escape may not have been difficult. The common excuse offered, that jails were too old and kept ill-repaired, could not have been said of Glasgow's tolbooth.

Rob was home in time to guard his family through a four-year emergency named 'The Hungry Years'. The twenty-five years of his life had been blessed with good harvest weather, interrupted by a few bad years widely dispersed. From 1696 to 99, four bad seasons came in a row. The crops were blighted by rain-storming summers, early bitter frosts, and autumn blizzards, accompanied by foot-and-mouth disease (then called murrain) among the cattle.[20] The effects were heightened by an increase in population following three decades of good weather, and the consequence was the heaviest mortality of the century.[21]

Rob knew, perhaps for the first time, the passion of protective will. His life had not been narrowly self-centred; he had been brought up to think of his people, who were not apt to think for themselves, but his brothers and sister had been older than he, and his father masterful; no young or weak members of family had relied on him for help and protection. The land's grim challenge would come as if it were a new thing, and stirred him as never before. He felt now that the lives of Mary and James were in his hands; at whatever cost he must save and shelter them. And since Mary would feel no differently about him and her son, the pair worked as one.

In MacGregor country as elsewhere no corn grew. In the few places where it did, the yield was too small to leave seed for the spring sowing. Sheep and cattle died by the thousand.[22] Goat meat was salted down for the first Martinmas, but that could not be done again, for the milk of the reduced stock had become invaluable, and no one had money to buy salt. The people tried to live off cheese, and old stores of oatmeal mixed with blood, but excess caused dysentery and supplies ran out. Failing barley and oatmeal, Rob's family and clan used every edible weed and berry available, from nettles to brambles, but no winter store could be had from these, nor sufficient meat for everyone from deer, fish, and birds. Nearly half of Scotland's one million people lived north of the Highland Line,[23] and outside the eastern Lowlands most of them starved. In the central Lowlands, Fletcher of Saltoun described two hundred thousand vagrants begging from door to door in 1698.

After losing most of their cattle, Rob and Mary relied on ewe's milk for cheese (daily summer yield, one pint), and goat's milk for drink (yield, one quart). They made oon by frothing up boiled milk with a cross-headed stick a yard long, twisted between the palms. The froth was supped off the top with wooden spoons, and again worked up and supped several times. No whisky could be distilled. Instead hot water was added to buttermilk, which precipitated a white curd that could be hung like cheese in a cloth, while the liquid could be kept for weeks or months while it fermented to the sparkling drink called bland. Another emergency food was everywhere prepared from the stored husks of oats. The husks were steeped in hot water for two days, when the liquor was sieved, stirred, and boiled while it thickened to a paste called sowens.[24] Snails were stored live for winter, when they were made into thick broth.[25] By these and other devices the people managed to survive the first two years. After that, a third or even half the parish populations were dying or emigrating.[26] Sir Robert Sibbald, writing in 1699, describes thin and feeble men with death in their faces begging by the waysides, accompanied by women with empty breasts and starving babies, until they dropped in the streets or lay dead by the bridletracks with grass in their mouths. The heavy death toll was caused not just by starvation but the diseases that found access to weakened bodies – typhus first and foremost in this particular famine, malaria, smallpox which was the main killer of children, and equally with these the influenza viruses.

Any disease that found a foothold in a Highland (or Lowland) settlement could enjoy a quick spread. Rob and Mary had a stone-built house, more likely mortared with clay than lime (which was rarely used); his tenants might sometimes have drystone houses, but nearly everyone here and throughout the Highlands built in turf, that being quicker and warmer. The walls were five feet high, often less and rarely more. Few had windows, the door was hardly four feet high, and when the fire was lit in the hearth the smoke poured out at every crevice, until the house looked like a fuming dunghill.[27] The smoke abated when the peats reddened. Inside, young children played naked among the hens. In good homes, the box beds were kept clean. A few had for chamber-pot a hole dug in the ground by the bedside, so that a man hastily rising had need of care where he put his foot. The speed with which virus diseases travelled through seventeenth-century communities in famine was thus accelerated by the housing.

While such bad times prevailed at home, Scotsmen were taking all the more earnestly to William Patterson's Darien Scheme. A Dumfriesshire man and part-founder of the Bank of England in 1694, he had conceived for Scotland an East India trade by the founding of trading stations on either side of the Panama isthmus, where the products of east and west could be bought, sold, and exchanged. King William, influenced by advice from England's East India merchants, disliked the scheme, and this served to increase Scottish enthusiasm. The people's imagination had been fired. The shares boomed as merchants, magistrates, and landowners flocked to invest. Four thousand colonizers enlisted. Men at the king's ear were bribed to secure the royal charter by a promise of two per cent of the profits. They succeeded, and the first company of twelve hundred men sailed from Leith in July 1698, dreaming of riches.

Men like Rob Roy, who might have been thought supremely fitted for colonizing work had they so chosen, could not in fact choose. Rob's land was his life, not in the sense that he owned it, but that it owned him. Between the bitterness of famine and the national euphoria over Darien, he held firmly to his own course, not fleeing the land's challenge but facing it. He would lead a free life as a cattleman in his own Highland country, in his clan society. He worked doggedly to that end through the four grim years. He raised his own cattle on clean ground, he travelled on foot through the Highlands buying small herds for the trysts, and he raised the necessary money.

Fortune began to smile. In 1700 the run of good seasons returned. The land relaxed and yielded. Rob's reputation as a man of trust had been tested and proven, and his wisdom too in the eyes of his landowning friends and neighbours who had now lost their Darien money. King William under pressure from the East India Company had ordered the English colonial governors to boycott the Scots settlement at Darien. When the Spaniards attacked, the colonists had been unfit to endure both war and disease. A few survivors of the first company had returned in 1699, followed by those of the second and third companies in 1700 – in all, only thirty of the original four thousand.[28] The starving refugees had been refused food supplies by the governor of Jamaica, while the ships' crews were refused naval help when they flew distress signals.[29] At home, thousands had been ruined. The *coup de grâce* came when the royal charter, which provided that damage by seizure of the company's men and effects would be made good by the Treasury, was repudiated. All blame was laid on William's shoulders, while the ruined Scots voiced rebellious thoughts. The Jacobites greatly profited and members of Parliament turned cold eyes on the advocates of union with England.

Rob had reason to congratulate himself that he had kept clear of Darien. Several of his family's friends had been trapped, and the only one to escape had been Colonel Alexander Campbell of Fonab. This man of character had befriended his late uncle Robert when most in need, and would one day help Rob likewise. Rob's good fortune was double-faced. While the Darien survivors straggled home, and the sun shone at last on ripening crops, his brother Iain died, victim of the famine's side-effects. Iain's elder son Gregor, aged eleven, was now heir to Glengyle. The boy was to be known throughout life as Gregor Ghlun Dhubh, or Gregor of the Black Knee, from a prominent birth-mark. He continued to live with his mother, and his brother Donald and sister Catherine, at Glengyle House under their chieftain's guardianship. But Donald's days were numbered. For all practical purposes, Rob Roy had become acting chieftain of Clan Dughaill Ciar, whose people looked to him alone for leadership. Kilmanan was impressd by the way he rose to the occasion, and in 1701, by deeds of 9 and 15 December, signed at Buchanan and Killearn, he sold to Rob Roy the township of Knockeild (Knockyle) between Rowardennan and Rowchoish, for the sum of 1200 merks and £40 Scots entry money, his son Hugh agreeing.[30] On these same dates he resigned in Rob's favour 'the whole of his land as purchased of Colquhoun of Luss together with the ten pound land old extent of Craig Rostan'.[31] The deed conveying the all-inclusive title was not registered until five years later.

Rob had become a man of substance. His might be poor land in the eye of an Atholl laird, but to the landless Gregarach his share, about 6720 acres, was princely. It extended from the Allt Rostan near the head of Loch Lomond eight miles down the eastern shore to near Rowardennan, including the entire west flank of Ben Lomond, its northern spurs, and the west end of Loch Arklet.

The ground fell steep and craggy from its undulating hill-spine to the shore of Loch Lomond, lightly wooded there in oak and birch, and sprinkled with hawthorn, not as now heavily forested on the lower slopes. It was inhabited by little townships whose people had cleared the land for grazing and lazybeds. Most lived near the shore, where the birlinns were moored and breached; some high on the flanks, where their broken walls still remain, almost lost in new plantations. The land looked gay in spring from the yellow and pale green of its leafing trees, and brightened further in June under the snow of hawthorn. High above the loch, and behind the first swell of the hills, lay three sheltered furrows, each a mile and a half long, with good grass for cattle, forming the glens of the Snaid, Culness, and Ptarmigan burns. A hundred and fifty families lived on Craigrostan.[32]

In effect, Rob and his wife's family, and his father, held dominion between the passes of Aberfoyle and Glen Dochart, and between Strathyre and Loch Lomond. They were jealous of large intrusion by other families or other branches of the clan, and felt resentment when Glen Carnaig in the Braes of Balquhidder was bought at this time by Iain Og of the Ladasach line. Glen Carnaig was one of the best of the glens. Widely open to the south, its gently sloping flanks were filled with sun and grass. Rob's cousin, Malcolm of Marchfield (son of MacGregor of Coilleitir in Glen Falloch), already held two farms nearby at the head of Loch Voil: Inverlochlarig, and Monachyle Beag, for which Marchfield was the inclusive name.[33] Rob having stocked Craigrostan was now grazing cattle on Malcolm's hill pasture. He had hoped in time to get Glen Carnaig or other land west of Loch Voil. Therefore, he determined to discourage Iain Og, who by repute was a rich man, from taking possession of the Carnaig glen. Kilmanan looked like drinking himself to death. Iain Og as a new, incoming chief – his line was senior to Roro, Balhaldie, Brackley, and Dughaill Ciar – might buy in his own name land that the Dughaill Ciar held to be theirs by right of occupation over the better part of two centuries – land that Rob now hoped to acquire in time from the profits of cattle-trading. In this field he had ability amounting to genius: his contemporary drovers described him as 'a man in ten thousand'.[34]

It seems probable that he made a round of the clan's chieftains, for all were now persuaded that Iain Og MacGregor should not be acknowledged as Kilmanan's successor. In justice to Iain Og, it should be said that there was no reason, other than Rob Roy's ambition, to think him unworthy. The domestic politics of the clan were against him. In justice to Rob Roy, it must be added that he laid no claim to chiefship. His branch was junior. But he wanted land.

CHAPTER ELEVEN

THE TUTOR OF GLENGYLE
1701–5

The death of Donald Glas

W HEN ROB ROY became 'MacGregor of Inversnaid and
Craigrostan' in 1701, he was aged thirty. He was in
full manhood, a very different figure from the bony youth of
eighteen. No portrait of him was ever painted, so far as is known,
although several have been wrongly described as his.[1] The two
best known are by Rob Roy's contemporary, Richard Waitt, who
was employed from 1713 to 14 by Brigadier Alexander Grant
to paint ten members of his clan. All were hung at Kinveachy in
Strath Spey. One, of Alasdair Mor Grant, the champion of the
laird of Grant, has been much copied and exhibited above the
title *Rob Roy*; the other, hung as *Rob Roy* in the Glasgow Art
Gallery, is posed precisely as for Alasdair Grant, and with clothing
in close accord, but with changed face. The gallery has no record
of origin to substantiate the title given. Imaginary portraits of Rob
Roy were done in later centuries for book illustrations, and none
was faithful to known fact.

No written description of Rob Roy was set down in his lifetime,
except by Daniel Defoe, who not having met him gave him a
beard a foot long. Sixty years after Rob Roy's death, several
accounts by men who had seen him in their childhood were given
verbally to Walter Scott, K. Macleay, and others. These agree in
their general terms.

Rob Roy was of middle height or little under – the average
height of Highlanders was 5′ 4″ to 5′ 6″[2] – spare and compact but
with an extraordinary breadth of shoulder. His strongly muscled
legs were likened to those of a Highland bull, both in light-footed
agility and thighs furred with red hair. No less remarkable were
the length and power of his arms. When Scott was told of this he
forgot about the Highlanders' peculiar sense of humour – a gift
for gross exaggeration, which they delight in using to point up
a general truth. Instead of giving Scott the prosaic fact that Rob
Roy had long arms, they said, 'Och, the man could tie his garters
without stooping', and Scott in writing passed this on to posterity

as literal truth. The more sober witness given to Dr Macleay is that a man unaided could scarcely hope to wrench anything out of Rob Roy's hands – he had been seen to seize a stag by its horns and hold it fast. His reach and strength of arm, when added to a trained talent, would account for his renowned superiority with a broadsword.

His head was well-poised on the neck, the face frank and open. Its normally cheerful expression became imperious at time of decision or danger. Thick red hair, now beginning to darken to its later auburn, was curled short across a broad brow and close over his ears. During the latter half of his life he wore a beard and moustaches. The record of his eyes says nothing of colour – most likely brown or hazel. They were uncommonly expressive, by nature bold, hiding little of his mind. By reason of his openness, most men liked and trusted him, provided they were able to give him cause to trust themselves. Such as could liked also his uncompromising speech. If asked, he said what he thought, and people knew at once where they stood. The quality was rare and made friends and enemies respectively of the wise and foolish. But he had learned when to hold his tongue, and his manners were those of a gentleman.[3] His voice was deep and speech fluent in Lowland Scots or native Gaelic. When aroused to serious thought or passion, his speech took the more elevated Gaelic idiom. He could then talk to men who were in disagreement with a disconcerting directness and vehemence.

All who met him had immediate recognition of a powerful personality and natural dignity. He owed this strong growth of character to its rooting in the house of a chieftain. Yet his elder brothers with equal opportunity had no equal vigour and ability. His alone was the latent potential, to which strong development was given by the good chance of birth and parents. He gained thus a dozen advantages: formal education apart, he heard from early days a higher level of discussion on the clan's affairs, learned tact and diplomacy in dealing with men and women; developed a natural courtesy; learned to accept responsibility for the affairs of tenants, and to have real concern for their welfare, on which his own depended; learned concern for stock and wildlife, on which people relied for livelihood and supplies; developed close observation, far beyond what is now thought needful, of all wild things and of men's living conditions; received discipline, for the chieftain's family had to set higher standards of behaviour; acquired the habit of foresight in farming and politics; won powers of command; and had the chance given by wide travel to know his country and its people, establishing thus personal relations with clan chiefs and merchants and a rich variety of men.[4]

Above all, he had a settled home and a happy one throughout childhood, and again during many years after early marriage. He naturally developed a deep love of the Trossachs and Loch Lomond homelands, with a complete knowledge of how to live there in bad times. The loss and starvation and misery that he and his families had experienced during the famine years sharpened his regard for the poor. His well-attested compassion towards them had this double base in a good home and personal suffering.

Rob Roy felt fully assured of his personal standing in the world, but not so of his clan's. He was too well-versed in their history not to be sensitive to the name's proscription, and in Lowland episodes resentment came out. There as everywhere, courtesy was one of his prominent characteristics, acknowledged by friends and enemies alike, but if given cause by any slight to his pride of name, he could switch to an impetuous ruthlessness. Kippen revealed an arrogant contempt for men who had certain defects he was lucky not to share – cowardice on that occasion; others illustrated in the course of his life were homosexual tendencies and corruption of good faith. His code was not thought out and full of anomalies. He could exact black mail for his Lowland Watches, and yet be scrupulous in honouring them. He could withdraw from a dispute or even a challenge to fight by calculation of the odds or the emptiness of the quarrel, and yet in this wise command of his passion, commendable in a celebrated swordsman whom no one thought to accuse of cowardice, he could be slow to make such allowance for others. One occasion on which he made judgment too hastily had a comic conclusion.

Rob Roy had gone to a summer party at John Buchanan's house at Arnprior, on the south side of Flanders Moss between Buchlyvie and Kippen, and there chanced to meet Henry Cunninghame of Boquhan, a Lowland fop, whose affectation was an effeminate delicacy of manner, dress, and speech.[5] When the whisky had loosened Rob's tongue, he found this poseur's company not to his liking and let fly an insult, not to be endured by a man of spirit. He was promptly made aware that he was meeting for the first time one of those exquisites (more numerous next century) who could combine deviations with high courage. He, the feared swordsman, was confounded to be instantly challenged. While they were fixing the meeting place at Shieling Hill, Cunninghame's sword was hidden by a well-wisher, hoping to save the poor boy from quick slaughter. Rob Roy strolled to the field and paraded there, amusedly relaxed, like some wild cat with whom a house-mouse had dared to make appointment. Cunninghame, after searching in vain for his broadsword, discovered an old rusty one and hurried to the field. Rob, with not a drop of adrenalin in his blood, was unprepared for what happened next. Cunninghame suddenly rushed him, wielding his blade with such fury, strength, and unexpected skill, that Rob gave ground, failed to recover a stance, and without blood drawn was driven off the field. The one man to rout Rob Roy – Boquhan might have dined off his story for the rest of his life, had he not been too diffident (as testified by a friend).[6] A long time may have passed before Rob Roy lived it down, for the tale was too good for a short life. Perhaps he told it against himself and had Clan Gregor rolling in the aisles.

Apart from this and one or two other incidents that must have been good for his soul, it was said of Rob Roy that he would not turn his back on a friend or an enemy. Nevertheless, he was unwilling to let a private quarrel develop to fighting point, for his swordsmanship was unmatched till late in life. Wanton quarrels like that of Arnprior were not repeated in a lifetime. Yet he was much challenged, often by men who wanted to measure themselves against Scotland's highest standard for the broadsword, knowing that if they lost they would live. The best-known challenger was Barra's chief, Ruari Dubh MacNeil, defeated as all others. Rob fought twenty-two duels according to Dr Macleay's precise informants, but some were bound to have gone unrecorded.

This then was the formidable, far-ranging man whom Mary MacGregor had chosen to marry, a man with a huge capacity for sin and virtue, and with wide scope for change and fulfilment in years ahead. While not overburdened with her husband's company, since like his father before him he was much on the move, she probably bore him at least ten children in their first twenty years, since five sons survived. Although he was much away from home, Mary was settled among friends and kinsmen of whom she would see much, and she could command all the help she needed from tenants owing services.

In 1702, Donald Glas died in Glen Gyle.[7] Rob Roy, his only surviving son, and Christian, his daughter-in-law, kept the watch on the corpse for four nights to allow guests to gather from as far north as Lochaber. They buried Donald in the old graveyard to the south of Glengyle House. The feast that night was a greater affair than for Gregor of Stucnaroy. Donald Glas had been known throughout the Highlands and Rob was now Tutor of Glengyle until Gregor Ghlun Dhubh should come of age. The boy was now 13. Rob was acting chieftain, his repute raised further by his clan's not recognizing Iain Og of Glencarnaig as heir to Kilmanan, whose insobriety had come to mean forfeiture of the chiefship in everything but name.[8] From Glen Dochart to the Highland Line (three hundred square miles), Rob Roy was master of the land and people, and his word weighty in other districts. The feast was hardly less in his honour than his father's memory.

Among the hundreds of visitors to Glengyle that night would be Rob's unhappy cousin John Campbell of Glenlyon, pauperized by his father, oppressed by his memory, embarrassed now by the presence of John and Alasdair Og of Glencoe, and thankful for the company of his father's friend, Campbell of Fonab; Coll MacDonald of Keppoch, whose aunt had been Donald's mother; Campbell of Glenfalloch, Breadalbane's nephew; Drummond of Comrie and Campbell of Duneaves, each in turn Iain's father-in-law; MacFarlane of Arrochar; Glengarry, a giant in size and strength, who had been Donald's good friend since Killiecrankie; and numerous representatives from other Jacobite clans, together with the heads of family from Clan Gregor and those of other name in all neighbouring glens.

Each and every day, since Donald's death, the women of Glengyle, Arklet, and Craigrostan had been busy in preparation, organized by Mary and Iain's widow Christian. Grain had been parched and ground, bread baked in huge quantities, reserves of milk, cheese, and butter pooled, and now the cooks were at work by fires lit along the banks of Gyle Water. Goats, sheep, cattle, and poultry were roasted in wooden barbecues.[9] The company gathered around them in the firelight, where most of the whisky distilled in Strath Gartney had been decanted into barrels. The common quaichs passed from lip to lip.[10] Each man could dip his own if he willed. The pipers and bards were out in force, the company willing to listen or dance once they were fed, and when dawn broke at last the scene was like a battlefield, for many had dropped where they stood.

Highland funerals were much used for conference between chiefs. Donald's was opportune. James VII had died the year before. His son James was only Gregor's age, too young as yet to be heard in his own interest, but old enough to stir hope in every Jacobite breast, and with hope the plots thickened. To complicate matters, Whigs, Tories, and Jacobites were plotting against each other as well, and in Scotland the greatest plotters of all were the four leading Whigs, James Douglas, Duke of Queensberry; Archibald Campbell, newly created Duke of Argyll; John Murray, Marquis of Atholl; and James Graham, Marquis of Montrose. Graham had newly bought the vast lands of the Lennox from the bastard duke of Lennox (a son of Charles II). Murray, Graham, and Campbell were mutual enemies, near neighbours of Rob Roy, and not averse to having the aid of his arm and ear. This strategic position of his land between these three princes, and his constant travel over their territories, commended Rob to the Jacobite leaders, who looked to him for intelligence.

William of Orange had died only a month or two before Donald. Anne was now queen. Although a daughter of James VII, she was despised by the Jacobites, who called her 'Queen of Cockneydom', and she, bored at thought of her northern province's affairs, had made Queensberry her Secretary of State. He had been William's Commissioner for Scotland, was a protagonist for the union of the two Parliaments, to which Atholl was opposed, therefore he and Argyll were rumoured to be meditating Atholl's downfall, and seeking to suborn Jacobite instruments to that end. Any sign of these great men cultivating relations with Rob Roy, as in fact they were, and he with them, caused interest. His schooling in diplomacy at his father's house stood him in good stead; he had to tread as delicately as Agag.

When tongues were loosened round the fires, the great scandal of six years earlier brought ribald speculation. This was Simon Fraser's rape of the tenth Lord Lovat's widow (Atholl's daughter). That old story had come again to the boil. Simon Fraser, sentenced to death and outlawed, had not yet been caught, and his scent being strong as a skunk's, he had fled to St Germain, declaring himself a Jacobite to get shelter. The Jacobites there seemed not at all embarrassed by the sudden adherence of this former arch-Whig. In the political morality of the times his trangression was venial. To men of Highland stock like Rob Roy, betrayal of trust and the expedient switching of loyalties were anathema. But not so to all Jacobites in exile. Among them were men of property great enough to give them power in the State and whose goal was that alone. Simon Fraser seemed to them less a traitor than a self-seeker, which made him one of their own. Their question was how best to use him, and within the year Rob Roy was to be involved in their machinations.

The master drover

When the guests had gone, Roy had a heavy reckoning to meet. Depleted supplies had to be made good, time given to the training of Gregor Ghlun Dhubh, and the year's cattle strategy planned. Throughout the Highlands, the cattle trade was growing year by year. Rob saw this trade as his life. He had talent, ambition, a true vocation for it. Success could bring status, modest wealth, and land. Above all it was venturesome, a challenge to shrewd calculation, to boldness of spirit, and to sound judgment. The risks were great, but so were the rewards if he could deal largely.

It was the custom of mountaineers trading in a small way – and Rob had been one of them in earlier days – to lay out the whole of what they were worth, or even three times as much, in buying a herd of twenty-five to one hundred head by travelling a circuit of forty miles from one small tryst or fair to another, living the while on bannocks and oatmeal, and lying out at nights on the heather regardless of weather.[11] The small profit had not given recompense. The hardships to such as Rob were small, but the time spent was too long for the money won. His father had trained him to deal in bigger herds, bought on loaned capital, but since Killiecrankie the merchants' money had been hard to raise until after his marriage. He had done well since then.

Men with money looked for certain qualities in the drover, apart from known honesty. These were: (1) an intimate knowledge of all country to be traversed, to avoid the dangers of rievers and weather; (2) a thorough knowledge of cows and their ills, and their market values; (3) good health and toughness in the endurance of hardships; (4) resource and initiative in dealing with every kind of impediment; (5) knowledge of men and the force of character to manage them; (6) an absence of scruple in dealing with over-hard bargainers, or the undue exactions that could be imposed by customs officers, or by landowners for grazing-stances on a journey south to England; (7) a strong sense of responsibility, with shrewd foresight in assessing the varied factors of buying and selling at widely separated markets, of planning long journeys and making all needed provision for them. The list might seem formidable, and to the great credit of the clan system there was no lack of qualified men, by virtue of their way of life, breeding, and heredity – and their ready transfer to an employer of the honest service given to their chief.[12] There were many men who could be trusted to drive small herds of fifty to three hundred cows, but the man who could drive a thousand to Crieff or England and keep a low cost per head required the attributes of a good general. The logistics hugely increased in complexity with the size of the herd and longer distance travelled, and so too the contingent circumstances affecting safety and profit. The men possessed of that order of organizing ability were rare, and Rob Roy was one of them.

In 1702, if not earlier, his ability was recognized by James Graham, the Marquis of Montrose. This young man was aged 22, and described by a contemporary as bearing himself 'with a sweetness of behaviour which charms all who know him; hath improved himself in most foreign courts; is very beautiful in his person'.[13] He possessed great estates in the counties of Linlithgow, Forfar, Perth, Stirling, and Dunbarton, but like other great landowners of Scotland had lost heavily on the Darien Scheme and was in no mood to lose more. He had that year paid a great sum for the Lennox, therefore his assessment of Rob Roy was cool, hard, and thorough. The result was that he advanced more and more money to their mutual profit, until his loans were annually approaching £1000 sterling.[14] Cows at that time were fetching a guinea a head at Crieff and more in England. Rob's skill and character having been proven, other men of town and country invested: Campbell of Blythswood, Graham of Gorthie, Sir John Shaw of Greenock, and MacFarlane of Inveruglas and Arrochar, among many more.[15] The money was given mainly on Rob's good name, but Montrose required also a bond on his property. Rob gave the security with misgivings. In all Britain there was no tougher arena than cattle-dealing. Rob had learned to trust few men, and none of them Whigs. He felt wary of Montrose more than most, for rich as that lad was in land, he seemed already obsessed by a need for more.

The large scale droving conducted by Rob Roy between 1702 and 1712 required the employment of many more men, not only drovers but marshalls or 'topsmen', and one annual expedition by-passing Crieff to fulfil English commissions. He had to be continuously in the field as general anywhere between the Outer Hebrides (then called the Long Isle), where he had developed a big trade,[16] and Carlisle, or perhaps Norwich. He now covered most of the low ground on horseback. A principal English destination was the small village of St Faiths, four miles north of Norwich, where the Norfolk graziers came to buy the 'Scotch runts'. On this rich meadowland nearly thirty thousand Scots cattle were fattened each year. 'They feed so eagerly on the rich pasture of its marshes', wrote Daniel Defoe, 'that they thus in an unusual manner grow monstrously fat and the beef so delicious for taste that the inhabitants prefer them to English cattle which are much larger and fairer to look at.'

The greater exertion, risk, and responsibilities taken for delivery to England won their reward. Courage and optimism were demanded of a head-drover coming all the way south from the Highlands, for the condition of the herd was deteriorating by fatigue, accident, and loss of weight, and the more so if grazing costs forced him to lengthen marches. He could be harassed too by uncertain market prices, caused by the brewing or breaking of political storms. Rob had his bad years; all in all he prospered. One reason for his well-doing was businesslike method. He kept close account of his dealings, even the smallest, as this letter to James Graham, writer in Glasgow, reveals.[17] He gave trust and received it:

Glengyle the 5 of July 1703

Sir

I wroat to you the last whyle concerning the ten kows that ye was to gett to the Marquess of Montrose. I told you I was not sure of them since I was not at home when I rect. your letter. Now I have bought them from [blank] on [condition that he] must have ready money befoir he deliver them. Send with the bearer Alexander Graham leatt McGre[gor] two hundreth and fyftie merks which is the pryce I agreed for and this lyne with his recit shall oblidge me to hold compt with you. Lett me know when ye shall desyre my lord stots to be sent. I rect. of the pryce of your own two kows a ginie and ane half so there rests to me as yett ten pund and 14 shillins. Give it to the bearer. This with my service to your self and lady. I rest, sir your assured friend and very humble servant

R. Campbell.

(A receipt for 250 merks is endorsed by Alexander Grahame sometime McGregor.)

He was not mean with his money. In March 1703, he bought from Montrose for his nephew Gregor, who was still impoverished after his father's death, 6400 acres of Glen Gyle. The charter dated 25 May gave the right of property to Rob Roy as attorney for 'James Graham' (Gregor's alias under the penal Acts), who would succeed when he came of age.[18] The deed does not give the selling price.

Rob Roy's name was now so well known in Scotland, he corresponded with so many men of high standing, and journeyed so widely, that his value to the Jacobites as an agent grew great. Equally, the Whigs with whom he did so much business were anxious to have his ear and lend theirs to him, sometimes to further their own enmities. In 1703, Simon, Lord Lovat, was back in the Highlands on a secret mission for the Jacobites in France. He had a plan to land five thousand French troops at Dundee to divert government forces while five hundred men were to land on the west coast, seize Fort William, and close the passes from the south and east until the Highlands had time to rise. His present mission was to discover what forces the chiefs might field. He found that they would field none. The time was not right, James still too young, and Lovat not trusted. Rob Roy was fully informed on these moves, his friends and allies being involved. The chiefs' negative decision was promptly shown to be right. Lovat, smarting under rejection, cast around to see what damage he could do. His enemy the marquis of Atholl had newly died, and his son John been created duke – to the chagrin of Argyll and Queensberry. So, Lovat put out feelers to the two latter, found himself welcomed, and to them betrayed his own plot and party. He persuaded them (unless they persuaded him) that their rival the duke of Atholl was not only in the plot but had corresponded with Louis XIV.[19] Lovat alleged that he could produce written evidence from St Germain if granted a pass back to France. Queensberry as Secretary of State was fool enough to sign the pass himself, and thus to secure his own downfall.

The intrigue was discovered. One of Lovat's or Argyll's agents approached Rob Roy and Robert Ferguson, a Jacobite of Aberdeen, with offer of a bribe for aid or false witness. Their revulsion was such that to get Atholl off the hook they disclosed to him what they knew. Ferguson acted first, in November, and Atholl went direct to the queen. His presentation of the case bore the stamp of innocence. Queensberry was dismissed. No evidence has ever been produced that John of Atholl wavered in loyalty to Anne. The Argyll Papers (Maidment), in recording their duke's effort to bring Atholl down, conclude with engaging frankness: 'and after all this intreaguing, he died in the armes of his whore, Ane Alison, in the north of England, 28th September 1703'.

Lovat on arriving in France was clapped into the prison of Angoulême, where he languished ten years.

Rob gave his own warning to Atholl, in supplement of Ferguson's, late and sparingly. He called at Holyrood House and saw the Duchess at the beginning of February 1704.[20] She wrote from Holyrood to the duke in London a letter dated 2 February, saying that she had seen Rob Roy and received information about the plot. She added, 'I am convinced he could tell more if he liked.' She had asked him to make a statement to Atholl's agent in Edinburgh, Mr Scott, but omitted to advise Scott, who thus incurred the duke's wrath by a failure to grasp the importance of Rob's evidence. Scott was obliged to write Atholl an apology on 22 February: 'I am sorry Robert Roy's declaration was so ill writt. I did it in hast not thinking it would be sent away. He is not now in town so cannot make it up and I really took it for stories of his own making & not materiall, which made me write it so carelessly, and that it was all hearsay, Kilmanan is still in town and I have been several times calling for him & either miss'd him or found him so drunk as I could not understand what he said.'

Rob Roy's relations with John of Atholl had been bad in the past and he hoped now to repair them. His rieving days were behind him, and although Atholl was a dyed-in-the-wool Whig, he was Scotland's most powerful chief, able to give aid should occasion arise – as indeed it might, since Rob's aid to Atholl had not endeared him to the Campbell faction. The new duke of Argyll was John, aged 25, and a promising soldier. He was already stirring up Campbell of Fonab to pull in recruits for his Independent Company, and Fonab had impressed two MacGregors of Glen Lyon, on Atholl land. Their people appealed for help to Rob Roy, since by force of character and repute he was at this time the most influential leader of the whole clan. He wrote to the duke of Atholl:[21]

Glengyle, ye 20 of May 1704

My Lord, – May it please Your Grace, In Your Grace's absence Fownab prest tuo of your men & sent them to Edr. for recruits; yr names be John & Duncan McEune Voire, late McGrigore in Glenlyone. Duncan liveing at ye time under ye Earle of Bradalbin was brought back. John remains still there. Your Grace was pleased to protect these two men formerly. Therefore I humblie beg that yr Grace may be pleased to liberat this poor man. who hath left a wyfe and maney smal children behind him. If not, Fownab May heirafter dispose of Yr Grace's men as if they were his

oune, beging pardon for this I am My Lord, Yr Gr/s most
humble and most obligded servantt.

Ro: Campbell

Since Donald's death, Rob Roy as Tutor of Glengyle made much
use of his late brother's house at Portnellan by Loch Katrine.
Gregor Ghlun Dhubh was a first care, virtually a foster son
although living with his own family in the chieftain's house.
He gave the boy the same disciplines he had received himself,
and a first-class job he made of it, judging by later reports on
Gregor.[22]

During 1704 and 1705, Rob and his fellow Scots came under
threat of political storms, which were about to discharge a
thunderbolt on the cattle industry. The trouble had started in
William's time. His government had inherited from the Stewarts
a constitutional defect, and that was the centring of monarchical
power in London while leaving Scotland to a puppet parliament in
Edinburgh. The defect had been exposed to public view during the
disaster of the Darien Scheme. The Scots had been awakened then
and thereafter to their deprivation of good government. There
were two ways out: the establishment of an independent Scots
parliament, or some form of joint parliament centred on London.
The Scots dreaded subordination to England, as seemed inevitable
in a partnership so unequal, and might have been united for
independence had this not involved the restoration of a Catholic
prince. The dire need of change, the divergent views on what
change was best, and the misgivings felt by all of whatever party,
had produced a national tension now ripe for explosion.

CHAPTER TWELVE

THE TREATY OF UNION
1705–12

THE THREE years preceding the Union of 1707 gave Rob his most searching test in mastery of the cattle trade. The storm clouds had begun to gather in 1701 when the English Parliament, without reference to the Scots, had passed the Act of Settlement declaring that on Anne's death the British crown should go to the granddaughter of James VI, Sophia, Electress of Hanover. The Scots Parliament, already resentful at English refusal to allow trade with their American colonies, especially when London's foreign policy had cut Scotland's 'auld alliance' with France and ruined her continental trade, replied to the insult by an assertion of independence. In 1704, under the guidance of Andrew Fletcher of Saltoun, they passed an Act of Security, declaring that if Anne left no heirs (her seventeen children had all died) the two crowns should not pass to the same head unless to a Stewart of Scotland's royal line, who must be Protestant and secure Scotland's free institutions of government, religion, law, courts, and trade.

Hostility between the two nations sharpened. A continued union of crowns after Anne's death fell in peril. The Jacobites' vehement opposition to a union of parliaments was now given the support of the Patriot party led by Fletcher. When the two parties joined forces in 1703-4, a civil war began to seem more than possible. The English Parliament lost its head and worsened a bad situation by passing the Alien Act, which provided that if the Scots had failed to accept the English Act of Settlement by Christmas Day 1705, their merchandise would be excluded from England and that 'all great cattle and sheep' exported from Scotland to England shall be forfeited.

Both nations began to prepare for war. Its declaration drew close in 1705 when a Scottish ship was seized on the Thames, where its presence 'interfered with English privileges'. Demands by the Scots Parliament for its release being ignored, they in exasperation seized an English ship named the *Worcester*, which had come into the Firth of Forth, and hanged the innocent captain and two officers on a charge of piracy. That such fat sparks failed to ignite the power-barrel was in part due to the dampening involvement of England, France, and Scotland in the War of the Spanish Succession, now in its fourth year, and in part to Scots Presbyterian reluctance to sever the union of crowns when James Edward was staunchly Catholic.

During these years of uncertainty, many drovers were bankrupted by the wild fluctuations in cattle prices. Rob Roy, and other notable dealers like McLaren of Brig o' Turk, were astute enough to keep their heads above water. One of Rob's methods for transferring the fluctuation risk to others was to buy herds in early spring for immediate resale to Lowland gentlemen, who fattened them on their own ground.[1] He accepted reduced income, and they the gamble. 1705 was for most the year of disaster. The threat posed by the Alien Act caused prices at the autumn trysts to fall by one third; as panic spread, by two thirds at the close of the Crieff tryst. All sellers lost heavily; even McLaren went under, and those who had bought early for the autumn sales lost all.[2]

Rob survived. He had the chance at the end to make a big killing, mainly to the benefit of Montrose. Scotland's three main exports were linen, coal, and cattle. England needed them. Salted beef was essential for armed forces engaged in prolonged wars. The Alien Act was as harmful to England as to Scotland. Therefore the English government had second thoughts. They resolved to repeal the Act well before Christmas. Montrose was a Privy Councillor, Lord of Exchequer, and Lord High Admiral of Scotland. He was now about to be nominated Lord President of the Privy Council. Since Rob had his money for investment, he assuredly had early notice of repeal. One or two others getting that notice were able to buy at Crieff at the rock-bottom price of 6s. 8d. a head and sell sky-high in England at £4 – their gross profit more than 1000 per cent.[3]

Eight months of the year having passed miraculously without war, Parliament met on 1 September, with Argyll as Queen's Commissioner, to debate a hypothetical treaty of union with England. Argyll had agreed with Godolphin, the Lord Treasurer of England, that this treaty would be to their mutual benefit. Late at night, when opposition members had left the chamber, Argyll contrived that the duke of Hamilton put a motion that the nomination of Commissioners to draft a treaty be left to the queen (which meant Godolphin). It was carried. Godolphin in name of Queen Anne appointed a commission of 64, 32 from each country. He picked the Scots to include heavy losers in the Darien Scheme, including Argyll and his brother, and then proferred a clause that would refund Darien losses out of the English Treasury. They met in the well-named Cockpit of Whitehall (a room in the palace), where in nine weeks' verbal battle they drew up a union treaty for submission to the two Parliaments. Its subsequent debate raised feeling in Scotland to fever pitch. The subject was highly complex. For this double reason, few were equipped to give it cool thought.

Rob Roy's frequent visits to Edinburgh and Glasgow, and his long journeys through the Highlands, Lowlands, Borders, and northern England, made him better aware than most Scots of every shade of opinion, prejudice, and rational thought on the dominant topic of his time. His own views are known – he considered the Treaty of Union obnoxious.[4] He was newly entitled to a vote in his county. Archibald of Kilmanan gave him his charter of Craigrostan dated 7 June 1706, registering in Rob's name the lands and barony with the office of 'baillerie' (magistrate), confirmed by a charter dated 14 May signed by Colquhoun of Luss as superior.[5] The land's value as purchased by Kilmanan in 1697 was 6500 merks or £4333 Scots. A 'barony' was the Scots term for a large freehold property even when held by a commoner. It gave power to hold a baron court, punish crimes, and the right to vote.

It is tantalizing to speculate what Rob Roy may have said of the treaty. As a cattle dealer, he must have welcomed the notion of free trade over the Border; as a Scotsman, shared his countrymen's deep sense of frustration at England's deliberate throttling of Scottish commerce in the interests of her own, for the Scots had few means of retaliation. The treaty's offer of free trade bore some likeness to a patronizing sop, and was viewed by Scots with resentment rather than welcomed as a bargain driven. As a Jacobite, he would approve the clans' loyalty to the House of Stewart, for any threat that posed to the Protestant establishment was overridden by two great fears: a Whig reinstatement of Campbell power and aggrandizement, and the erosion of the Highland way of life. He would share too, since William's reign, the common exasperation at the subordination of Scotland's traditional foreign policy to England's preoccupation with the balance of European power, which had made Scotland a recruiting ground for successive wars against an ancient ally. Policies might rightly change, but the Scots had not been given a choice.

Since the Scots of 1706 had a much stronger sense of their national identity than now, it might seem strange that they could even contemplate the loss of their own Parliament, forfeiture of an independence for which their ancestors had fought with much fortitude, and reduction to a region. The answer is that they did not agree. They could not elect their members of Parliament – and the latter might well have replied that the people were too ignorant for such a privilege, quoting in support (but out of context) John Dryden: 'If by the people you understand the multitude, the *hoi polloi*, 'tis no matter what they think; they are sometimes in the right, sometimes in the wrong: their judgement is a mere lottery.'[6] Their betters could do no better – but that was a point to which all were blind. Since Rob Roy could think for himself, and notoriously cut through dross to the heart of a matter, his summing up might have been worth hearing.

He had probably small respect for the Scottish Parliament as it then was, less because it was a feudal oligarchy than incapable of seizing initiative from the Crown and its privy council executive. On rare occasions it had offered criticism, and did act boldly over Darien and the Act of Security, but could not maintain the role. To Rob and his Highland contemporaries, the loss of Parliament's existing constitution was not of concern, but the loss of Parliament itself certainly was. A nation without that potent instrument is castrated. It has no means to generate its national evolution. To Lowlanders, it seemed less severe a loss than that of the royal presence from Holyrood in 1603 – when the disappearance of the Edinburgh court cut off the arts and commerce from a chief source of nourishment – but still a deprivation, both psychological in a lost sense of self-responsible purpose, and in the loss to the country's institutions of men of initiative, who to fulfil themselves go where power lies.

Such finer points may not have been widely appreciated in 1706. The idea that national identity could be emasculated over future centuries did not come to the fore in men's thinking. Proposals for union had been made four times during the last century, twice on Scottish initiative. It was argued that Scotland under the treaty lost no more sovereignty than England, since both would lay it down to take it up anew in unity. That academic sophistry stood no chance with men like Rob Roy. The Scots would have 45 seats in the Commons among 568 English, and only 16 in the Lords among 206. Scotland's yield in tax was barely one fortieth of England's although her population was one fifth. Equality under these conditions was an impractical ideal. The partnership would be grossly unequal.

There were other hard facts to be faced. A continuation of

the existing system was hardly to be borne. Three choices were open: (1) parliamentary union with a guarantee of Scotland's civil and religious liberties; (2) a looser federal union; and (3) complete independence. These were the subjects of debate when the last Parliament met on 3 October 1706. The Scottish people had rarely been in greater excitement.

Rob's presence in Edinburgh during the course of the great debate is certain. The importance of the issue for cattle dealers, Jacobite leaders, and clan chiefs, made frequent conference essential. He probably lodged at Kilmanan's house, and for several years thereafter was a well-known figure at the Exchange coffee-house.[7] His trade creditors were nearly all Whigs. Their confidence in Rob had redoubled on seeing him weather all storms. At the same time, the Union debate had bound him still closer to the Jacobite party, their dedicated agent. When that too became widely known, it sowed in Whig minds a seed of distrust, dormant as yet, waiting for rain.

The debate was heralded by an event more splendid than any in Britain except a coronation – the Riding of the Parliament. The duke of Queensberry, after three years in the wilderness, was back in office as Royal Commissioner. However noble the sight and heart-warming the blaze of colour offered to the public on this great occasion, the members after three months' debate snuffed themselves out.

The debate made clear that a majority could be found for a federal union rather than any one of the other alternatives, and equally clear that England would have no less than full union. England's people cared not at all, but her Tory ministers, Godolphin, Sunderland, and Harley, with a foreign war on their hands and most of the army abroad, required union to end dispute on the succession. To try to be sure that he got it, Godolphin had employed Daniel Defoe as a secret agent in Scotland throughout 1706 to buy the votes of susceptible members of Parliament.[8] Over the Scots sitting in Parliament House hung the menace of commercial blockade, continuing domestic division, and repeated dynastic wars. They gave voice to the perils, and arguments grew so angry that bloodshed under their own roof seemed often imminent. Montrose, Mar, Queensberry, and Argyll (the latter on leave from Flanders), were prominent in support of the treaty. It was alleged that leading men had been bribed by promise of office and money – Montrose was afterwards made duke; Mar, Secretary of State and Privy Councillor; Queensberry, duke of Dover and marquis of Beverley; Argyll, knight of the

Garter (having already been given the earldom of Greenwich and promoted major-general); and so with many others – and now there was revealed the clause in the treaty providing that England would pay nearly £400,000 to meet arrears of government pay and to reimburse the losses of the Darien expedition, in which very many members of Parliament had been shareholders, Argyll first and foremost. The sum was termed 'The Equivalent', but outside Parliament House the people spoke more plainly.

The duke of Atholl in a brave attempt to bring counterpressure to bear on Parliament, raised four thousand Athollmen in arms, but could not get enough support from fellow nobles and had to disband them. As the debate swung in favour of accepting the treaty, the country was roused to fury. Revolt in Glasgow had to be quelled by the army; Dumfries burned the treaty in the streets; at Edinburgh the people stormed Parliament House but failed to break in. They stoned Queensberry, the 'Union Duke' as they called him, when he drove through the High Street. The same story of riot came from all parts of the land. A minority thought the treaty wise. The great majority rejected outright the end of their nation's independence.[9] Argyll took command of the Horse Guards and packed the High Street and Parliament Close with troops.[10] On 16 January 1707, the members of Parliament, who had not been elected by the people, approved the treaty by a vote of 110 against 68.

Queensberry touched the paper with the sceptre, and it was law. It was also expedient, given the state of the nation in 1707. But the people were not placated. Independence, they felt, had been lost for insufficient cause – the religious beliefs of James Edward. Gross though that simplification might be, dislike of the Union grew at all levels of society.[11] The members of the Commons grew wearied and somnolent from debate without relevance to their nation; the Scots lords, enraged by the denial to them of privileges granted to English nobles; the clergy, angry and afraid at the restoration of patronage, in violation of the Treaty of Union; taxpayers one and all, incensed by a new officious breed of tax-collectors sent north from England, who insisted on prompt payment where the Scots taxmen had allowed long months of grace; and everyone, angry at a threatened malt tax that would raise the price of the common man's drink. Relations between England and Scotland were no better after the Union than before, and often worse. As for the Equivalent, when that arrived at Edinburgh in 1707, in twelve waggons guarded by one hundred and twenty dragoons, the people stoned it through the Leith Wynd, Nether Bow, High Street, and Lawnmarket, and all the way up to the castle.

The Jacobites having done all they could to prevent the Union were now the only people in the land to feel any comfort in the result. Their numbers and enthusiasm grew with the discontent. So evident was the general unrest that Louis XIV thought to seize this chance, heaven-sent he hoped, to strike at England through her back door. The strategic plans were laid, the Highlands warned, the clan chiefs consulted, action concerted with the Jacobites of England and the Lowlands, and James Edward released from service with the French army. From Anne's succession to the 'Forty-five, almost every responsible statesman of the United Kingdom intrigued with the Stewarts at some time in his career – Sunderland, Marlborough, Godolphin, Argyll, Mar, Bolingbroke, Oxford, Ormonde, Newcastle, Strafford, and these were only a few among other great names. There seemed good chance that a successful landing made now would take Scotland and be consolidated. Breadalbane gave the French much encouragement. Although wisely refusing to commit himself on paper, his verbal assurance had strong influence on the western clans and his MacGregor neighbours. Hopes were high that Atholl would join. The invasion was now planned for the spring of 1708.

Rob Roy and Gregor Ghlun Dhubh who was now eighteen, were closely involved in the plotting – they could put several hundred men in the field. Like all the chiefs they were discretion itself. Apart from the need of war-secrecy, Rob Roy had private reasons for caution. Past experience had taught him to be sceptical, not about the worth of the cause but the military abilities of those who might lead. He was committed as never before to keeping the peace of Glengyle and Craigrostan, not only for the sake of his growing business and family – his first son James had been followed by Coll, Duncan, and Ranald – but the need to provide for his brother's widow and her children, Gregor, Donald, and Catherine. The office of Tutor laid on him responsibility for the clan's welfare as well as Gregor's. At this point in his life, he was more content to follow his trade and rule his clan's land well than embark on war, unless an assuredly victorious war. He, although as ever on the move, waited to see.

Falkirk tryst opened for the autumn sales of 1707. This was a more convenient market than Crieff for English dealers, who were now coming north in growing numbers, feeling more self-confident under the treaty, which had come into force on 1 May.

Customs duties on cattle had ended. The droving that year gave
Rob Roy good opportunities for furthering the Jacobites' ends
while pursuing his own.

At Gengyle, Gregor Ghlun Dhubh was wanting to marry
Mary Hamilton, the daughter of James Hamilton of Bardowie,
with whom Rob had arranged a marriage contract four years
earlier.[12] On 12 November that year Rob wrote to the earl of
Breadalbane, saying of Gregor, 'he is a young man so my lord
give him your advice he is Bigging his house and I hope your
Lordship will give him a precept for the four trees your Lordship
promised him . . . .'[13] (The world 'bigging' here means building,
not begging).

Big timber was needed for the roof. It would appear that he
rebuilt Glengyle House, for his first son, John, was born there next
year. He then assumed chieftainship and command of the Watch,
for he wrote in his own name to Montrose 'offering to take care' of
his estates.[14]

Gregor's brother Donald, now seventeen, had to be given
farmland. Rob Roy acquired for him from Atholl the tack (lease)
of Monachyle Tuarach on the south side of Loch Doine in
Balquhidder.[15] Its grass and arable land sloped gently to a short
river linking Loch Doine to Loch Voil. The bare hillside rising
steeply above gave indifferent grazing. The neighbouring lands
of Inverlochlarig, Monachyle Beag, and Wester Invernenty, were
held by Rob's cousin Malcom of Marchfield on feu-charters from
Atholl, the last dated 7 February 1707. This western half of the
Balquhidder glen had long been in Gregarach hands, mainly of the
Glengyle branch, except for one MacIntyre township at the foot
of Glen Carneig, held by Iain Og, although Iain by Rob's order
could not yet take possession. Donald's new farm appears to have
been managed for him by a man named MacDonald, whom Rob
employed as a drover.[16]

The winter was a busy one for Rob as the invasion date drew
nearer. Early in the New Year of 1708, Louis assembled 26 ships,
five of them big transports and the rest frigates, at Dunkirk, where
four thousand troops embarked in March. His best admiral commanded, and James Edward sailed with him. The plan was to enter
the Firth of Forth, seize Leith, and besiege Edinburgh.[17] The time
was well-chosen. Scotland had only a small force of government
troops, totally incapable of stopping a French landing while the
Jacobites rose in the Highlands and Lowlands. The government's
secret service knew of the plot, yet the only measures taken on
the eve of invasion were imprisonment of some clan chiefs and a

token imprisonment of Atholl at Blair – he could have raised six thousand men.[18] Ministers of the Crown had held their hands so far as they dared. Granted this unprecedented opening, the French naval officers failed their last test: in the dark they sailed past the Forth. They discovered the error and doubled back, too late. While they beat slowly into the outer firth, the grey dawn skies behind the Isle of May were pricked along the horizon by the skysails and main royals of the English navy, advancing under Admiral Byng. The French fleet had nothing like its fire-power, had no time to make landings, and did well to slip aside into the North Sea. As always on these occasions the war-god's breath blew for England. A storm overtook the invasion fleet, wrecked the ships, and drowned most of their men.

Rob Roy, like many another man of higher station, must have heaved a great sigh of relief that he had not declared himself.

CHAPTER THIRTEEN

TIME AND CHANCE
1708–15

ROB ROY prospered over the next four years, 1708 to 11. In 1710 he bought Ardess, the farm at Rowardennan, from Robert Stewart of Coille Mhor.[1] His further good fortune seemed assured. His sound business sense had become known across the country. His record of seventeen years' trading free of any serious mistake had been distinguished by prompt settlement of debt and promise kept. That gave him the trust of all, from numerous Lowland gentlemen with funds to invest down to his tough, hard-working drovers earning their shilling a day. Another credit to him was Gregor Ghlun Dhubh's coming of age in 1710. Gregor was acknowledged by all to be a handsome young man of good mind and physique. His high standards of conduct and discipline were already winning happy auguries for his chieftainship – and they were to be borne out to the end of his long life.

Rob had given much time to his charge, and now that the tutorship had ended he could devote his energies to the direction of his cattle-trade and promotion of the Jacobite cause. His interests had become so numerous and widely spread through the kingdom that his advice was much appreciated by the Jacobite leaders.[2] His relations with them were intimate. But travel was slow, and Rob had to delegate as much work as he could to others. In business, he gave much trust to his chief drover, his great-nephew's man MacDonald in Monachyle Tuarach, to oversee the droving and to buy and sell cattle when Rob was engaged elsewhere.[3]

In the summer of 1711, Rob Roy thus stood at the peak of his fortunes, and with fair prospects for increase of his stock, land, rents, and profit from cattle. During the back-end of the year he raised £1000 sterling (a huge sum in these days) from the duke of Montrose and other clients under commission to buy cows and collect herds for fattening in the Lowlands before the summer and autumn trysts of 1712.[4] In April, he despatched MacDonald with drovers to bring in the stock, and gave him the bills of exchange. At Craigroston in May, his tenants were in good heart, for the harvest of 1711 had been plentiful, and April sowing had passed off well, and the lambing snows that came as usual in the first week of May had dusted Ben Lomond only above its Ptarmigan shoulder. Now the sun was out and everyone revelling in a West Highland heat-wave. The cuckoos were calling from the gaily crowned oaks at the lochside, where men were fitting out the birlinns. Others were moving up the Culness burn to the peat-banks in the upper corrie, and the women were talking at their low doors of an early flitting up to the Snaid shielings. All seemed well with the world, and Rob may well have been thinking so when a gillie arrived hot-foot from the north. He was one of Rob's drovers, beaded in sweat and garrulous in the Gaelic. Rob listened, stupefied by the tale he bore. He himself had so long been accustomed to holding large funds on trust that he had given no thought to MacDonald's temptation. The untold wealth in his deputy's hand had toppled his honour. MacDonald had absconded.

Bankruptcy

Montrose had been driving hard bargains with Rob Roy. Profits were shared equally, but losses were Rob's responsibility alone, and Montrose had secured his advance of money by a wadset (mortgage) on part of Craigrostan. Rob had presumably agreed to this one-sided contract with creditors as the only way to get the large sums needed for market. Montrose's hard line had long since limited trust and alerted him to danger. Montrose had become a 'man on the make' without a share in the talents of his great forebears, yet burning with twin ambitions for dominion over vast properties that would rank him with Argyll and Atholl, and for power in the State. Such men are ruthless. Rob had learned at his father's knee the means, like the foreclosing of mortgages, by which they dispossess victims. He had taken precautions to safeguard his own interests. While giving Montrose his mortgage, he had wisely put one half beyond his grasp by making it over to his nephew's father-in-law, Hamilton of Bardowie.[5]

At one stroke he was insolvent, and his good name lost unless Montrose would hold his hand. He had reason to suppose he would. His land-holding was hopefully too small for a Graham to covet, and he had won for Montrose profits exceeding this debt, notably in 1705. He could do it again. Given time, all was not lost, for his debtors owed him large sums.[6] His reputation as an able, straightforward dealer had been built up and maintained so long untarnished that if only he could keep it so he could still hope to repay. Montrose must surely see that. Otherwise Rob was ruined and the creditors' capital lost for good.

Meantime, there was a chance that MacDonald could be traced. There was not a moment to lose. It is evident that Rob took off on his trail, for he left home abruptly, and his first letter to creditors was dated nearly a month later.

An unsolved mystery surrounds this MacDonald, of whose crime there is no contemporary written record other than Daniel Defoe's. The evidence of his theft is oral, given by men who had known Rob Roy to historians late in the century.[7] Rob's three surviving letters on the subject, sent in June 1712 to one of his chief creditors, James Graham, a writer in Glasgow, and to the laird of Dougalstown and the duke of Atholl a year later, say nothing of MacDonald's part. That the theft did occur appears to be true, for Rob Roy could hardly have lost so large a sum in cattle in the early months of a season free of disease, and he certainly did not make off with it himself. The fact of that is not only evident from the course of his life to date, his clan and family responsibilities, and his known record of honesty,[8] but is established by the record of the Montrose Estate Papers. He strove to repay. It is not known with what sum MacDonald made off. Apparently he had bought the cattle on bills of exchange and then resold them. Rob's search was fruitless, and no more is heard of MacDonald – his only safe course was to disappear into England.

Much harder to understand is the precipitate action now taken by the duke of Montrose and his fellow creditors. Forgetting Rob's good record, remembering only his ardent Jacobitism and his party's endless need of money, they allowed the seed of distrust to shoot wildly.

When Rob left Inversnaid in hot pursuit, he took no time to send word of the disaster to creditors. By whatever means, Montrose swiftly had the news, and by the time it reached him it was already garbled. 'The money has gone and Rob Roy has lit off' – something like that. Montrose could equally swiftly verify it without hearing the essential corrections. It is unlikely that anyone at Craigrostan knew well what had happened, far less at Buchanan or Edinburgh. Montrose's first and wrong impression is recorded in his family papers of 1712: 'He (Rob Roy) addressed himself at Glasgow and other places to such as he knew had occasion for black cattle and by this means gott together to the value of £1000 for which he gave his obligations to deliver the value in black cattle in the months of May and June following, as he had been in use formerly to do ... when time for delivery was come, the persons who had payed the money sent him their servants to receive the cattle and then it was known, and not till then, that he was gone with the money to the Western Isles, to wait his opportunity of conveying himself away with his money, and that he had settled his land Estate in the persons of some of his relations and confidents, some few days before he entered into the above-mentioned Contracts ... thereby to disappoint his creditors ...'

The work of embellishment was then taken over by the 'grapevine'. Malicious tongues wagged in the Glasgow and Edinburgh coffee-houses; yet no one was foolish enough to think that Rob Roy might have stolen money for his own pocket – it was put about that he had seized it for Jacobite war-funds. The king of rumour circulating in Edinburgh was reported by John Douglas, the duke of Atholl's law agent in Edinburgh, in a letter of 25 June to his master: 'Rob Roy has gone off with 1000 lb ster of My Lord the Duke of Montrose's money and other gentlemen's money and has been gazetted.' He went on to report the Edinburgh gossip that Rob had made his way to the Pretender, and had recently been in conversation with Atholl, Huntly, and many others of Highland clans – 'which I am confident is altogether false'.

False or not, he warned Atholl, 'Montrose is making search for all imaginable ways and conversations of Rob Roy since he went away.' Atholl's brothers and sons were Jacobites, and he himself was unjustly suspect; he had strongly opposed the Union, which was now in such bad odour that ministers of the Crown were on edge and fearful of Jacobite plots and plans. The warning was timely. Montrose had office and might open a season of witch-hunting. Rob Roy was already one victim, for Montrose knew well his intimacy with Jacobite nobles and had jumped to the wrong conclusion. On four successive days, 18 to 21 June 1712, he had Rob Roy gazetted in the Edinburgh *Evening Courant*. The advertisement for his apprehension read:

That Robert Campbell, commonly known by the name of Rob Roy MacGregor, being lately entrusted by several noblemen and gentlemen with considerable sums for buying cows for them in the Highlands, has treacherously gone off with the money, to the value of £1000 sterling, which he carries along with him. All Magistrates and Officers of his Majesty's forces are entreated to seize upon the said Rob Roy, and the money which he carries with him, until the persons concerned in the money be heard against him; and that notice be given, when he is apprehended, to the keepers of the Exchange Coffee-house at Edinburgh, and the keeper of the Coffee-house at Glasgow, where the parties concerned will be advertised, and the seizers shall be very reasonably rewarded for their pains.

It is important to remember that this advertisement had been hastily put together on hearsay only, and not on evidence that Rob Roy had the money as alleged. It is notable that no description of Rob Roy was thought to be needed. Every man knew him. He was in any gathering conspicuous, and less by his red hair than his bearing and eye and breadth of shoulder.

Rob was indeed in the Outer Hebrides as Montrose had heard, but for reasons quite other than Montrose suspected. He had abandoned the search for MacDonald in favour of a search for his two principal debtors, who had absconded immediately on hearing his need. He was a deeply worried man, as shown in the hastily written, unpunctuated letter he sent in July to his creditor James Graham in Glasgow.[9]

Sir
I am sorry that I have putt you behind soe much as I have done or any man that had such trust in me as I am confident you had. I believe people may take apprehension that what come upon me was partly designedly but I tell you upon my honesty that I will let you see to the contrary of that That what free gear I have I shall give it so long as a groat of it lasts what money I have to the fore I have left it here in the highlands in order to be given you and what geir I have in else where I have designed to give it as farr as it will goe for what money is to the fore is of your money I am in persute of two of my debitors there is one of them away to the Long Island and other of them to South Uist I am informed they have disposed upon their geir and has considerable soumes of money with them Ill never return to my own countrey till

Ill know what to doe with these people For if they will stay
in Scotland or Ireland with Gods assistance I will gett a grip
of them for all the high lands has such a kindness for me in
generall that they will assist me what ever place I will gett
them taken Before I can return I am sure it will be the latter
end of Agust altho Ill gett no reparation of those that I made
bargain with Ill have as much geir as will putt one and all of
you very near your own unless you ll heap expenses which
ife ye ll doe I ll let you pairt it among you for I'll never offer,
altho I should beg, to keep a groat of what I have from you
so that I intrust you to speak to them all for if I'll gett leave
to goe upon the road I'll know I'll gett much more done for
you for the Highland lairds my Lord Bredalbine & my Lord
Drummond is content to make a collection for me before I
should goe out of the countrey. This is much better for you
nor to keep me out of the way or to throw me in prison soe
again I return I hope you'll have your answer to me
I am
Yours
     Ro. Campbell

The letter was endorsed, 'Come to hand upon the 5th Jully
1712.'

His wrath on return to the mainland, when he learned of the hue
and cry published in the *Courant*, hardened his tender regard for
his creditors. He returned briefly to Craigrostan, and appears to
have seen Grahame of Killearn, with whom he made arrangements
for repayment as far as he could. Then he was off again to try to
round up debtors, and to give the true story and what assurance
he could to Highland stockmen who held his bills of exchange.
Montrose's reaction, when he knew of Rob Roy's return and
letter to James Graham, and discovered that his first assumptions
had been false, was not to hold his hand and give Rob a chance
to work off the debt, but to sue him in the Edinburgh courts.
Whatever 'sweetness' of disposition Montrose had enjoyed in his
twenties had been wrung out of him by his thirties. His avarice had
flowered on the richness of his landholdings. He must have coldly
calculated that his too early gazetting of Rob Roy had sufficiently
injured his trading credit to make it likely that he, Montrose,
might now recover more by seizure of Craigrostan. The acqui-
sition of real estate had become in Montrose a lifelong passion.
The legal process accordingly went ahead, and Rob Roy when

summoned to court did not appear. Montrose's insistence on immediate repayment had given Rob a deep distrust of his motives, for the demand was unreasonable, Montrose being well aware that Rob could not repay then and there. Rob knew that if he went to Edinburgh he would end up in the Tolbooth, where he could do nothing by way of repayment, while his land was taken, and his life drained away like his father's and brother's. Nor could he afford to engage lawyers when every merk counted. He felt that defence in court was time wasted and not to the point – wasted because there was no legal case to win, the money having indeed gone, and not to the point since that was repayment – for which his most strenuous efforts were needed outside court or tolbooth. Finally, debtors and bankrupts at Edinburgh were treated with a harshness unconformable to a just penal code: liable to be put in the stocks and scourged. He had seen them nailed by the ear to the pillory.[10] An Edinburgh court would be diligent in revenging a loss to the pocket of the Keeper of the Privy Seal.

Montrose appreciated Rob's reluctance to come to Edinburgh, and wrote offering protection from arrest. But Rob preferred to go to the core of the trouble and raise money. He began to make payments through Grahame of Killearn, who was pressing him hard in his master's interest.

Montrose had more troubles on his mind than Rob Roy. John of Argyll was one of them. The Campbell and Graham houses had been at strife for a century: the Graham's plundering of Lorn, the defeat of Campbell at Inverlochy, the Campbell's final triumph on Graham's execution, these were just three incidents in a bitter tale. Montrose was ambitious for power and his appetite whetted. But now the War of the Spanish Succession was drawing to its close and Argyll was home, his reputation high from great services under Marlborough at Oudenarde, Malplaquet, and other battles. He had been Queen's Commissioner to the Parliament of 1705, been one of Scotland's commissioners at the Whitehall Cockpit and a principal promoter of the Union at the last Parliament. His record was clean. Montrose no longer had a clear field in Scotland. Argyll was here, free for high office, and much the same age as himself. Montrose took thought, searching his mind for a means to cloud Argyll's bright prospect. He recollected that ten years ago Queensberry and Argyll's father had made a brave effort to besmirch Atholl with treason, and although Atholl had given disproof, he had not again held office. Montrose had never corresponded with Jacobites, but so many other ministers had, at least with James's half-brother, the duke of Berwick, who was Marshall of France, if not with James himself, that Montrose knew it likely that Argyll had too. If only proof could be found that he had even given ear to some Jacobite advance, that would be enough for his purpose. Where to get evidence? Montrose thought of Rob Roy. He would be aware that Rob had rejected Archibald Campbell's earlier offer to bribe or suborn him, but times had changed. Rob was a broken man, even if as yet he did not know it. When he felt the screw of the law-courts he could be made to talk.

So, the order went out to Grahame of Killearn to dun Rob more harshly, and to the lawyers to press court action. Rob did his best to meet the demands before Michaelmas. A letter from Grahame to Montrose records that he had got £50 from Rob Roy at Whitsun, 'which was all that he had at the tyme, but promises the rest in a fortnight or twenty days'. News of that kind was no longer to Montrose's liking. Had Rob Roy in truth been promised money by Breadalbane and Drummond, or by the alcoholic Kilmanan? Could the latter have such a love of his protégé that he would help to salvage Craigrostan? Or had Rob found his debtors? Montrose took his lawyers' advice. He ordered Grahame to contrive a refusal of the bond's redemption by presenting a bill for interest and expenses above any sum offered, and at the same time applied to the Lord Advocate, Sir James Steuart, for a special summary diligence. This could only be had by a gross misrepresentation, which Montrose did not scruple to use. The Lord Advocate responded in early October by issuing a warrant for Rob Roy's arrest.

By Her Majesty's Advocate

These are to require and warrant you to sease and apprehend the person of Robert Campbell, alias Rob Roy M'Gregor of Innersnait, a notorious bankrupt, and who by open fraud and violence hath embezzled considerable sums of money, refusing to come to any account, or subject himself to ane tryal or diligence, but keeping himself with a Guard or Company of armed men in defiance of the law, conform to a written information exhibit to me thereanent, and that you secure him in the next sure prison in order to his trial.

Given at Edinburgh the third day of October, 1712
                    Ja. Steuart

To all Her Majesty's Officers of the Law whom they may concern.

Four false accusations deliberately made by Montrose and his lawyers had won this warrant. (1) Fraud: this was not Rob's crime; he was striving to make good the loss and Montrose knew it. (2) Violence: no one had used it. (3) Refusal to come to account: to the contrary, he had acknowledged his debts and begun to make repayments, which Montrose had at first accepted although trying now to prevent their completion. (4) Keeping an armed guard in defiance of law: Kilmanan's Watch, which Rob Roy led, had been formed and armed with the sanction of the Privy Council, and Highland drovers were by law entitled to carry arms. The master drovers like Rob had certificates.

It becomes plain from all evidence that perjury with intent to defraud was Montrose's crime, not Rob's, and falls into place with his plan to ruin Argyll, disclosing his bent.

Montrose had still no warrant to take Craigrostan, but the legal process went forward. Campbell of Fonab, commanding Argyll's Independent Company, received orders from Steuart to bring in Rob Roy. Montrose calculated that he now held Rob Roy in a legal nutcracker. The squeeze began. Rob was offered through Killearn cancellation of the debt if he gave proof of Argyll's past or present communication with Jacobites.[11] This attempt to suborn him failed. When put to the test in early winter, he was not, after all, a nut to be cracked. If he had the information wanted, he would certainly feel the temptation. He owed nothing to the duke of Argyll, whose great-grandfather had betrayed Clan Gregor. Betrayal, however, was not in Rob's nature; nor was the giving of false witness. He rejected Montrose's overtures for the same reason as he had Lovat's. He and they lived in different worlds: they so imbued with ideas of self interest and national politics that Highland scruple seemed to them irrational; Rob Roy imbued with the loyalties educed by communal life. Montrose could at least gauge Rob's love of his land and the terrible injury its loss would mean. He must have felt that that would surely tip the balance. As it proved, there was no balance to tip, or not yet.

Rob Roy took the only two actions now open to him. He appealed for help to Montrose's rivals, the dukes of Atholl and Argyll. He had reason to hope that Atholl, who at last was back in favour at Court and newly appointed High Commissioner in England, would reciprocate the help that Rob had given him in 1704. His letter to Atholl assumed his general knowledge of the injustice:

Port'nellan, 27th Janr 1713

May it please Your Grace, – I am hopeful your Grace Has heard how ye Duke of Montrose is offering to ruine me upon the accompt of cautionrie yt I engaged to his Grace. I have offered him the whole principle soume with a yeir's rent, which he positively refuses ye same. The reasons why he did refuse it was, he sent me a protectione, and in the meantyme yt I had ye protectione, his Grace thought it fitt to procure ane order from the Queen's advocate to Funab, to secure me, and had a partie of men to put this order in executione against me. This was a most rediculous way to any nobleman to treat any man after this manner.

Funab is still promesing to put this order in executione; but if I can his Grace & he both will not doe it: God knowes but their is vast differs between Dukes. Blessed be God for that it is not ye Athole men that is after me, Altho' it were if your Grace would send to me the least foot Boy I would come without any protectione. Your Grace was always charitable and kynd to me beyond my deservings. If your Grace would speake to ye advocate to countermand his order, since its contrary to Law, it would ease me very much off my troubles, and I beg pardone for this trouble and for the superscriptione hereof, and I am

Your Grace's servant while I am alive, Rob Roy.

His second act, to which he dropped a hint in the letter – 'if I can his Grace and he both will not doe it' – was to warn Argyll of Montrose's mind to traduce him. Argyll called off Fonab, who took no further action despite all instructions from the Lord Advocate.[12]

The letter to Atholl brought no response. Perhaps he recalled Rob's depredations on his Tullibardine lands, or he reflected that this was no time, when so newly in office, to be heard in support of a known Jacobite, and least of all when the rights and wrongs of the case were to him not quite clear. He may well have referred to Montrose, and Montrose would most certainly hear indirectly from Argyll, who with at least four thousand men at his call was no man to mince his words. The end result was that Rob had brief respite, but no positive help from anyone. He used his respite to travel to England, collecting moneys due on bills in his own favour, not knowing that the law had run its course.

Put to the horn

On 28 February 1713, the first of five adjudications of his goods and lands was given against 'Robert Campbell' in favour of Sir John Shaw of Greenock, the duke of Montrose, Graham of Gorthie, James Graham, writer in Glasgow, Campbell of Blythswood, MacFarlane, Buchanan, and Montgomery.[13] To these were added letters of horning and caption, which proclaimed him an outlaw.

Montrose seems to have been thirsting for vengeance. As Sheriff, he acted fast by directing Grahame of Killearn to lead the troops placed at his disposal into Craigrostan, to evict Rob Roy and his family, and to take possession of all movable stock and property. This was done early in March, a month when the snow lies most heavily on the hills, and the cold is worst. The record is bare but grim. Mary's four sons were James, aged eighteen, Coll fifteen, Duncan nine, and Ranald seven. Not all would be there at the time, for the two younger were school-age, but those who chanced to be at home were ejected along with their mother, the house stripped of furnishing, clothes and bedding, and the outbuildings of all stored and stacked grain, farm-equipment, and every bit of movable gear. The house was partially destroyed, which may mean that only the walls were left standing. Although not fired, the whole was rendered uninhabitable. Mary's anguish did not allow her to stand idly by. She gave the troops the lash of her tongue, if not more. The story handed down is that she was roughed-up, raped, and branded with hot irons.[14] The rape and hot irons are certainly embellishments, for if true, Grahame of Killearn would not long have survived Rob Roy's return. That she took blows was inevitable. No woman of her spirit would see her home wrecked without trying to fight. The entire action by Montrose had been heartless, but the eviction had been malevolent. He would have lost not a penny by waiting for warmer weather, and he knew the substance of his accusation to be false in a main essential. Why then such mindless fury? This had surely been evoked by more than a money-loss: perhaps by Rob's expression of contempt, compounded by his warning Argyll. Montrose had now taken his revenge, for what it was worth. It was to cost him many times the money owed by Rob Roy.

The tale as told by Georgian and Victorian writers continues with Mary and her family wandering like lost sheep across the winter hills as far as Glen Orchy, seeking shelter in vain.[15]

The reality was quite different. At Corrie Arklet, Comer, Loch Katrine. Glen Gyle, and Glen Falloch, her kinsfolk were thick on the ground, and her chieftain Gregor one of them. Shelter, care, and sympathy were hers without asking. She had need of them all, for her man was ruined, and she and her children with him.

Rob Roy came home from the south in windy March weather. Ridding north on the high track over the Stockie Muir, he could see his land of Craigrostan fifteen miles ahead. The Ben rose massively out of the Loch Lomond depression, at this time of year either with hard, sparkling edges, or ghostly, hunched on its Ptarmigan shoulder, blurred by spindrift. On this high ground an east wind would pierce even his plaid doubled over the chest and pinned close to the throat. The gillies trotting by his side were better off than he. This was the half-way point out of Glasgow, now 23 miles behind him. He would have left as usual at five in the morning with a big breakfast inside him, and not think to eat again till he sat by Mary's hearth-fire. Inversnaid might be hidden by the white mass of the Ben, but in his mind's eye he looked straight through it, through the thick wall of his grey stone house to the peats' red glow, and the stew-pot hanging black on its thick chain. The boys had probably been skating on Loch Arklet and their appetites would be huge – like his own by the time he joined them at nightfall. He was not expected, but there was still meat in the barrel and plenty of grain in the kist. James would have seen to that in the autumn. He was a good boy, tall and well set-up. All too soon he would be begging his stock. Rob had hoped to buy him a farm in Balquhidder, and settle the other boys there when their turn came. But now all was again in the melting pot. Rob was not yet depressed in spirit.

He had collected some part of his debts. Montrose would get his money if only he'd bide his time. The fact that he had repaid would be known in time and his business recover much of its old prestige.

It was only when he passed through Buchanan in the early afternoon that the news was given him. His house was ruined. Mary and the boys had been driven out, and no one knew where they were. He was outlawed. His lands and goods had been attached. His name had been put to the horn.

He might well have been sick at heart but for anger. This had been done while he was actively demonstrating his will to repay the investors. To them he was morally responsible, but not, in justice, to his exclusion from all human rights and freedoms, nor to the reduction of Mary and their sons to beggary. He hastened on, his angry despair growing with the miles. At Craigrostan, he heard that Mary was safe at Portnellan, but not till he stood at last by the Snaid burn and saw by twilight the desolate walls that for twenty years had been their home, could the enormity of the wrong strike his mind. Here he had been established by his clan's chief, well founded in land with house, gear, and stock, married to a woman he loved, and their lives filled with work. He had ruled his clan well, received their kindness and respect, and given it back to them doubled. He had built a thriving cattle trade, and many of his people had shared in work and profit of value to any clan, for always they had more men than could be employed on the land. They had needed him, as much as he them, for strong leaders were few.

He was now 43. Apart from the total loss of everything that Mary and he possessed, his outlawry (an all too common sentence for debt) meant the loss of land and rent, their divorce from their clan's lands, the loss of tenants' services, exclusion from Lowland society, and the loss of all the cattle work in which he had most interest, knowledge, talent, and satisfaction. His stature as a man had been diminished. He could and would have gained for his family and clan big landholdings. The discovery that he had the means and drive to get these had excited him. Life had been bright with promise. Now he was nothing, could do nothing.

He was gripped by a wild rage of spirit. They, the men of stone, had done this harm to him and his, as they had done it to his name and clan and race for centuries: men of law, state, property, and of stone hearts. He would fight them till he died. They had not destroyed him but changed him. Never again would he live his life as a straightforward Highland cattleman or trusting patriot. These men like Montrose, so secure in great properties or positions that they felt free to wring human dignity out of men, and debase them for a quick gain, were an enemy worthy of hatred. He could outmanœuvre them. He could strike at them without compunction. Never need he scruple to turn against them their own weapons of deceit, faithlessness, and dissimulation – new arts to him but learned from masters. Montrose had sown the wind and would reap the whirlwind.

His friends at Craigrostan, who had come up to stand beside him under the Snaid glen, would speak to him gently in soft Gaelic voices, but their words of comfort, hope, assurance, dismay, fell on deaf ears. They sensed his passion of will and gave warning. Montrose's soldiers had been scouring the country for him under the guidance of Grahame of Killearn. They would have heard now of his passage through Buchanan. He would be safe at Portnellan tonight, but not longer unless scout patrols were sent out by Gregor Ghlun Dhubh. When he had heard them out, he pulled his blue bonnet over his brow and took to the hill up to Arklet. Seven more miles. But men had gone ahead to shorten his journey. They held a galley for him at Loch Katrineside. An hour later, Mary fell into his arms weeping.

CHAPTER FOURTEEN

PRELUDE TO WAR
1713–15

The Outlaw

IAIN GLAS, the earl of Breadalbane, was 78 in 1713, but still a potent force in Highland affairs. Much as his reputation had suffered from the massacre of Glencoe, for which he was held partly responsible by advice given to Stair, his wisdom, or at least his cunning, remained proverbial. He was alive in mind, could field one thousand two hundred men if he had to, and his political sympathies were Jacobite. Rob had ready access to him on this last score, for to such as Breadalbane with much to lose, men of trust were not expendable, and Rob's mother had been his first cousin.

Rob arrived at Finlarig Castle in April and told his story. Breadalbane was a tight-lipped man. His broad face had the impassivity of a barn wall. A moment's abstraction may have shadowed those hard eyes while he weighed the pros and cons of granting protection; if so, they soon brightened in a crinkle of shrewd distress, and the obligatory cluck of sympathy was uttered. He gave Rob the lease of a house and land at Auchinchisallen (also in some papers spelt Auchinchallan) in Glen Dochart, about five miles east of Crianlarich.[1] That Montrose or Killearn would soon learn of his new refuge was not of moment to Rob Roy or Breadalbane. The Grahams could not or would not dare to come with force into Campbell territory.

It suited Breadalbane well to have on his land a man of Rob Roy's resource, the more so when outrage had maddened him against that obnoxious Whig Montrose. Like most other great men of the Highlands, Breadalbane had use for a body of men living in contempt of the law, provided they were sufficiently resolute to savage the lands of his enemies, and disciplined enough to give him no trouble at home. James Graham was a man to be brought down if that could be done, and Iain Glas relished the idea of providing a base of operations for Rob Roy. If Montrose were ineffective in defending his own land, who would trust him with the nation's? Government of course would know that Breadalbane could halt his raids if he chose, and that would enhance his negotiating position in certain affairs.

Rob Roy was pleased with this new refuge for Mary and the family. The house stood on a grassy terrace (an old moraine) on the south side of Glen Dochart at a height of six hundred feet.[2] It faced north to the mountains of the Mamlorn Forest. Close behind to its south-west, Ben More towered above to 3800 feet, lightly wooded on its flank, under which the Allt Coire Chaorach cut a deep glen that gave access over a high pass to Balquhidder, where his cousin Malcolm and nephew Donald lived near the head of Loch Voil. The distance to Balquhidder was only six miles walked in two and a half hours. Glen Gyle could be reached in six hours (fifteen miles), and Inversnaid in six by Glen Falloch. The house overlooked the flat grass-lands of the river Dochart about a hundred feet below. Along its banks went the drove road used by the Skye and Lochaber herds, with a night-stance at Luib one mile east. The house was well sited for gathering news. Mary and the boys would have company at the numerous communities of Clans Gregor, MacNab, and Campbell, spread along the fourteen miles of river between Crianlarich and Killin.

By the early summer of 1713. Rob and his family were established at Auchinchisallen, and Rob had reorganized his life. He did so most efficiently, for he grasped the simple principle on which he had to work, and applied it methodically. For him, the king's law no longer ran. Its rejection had to be mutual. He would substitute for it his own conception of natural justice as he had been led to see it (amending it over the coming years in light of experience).

Lowland society had outlawed him; therefore, since he had no means of living or supporting dependents other than by the life of an outlaw, that should be his profession, and his prey those who had unjustly imposed the outlawry. The lands of Montrose were the prime target. They stretched from the Campsie Fells to the Trossachs, and from Stirling to the Clyde estuary – mostly arable and meadow, yielding abundant rents from a host of tenants. The duke's harvest must now provide for Rob Roy and his followers. He included with a sweep of his mind the lands of all rich Whigs, enemies of his king and of Scotland's independence. Their property should be laid under tribute in three principal ways: the lifting of cattle, the confiscation of grain, and the exaction of black mail. The effective execution of the work required a large band of men, young, trained to the field, and well-directed. The men were freely available. First, his drovers who no longer had work; second, the young men of his clan, who would eagerly seek his leadership as invaluable training for later life, whether in droving or campaigning; third, the men of the former Watch; and lastly, the large reservoir of the unemployed.

In 1713, half of Scotland's population of 1,050,000 lived north of the Highland Line, of which half again lived in the Highlands proper.[3] The full-time work available in farming, shipping, fishing, and all trades, engaged no more than half the adult male population of sixty thousand in the Highland region, leaving thirty thousand men with only seasonal work in droving, harvesting and shearing and the like in Lowland country. They were fit to bear arms, and at the service of any who knew how to lead them on profitable expeditions – subject to the approval of their chiefs. In the Trossachs country, such men were present in numbers sufficient for Rob to be selective in his choice of fifty or sixty, and to have them available on call when the opportunities arose. He could double that number given notice.[4]

Having made this plan, Rob was reluctant to act on it. After his first rage had come sober thoughts. Therefore he made one last effort to bring Montrose to reason. Granted time and freedom, he could hope to repay his original debts with interest, but not the legal fees piled on top. He wrote civilly in these terms to Montrose's friend, the laird of Dougalstown, asking for his intercession:

Sir

The circumstances of my afairs not aloweing me to waitt on you to ask your advyce and assisstance I hop ye will pardon the freedom of giveing you the trouble of this lyne, representing to you that I being now settled in this country with a resolution still to do all justice to my creditors that possibly I can upon the effects I have, my misfortunes haveing brought me to the condition Im [torn] necessitat me to this method to settle [torn] creditors resolveing in the first place to [satis] fie the Duke of Montrose. I hope ye will be pleas'd to give your advyce to his Grace to take what Im able to do which is truly the offer I made before. If it were in my power to do any more I should not neid to be press'd to it there being nothing more I desyre than to have his Grace satisfied. The offer I made his Grace was to pay the principall sum I had from him with ye interest since receipt and to asigne his Grace to my dillgence against Dunchea and to serve him as far as power to gett the saume made effectuall. If ye can get his Grace to accept this offer which is all I can do unless I give others nothing, I shall be ready on all occasions gratefully to acknoledge your kyndness and ever be a servant to you and yours. So hopeing ye will be att the paines proposed and excuse the trouble

    I remaine

    sir

    yours to serve you att comand

    Ro: Campbell

Tynedrom 3d June

1713

Dougalstown forwarded Rob's letter to Montrose.[5] Either no response was made or else it was negative.

Rob took his final decision. He moved south into the Trossachs to pick and organize his men. He appointed lieutenants, of whom the principal was Alasdair Roy, celebrated for his markmanship with gun or pistol.[6] He had no settled headquarters, but could be found most frequently by Loch Katrine, from which he still headed letters 'Portnellan'. The company could not be assembled and held as a unit unless on rare occasions, for neither Breadalbane nor Gregor Ghlun Dhubh would accept so large an independent force in his territory without resentment. When the whole force had to gather, it met either in secret or at a rendezvous outside clan lands near Callander, Doune, and Aberfoyle. And this could not have been often necessary, for Rob Roy organized his company in sections, giving each its specific task. His information on his targets, and the detail of events in Menteith and the Lennox, was so good that he must have had an intelligence unit ably directed, and perhaps inherited from the former Watch. Every landholder was listed, his boundaries known; the amount of rent due in kind and money, the place, dates, and times of rent-collection by the factor, almost every move the latter made, the stores held in the landowners' girnels or granaries, where grain-rents were collected, and every important detail of livestock, were noted.

By late summer Rob Roy was ready for action. He waited till the harvest was in, for at this time there was work for everyone, and then made his first descent on Menteith and the Lennox in role of rent-collector at Michaelmas, over a month ahead of Montrose, who collected at the November term.[7] He struck only against principal tenants, too widely separated to help each other by warning or reinforcement. His company was divided into some ten detachments of five or six men. They stole quietly through the countryside, arriving at their targets by sundown. Surprise was complete and no resistance met. From each they collected rent at dirk and pistol point, giving in exchange a receipt signed by Rob Roy, declaring that the rent due to Montrose had been paid in full.[8]

That kind of operation could be repeated annually, modified by change of contributors on a rota system. For his regular income, Rob relied on cattle and sheep lifting and receipt of black mail. He took little from the smaller tenants. beyond what he judged they could spare, and nothing from those living near subsistence level, who by one bad season could be thrown into arrears of rent. Grahame of Killearn was notoriously a harsh factor. When Montrose felt the bite of Rob Roy's raids, he required Killearn to exact without remission all rents due from smaller tenants spared, and to take it in kind by summary diligence if he had to thus causing the occasional oppression of subtenants and cottars. When Rob had news of this, he intervened as need arose. His long training in responsibility for his actions, and for the people affected by them, appears to have kept his conscience alive. From this time began the many acts of compassion for the poor that gave popular comparison to Robin Hood. They were attested by contemporaries and no legend of romance.[9] If the poorer people had been left too short of winter grain taken for rent, Rob raided the Buchanan girnels and distributed grain where most needed. His charity no doubt began at home, but it spread out. It is easier to be generous with other people's property than one's own, but Rob had no property of his own, apart from the clothes on his back, and his sword. dirk, gun, and pistols. In the days when he did have money, he had been generous with that too. He can be given credit, then, for staying true to himself.

Rob had a natural gaiety of heart that he might deny in rage or disaster, but never suppress in the end. He showed time and again a remarkable ability to live in the present moment, and enjoy of life what there was to enjoy. His ambition to acquire lands and property had been forcibly taken from him, and with that his purpose in life must for a while have seemed to be lost. But maybe this was not so. However badly he felt all his wrongs, frustrations, and his family's deprivations, these made him more aware of other people's, and now he was at least free to rectify wrongs without feeling beholden to 'laws' that tolerated them. That his generosity could be disinterested was borne out in countless incidents, when he gave himself no small trouble without gain to his pocket. One well-attested action occurred near Balfron, where a cottar threatened by court action for arrears of rent appealed directly to Rob Roy 'for auld lang syne'.[10] He must have known her in his youth, and when he went to see her, discovered that Grahame of Killearn as deputy-sheriff had fixed the day for seizure of all her possessions. Early on the day appointed, Rob arrived at her door with the money, and told her on no account to let the bailiffs go without getting a full receipt. The bailiffs were of course ambuscaded on their return journey to Stirling, and Rob's money refunded.

The Highland dilemma

During the winter close-season, Rob was involved in political affairs both at clan and national level. The Union was going so badly that many of its former supporters were turning against it, including the Scottish nobles, and notably the earl of Mar – a motion in the House of Lords to dissolve the treaty was negatived by only four votes. Demonstrations in favour of the Stewarts were more openly held. When Campbell of Lochnell died in January 1714, the western clans used the funeral as cover for a gathering to test their strength and get opinion. Rob, who was related to Lochnell's daughter Sarah, led a large company of Breadalbane Campbells to the funeral, which was 'attended by 2500 men well armed and appointed'.[11]

The government had been so dreading Jacobite action since 1707, that to keep the chiefs quiet Queen Anne had been paying them bribes, euphemistically styled 'pensions', of £360 sterling a year. The death of Archibald of Kilmanan in 1714, the last of the Glenstrae line, put succession to the chiefship of Clan Gregor in question, and raised a plan to get Anne's pension. By primo-geniture, the chiefship should go now to Iain Og, Young John of Glencarnaig, presently calling himself Murray since he lived on Atholl land in Balquhidder. Having now made his fortune, he would not risk it in open support of the Jacobites, although he gave help secretly.[12] Rob Roy like his father had long believed that chiefship should not go by birthright to the first-born, but to the most able of the ruling families by election, thus reverting to the ancient rule of the clan system, the abandonment of which had been a major cause of its deterioration. In order of seniority, the possible claimants after Iain Og were Gregor of Roro, Alasdair of Balhaldie, Gregor of Brackley, and Gregor of Glengyle. These four agreed with Rob Roy that the chief should be elected. Balhaldie, it is alleged, persuaded the others to stand down by resigning to them, as he could well afford to do, the pension if obtained. It had been further alleged that he bought off a claim by Rob Roy, but that is nonsense. Queen Anne would have paid no pension to an outlaw.

Fourteen leading men of the clan met on 20 July 1714, at Auchinchisallen, where they elected Balhaldie, and signed a bond of election, which was witnessed there by the Gregarach and again a week later at Dunblane (Balhaldie's land was by the Allan Water) before Cameron of Lochiel and the Reverend Duncan Comrie (the former minister of Inchcailleach). Balhaldie, calling himself Alexander Drummond, agreed by deed to pay Glengyle, Brackley, and Roro: 'If it shall please the government to give him a pension as other chiefs get, then and in that case he shall bestow and designate a third part to each of them, as a just and equal share of the said pension.'[13]

The ink was hardly dry on the paper when the three Gregors lost their reward. Queen Anne died. She could hardly have done so less opportunely for the Jacobite cause. Bolingbroke had superseded Oxford as leader of the Tory government, and realizing that the only hope of his party's survival if Anne died was the securing of James's succession, he had been corresponding with James over the last two years, and trying to persuade him to turn Protestant – when the crown would have fallen into his lap. He had the support of the duke of Ormonde commanding the army. All important military and civil posts were in Tory hands. The repeal of the Act of Settlement could be pressed and won; for that he had the tacit support of the queen, either from regard for her brother or dislike of George of Hanover. On the eve of this Jacobite triumph, she inconsiderately died. Bolingbroke had a majority in the Cabinet and the Lords, but had not had time to change the Whig bias of the Privy Council, which quickly met and proclaimed George of Hanover king – and Montrose a regent of the kingdom.

The Whig's promptitude caused the utmost confusion in the Tory and Jacobite ranks. When George arrived in September, he at once attached himself to the Whigs, and dismissed Bolingbroke. Among those who fell with him were Atholl, and John Erskine, Earl of Mar, whose place as Secretary of State was taken by Montrose.

The duplicity of Scottish and English statesmen and nobles of Rob Roy's time verged on the incredible. They lied, bribed, and betrayed their fellows freely to gain or hold office. They were corrupt, and John Erskine was one of them, but with less humbug. He was dubbed 'Bobbing John', having been a Whig at the time of the Union, which gave him a seat on the Privy Council and keepership of the Signet, then a Tory, which gave him a secretaryship of State, and was now making overtures to the Whigs in hope of retaining office under George. But in lack of scruple he was a tyro compared to turncoats like Godolphin and Marlborough. Mar was more tolerable by his openness. George could and should have made use of his able mind, and would have been well served if he had.

George I came to London without English, without knowledge of the unhappy relations between England and Scotland, and without understanding of the political dangers. His pronouncements were tactless and sounded despotic. No rising occurred in 1714 only because everyone had been taken by surprise and no Jacobite leader had as yet emerged. A great number of Scotland's people and nobles had been willing to accept Anne as a daughter of James VII; but not the German speaking elector of Hanover, whose relationship to James VI (great-grandson on the female side) seemed too remote. The number prepared to speak out, however, was much thinned down by fear of death or forfeiture of land. Without a fully convincing leader, no one dared move, or make open declaration. The clan chiefs played for time by accepting a proposition from Mar that he submit in their name a humble address to the king, professing their welcome. He tried to present this monumental hypocrisy to the king on his arrival at Greenwich. He was rebuffed, the king saying that he was 'well assured that it was prepared at St Germain'.[14] (The address had in fact been written by Mar's brother, Lord Grange.) George was ill-advised. He had chosen for counsellors statesmen of the second rank – Townshend. Montrose, and Stanhope. They should have known and taken care not to provide the Jacobites with a leader from the ranks of dismissed ministers. But so concerned were they all with 'proving' Jacobite sympathies against former or future political rivals, making no allowance for the current venalities of life, that they pushed opposition statesmen to the brink.

Mar, the duke of Ormonde, Bolingbroke and other Tories, might have expected a cool reception at Court in the autumn of 1714, but after the New Year George was showing positive intolerance. They had wind of the new ministry's compiling information that could lead to impeachments. It could be used either to persuade them to sink into obscurity, or to destroy them with charges of treason. Bolingbroke and Mar, faced with such hazards and now convinced that their ruin was determined, both opened correspondence with James. They wanted to know if the Jacobites were strong enough for a rising.

In Scotland, the pot of rebellion if not on the boil in late 1714 had begun to simmer. Montrose knew it. His would be the task of suppressing a rising, and the Crieff tryst, where disaffected men were gathering from all over the Highlands, was a likely tinder-box. So he filled the town with his troops and spies. That being known to all, the clansmen were out to needle authority. Rob Roy came to sell Montrose's cattle, with a bodyguard strong enough to ensure safety. Comic situations developed, in which both sides played rough games that could turn at any moment to tragedy.

On the very first evening a gauger (exciseman) came upon ten or twelve Clan Donald drovers refreshing themselves behind a dyke. Relying unwisely on the army's distant presence, the gauger thought to put these Hielan' tykes in their place. He declared the gathering a public session with tax due on the whisky, which he tried to confiscate. Unluckily for him he was not seen as a fellow Scot but an officer of the usurping 'German lairdie'. The MacDonalds forced him on to his knees, made him drink a quaich of their whisky to the health of King James VIII, and cut off an ear. The incident was reported to Montrose by Sir David Dalrymple of Hailes, the Lord Advocate.[15]

Its sequel featuring Rob Roy was reported in a letter from Haldane of Gleneagles.[16] Rob seized the occasion of the gauger and the heavy presence of troops for a jest at Whig expense. Under a clear moon on the following night, he led thirty armed men to the cross of Crieff, which had marked the town's erection by James VII to a royal burgh, until the Whigs in 1688 had cancelled that in a fit of pique. When the parish bell tolled midnight, the MacGregors formed a circle round the cross, broached a keg of whisky, and to loud cheers that awakened the slumbering townsfolk, drank a series of treasonable toasts, recorded by Haldane: 'To His Majesty King James the Eighth'; 'Success to Tullibardine and confusion to Montrose'; followed by others to Jacobite nobles, and to the damnation of enemies. The town rang to the shouts and piping, and laughter, until the army's duty officer thought the rising had begun and sounded the alarms. The soldiers mustered to tuck of drum. Haldane reported that Rob Roy gave a final toast, 'To the health of those honest and brave felons cutt out the Gadger's ear', after which they dispersed before the troops could charge.

The seemingly trivial incident became the talk of the tryst next day, and spread with embellishments all over the country, provoking a dozen repetitions, notably by noblemen at Falkirk. It became a rage to drink the true king's health in public, above all in the streets and taverns of the capital, which that winter was such a hotbed of disaffection that Montrose dared not enforce the law against offenders for fear of open revolt.

The Crieff affair is further evidence that Rob's allegiance did lie with the Jacobites, for this was called in question now and later. Only next year could the allegation seem to have substance. An important doubter was the Lord Justice Clerk, Adam Cockburne of Ormiston. Atholl had written to him about the alarming state of the country, advising him to have Rob Roy captured at any cost, for although he lived in the wilds under the Campbells, he 'knows much of the transactions in the Highlands'. His interrogation, thought Atholl, would open up all the intrigues. Cockburne's knowledge of Highland politics was as vague as any other Lowlander's; he assumed that Campbell's protection meant Argyll's, when in fact it was Breadalbane's. And Breadalbane was no friend to Argyll, who was King George's man. Cockburne, unaware of his error, and knowing that Rob Roy had refused Montrose's bribe to betray Argyll, came to the conclusion that Rob Roy held with the hare and ran with the hounds. In a letter to Montrose he swore that 'Rob imposed upon both partys'. Rob Roy in fact had no protection from Argyll in advance of the rising, or any other obligation.

Rob went his own way. He could stand up to Breadalbane or Argyll no less than Montrose. On one occasion, Iain Glas had employed as land agent a gentleman of Argyll's family, and given him more authority than his due. That man evicted a family of Clan Gregor from its smallholding in Glen Dochart, allegedly for insufficient cause and its seeming easy prey as one of a broken clan. The property and stock had been taken when Rob Roy on appeal had the agent seized and brought before him at Tyndrum. He obliged the man to sign papers restoring the property and reinstating the clansman, and then had him ducked in the pool of St Fillan, midway between Tyndrum and Crianlarich. A chapel stood there by the river Fillan. The holy waters were believed to cure lunacy and other disorders – numerous cairns around were covered with the rags of bathers' clothing. The Campbell agent was given the cure, which included roping him overnight to a wooden frame with St Fillan's bell set on the crown of his head. The incident gave affront to Argyll as well as Breadalbane.

Perhaps to give them time to cool, Rob Roy removed for a while to Craigrostan, but more likely to organize his Martinmas raids on Menteith.

The extreme discontent of the country had given the Jacobites yet another golden opportunity, if only they had been better. prepared. The arrival of King James, now aged 27, was eagerly expected for March 1715, but the months slipped by and Louis XIV was not yet ready with the promised support, nor had the Jacobites found a general. Both in the Lowlands and Highlands they were arming and plotting in secret. Grahame of Killearn wrote from Buchanan House on 14 June to Montrose, summarizing a scout's report: 'The Highlanders were active: ten thousand targets were prepared, broadswords and belts having been procured from Glasgow, Dunblane, &c, the Captain of Clan Ranald had been communing with Lord Antrim, and had one hundred guineas from him; Rob Roy had to lie close at home, he and the Laird of Lochbuy being distrusted for sending intelligence to Argyll and Islay.' This rumour of distrust was nonsense, as soon shown by the exceptional trust given to Rob by the Jacobite leaders, including Breadalbane.

In London, the former Tory ministers had their fears of impeachment confirmed. Bolingbroke had fled in March to France, and in July became secretary to James. Mar was now in great danger. He was aged forty when he took his decision to lead the rebellion. On 8 August, disguised as a workman, he stole aboard a collier on the Thames bound for Newcastle, where he chartered a new ship and sailed to the port of Elie in Fife, a Tory stronghold. From there, without pausing to tell James, he despatched letters by a host of couriers across the kingdom, appealing to Jacobite leaders for support in a rising. He threw himself into the work with such swift energy, displayed such a gift for administration and the conduct of interviews, could arouse such enthusiasm by the words of promise and baseless hope of French aid, that the Jacobites found in him their long-awaited leader.

France had not long since accepted the treaty of Utrecht, in which she promised to withhold aid from the Jacobites, and Bolingbroke as a prime author of the treaty had signed for Great Britain. The irony of that would not escape Mar when he at length corresponded with James's new secretary. Louis XIV was now on his death-bed (he died on 1 September), and Mar knew that the regent Orleans would refuse help to James. Yet he stirred Jacobite hopes. feeling perhaps that self-confidence would count for more than French arms. The chiefs of the western clans could not be thus deceived. They knew France better than he. They distrusted Mar, felt despondent at thought of his leadership, and felt justified respect for the military abilities of *Iain Ruadh nan Cath*, or Red John of the Battles, as they called John, the Duke of Argyll. He was Scotland's best soldier. Rob Roy held strongly to the same view. Lochiel, Appin, and Glengarry took the extraordinary step of writing to Argyll's righthand man, Colonel Alexander Campbell of Fonab, proposing 'that if he could promise them the duke's friendship they would, as soon as they could, get their men together, march them to Inveraray, and join his men, who were in arms for the King'.[17]

When Clan Gregor, in the persons of Rob Roy, Gregor Ghlun Dhubh, and Balhaldie, had news of this *volte-face*, unprecedented in the military history of the Highlands, they had to sit down together and take thought for their clan's welfare, as well as their own. They had each received Mar's appeal.[18] In principle, they were all for the rising, Rob Roy whole-heartedly, for quite apart from Jacobite sentiment, only by triumph of his natural prince could his own wrongs be righted, and his land restored. The accession of James would end his outlawry and destroy Montrose. But none of them knew Mar save as Bobbing John – a short man of fair complexion with a hunchback. Worse, he had no war experience. He had made a good secretary, but could he direct a campaign? On a field of battle, he would be no match for Red John, but he would surely not want command in the field. The man for that was the king's bastard brother, James Duke of Berwick (whose mother was Marlborough's sister). If Berwick came, the chiefs' doubts would be gone, the rising won. He was Europe's best general. But he was Marshal of France, and the rumour was that France would not release him. The chiefs had been right to hesitate, but to throw in their lot with Hanover, and precipitately take up arms with Argyll – that was more than Rob Roy and Clan Gregor could stomach.

The western chiefs' apparent rejection of the Stewarts was an act not of realism but despair. They were all bewildered by the too many changes of the last twenty-five years, the too many options, the too many calls for decision when no one could foresee the future. Their minds had revolted and damned the Stewarts, in cold hypocrisy turned to Hanover, and in bitter cynicism offered service to Argyll. Rob Roy's mind would hardly be boggled by the quick dishonour, for matching examples were continually given by great men of his day, but in such a climate the germinating seed of his own cynicism shot fast. It fed not on doubt of the

Jacobite dream, but deep distrust of the Tory leaders (supposing they *were* Tory and not Whig). He kept his head and his own counsel. Whether he and his clan fought for James or George, they would now be confronted on either side by some of their best friends. So he resolved to play his own hand. For once he would look to his own interest, to the safety of his family and clan. The resolve then made, either by Rob Roy alone or in concert with Gregor Ghlun Dhubh, was to commit the clan openly to neither party until the position clarified, while Rob for his own part determined to play Mar against Argyll and to keep his options open by offering service to each. He would not have compromised thus in youth. The world's blasts had withered some early ideals.

His approach to Argyll, made either direct to London or to Campbell of Fonab at Inveraray, and most likely to both, was immediately taken up. Argyll was placing agents in Mar's camp, and Rob Roy appears to have accepted position as one of their number. That much is evident from Rob's letter to Argyll of 21 November 1715 (see p.193),[19] in which he gave information of no real value and after news of it must certainly have reached Argyll from his own spies. His true allegiance remained with James Edward, as repeatedly shown by his acts in the field, and by his own words spoken in confidence long after.

His approach to Mar was met by immediate summons to Braemar in mid-August.

CHAPTER FIFTEEN

THE 'FIFTEEN
1715

MAR HAD moved north to his Aberdeenshire estate, where he had called a tinchell, or great deer hunt, on the Braes of Mar for 15 August. Under its cover, 26 Jacobite chiefs assembled for a council of war. When Rob arrived he found that Mar had a job for him. Ninety-three years ago, Rob's grandfather had led three hundred men of Clan Gregor to Morayshire, and some had settled near Aberdeen. They were now a considerable body of men, and Mar wanted them. He gave Rob Roy the mission.

Near the end of the month, Rob was in Aberdeen. He stayed with his cousin, Dr James Gregory, the professor of medicine at King's College.[1] His son James, then eight and destined to become professor of medicine like his father, later in life told Sir Walter Scott that Rob Roy had taken his father aside and praised that fine spirited boy, whom he would like to take away and train to manhood, rather than see him languish in Aberdeen. Rob had spoken out of gratitude for the hospitality given, and wanted to repay his cousin generously. The embarrassed father tried to hide his belief that Rob was sponsoring his son for the gallows, but Rob would take no excuse and swore that the boy should be taken, until Gregory, pleading his son's youth and doubtful health, at last persuaded Rob that in a year or two he might be fit to follow the brave career that his cousin opened out. On this agreement, they parted. In after life, when James won his chair, his every foible earned the reproach that it came of losing Rob Roy's tutorship.

Mar's council was summoned to a final meeting at Aboyne on Deeside on 3 September.[2] They resolved on a national call to arms. On 9 September, Mar proclaimed James by manifesto and unfurled his standard at the Castleton of Braemar. He had planned to heighten the effect with the simultaneous capture of Edinburgh Castle. The plan was the brain-child of the duke of Perth's son, Lord Drummond.[3] His agent, a former officer of the Scots Guards named Thomas Arthur, bribed Sergeant William Ainsley of the castle garrison, and two sentinels, to let down lines from the wall-top and hoist up broad rope ladders by which several men could climb abreast up the rock and wall. The storming party of one hundred Jacobites (fifty from Drummond lands and fifty from Edinburgh) gathered under command of Balhaldie at midnight of the 8th by the west wall near the Sally Port. The lines came down and the ladders were partially hoisted. They were too short, for the lower halves had still to arrive. And that was at least a lucky chance – for while they impatiently waited for the late-comers, the alarm sounded up at the castle. It was the old story. Arthur had not held his tongue. He had told his brother, a doctor in Edinburgh, and the fool had told his wife. She had sent a note to Cockburne, the Lord Justice Clerk.[4] The prize lost to Mar by Arthur's folly included huge stores of arms and ammunition (but not the Equivalent, which had been paid out), and above all the rousing shock he might have given to the nation, calculated to bring in the ditherers, shake the government, and cripple Red John.

On that same day, John of Argyll rode north out of London. He had been appointed commander in chief for Scotland. Five days later he arrived at Edinburgh, and on the 16th reviewed his army stationed at Stirling Castle under General Wightman. He had only 1840 men, too few for action.[5] Having heard the good news of the western clans from Fonab, Argyll tried to demoralize them further by getting Montrose abruptly to summon all heads of Jacobite clans, including Rob Roy, to appear forthwith at Edinburgh, there to give assurance and bail for their loyalty on pain of outlawry and forfeiture – Parliament had passed the enabling Act on 30 August. The governor of Fort William simultaneously threatened to ravage the lands of any Lochaber clan that joined Mar.

Argyll's bluff was called by Iain Glas of Breadalbane. The old chief, in one of the well-timed, decisive acts of his life, sent the fiery cross round his clan, raised five hundred men overnight, and sent them under John Campbell of Glenlyon into Argyll.[6] His orders were to recruit Clan Campbell for James Edward. The plan had been made in concert with Mar, whose own orders to take Inveraray had been dated 1 September.[7] The effect was electrifying. At least it was so everywhere except in mid-Argyll. Although Breadalbane's five hundred penetrated to the heart of Argyll, few men there would cross the will of MacCailein Mor. On 9 September, Mar renewed orders 'to the king's forces in Argyll' that Inveraray Castle and town should be seized.[8] But Campbell of Fonab had put himself at the head of Argyll's militia and confronted his old friend's son. Between these two no fighting was possible. They shook hands on that, and Glenlyon withdrew.9 But the move had done its work. The clans had always dreaded the foresightedness of Iain Glas, which had passed into legend. Where most others had lost land or status in sixty years of national upheaval, he had maintained his. Their doubts had gone. The old earl would be the last man to stake all unless he was sure.

His act gave the spark needed. All across the country, vigorous men deadened by repression of natural instinct could see this smoke-column curling up into the skies of Breadalbane, signalling that an old man had burnt his boats. The chiefs felt as if some unholy incubus had lifted off their spirits. Of one accord they rose up and gave allegiance to James. The day of the coward had ended. Out of fifty chiefs ordered by Montrose to Edinburgh, only two went. Mar backed Breadalbane by sending the Earl Marischal to proclaim the king at the cross of Aberdeen, Gordon likewise at Elgin, the earl of Southesk at Montrose, the earl of Panmure at Brechin, the marquis of Tullibardine at Dunkeld, Macintosh at Inverness, and Graham at Dundee. When he marched south through Angus, men flocked to his standard. He took Perth on 18 September. Argyll's small army at Stirling alone opposed his crossing the Forth.

In the West, Clans Donald, Cameron, Maclean, MacDougal, Stewart, and MacGregor mustered for war.

Glenlyon made his way out of Argyll in late September by way of Glen Orchy, and found Glengarry and Glenmoriston already encamped at Achallader with five hundred men. Each had received Mar's orders: Glenlyon to join the army at Perth, and Glengarry to move ten miles south to Strathfillan, there to await near Tyndrum a gathering of the western clans. Their commander would be Lieutenant-General Alexander Gordon of Auchintoul. His task would have double purpose – overtly to belittle Argyll in the nation's eyes by capture of Inveraray; and covertly, to find therein excuse for a strong force held poised in the west to secure the landing of King James. His secret arrival on the Clyde was expected by Mar in October.10

Rob Roy had returned to Glen Gyle in mid-September. Iain Og, although a Jacobite, was taking no active part in the rising. He at this time changed his alias from Murray to Campbell, out of respect either for his wife, a daughter of Campbell of Lix, or for Iain Glas, his most powerful neighbour. Leadership was taken by Gregor Ghlun Dhubh, with the help and counsel of his redoubtable uncle, who dominated naturally any company in which he found himself.[11] Upon Rob's arrival, the fiery cross was sent round Clan Gregor. Three hundred of their men mustered on the 27th at Loch Arklet, where they were reviewed by Glengyle, Rob Roy, and Balhaldie.[12]

Rob is said to have had a plan to take Dumbarton Castle.[13] This was at least possible, for its governor, the earl of Glencairn, had written to Montrose of its bad state of repair, and to Marlborough pleading for armaments, since he held for its defence only 'some olde rusty bulletts and matchs'. The castle was the key to the Clyde, third in importance to Edinburgh Castle, where Balhaldie had been mortified a week before. Rob, a past-master of surprise by good planning, might hope to do better.

Mar would give no support for a move on Dumbarton Rock. Its capture would arouse Lowland forces when he wanted the coast clear for King James. He had another plan. When James landed under Gordon's protection, Mar proposed to march across the Forth into Menteith, whence the King would lead his army into England.[14] As a first step, he felt a need to deny Loch Lomond to the enemy, who might otherwise use it to harass him in Menteith. He accordingly ordered Glengyle to seize all boats on Loch Lomond, and to raid into the Lennox ostensibly to embarrass Whig lairds, after which he must join the clans gathering at Strathfillan for the march on Inveraray. Mar had already written to Grahame of Killearn, urging him to forsake Montrose and come out for King James.

Before Glengyle's skirmish opened, Mar recalled Rob Roy to Perth, where he arrived in late September to be closely questioned on what local support Mar might gain in Menteith, the food supplies available for an army, and the strength of hostile forces. He was then given the task of transporting Jacobite coin to Breadalbane.[15] The army's pay was threepence a day and three loaves, or the same amount of meal in lieu of bread.[16] Gordon and Breadalbane were short of all three, and in need too of arms, ammunition, and general supplies for over two thousand men. No one could be better qualified than Rob Roy for safe conduct of the treasure-chest, since he knew every raider's trick. The trust given him dispels Cockburne's gossip of distrust. Thereafter, he repeatedly carried Mar's orders to General Gordon, and the latter's despatches to Mar.

Meanwhile, on Michaelmas Day, 29 September, the three hundred MacGregors under Gregor Ghlun Dhubh came down on Montrose's lands. They were organized in three companies. One of seventy men came by galley and seized all boats on Colquhoun's shores at Luss, the mouth of the Leven and Endrick, and the shores of Buchanan. This done, they took the isle of Inchmurrin, owned by Montrose, from which they sailed at midnight down the Leven to Bonhill, where they landed three miles above Dumbarton. The second and third parties, led by Glengyle and Malcolm MacGregor of Marchfield, fell upon the Heads of Menteith and Buchanan (Callander, Port of Menteith, Aberfoyle, Drymen, and Buchanan House), where among other stores they captured 22 government guns.[17] They too then advanced by night on Bonhill. The country took quick alarm from the ringing of church bells and the firing of warning guns from Dumbarton Castle. Glengyle decided not to risk his plunder in daytime skirmishing. His real job – the seizure of the boats – had been done. He called off his forces, but sent the galleys back to Inchmurrin to strip the isle of its livestock, mainly cows and deer, after which they all forgathered at Inversnaid. The boats were dragged and lifted high above the shore and hidden among the undergrowth and bushes.[18]

As soon as the plunder had been distributed, Glengyle and his three hundred men joined the camp at Strathfillan, where Clanranald arrived with seven hundred men, accompanied by more from Glencoe. But General Gordon was not ready to move on Inveraray: only half his expected clan muster had arrived. Lochiel in particular was having trouble in raising the Camerons, whom the governor of Fort William had been threatening.[19] Glengyle and his men therefore returned to Craigrostan, where they mustered on 10 October to menace the Lowlands. This turned out badly. Argyll knew of Mar's plan to raid Argyll – although not the hidden reason, which no one had ever betrayed – and on 6 October had sent his brother Archibald, Earl of Islay, to Inveraray to prepare its defence. At the same time he sent an urgent request to the earl of Kilmarnock, whose troops were in garrison at Cardross, Drumakill, and Gartartan, to raid Craigrostan and retake the boats, and requested the naval commander on the Clyde to give aid.

Rob Roy arrived back at Strathfillan on 6 October. He bore a long letter from Mar to Gordon. An excerpt reads:

From the camp at Perth, Oct 4, 1715

... I have ordered Glengyll, Rob Roy, Ballhaldie, & the M'Grigars with them to join you, and to follow the orders you give them ... The service you are going about is of great consequence, and the more because of the arms Glenderule

writs me are lately put into Inveraray; therefore you are to
lose no time in going about it with all expedition, but you
would take care that you be sufficiently able to execute it,
and out of danger of being affronted. I will not begin with
burning houses, so I hope you will have no occasion of doing
that to the house of Inverary; and tho' you may threaten it,
you must not put it in execution . . . Mar.[20]

Gordon was unable to move, frustrated by the non-arrival of
clan chiefs. Rob Roy arrived to find Glengyle newly away to
Craigrostan, whither he followed next day, but immediately
returned to Perth on Mar's instruction.[21] Mar was about to launch
east of Stirling an attack on the Lothians led by Macintosh of
Borlum while he, Mar, advanced west of Stirling. He needed Rob
Roy's guidance on the fords across the Forth, especially by way
of Fords of Frew.

The advance had become the more urgent by receipt of a
message from France that James Edward might shortly be on
his way to the Clyde coast. Mar sent off a despatch to Gordon
at Auchtertyre in Strathfillan:

Taymouth, 8th October 1715, Ten-o-Clock in the morning

Sir, Since writing this Morning, I have got Part of my
Letters deciphered, and by what I can judge, I think the
most probable Place where the King will land is somewhere
near to *Dumbarton*, about Lochlong, and I know not but he
may be there before you can reach that; This you will soon
see makes it absolutely necessary for you, and the People
with you, to finish your Business without Loss of Time in
Argyleshire, and to march straight towards Dumbarton,
and there to expect him, or further Orders from me. I
have ordered Lord Broadalbine's two battalions that were
coming here, forthwith to join you . . .

I have ordered the whole Army here to march Tomorrow
Morning towards *Stirling*, which the Enemy will get Intelligence of, so will not adventure to give you any Disturbance
either to our friends about Edinburgh, or to you in the *West*
. . . Mar.

Gordon could still make no move. Glengyle now rejoined him, for
his further action in Menteith and the Lennox had been stopped
by the news that the country there was in arms, and by Rob Roy's

passing on Mar's order not to court a reverse while the Jacobites were still recruiting. The earl of Kilmarnock's men had assembled at Dumbarton to a number of four hundred, to which were added on 11 October a hundred and twenty Paisley men from Dumbarton Castle, and over a hundred well-armed seamen. The Clyde fleet sent to Dumbarton Quay at night three longboats and four pinnaces, armed with four pateraroes (guns for discharging pieces of iron and stones), and a larger boat from Port Glasgow with two 'screw guns' (rifled barrels). Another three large boats of Dumbarton joined in the morning, when the small fleet was towed up the Leven by horses to Loch Lomond. The infantry then marched up the west side of the loch accompanied by a train of mounted gentlemen under John Campbell of Mamore (Argyll's uncle). They stopped that night at Luss, where Sir Humphrey Colquhoun joined, 'followed by forty or fifty stately fellows in their short hose and Belted Plaids, armed each of them with a well fix'd Gun on his shoulder, a strong handsome target with a sharp pointed steel of above half an ell in length screwed into the Naval of it, on his left arm; a sturdy claymore by his side, and a pistol or two with a Dirk and Knife on his Belt'.[22]

On the morning of 13 October, there were seven hundred men and ten boats at Luss. They sailed to Inversnaid, which appeared deserted. Captain Clark loosed off his great guns and drove a ball through the thatch of a house on the hill-flank, 'whereupon an old wife or two came crawling out and scrambled up the hill'.[23] But still no enemy appeared. Thus reassured, 'a hundred men with the greatest Intrepidity leapt ashore'.[24] They still found no one, so they beat drums, fired guns, and stood about for an hour. They found no sign of the boats they had come to recapture, until by chance someone stumbled on ropes, anchors, and oars hidden among shrubs. That led them to a thorough search and the discovery of eighteen boats. They sank five that were damaged and carried off thirteen to Dumbarton.[25] They had certainly not found half; it may be that the others were hidden ashore farther north. Their commanders deserve all credit for not plundering or firing the Clan Gregor houses.

Glengyle had withdrawn his men to Strathfillan at Gordon's request. Rob Roy rejoined them there on the 16th bearing letters from Mar to Breadalbane, Gordon, and Glengyle, dated 14 October. He had stopped en route at Finlarig Castle to give Breadalbane a letter expressing Mar's regret at Islay's presence at Inveraray and the enemy's counter-measures on Loch Lomond. He wished they could be stopped. But Breadalbane with most of his men away could do nothing. The letter to Gregor Ghlun Dhubh read:

> Sir, I am very well pleased with the account of your securing the Boats on Loch Lomond and the other good services you have done since you was with me; General Gordon, Glengarry, and Glenderule are desirous of having you, your uncle the bearer and the men with you with them on the Expedn they are going about, therefore you must lose no time in going to them and follow such orders as you shall receive since your uncle is the bearer I need say no more. Mar, from the Camp at Perth Oct 14.

On the same day (16th) Gordon at last heard that Stewart of Appin, Maclean of Duart, and Campbell of Glendaruel were coming in with eight hundred men, which would bring his numbers to two thousand four hundred. By the 18th, all had arrived, and that morning they marched to Loch Fyne, where half the number invested Inveraray at midday of the 20th. The too long delays had ruined their enterprise. Islay during the last twelve days had raised two thousand men for Inveraray's defence, and in two and a half days they had built a dyke surrounding the town. General Gordon's force advanced to within gunshot, and during the exchange of fire Rob Roy was wounded.[26] There is no report how badly.

Gordon felt unable to take the castle, but seized immense plunder up and down Loch Fyneside – Glengyle wrote to Gordon at the Parks of Inveraray expressing difficulty in getting all he had seized to camp. On the other hand, they were scrupulously fair in dealing with people other than Campbells. When boats unwittingly landed cargo for Clan Campbell, the invaders while helping themselves to the stores paid for all they took.[27]

Gordon now received further orders from Mar. One dated the 16th required him to march at once to Menteith; a countermand dated 19th ordered him to Perth – James Edward had been unable to get away from France. Gordon started withdrawing on the 23rd. By the end of the following week, his battalions were at Drummond Castle, near Crieff, and Rob Roy was with them, his wound sufficiently healed. Battle was imminent.

Mar was master of Scotland from John o' Groats to the Forth. His taking Perth with five thousand men of Atholl, Braemar, Breadalbane, and others of Perthshire, had greatly strengthened confidence by securing all the country to his north and west, so that followers were easy in mind about the safety of their families and communication with France. He had been joined on and after 5 October by the marquis of Huntly with two thousand foot and five hundred horse, by the Earl Marischal and Seaforth, the dukes of Perth and Hamilton, Macintosh of Borlum, and others, who brought up his strength to nine thousand men, to which Gordon's two thousand four hundred had still to be added. Argyll opposed him with under three thousand.

Argyll had not been getting the support he should from Montrose, who had been lulled to Argyll's critical position by Stair's advice from Paris: 'I would not indeed advize to runn one's head against them when they have their bellys fill of beef and their heads fill of strong beer. By the time they have layn a week under a hedge in the end of October or the beginning of November it will be easie dealing with them.' From his enmity to Argyll he was all too ready to listen. He could not dispense with a general so competent, yet dreaded Argyll's rise to power if successful. He gave Argyll slow and grudging aid, arguing that 'the royal force is too weak to attack Mar and should simply observe his movements'.

It was evident to everyone that Mar should promptly grasp the opportunity that providence offered, advance into the central Lowlands, and thus give the strong moral and material support urgently needed by the Jacobites of England. He knew all this, yet in hope of James's arrival delayed at Perth all through October into November. Early in October, he had formed with the English Jacobites the compromise plan of sending his veteran Brigadier Macintosh of Borlum with two thousand five hundred men through the Lothians into Dumfries and Northumberland, where risings had already occurred, to gather in the rebel forces there and march south through the western counties.

Mar had another reason for delay. Although he had an able statesman's mind, could forecast national sentiments and actions, form bold plans, and with immense energy organize all preparatory work, he was not a soldier. He was known to be a good swordsman.[28] As a young man he had been brought in to the Privy Council, received command of a regiment of foot, and been invested with the Order of the Thistle, all helpful to further power and higher station in the body politic.[29] But he had neither battle experience nor a talent for war. He had early trusted to gain the services of the duke of Berwick, recognized by all as one of the greatest generals of his time, having successfully commanded in nearly all European theatres of war, and won great victories by his cool self-possession allied to bold swiftness in action. His armies trusted him. The stern discipline he imposed was balanced by a real care for their lives. This was the ideal man to command in Scotland. If Louis XIV had lived Mar would have had him. But Berwick would not come without consent of the duke of Orleans. So Mar in the end stood alone, forced to take a command for which he must secretly have known himself unfitted. From this stemmed all his hesitations. He had a far greater army than Dundee or Montrose had been able to gather, but now had to substitute for generalship a blind trust in numbers, which could never be high enough. Apart from launching Macintosh across the Forth, he delayed at Perth week after week, seeking advantages that would still further boost his four to one superiority over the enemy. He tried to win over Atholl, who all the while was passing minute detail of Jacobite numbers to Montrose.[30] He seemed to be prepared to await indefinitely the advent of James Edward, and to cultivate ever more promise of support when the need was battle. The very virtues of the politician became vices. His address and subtlety of mind, his patience, his skill in proselytizing, were turned to procrastination, dilatoriness, and irresolution to the point of folly. Forgetting the moral courage he had shown, some thought him a coward. He could bring himself to use all the force required for a rising except brute force. From mid-October onwards, the Jacobites' misfortune had become apparent to all at Perth and Stirling.

The discovery was made too late. Argyll had learned from his spies of Mar's plan to land on the Lothians and took appropriate steps. The Royal Navy occupied the Firth of Forth, and his army detachments guarded the shores of the estuary. Macintosh, who had great experience in the French wars, matched him in skill and quick decision. After analysing intelligence reports, he came fast down the Fife coast while scouts reconnoitred available boats, made a feint to embark at Burntisland opposite Leith on 12 October, but instead embarked at night with one thousand six hundred men in open boats, which he had seized at Elie, Crail, Pittenweem, and other ports opposite North Berwick on the outer firth. The wind favoured them and they slipped past the naval patrols, crossing sixteen miles of open sea before the royal fleet sighted them too late. They landed along the shores of East Lothian, reformed at Haddington, and took Leith. The Jacobites in Edinburgh had been warned, and Macintosh marched on the capital, expecting them to rise.

As soon as Argyll heard the naval reports, he mounted a force of two men to each horse and sent them speeding from Stirling to Edinburgh, which they reached just before Macintosh. This should never have been possible, for Mar had engaged to move on Stirling while Macintosh was embarking, thus to draw Argyll's forces, but, through waiting for intelligence that never came, was a day late in acting. That cost him Edinburgh. Macintosh, undeterred, retired to the old fort at Leith, and held it for a space while Mar marched and countermarched between Perth and Dunblane to draw Argyll off. When that proved vain, Macintosh headed for the Borders, picked up the rebel forces from Dumfries and Northumberland, and marched south into Lancashire.

Mar continued to waste time at Perth until November, to no one's gain except Argyll's. All this while, Rob Roy and the MacGregors were with Gordon first at Drummond Castle and then at Auchterarder. Rob had been called to Perth for interview by Mar on the night of Macintosh's march on Edinburgh, and now was called in again at the beginning of November to give expert advice on the several fords across the Teith and Forth rivers, but for reasons unknown was unable to go.

On 4 November, Mar despatched a letter from Huntingtower to General Gordon: '. . . I wonder what keeps Rob Roy from coming to Perth as I ordered him. Pray send him there immediately, for I want very much to speak to him; and if there be no alarm from the enemy, I would have you come to Perth tomorrow morning that I may concert some things with you as to our March.'

It may be that Rob like everyone else had become exasperated by Mar's procrastinations. Not until 9 November did Mar call a council of war. The land was now gripped by hard frost. The weather might break at any time and bring the winter's first snowfall. The chiefs were determined to advance. When the decision was made and announced to the army, such was the men's relief that they tossed their bonnets in the air.

~

CHAPTER SIXTEEN

SHERIFFMUIR
1715

Mar's plan of advance was to by-pass Stirling and cross the Forth by detaching Gordon's three thousand men to make feints at Abbey Ford and Drip Coble, below and above Stirling Bridge, while he with the main army crossed farther up at Fords of Frew. Rob Roy was to be sent there on detachment with an unobtrusive force of two hundred and fifty MacGregors and MacPhersons, with what orders is not known – presumably to reconnoitre and guard the fords, or to form a bridgehead on the south bank.[1] Meanwhile, Mar sent an express to Gordon, ordering the western clans to join him on the march, and broke camp at Perth on 10 November. He advanced fourteen miles across Strathearn to the muir of Tullibardine. When Gordon joined him, he received orders to take Dunblane, five miles north of Stirling, preparatory to making his feints, and to post Rob Roy to the Fords of Frew. Mar then delayed one more day.

Argyll had been informed of Mar's plan, and watched with thanksgiving the leisurely approach, so unlike the lightning strikes of the old Graham leaders, who before he knew would have had the rebel army into Lanark and West Lothian, and Stirling isolated, communications cut. Mar had even chosen this moment to leave his advancing army and visit Breadalbane at Drummond Castle, still preferring plotting to battle-action. He had lost one thousand three hundred men by desertion on the march, but was still fielding nine thousand including eight squadrons of cavalry. Argyll's army now numbered three thousand five hundred, including ten squadrons.[2] Thus outnumbered, he racked his brains to find some way of improving his position. He seized the chance, now offered by Mar's fatal delay, to advance north to the Sheriff Muir above Strath Allan, knowing that his own well-trained and heavier cavalry, on which he relied to offset his lesser infantry, could not have been effectively used along the river banks of the Forth, whereas the open moor gave good ground for his horse, and was known to him from earlier use as a training field. He offered his inferior numbers as bait.

Both sides moved on the 12th. Argyll's advance guard forestalled Gordon by taking Dunblane, while his main army coming up behind occupied the hill-ground to its south-east above Kippenross – a sheltered position in the glen of the Wharry Burn, at a height of six hundred feet, close under Lynns farm.

Rob Roy's detachment had meanwhile marched south-west out of Strath Allan, heading for the Braes of Doune, from which it would cross the Teith to the Frew fords.³ Gordon came down Strath Allan itself, and had marched barely an hour when he had the news (sent by Balhaldie's wife) of Dunblane's capture. He halted at Ardoch to warn General George Hamilton, who commanded the main army coming behind. He then advanced to the farmlands of Kinbuck, two miles from Dunblane, where he fired two signal guns in prearranged confirmation to Hamilton that Argyll held the town but the way was clear thus far. The main army came on and all bivouacked that night at Kinbuck by the Allan Water, where Mar rejoined them.

The two armies thus lay within three miles of each other to either side of Sheriff Muir under the Ochil Hills. Both lay by their arms in battle formation. Hoar frost formed thick on the plaids and beards of the sleeping men.

Some detailed account of next day's battle is required to refute allegations of Rob Roy's part in it, for these were incorrectly made by early writers, and then by later who accepted the early reports to his detriment without reference back to the facts.

Mar was the first to move that Sunday morning – his Highlanders were inured to extreme cold and quickly fed. They crossed the whitened stubble-fields by the Allan Water, which like the Forth had partially frozen, and marched east across the grassy Muir of Kinbuck, beyond which the ground rose three hundred feet on to the heathery Sheriff Muir. Argyll, warned by his scouts who had been watching overnight, rode north out of the Wharry glen at sunrise with General Wightman, and crossed the broad back of the ridge that fell from the Ochils to Kippendavie. They came to the point where the Gathering Stone now lies on the wide moor at eight hundred feet. They rode a few hundred yards further until the ground fell away and allowed them a sight of the enemy's movement and battle order. To west and north, they saw the moor fall away some two miles to the low ground of Allan Water; eastward it rose gently across Sheriff Muir, then steeply to the crests of the Ochils. Along the top edge of the moor ran the drove road to Bridge of Allan. The enemy were advancing widely spread and holding to the level farmland below the rise to the moor. They were moving slowly south, and finally halted. Mar, it seemed, was holding a council of war.

Mar had halted on sighting Argyll's group outlined against the sky on the Kippendavie ridge. He ordered the Earl Marischal to advance with two squadrons of horse and Sleat's battalion and dislodge them. Before this movement began at 11 a.m., Argyll came down to the Wharry Burn and ordered all drums to beat the *General* (call to march). Frozen to the marrow, his men were slow in forming. It was nearly eleven-thirty before they were ready for action. Meanwhile, the Earl Marischal had reported Argyll's position on higher ground than Mar's, and Mar now abandoned his strategic plan of by-passing Stirling by Fords of Frew.[4] He resolved to give battle on Sheriff Muir. This change was exactly what Argyll had tried to invite. His scouts soon after reported that Mar had suddenly changed direction to breast the higher hill ground on Argyll's right towards the drove road, and so take him at disadvantage before he could climb out of the Wharry glen. He at once ordered the army to face about, stretch out to the right, and march up the gently sloping south-west side of the Kippendavie hill in front – an ascent of two hundred and fifty feet in under a mile. His urgent need was to gain Sheriff Muir before Mar could attack.

He succeeded. When he had breasted the rim on to the flat ridge-top and advanced a quarter of a mile north-eastward, he saw that the enemy were over the other flank of the ridge and within pistol-shot. Both armies were in some disorder after their fast climb – their left wings in particular – and hastily re-formed in battalions with colours flying. Mar at this point made a momentous mistake by allowing or directing several squadrons of cavalry, which had previously been out on the wing-tips, to move around and in to the centre, leaving the right wing with a bare two squadrons and the left with none.[5]

Argyll's right and left wings were each of four battalions of foot, with four squadrons of dragoons at their tips and one behind. The right wing foot were commanded by General Wightman, the left wing by General Whitham. Argyll took personal command of his right wing cavalry.

Mar opposed him with twenty battalions, ten to each wing in double line, with two squadrons of horse at the right wing-tip, and six squadrons at centre under the duke of Perth. His left wing opposing Argyll's right was under Hamilton; his right wing

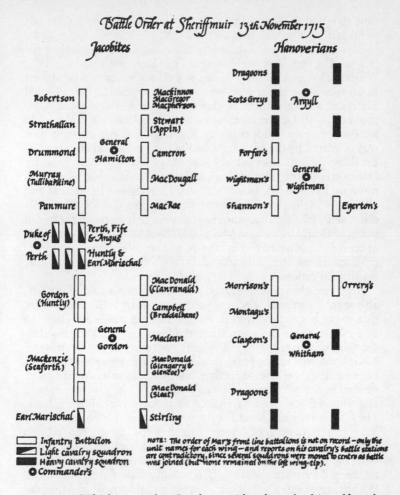

Battle Order at Sheriffmuir 13th November 1715

Jacobites   Hanoverians

Dragoons

Robertson   Mackinnon   Scots Greys   Argyll
                   MacGregor
                   Macpherson

Strathallan   Stewart
                   (Appin)

Drummond   General Cameron   Forfar's
           Hamilton   General
                                               Wightman
Murray   MacDougall   Wightman's
(Tullibardine)

Panmure   MacRae   Shannon's   Egerton's

Duke of   Perth, Fife   Morrison's   Orrery's
           & Angus
Perth   Huntly &
           Earl Marischal

Gordon   MacDonald   Morrison's   Orrery's
(Huntly)   (Clanranald)

                    Campbell   Montagu's
                    (Breadalbane)

           General Maclean   Clayton's   General
           Gordon   Whitham
Mackenzie   MacDonald
(Seaforth)   (Glengarry &
                    Glencoe)
                    MacDonald   Dragoons
                    (Sleat)

Earl Marischal   Stirling

☐ Infantry Battalion
◣ Light cavalry squadron
■ Heavy cavalry squadron
◉ Commanders

NOTE: The order of Mar's front line battalions is not on record – only the unit names for each wing – and reports on his cavalry's battle stations are contradictory, since several squadrons were moved to centre as battle was joined (but none remained on the left wing-tip).

opposing Whitham under Gordon, with whom he himself took position.

The battle went rapidly out of both generals' control, since neither had taken central position. Each on his own right wing knew too late of the fate of his left.

Argyll's left wing regiments had been last in coming on to the field, and were still straggling but trying to close up on the move when they came on Gordon's battalions, hitherto partially concealed by a swell of the heathery ground. Whitham had barely

time to see with dismay that Mar's horse were riding farther out
to his left, as if to take him on the flank, when the clans fired two
volleys at close range with deadly precision. Gordon sounded the
charge. The time was twelve noon. The clans' swift onslaught cut
Whitham's foot to pieces. Those not taken prisoner were driven
in on their own dragoons, who fell back in confusion. Colonel
Harrison, an eye-witness, declared that in seven or eight minutes
the rout of all Government units was complete. Whitham could
not see what was happening to Argyll's wing, for all sight of it
was obscured by the eddying cloud of four thousand Highlanders
breaking through his centre. He could only think that the entire
Hanoverian army was defeated, and that once Mar got behind him
he could have no line of withdrawal. He sounded the retreat and
all fled to Stirling, where they arrived at three o'clock. Gordon's
clansmen with Mar in attendance pursued only as far as a little hill
south of Dunblane, where Mar called them off.[6] Had he remained
at centre and ordered the cavalry to fall on, Whitham's regiments
must have been utterly destroyed. Instead, the cavalrymen sat idle,
waiting on orders.

Argyll's right wing had fared well after a bad start. Mar's left,
although disordered, had engaged them with well-directed fire
that made his dragoons reel. Argyll ordered the Scots Greys to
ride out to the right and attack the clans' flank, and this they
did with such spirit, while Wightman's front-line regiments gave
disciplined fire in support, that the clans gave ground. Argyll
kept up the pressure, directing his heavy cavalry where most
needed in support of Wightman's advance. He gave no respite,
and allowed the clans no chance to re-form their broken lines.
They never regained the advantage that superior numbers should
have given them. They were forced back on to the moor's
down-slope, and then consistently pressed back in three hours'
hard fighting entirely against the five hundred cavalry who now
interposed between them and Wightman's foot, never routed like
Whitham, repeatedly rallying – ten times, said Argyll – so that the
battle eddied back and forth. They allowed Drummond's cavalry
every chance to come in and turn the tide, but Drummond's
and the Earl Marischal's squadrons were easily beaten off by
Wightman's battalions. Another eye-witness said, 'The cavalry
behaved shamefully, making inexplicable blunders in taking
up positions, deserting the infantry who fought admirably,
and failing to rally through confusion.'[7] He omits to add
that Drummond's squadrons were wretchedly mounted and
equipped, and without previous experience.[8]

The left wing clans were finally defeated by the banks of the Allan Water around four o'clock in the afternoon. General Wightman wrote of them afterwards with admiration: 'I never saw Regular Troops more exactly drawn up in Line of Battle, and then in a moment; and their officers behaved with all the Gallantry imaginable.'[9]

Mar's victorious right wing had all this while been inactive. Mar having left the battlefield to follow the desultory pursuit, Lord Sinclair had to send expresses to bring him back.[10] They found him watching a body of Highlanders dispersing a small enemy force trying to re-form. Hearing of his left wing's defeat, he marched back up the hill of Kippendavie. The cavalry and clans to a number of four thousand were re-formed on the north side, where the open moor fell away to Balhaldie farm and Kinbuck.[11] There they remained for nearly three hours. Later in the day, they moved half a mile down the Kippendavie slope to see better.

Argyll on approaching the Allan Water might have pursued until dark had not Wightman sent an *aide-de-camp* to report Mar's presence on the hill behind. Argyll called off his cavalry and with Wightman advanced to within half a mile of the enemy. This was bold – folly had Mar attacked – for they had now only three battalions and five tired squadrons.[12] Along the foot of Mar's hill were earth walls and ditches, which Argyll's men used for breastworks.[13] He placed cannon to right and left, gave battle orders, and awaited attack. Mar made no move. His nerve had gone. Argyll had later report that he consulted Glengarry, whose answer was 'that the clans had done enough and that he would not hazard them to do other People's Work' (referring to the inaction of cavalry).[14] When darkness fell, both armies retired, Argyll down Strath Allan and Mar up.

Mar's extraordinary misconduct can receive no adequate account without personal knowledge of the man. His tactical errors are more easily read. He did not lose the battle, he threw it away. He should in the first instance have given the right wing to Gordon and acted as central commander-in-chief. His desertion of the battlefield in vain chase after Whitham's broken horde was a shedding of generalship. He could still, when he returned, have advanced with his elated four thousand and well-rested cavalry to attack Argyll's rear while he was battling so slowly down to the Allan Water. There was ample time. Having chosen to stand his ground and await what befell, he had yet one chance more, to attack Argyll's last advance under the Kippendavie hill, and deny him the breastworks. All that was asked of him was one strong effort to bring his right wing under command, to issue clear orders, and so rally the clans and cavalry for a final battle. He had overwhelming strength.

The contemporary historian of Sheriffmuir, Peter Rae, declared: 'The want of a commander who could seize on that decisive moment when the line of Whitham yielded, ruined the Jacobite cause. Mar's incapacity became conspicuous to the meanest clansmen . . . Without command, without common action, the clans stood astonished in the places to which they were appointed at the beginning of the battle, and the forces opposed to them being beaten back, knew not what they should do next . . . the imbecility of the leaders so effectually counteracted the warlike spirits of the clans that they stood in helpless amaze.'

The MacGregor battalion had been divided before battle began. Balhaldie's contingent was posted to the left wing with the Camerons. He and his men disputed every yard of the way until most were killed. Balhaldie was lucky to escape. His house by Allan Water stood only a mile off the line of retreat. As he made for home, dragoons rode up and almost had him, when they were attacked and killed by a troop of retreating horse.[15] Rob Roy's posting was ten miles off at the Forth crossings, and the earliest likely moment at which he would hear of Mar's change of plan was one o'clock. That he did get his recall is plain, for he marched at once to Allan Water by way of Doune, arriving on the banks near Kinbuck around four o'clock, just in time to see the Camerons and Appin Stewarts – recognizable by their crowberry and oak cap-badges – driven across the river by Argyll's cavalry. John Cameron, Young Lochiel, reports the meeting:[16]

> I rallied there all I could meet with, and caused such of them as had fyred to change their pieces. At the same time I perceived Rob Roy Mcgrigar on his march towards me coming from the town of Down, he not being at the engadgment, with about two hundred and fifty, betwixt Mcgrigars and Mcphersons.
>
> I marched towards him wt the few I had got together; perceiving Argyll opposite to us, I intreated, he being come fresh wt these men, that we would joyn and cross the River to attack Argyle; which he absolutely refused; so that there was such a very small number left when Rob Roy went off, and not knowing well then what became of our right, could not attempt any thing with that number.

He was writing perhaps to mollify his formidable father, now aged

86, outraged at a Cameron retreat in face of an enemy. Young Lochiel had in fact been lucky to get the chance of escape up-river that Rob Roy's arrival gave him. Struan Robertson, the chief of Clan Donnachaidh, witnessed the meeting: 'As soon as they passed the water of Allan, having met with a party of MacGregors going to join our army, they drew up, and the enemy thought it proper to leave them.'

Immediately afterwards, Argyll called in his cavalry and faced about to confront Mar on the hill behind. Rob Roy's refusal to attack Argyll was in the circumstances a rejection of insanity. It was also in accord with his early resolution to be no general's fool, least of all Mar's. He made the decision to be ready for whatever opportunity the last hour of daylight offered, and crossing the river followed Argyll's rear over the moor of Kinbuck. He was then in good position to aid effectively a Jacobite attack if Mar came down, which he never did. The presence of Rob's force was spotted by Mar's officers on Kippendavie hill.[17]

The historians of the time, unaware of Rob's position or the witness given by Cameron and Robertson, placed him for want of evidence on Kippendavie hill, presumably because he had been under General Gordon's command for two months past. His consequential defamation has come less from his enemies or from malice than the blind repetition of ignorant gossip, first by the Reverend Robert Patten when he wrote his account of the battle, and finally by Sir Walter Scott. Scott's defamation, which repeats and embellishes Patten's, records the rout of the two wings and continues: 'During this medley of flight and pursuit, Rob Roy retained his station on a hill in the centre of the Highland position; and though it is said his attack might have decided the day, he could not be prevailed upon to charge . . . While the favourable moment for action was gliding away unemployed, Mar's positive orders reached Rob Roy that he should presently attack. To which he coolly replied, "No, no! if they cannot do it without me, they cannot do it with me." . . . Rob did not, however, neglect his own private interest on this occasion, he enriched his followers by plundering the baggage and the dead on both sides'.

Scott's account is fictional in the worst sense. Fiction can illuminate truth. Scott here falsifies it. He had not even troubled to visit the battlefield. His 'hill in the centre of the Highland position' does not exist. All is gently rolling moorland. Even supposing that Rob had been present on Sheriffmuir, Scott has not paused to reflect that by the time Mar was back on Kippendavie hill, with

a first chance to give Rob orders, his left wing was in full retreat
to the Allan Water. Had Rob's small contingent been present,
would Mar have given him an order to attack which he never
gave to his right wing battalion commanders or cavalry? Only
they had the strength of four thousand men to advance on
the rear of Argyll's regiments. Rob Roy's tiny force could not
have drawn blood before Argyll's squadrons brushed them off
or Wightman's unexercised regiments shot them to pieces. The
words that Patten and Scott put into Rob's mouth could have
been Glengarry's (unless he too was misreported), and the scene
where he refused Young Lochiel's proposal has been transferred
from the Allan Water to the top of the Kippendavie hill.

The second accusation, that he plundered the dead, came to
be fastened on Rob Roy by Murdoch McLennan, a ballad-writer
who no doubt picked him out as a 'name' on whom a comic verse
could be hung:

> Rob Roy he stood watch
> On a hill for to catch
> The booty, for aught that I saw, man;
> For he ne'er advanced
> From the place where he stanced
> Till nae mair was to do there at a', man.

The verse is only one of many that nicely satirize the rival claims
to a victory.[18] It was published in 1819 by James Hogg, a friend
of Sir Walter Scott. That this particular verse is an innuendo
McLennan lets slip in his second and third lines. The two armies
left the battlefield after 4.30 p.m., so that by the time there was
'nae mair to do' it was dark. Neither side carried baggage on to
the battlefield, and the troops wore nothing of value except their
arms. The only weighty plunder gained was by Argyll's victorious
wing, which captured four cannons, seven covered food-waggons,
arms, colour-standards, and prisoners of quality down by the
Allan Water.[19] It is commonsense on a field of battle to seize
arms and equipment that one lacks, and Rob Roy's men would
have been unwise not to pick up what they needed, if chance
offered. More fighting lay ahead, in which they were to play a
fuller role. The innuendo is not that they, like all others, took
gear wanted for campaigning, but that booty in the wider sense
was the purpose of Rob Roy's presence and inaction following
Whitham's defeat. The disproof of that is plain.

When night fell, Argyll withdrew to Dunblane and Mar to

Ardoch, neither knowing who had won the day.[20] Argyll's official list of losses showed 133 prisoners, whom Mar soon freed without stripping them,[21] and 477 all ranks killed or wounded. The Jacobite list showed 82 prisoners and only 150 killed or wounded, largely due to Argyll's orders on the field 'to spare the poor blue-bonnets'.[22] Each side claimed a victory for propaganda purposes.

Rob Roy followed Mar's retreating army, imagining that after the drawn battle they would re-form next day, either to resume battle or to cross the Forth as originally planned, and advance into Stirlingshire, drawing in the skirmishing parties now operating in the central Lowlands. He soon discovered that his services at the Forth crossings would not be wanted. Mar fell back to Ardoch so precipitately that Rob could see artillery, already rimed by frost, lying abandoned by the Allan Water. He must have wondered why. Their forces were superior and no enemy harried the rear. Perhaps a line from the Book of Proverbs came to mind from his schooldays: 'The wicked flee when no man pursueth.' Mar, if not wicked, was demoralized.

Mar now knew consciously what all Scotland knew, that he was no general. He was never to receive the sympathy or charitable regard that he deserved, having summoned up much courage to launch the rising, planned well, worked hard, and although ignorant of war, been left as general by default. He had accepted that too readily, not understanding that a would-be general needs much previous battle-experience to interpret the field's bewildering chaos; to appreciate what is happening to whom when twelve thousand foot and horse are flowing back and forth; to anticipate what is to come, and to know what to do and how. He needs a quick, cool mind backed by a brutal will. He needs much more besides – at least an air of personal assurance that can impose itself on subordinate commanders and men, and in battle that can only happen if real. Humbug does not pass.

Mar at Sheriffmuir had to overcome a further difficulty that did not afflict Argyll. A Highland army was not fully subject to the subordination of lesser commands to superior as practised in a regular army. The men looked first to their own chiefs, who might hold independent ideas on battle-action, accepting the general's as they chose. A general to impose his will had to do so not by rank but by a real and recognized human superiority, the ingredients of which were a mix of ability, experience, and the force of character that creates trust. Mar could not do this. Without either authority or ability to direct his chiefs and cavalry commanders, he had no choice but to leave his left wing to its fate. The lack of central command allowed Campbell's escape; it lost the day and the days to come.

Mar remained on the 14th at Ardoch, then ordered a retreat to Auchterarder, excusing it on the loss of his food-waggons, although every man knew that he could have fed well in the Carse of Stirling. The real victor emerged on that Monday morning by self-selection, for while Mar rested, trying to find food, Argyll advanced to renew battle. He came with only two thousand men, outnumbered, knowing that yesterday he should never have escaped. He had courage. His small army paraded at Sheriff Muir, astonished and relieved to find the enemy vanished into thin air. His men collected the spoil, which included oatmeal to a total of many bolls, tied up in the plaids of fallen Highlanders.[23]

Mar had no plan, therefore could not screw up new courage. His demoralization afflicted his army and groups began to desert. The men of his broken left wing, having all lost their plaids, had to go home to reclothe.[24] While many failed to rejoin, many did so and the main force stayed with him, including Rob Roy, Glengyle, and their MacGregor following. The chiefs, though disillusioned, had nothing more to lose and could still hope for some retrieval of fortune. If Mar would not or could not fight, at least he was a diplomatist, and might be able to negotiate a peace with the Hanoverian government. After they saw him established at Perth, they insisted that he act. Their determination had been strengthened by disastrous news from England. On 14 November, the English Jacobite army had surrendered at Preston.

Rob Roy was in broad agreement with the chiefs. Neither he nor they had abjured the Jacobite cause, to which they remained devoted, but they were not if they could help it going to be made a sacrifice by inept generals, as they had been too often since the great day of Dundee. Rob as before took a line of his own. He would salve what he could from the situation and look again to his own interest. He had through life been trained to make provision for seasons ahead. All too clearly he saw that Mar's days in Scotland were numbered, that his own hopes of regaining Craigrostan were lost, that James Edward's supporters would be singled out after attainder first for forfeiture and then retributive punishment. One of the first to fall must be Breadalbane. It behoved him to take out some insurance with Red John, that Mary's home might be passed by in the burnings. She was again pregnant.

One week after Sheriffmuir, while billeted at a farm in southern Perthshire, he searched his mind for some more innocuous information that without harm might be passed to Argyll. At last he found it. Both sides had claimed a victory and were putting out propaganda in hope of raising men, means, and morale. Town- and country-men were soon to hear and enjoy the comedy of the rival claims sung by Murdoch McLennan:

> There's some say that we wan,
> Some say that they wan,
> Some say that nane wan at a', man;
> But ae thing I'm sure,
> That at Sheriffmuir
> A battle there was that I saw, man.
> And we ran, and they ran,
> And they ran, and we ran,
> And we ran and they ran awa', man.

Mar and Argyll were each sending men into the towns to proclaim his own triumph. More than that, Mar to soften up Argyll for armistice negotiations was leaking news that his army looked like doubling in size. Knowing that Argyll and Montrose must swiftly hear of the proclamations from their corps of agents, Rob Roy wrote to Argyll:[25]

May it please your Grace. The Bearer of this will give you sufficient Intelligence upon the late movements of the people here and as I cannot put down on paper I hope you will forgive me at this Juncture but must take the risque of the messenger coming at you, – I hope that nothing will come out, that will make so much turmoil as I do not think the army of Mar can come to so much against your Grace's men if they only all come out. As to what your Grace may know about the people here from other people be very careful as MN and GD were sent yesterday to make false news to the people in the district from which I know that they have sufficient designs to make grievous injury to the forces under you if they can. They were both sent with Proclamations to be issued and as I send this by a quicker route you shd give orders to detayn them at the Bridge or wherever found.

I shall have mair for you when I get the matter on hand settled with them. –

> I remain,
> Your Grace's humble and obedient servant
> Ro Campbell
> From the farm at Inverarlich place please address me
> 21 November 1715

There was no quick way that would save a whole day between Perth and Stirling, and Mar's messengers were put to no greater risk. Argyll must have wondered why Rob Roy sent him such useless crumbs. If Rob's motive had been his own safety rather than Mary's and the children's, he would now have followed the lead of so many others and withdrawn from Mar's army. He had already taken part in the invasion of Inveraray, had plundered Argyll's land, and been wounded there. He had given Mar valuable service and knew that Argyll knew. Yet he still intended openly to aid the Jacobites, to plunder Whigs for his winter's mart, which he and his following urgently required for their families, and for which golden opportunities were now offered, and at the same time to give Mar real aid, distinct from his mock aid to Argyll. It might be said that now indeed he ran with the hare and hunted with the hounds, but the act looks much like an impersonation. He had staked more on the Jacobite cause than Argyll knew. It was not his heart that had changed, but his hopes. He had thought it well to cast this breadcrumb on the Stirling waters. No one knew better than he the off-course swervings of fate.

On St Andrew's Day, 30 November, Montrose received a note signed 'Charles Cokburne' (son of the Lord Justice Clerk): 'Mar by the consent of all the heads of his party, has sent proposals of peace through Colonel Lawrence. The report that Mar would be 18,000 strong in a few days, and that his aim now was to get back his deserters, is wrong. Perhaps, however, he is looking after a better bargain, as was the policy of the rebels under King William in 1690.'

This Colonel Lawrence had been captured by the Jacobites at Sheriffmuir. At Perth, he had been allowed to see the true state of Mar's army and to hear the discords and disenchantments of the chiefs. Mar's choice of him to convey treaty proposals to Edinburgh was extremely negligent. Argyll rejected the plea outright, and for once Montrose could agree with him.

CHAPTER SEVENTEEN

TEMPTATION IN THE WILDERNESS

1715–16

The first temptation

MAR TOOK thought how best to bring Montrose to think on the merits of peace. To that end, he gave Rob Roy orders in early December to lead two companies of Clan Gregor into Menteith and the Lennox and there harry Montrose's land. He asked Rob, whom he had found a man of address,[1] to contrive a meeting with Grahame of Killearn, and try again to win him for the Jacobites. He was unaware that his letter of two months ago had been sent by Grahame straight to Montrose, who read it to the king. In accepting this commission, Rob no doubt argued that Montrose's enmity was in any event assured, while his family's safety rested not with him but Argyll, whose equanimity would not be disturbed by pinpricks to Graham country.

His arrival in Menteith on 7 December was mild, that Killearn might not suffer personal affront. A report was sent to Montrose in a letter dated 9 December from Charles Mortland: 'On Wednesday morning between one and two o'clock, Rob Roy arrived with 100 men at Drunmon (Drymen), marching through Buchanan to Craigrostan without attempting anything upon the garrison of Drummakill, and having done little at Drunmon but proclaimed the Pretender and tore the guager's books.'

Next day he again spared Buchanan. He and Malcolm of Marchfield raided Luss instead, crossing the loch in a fleet of galleys, which the Loch Lomond expedition had failed to find.[2] He captured two of Colquhoun's men, holding them as hostages for four men of Clan Gregor, who during his absence had been imprisoned in Dumbarton. During the following week, he was able to meet Grahame in Buchanan. Montrose had asked Grahame to try once more to win from Rob Roy some evidence that might implicate Argyll in Jacobite plotting.[3] Argyll must certainly have been approached by the Jacobites, as almost all great men had been, and any proven 'approach' could be twisted to imply its invitation. The bribe as before was Craigrostan and freedom. The meeting must have been short, cool, and for their noble sponsors of treachery disappointing. Montrose would feel mystified that a secret agent could have this sense of honour, not appreciating that Rob posed as such to serve a private end. Rob now felt free to raid Menteith and Buchanan. He began by lifting cows, sheep, horses, and three more hostages in the persons of John McLachlan of Achintroig and his two sons. He took the house by firing the door.[4]

Montrose riposted by sending in the navy, who landed a hundred seamen at Dumbarton, where they were joined by a company of local militia. Their orders were to bring in Rob Roy.[5] Grahame took command at Loch Lomondside and embarked a hundred men for Inversnaid, where they found that Rob Roy had moved to Strathfillan.[6] The militia followed at night ten miles through Glen Falloch. In the early hours they learned that Rob Roy was sleeping in the Crianlarich change-house. Twenty of his men occupied the barn, and the remaining eighty had gone eastward on a *creach* under Alasdair Roy. Grahame bolted the barn door from without. Rob Roy's capture seemed assured, but before the attempt could be made he awakened. The change-house door was too low and narrow to be rushed. No one could get through against his sword, and the bodies of those who tried soon blocked the threshold. His aroused men burst the barn doors open by weight of number. Hackles up and weapons out, they drove back the civil militia. Rob Roy joined them. Grahame rallied his men out of pistol-shot, but Rob's marksmen picked off leaders with their flintlocks, and the rest fled before a broadsword charge.

On 17 December, Mar recalled Rob Roy to Perth.[7] Rob had spent a few days with Mary and the boys at Auchinchisallen, and before leaving released his five hostages. McLachlan of Auchintroig pleaded for the return of his cows, sheep, and horses, and must have been facing real hardship for Rob gave him back the stock intact.[8] The weather at harvest time had been so bad that men had failed to get in any crops. Rob Roy's compassion was shown repeatedly in the records of the period when he was most harassed. Men under extreme pressure are not merciful, unless by nature openhearted.

He arrived at Perth in good time for the most embarrassing moment of Mar's life. On Christmas Eve, a horseman rode in with the news that James Edward had landed with five companions at Peterhead. To escape the vigilance of the duke of Orleans, he had slipped away from Dunkirk disguised as a fisherman. James had never before set foot on his 'native' land. He looked to Mar for its conquest and Mar's heart was bitter. He had stood so long alone, expending his courage for this prince – who had been trysted for last March, then for June, then October – all the while trying to hearten his countrymen (who needed confidence less than he), ascribing to them fears that were really his own in dire warning to Bolingbroke, 'they will give over all hopes of him forever if he be not with them before the hooke goes into the corne', and yet the year had ebbed away without encouragement from France. The summer had gone, the harvest failed, Sheriffmuir been lost, thick snow fallen over the land – and here now was the prince, expecting miracles of a man whose spirit had been drained away. If only he had sent his brother Berwick instead!

Before riding north with the duke of Hamilton and the Earl Marischal to meet James Edward at Fetteresso, Mar posted Rob Roy and a hundred and fifty MacGregors, under command of Glengyle, to Falkland Palace in central Fife. They took possession on 4 January.[9] The Perthshire Lowlands, Angus, and all of Fife except the Forth coast, were firmly in Mar's hands and controlled by self-supporting garrisons. Rob Roy provisioned Falkland by sending detachments far and wide to plunder Whig lands and take what they wanted in food, clothes, and all else. Rob as Gregor's deputy had the ordering of these units and found himself in his element. His excursions were so efficiently conducted, and during the most severe weather of the winter moved with such pace, never long in one district before appearing in another at great distance, unpredictably, that his name became the terror of the eastern lowlands. As before, he spared families unable to afford depredations; there is record of aggrieved small-holders appearing in Falkland to receive from Rob Roy the return of their stock.[10] Alexander Archer, a candle-maker in Hamilton, received a series of letters dated January to March, from his brother at Leslie. He remarks that Rob Roy and his men were all armed with sword, gun, dirk and targe. He heard Rob say he 'never desired a more pleasant and satisfying breakfast every morning than to see a Whig's house in flames'. The words had been only a growl, for the writer added, 'Yet George told me he was the fairest and most discreet (discerning) among them that he knew.'

On 20 January, Rob and his hundred and fifty men took and garrisoned the Tower of Balgonie (a seat of General Leslie, the earl of Leven), set on a hill near Markinch about five miles from Falkland. On that same day he surprised, surrounded, and captured at Markinch a mixed force of Swiss mercenaries and Kirkcaldy militia. He imprisoned all in the tower.[11]

The MacGregors shared with other clan units under Lord George Murray (Atholl's son, who had newly come of age) the task of checking incursions by Hanoverian troops. Argyll had received heavy reinforcements under General William Cadogan, Marlborough's most distinguished Irish commander. Cadogan was now Argyll's second-in-command, and planning to advance his line up the sea-coast, while bringing northern forces south from Inverness to Lochaber. He was probing Fife with Swiss and Dutch mercenaries and local militia based on the Forth towns, all of which were in Argyll's hands. Rob Roy resented Cadogan's use of foreign troops and made life hard for them in unremitting attacks. Cadogan was said to be furious at Rob Roy's seizure of Balgonie, which he had meant to use in his planned advance.[12] Rob had ruined it, after using it first as a prison for Swiss and other captives. Cadogan's anger at Clan Gregor may none the less have been real: incessant pinpricks are unwelcome. His revenge was to come.

James Edward had moved south to Dundee on 6 January, then set up his court in Scone Palace at Perth. Proclamations were made that the king would be crowned at Scone on the 23rd. The gesture was empty. Everyone had given up hope. A strong army had been raised, but without head or heart it was impotent. Desertions were reducing it daily. Ammunition was running short, no coal could be had north of the Forth, and the troops were suffering extreme cold; Argyll's too, for he reported on 25 January that everywhere north of Dunblane 'the snow was so heavy it was up to the horses' bellies'.[13] The king went among the men with stony looks, made processions in towns, required thanksgiving services, and demanded that the Church offer up prayers for himself (but not for his followers, who had sacrificed all). There was little he could do to halt Argyll, who was now about to advance on Perth, other than issue a particularly cruel, self-regarding order that Auchterarder, Blackford, and other towns between Dunblane and the Tay should be burned, and their stocks laid waste to deny Argyll provisions. These towns had been loyal to James; the weather was wild, the cold penetrating, and Argyll's 35-mile advance not halted thus by more than a day or two.

Mar's evacuation of Perth, and withdrawal to Dundee and Montrose, was resolved upon towards the close of January. He issued final orders to "The Laird of Glengyll Commanding Officer of the Garrison of Falkland', and signed them at the court of Scone on the 27th.[14] They directed Glengyle to call in all detachments out in garrison and to march with the battalion of the name of MacGregor 35 miles to the Teith valley west of Dunblane, and there prevent the enemy from collecting provisions. If necessary, he was to call for reinforcements from the garrison at Braes of Doune. He was ordered thereafter to march with his whole force 43 miles east to Naughton on the Firth of Tay, where boats would be ready to ferry his men across to Dundee on the farther shore.

Rob Roy on this expedition distinguished himself near Stirling by lifting from under the nose of their guards the cattle and stores gathered by the castle garrison. On the return journey to Naughton, he received orders to burn Leslie.[15] Revolted, he refused the order and marched on to the Tay coast. At Dundee, he heard that Mar and the prince had reached Montrose on 3 February, and that same night had ordered the army to march to Aberdeen. While the army slept, they had embarked on a French ship. Rob hastened north with his force into Aberdeenshire, then west to join the MacDonalds of Keppoch and Sleat in Strathspey which they plundered. The prince on sailing had had the grace to send off a last letter of thanks to the army, on receipt of which the clans marched into Badenoch and dispersed.

The burning of Auchinchisallen

While the MacGregors were finding their way home from Ruthven in Speyside, which they left on 16 February, Argyll and Cadogan were in strong disagreement on the best policy for the pacification of Scotland. Argyll appears to have felt a genuine sympathy for his fellow Highlanders, despite their plundering mid-Argyll, perhaps because Inveraray had been spared, and Clan Campbell itself divided on the rising, and maybe from distaste for the political expediency that alone had brought George I to the throne. He wanted clemency, Cadogan retribution. In opposing Argyll, Cadogan correctly gauged the will of Montrose, Townshend, and the little men about the king, for blood and flames. He had been offered a peerage, and would rise on Argyll's fall. He now acted in concert with Montrose to that end.

Parliament had passed an 'Act declaring the persons following to stand attainted of High Treason from 13th November 1715 unless they surrender themselves to Justice by the last day of June 1716'. The list of only 49 names included 'Robert Campbell alias

MacGregour commonly called Rob Roy', but not his chieftain Gregor Ghlun Dhubh, who was overlooked by reason of his uncle's greater name. Cadogan saw no reason to wait for the chiefs to accept the amnesty, but went after them. He marched through the snows of Perthshire straight to the heart of their strength in Lochaber. And there his Swiss and Dutch troops burnt houses, drove off and killed cattle, and shot any who resisted. This was done during the months of February and March 1716, when Argyll was recalled to London.

Rob Roy by that time had withdrawn to the Trossachs. Although aware of the division of army command, he had not imagined that Cadogan would be allowed a free hand in any Campbell country, or that Red John could now be a falling star, on the defensive against Montrose's reports to the king of his suspect leniency, and dared not be seen to protect the lands of Breadalbane. Rob accordingly went raiding in Stirlingshire with some two hundred men of the disbanded war-muster. Montrose, being suddenly given cause to remember him, saw to it that Cadogan did not forget him either. His punitive regiments returned south in late March across Rannoch to Breadalbane, where they took Finlarig Castle and left a garrison under Colonel Russell. Breadalbane, now aged 81, lay on his death-bed, and although placed formally under arrest was not disturbed. His following suffered in his place. Montrose had arranged with Cadogan that an officer named Peter Robison should have charge of the detachment detailed to burn both Rob's house and his nephew's. Robison had been given careful directions, but since then had received a wound in the hand, causing his withdrawal to Stirling Castle.[16]

When Rob heard of Cadogan's westward march, he rightly feared for Clan Gregor's safety, and led his band to Glen Gyle and Craigrostan. He stationed them there to guard the homeland, then went on with a dozen men only to Glen Dochart and Loch Tay to keep watch. On the capture of Finlarig, he sent Mary, whose time for delivery was near, back to Glen Gyle under protection of Alasdair Roy. On the night of 4 April, word at last came to him from the Campbells at Finlarig that Colonel Russell had ordered the burning of his house. He at once sent a gillie to Alasdair Roy with orders to bring in two hundred men, but was too late. A company of Swiss mercenaries (65 men and officers) set out for Glen Dochart early next morning, led by a local guide. Rob set an ambush at Auchinchisallen. Behind the flat terrace on which the house stood were two craggy mounds, providing dead ground over the short passage to the mouth of Glen Chaorach, which gave access over the hills to Balquhidder. Rob disposed his men there and waited.

Across Glen Dochart, the high tops of Meall Glas and Sgiath Chuil were at this time of year always covered in snow. Down below, men and women would be working on the fields of Auchessan farm across the river Dochart, harrowing and sowing. At ten o'clock in the morning, the scarlet and white caterpillar of the Swiss company was sighted, crawling along the drove road from Killin. It was too strong to attack. Rob had to watch in helpless wrath while the troops carried out from the house all his furniture, clothes, and stores; but when they prepared to fire the thatch and grain stacks he could endure no more and ordered his men to open fire. The range was a hundred yards. Twelve to fifteen of the merceneraries fell. The company returned the fire and Rob had several men hit before his small band could retire into Glen Chaorach. The Swiss did not risk a pursuit, but carried off all his stock and goods, and burnt his house to the ground. Since Rob's cattle were capable of walking, they were probably a *spreidh* brought in from Menteith.

That same day, Colonel Russell sold the stock to Iain Og MacGregor of Glencarnaig. Russell's receipt survives.[17]

I doe hearby Certifie that John Oge Campbell has bought and payed for all the Cattle which was brought or taken from the House of Rob Roy by the party sent thither from Finlarig Castle, and if any of the said cattle strayed from the party as they came along which several of them did, the said John Oge Campbell is intitled to them as his owne proper goods soe may take ym up as such.

Given at Finlarig Castle this 5th of Aprill 1716.

Chris. Russell

I doe likewise oblige myselfe yt the said John Oge Campbell shall not have ye said Cattle taken from him by any who shall pretend a writ by law, or otherways as mony due to ym by the said Rob Roy any manner of way.

Chris. Russell

Rob Roy returned to Craigrostan in vengeful mood, gathered his men, and made a big raid on the grazings of Duntreath Castle above Strathblane. Grahame of Killearn wrote at once to Mungo Graham of Gorthie, Montrose's chamberlain, asking him to get a new punitive order from Cadogan, since Robison had failed them:

Killern 11 April 1716

Sir – I was enquyring about Rob Roy's story, which is, as it comes from his own friends, that on Wednesday last he was informed that a partie was to be sent from Finlarig to his house, he sent of ane express immediatelie to his people in Craigrostan to come as quicklie to his assistance as they could and thought fitt to absent himself when the party came because he found he had not force to resist. The party caryed off his whole plenishings and goods, except a few wild beasts that ran away with the fyring, and burnt all his houses save one little barn. But Robert was not able to bear all this without attempting some revenge. Therefore with a few of these he could gett readiest, his Craigrostan folks not having tyme to come up, he fyred from some rocks and passes upon the partie and killed two or three, and has wounded ten or twelve, ther's lykwise one of his killed and several wounded, but all the booty was carried off. This is the most distinct account of the matter that I have yet gott. Now its certain this partye has not been commanded by P. Robison, for they returned to Finlarig: if it had been Robison he would have marched to Glengyle sae that you see that concert failed, wherefor its most necessar' you consider hou to make a new application to the Generall to take a course with these villains whose insolence is not to be born any longer. They have just now stolen a good deall of sheep of the Muir of Blane above Duntreth, and daylie threatens more mischief to all the country.

The second temptation

Rob Roy knew well that hard times lay ahead for Mary and him. The government's offer of amnesty expired in two months, after which, if he had not surrendered, he would be hunted – the troops were available. But to whom could he as an outlaw make submission? Certainly to no officer of the government while Montrose held power. His best hope was some great man's protection. He could no longer look to Breadalbane. Atholl was a Whig and Argyll Montrose's general. To whom could he turn? Montrose supplied the answer. His work at court to smear Argyll as a Jacobite sympathizer was bearing fruit. He had used Cadogan's witness to show that Argyll had been lenient to rebels, and to suggest that with Breadalbane as kinsman he had been early acquainted with Jacobite plots, with which he was not out of sympathy, thus earning Mar's light touch at Inveraray. Argyll was now opposing the ministry's trial of Scots rebels at Carlisle, damning it as unjust and a flagrant breach of the Treaty of Union.[18] His skill and courage at Sheriffmuir, which had helped to save the throne, were belittled by Whigs ignorant of battle. He was dismissed from his command in favour of Cadogan. Montrose, still not satisfied, wanted Argyll forfeited. Rob Roy could help to that end and must have his price, were it not that his personal hostility overrode approach by a Graham. It must be made by another, and Montrose prevailed upon Cockburne of Ormiston to act.

Cockburne in May sent an express to Rob Roy at Craigrostan, proposing a meeting at Cramond Brig on the Almond Water, five miles west of Edinburgh. Rob took the bait, for no chance of his rehabilitation could be let slip. Mary had now given birth to Robin Og. After the christening, he went to Cramond and made a reconnaissance, found no trap, and sent a gillie into Edinburgh. Cockburne came. According to Rob Roy's written word, the Lord Justice Clerk tried to suborn him into false witness of Argyll's treason, offering life and fortune in exchange.[19]

Rob concealed his revulsion and heard him out. Mary and his five boys could not go on living the way they were. Nor he himself. They had been living a wretched half-life, and worse times would be coming. If Craigrostan were theirs again, all would emerge from dark to light, as if to a new day. The chance of winning back his rightful place and honour, offered by a Jacobite success, had been destroyed at Sheriffmuir by Campbell of Argyll – and yet here was offered again as though fate were insisting. Such far-out chances almost never recurred. To regain all that was lost, he need only bring down his clan's ancient enemy. Only a fool would say no.

Cockburne gave him all the leads, with which he was already familiar. Since King William's death, most great men of the State and Army had sounded out the Pretender at one time or another. Surely Red John had been involved? Mar last year had given express orders that Inveraray should not be burned. Surely there was collusion? After Sheriffmuir, Red John had held his hand against the rebel clansmen. Was there not here some ground for the charge of collaboration? There was more of the kind. Rob was reminded that MacCailein Mor was a man every MacGregor should hate. But Rob could not. This Red John of the Battles

had broken Mar by self-disregarding courage – had put trust
in his light and given all. Rob honoured the man. Cockburne's
crookedness reminded him that the Lord Justice Clerk would not
be here without strong-arm men in waiting, and that arrest would
follow a too blunt refusal. He dissembled, letting Cockburne
understand that he had the evidence needed, and might produce
it on return to Inversnaid.[20] The two parted, each with a ray of
hope in his heart – for Rob had seen a way to better himself.

Cockburne, like Montrose and most highly placed men, knew
of the Highlanders' ambition for land, but not that the motive
differed from theirs – hence their difficulty in understanding
Highlanders of Rob Roy's quality. The close social communities of the glens required of their people an essential virtue,
trustworthiness, without which their way of life could not hold.
While everyone including Rob might fall short and temporize,
men of clan family like Rob Roy were deeply imbued with an
abhorrence of treachery. This virtue was buttressed by a second
that came naturally to hill-peoples – superiority to want.[21] Despite
general poverty and recurrent starvation, they were indifferent
to worldly riches, even scornful of luxuries, yet their unstinted
hospitality was a by-word among travellers. Land-loving as they
were, the Highlanders had no spurring ambition for power and
money, hence were not corruptible by such as Cockburne.

The men of great Lowland estate could bring themselves on
occasion to fight and die for religious convictions or political
beliefs, but lived divorced from the people, unable to bridge
the social gulf as Rob Roy could from his life in the clan lands.
They were careless of the plight of the lower orders. They turned
a cold eye on men, women, and children, whom they considered
public trash, without human rights, and not like cattle to be held
in some esteem. Rob Roy was a more civilized man than the lords
of his day in one important respect. His concern for the common
man was unfeigned. He had lived as they did. He could not have
brought himself to inflict on people the inhumanities approved by
men of power.

The greatest of the Highland landlords shared in that disregard
for the Lowland workers, and for the same reasons. The earl
of Mar, while Secretary of State, had been one of Scotland's
bigger coal-owners, employing – like Atholl, Argyll, Gordon of
Aberdeen, Lothian, and many another – miners as slaves, who
were served at the coal-face by women and children of four
years and upwards. The miners had to pay from their own
pittance the women who bore the coal to the surface. They

worked twelve hours a day and more below ground for six days a week without holidays. All were bound for life and transferable with the property. Insubordinate miners were scourged and put in iron collars chained to the pit-props, and protesting women tied by the hands to the gin-horse's neck, being thus forced to run backwards before the horse round the gin. A woman's daily work at the shaft-stairs equalled the carrying of a hundredweight from Loch Lomond to the top of the Ben. The girl children of eight or ten carried the same weight over shorter distances. The women developed 'a peculiar type of mouth . . . wide, open, thick-lipped, projecting equally above and below . . . like savages . . . they cried like children under their load.'[22]

When Rob Roy showed a warm heart for the poor, and went out of his way to help, men like Montrose and Cockburne thought him stupid, and so too on his rejection of bribes for betrayals. Nor could they appreciate that in Rob Roy's 'lawless' mind, as in the common people's, the king's law was not identified with justice. An ideal of justice informed the law – but the laws of the time were made and interpreted by privileged men for their own advantage. While justice had men's respect, no respect could be extended to a legal interpretation that led to cruelties and rewards for perjured evidence. Rob Roy therefore interpreted the law for himself, and was named a barbarian by Montrose, but he was not so named by the common people.

Rob turned the Cramond Brig trial to the best advantage. His Grace the Duke of Argyll might be out of office in London, but in Argyll MacCailein Mor was God; to him he would submit.

The amnesty required a surrender of arms. Rob Roy had no intention of giving these up and negotiated in advance with Alexander Campbell of Fonab, who was still Argyll's right-hand man. It may be inferred that Rob informed them both of the Cramond meeting, for Fonab advised Rob to report at Inveraray with forty or fifty men, which he did in June – Fonab was a man to be trusted. They came armed with the most ancient, blunt, and rusty weapons that Clan Gregor could find, but Fonab's keen eyes saw numbers only. He gave Rob a signed paper declaring Argyll's protection for Rob Roy and all his men, and after that brief ceremony there followed several days of feasting at Inveraray, where the Gregarach were honoured guests of Clan Campbell.[23]

Rob Roy returned to Inversnaid, for Mary and the younger boys were dearly wanting a home of their own. He rebuilt the old house, and having seen them installed raised a force of two hundred men.[24] For his own protection he was attended constantly by a bodyguard of ten or twelve picked gillies and wore a steel plate in his bonnet. All that summer his men ranged undisturbed over the lands of Montrose and his neighbours, levying black mail, lifting stock, and using the granaries as their own. Cadogan and Montrose were in London, and the former's command in Scotland had been taken by Lieutenant General George Carpenter. Grahame of Killearn implored Montrose to retaliate, and at last this was done. A tale survives that Glengyle House was burned during the summer by a company from Finlarig.[25] There is no hard evidence that this happened, but Montrose returned to Scotland in September, and prepared to make an end of Rob Roy.

The second burning

The army's assistance was assured by the latest of Rob's exploits. The Finlarig garrison had arrested one of Clan Gregor, found lurking nearby and illegally bearing arms. The dragoons detailed to escort the prisoner to Perth were ambushed by Rob Roy at Loch Earnside, and after a short, sharp fight disarmed. He freed the prisoner and dismissed the escort. Its officer was later court-martialled.[26] When Montrose asked Carpenter for an expedition against Craigrostan, he co-operated with alacrity.

On 27 September, three detachments of troops, each of eighty men, were sent out from Glasgow, Stirling, and Finlarig.[27] Their movements were timed to bring them all on foot to Inversnaid at 5 a.m. on the day appointed. The Glasgow and Stirling companies met at Buchanan House under command of Major Green of Hotham's regiment. They were attended by Graham of Gorthie, and Grahame of Killearn as Sheriff-depute of Dunbartonshire, who were to guide them up Loch Lomondside. They started out around eight o'clock at night, for they had sixteen miles to cover on bad tracks, which over the last seven along the base of Ben Lomond would be very hard to follow in the dark. Surprise was essential, and hopes of catching Rob Roy at dawn were high.

The parties had not long been gone when the skies opened. Torrential rain drove across the loch all night. The bridgeless burns rose in spate and caused great delays. It was broad daylight before the bedraggled companies won through Craigrostan to Inversnaid, chilled to the bone, the water squelching out of their black shoes. Rob Roy had reports of their coming before they ever entered Craigrostan. He had withdrawn his men up the hillside to the shelter of crags and bushes, and the women and children over to Arklet. Major Green and his troops found nothing but empty houses. Rob Roy had too few men at Inversnaid to attack 240 soldiers, but made his presence known, perhaps to draw them off. The troops shot at them – with what effect was never known.[28] The MacGregors then fired a volley that brought down several men and killed a grenadier. Major Green dared not risk an attack up the hillside through crags and trees. Instead, Killearn and Gorthie directed his men to Rob Roy's house. This they put to flames with all it contained. For the second time in six months Rob Roy was left homeless.

He returned briefly to Loch Katrine to join Mary and their three younger sons, Duncan aged twelve, Ranald ten, and Robin Og only a few months. The two elder, James twenty-one and Coll eighteen, may have accompanied their father from Sheriffmuir onwards. Rob could not now settle with his family at Loch Katrine, or anywhere else in its neighbourhood. His very presence had become a danger to the clan. Repeated military incursions threatened them all. Montrose and Carpenter, having been balked and discomfited, would try again while troops were available, this time seeking wider reprisals. Rob had no arable ground on which to feed his family, nor stock at pasture. His only support could be rieving, which made reprisals on the district that harboured his band still more certain. In these circumstances he resolved to withdraw from home ground and seek refuge where safety was assured, and that could no longer be in Breadalbane (Iain Glas died in March 1717), but with MacCailein Mor. Gregor Ghlun Dhubh no doubt added his persuasions, if they were necessary. His uncle's presence had become for all his people a liability. Much as they admired his revolt against Whig authority, sympathized with his misfortune, and liked him personally, their approval could no longer be open.

Rob relieved them of his presence early in October. Argyll agreed with Fonab that he be given leave to build a stone house at seven hundred feet in upper Glen Shira.[29] This glen lay five miles above the head of Loch Shira, the bay of Loch Fyne on which Inveraray was sited. Rob moved in with six gillies and built the house with a living room and byre separated by a wattled partition,[30] at the very edge of a steep bank that fell fifty feet to the Shira burn. (Its ruined walls remain there today.) The bank below the house was wooded in alder, oak, rowan, and sycamore. No more safe and secluded spot could well have been found. Apart from the one easy approach up Glen Shira from Inveraray, the only access went east and west by empty straths through eighty square miles of trackless hills. Yet by these routes he could reach Loch Awe in two hours and Loch Lomond's head in four.

Rob and his men brought in corn and cows. Fish could be had at Inveraray, for Loch Fyne at that time abounded in herring shoals. The Campbells swore that their sea-loch was three parts fish to one of water.[31] In Loch Shira alone, nearly five hundred boats were out fishing in summer, when many of the four-man crews lived aboard. They worked at night. By day they either slept aboard under a sail-cloth, which was stretched over the boom, or repaired nets to pipe-music and song. At evening they sailed out to form a line six hundred fathoms long, uniting their nets, which were buoyed with blown bladders. The gutted fish were salted in barrels for export to Glasgow, Dumbarton, and Stirling. Rob's men could be sure of fresh fish until November, but the duty on salt had been set so high that no one could afford any longer to buy salt for winter mart or export of fish unless he gave a bond to the Clyde Customs, which allowed him duty-free salt on condition that he later produced the cured fish in evidence of use, and returned any salt unused. This bureaucratic insanity was now breeding a big new smuggling trade between Argyll and Ireland, where salt was duty-free. Rob Roy most likely tried for a share in that – he was well liked at Inveraray.

At Glen Shira, there could be no adequate provision for Mary and the children. She remained by Loch Katrine, and later stayed with her nephew Donald at Monachyle Tuarach. The *Argyll Records* have no mention of her save that Rob 'went to Balquhidder now and again to see his wife'.[32] It would appear that the younger boys were sent to school at Acharn by the foot of Loch Tay, because Rob presented the school with a bronze bell, which he carried off from the kirk at Balquhidder.[33] Taymouth having been his mother's country, the boys could then be boarded with relatives.

Rob used the Glen Shira house during the next several years, but for no more than a week or two at a time. There is record that he built a fank (or fold) to which he drove cattle and sheep lifted from Montrose, selling them later at trysts in the west and north-west Highlands.[34] Glen Shira for Rob was a very useful marketing base and occasional bolt-hole. Here he was safe from all enemies. But he had no intention of making this a family home, or forsaking his clan's land, or leaving Montrose at peace. Meantime, he had Mary and the boys to look after, so tightened his belt, and set out to make the best provision he could.

CHAPTER EIGHTEEN

THE DUEL WITH MONTROSE
1716–17

Chapelarroch

R OB ROY reappeared in Craigrostan at Hallowe'en, when the hill-tops close by the glens were flickering with bonfires. The young people would be dancing up there, while their elders down at Inversnaid were fixing rowan branches at their doors to ward off witchcraft. This was the old Celtic celebration of *Samh'uinn*, the 'peace fires' lit in thanks for harvest and in hope of an untroubled winter.[1] Rob Roy had no illusions about his own prospects that winter. He came back in fighting form, determined to accept Montrose's challenge. He would make that man understand that it paid better to accept Rob Roy's annual levies than to keep on slashing at him.

He found that his reputation had suffered in his absence. His disbanded men had gone marauding on their own in Stirlingshire. Without the discipline imposed by his leadership, some had run through the gamut of violence, the blame for which had been laid on himself. He brought the roughnecks under control, but the blood-money now put on his head was attracting broken men, so that he had to move with more circumspection than ever. For this and his clan's sake, he had to deny himself any settled abode or township life, and take instead to living in caves and fast places along Loch Lomondside and Loch Katrine. To these he called in his men to a number of forty or fifty, and planned a new coup. He needed one that would singe Montrose's periwig and set up Mary and the boys and his whole band for the winter. Providence seemed to lend an ear and give the occasion.

Every year at the November term, Montrose's rents fell due and were collected from his tenants during the course of the month by Grahame of Killearn. These were in large part paid in kind, the remainder in money. The money rents for the Menteith estate amounted to £1000 sterling,[2] one half of which was this year to be collected at Chapelarroch on the Kelty Water, where Grahame had a farmhouse on the road between Drymen and Gartmore. It was named from a ruined chapel close by, dedicated to the Virgin Mary. He would be there for two or three nights from 20 November. Rob Roy elicited the detail with customary skill, and planned his descent. He lay low, and let it be known in Menteith that he had fled for refuge to Ireland.

At nine o'clock at night on the 20th, when most of the tenants had gone to Chapelarroch, paid their dues, and were still there at the whisky, and Grahame still at table was accepting the last of the money from one or two late-comers, they heard a cry of alarm from one of their number outside. The windows were smashed in and guns presented by bonneted figures. An instant later, the door was flung wide and in walked Rob Roy with his bodyguard, all with cocked pistols. Grahame with great presence of mind had seized the moment of commotion, between the cry and the candles' guttering, to sweep his books and money into a bag and throw them up to the loft.

Rob walked to the table and asked, with a show of courtesy, if the rent-collection had gone well. Grahame tried to bluster. Rob cut him short. He told him he would be taken into the hills and held for ransom. Graham of Gorthie would too, when he laid hands on him, and had burnt his house as Gorthie had burnt his. The loft was then searched and the cash and books were found. Rob sat down at table, counted out some £3000 Scots, and issued fresh receipts to the tenants signed by himself in the duke's name. Finally, he made Grahame write out a ransom note to Montrose, who was living now in his splendid new house, built that year in the Drygate of Glasgow, near the Cathedral.

Chapellarroch, Nov 19th (sic), 1716

May it please your Grace, – I am obliged to give your Grace the trouble of this, by Robert Roy's commands, being so unfortunate at present as to be his prisoner. I refer the way and manner I was apprehended, to the bearer, and shall only, in short, acquaint your Grace with the demands, which are, that your Grace shall discharge him of all soumes he owes your Grace, and give him the soume of 3400 merks for his loss and damages sustained by him, both at Craigrostan and at his house Auchinchisallen; and that your Grace shall give your word not to trouble or prosecute him afterwards; till which time he carries me, all the money I received this day, my books and bonds for entress, not yet paid, along with him. The soume I received this day, conform to the nearest computation I can make before several of the gentlemen, is

£3227. 2sh. 8d Scots, of which I gave them notes, I shall
wait your Grace's return, and ever am,
            Your Grace's most obedient, faithful,
                        humble servant,
                        John Grahame.

Rob despatched the letter by one of Grahame's servants. Its tem-
perate terms are notable by comparison with twentieth-century
barbarities. He had no intention of taking Grahame's life, so
made no threat of it, even though it weakened his demand. The
omission would not escape Montrose.

Having wound up his accounting at Chapelarroch, Rob conducted his prisoner through the pass of Aberfoyle and up the
shores of Loch Ard to Stronachlachar, where he ferried him on
to the nearest islet of Loch Katrine; Grahame was throughout
treated with firm courtesy, and warned only of rough handling if
pursued. It is unlikely that the islet had more than a herdsman's
hut, but if Grahame suffered from the November cold he made
no complaint – he had inflicted worse on Mary MacGregor.

Montrose received Grahame's note on the following night, 21
November – and not just with surprise. He was stung to the
quick. After questioning the messenger, he had such a head
of steam to let off that he sat down and let fly five long
letters – to Viscount Townsend, Secretary of State for the
Northern Department; Robert Pringle, Under-Secretary of State
at Edinburgh; and General Carpenter at Montrose. Three of these
were to Townshend, but only the most concise was sent. One of the
others, rejected as wordy, says so much in confirmation of Rob's
activities and of Montrose's point of view, that it must be given
in full (after omission of two paragraphs of polite preamble).[3]

                        Glasgow, the 21st November, 1716

My Lord, – ...
Mr Graham of Killearn, who has the charge of my estate
in the Highlands (the same person to whom the Earll of
Mar wrote a letter, in winter last, to debauch my tennents
to the service of the Pretender, which I had the honour to
read to His Majesty), haveing gone into that countrey on
Munday last, as he uses allways to do at this season of the
year, to gather in my rents, as he was in a countrey house
with some of my tennents about 9 o'clock the same night,
was attackt by Rob Roy, that notorious robber, with a
party of ruffians whom he has still kept about him since

the late Rebellion, and was carryed away prisoner by these barbarians to the hills, with what money he had gott, his books, papers, and bonds to a considerable value, and is now in their hands to suffer all the injurys that a desperate wicked crew of bandits shall be pleas'd to put upon him without my being able to foresee any manner of way how its possible to rescue him.

That you may the better comprehend this matter, I must inform you that this Rob Roy has of a long time putt himself at the head of the Clan M'Gregor, a race of people ever obnoxious to all governments for their robberys, depredations, and murders. From the revolution to this moment, this fellow has taken every opportunity to appear against the Government, but allways with ane eye to rob the countrey, never having done ane single action of good service to the party he pretended to favour; and he has actually committed more villanys and ravages in the countrey than all the other Highlanders have done. Some three or four years ago, haveing contracted a great many debts, he left his usuall residence, and went some 12 or 16 miles furder into the Highlands, and putt himself under the protection of the Earll of Breadalbin. When my Lord Cadoggan was in the Highlands, he ordered his house at that place to be brunt, which obleiged him to return to the same place from whence he first came, being hard by my estate at Buchanan, in a rugged inaccessible countrey of about five or six miles in length, upon the side of Lochlomond, full of rocks and precipices. Being intended to make this place his residence, where all his friends and followers were, he judged very rightly that it was possible for all this that he might be surprised, especially by the Highland independent companys if they should be hearty in it. For this reason, no sooner was my Lord Cadoggan in Edinburgh in his way to London, but he and Collonell Campbell of Finnab, commandr of one of the said Highland independent companys, so contrived it as that this notorious rogue, with about 45 of his followers, went to Inverary, made a sham surrender of their arms to the Collonell as one of His Majesty's officers, and notwithstanding that he was actually attainted by the Parliament a good while before, he was received by him as a commoner, and he and all his men had particular protections given them sign'd by the Collonell.

After two or three days very kind intertainment given him at Inverary by the Collonell and some others their, he return'd to Craigrostan (that's the name of the Countrey I mentioned before he was now to reside in), when it was not long before he had occasion to give proofs for the sincerity of his submission, for in a very short time after, he appeared hostile at the head of about 200 men well armed in opposition to the King's troops who hapned to be in the countrey thereabouts in executing orders. At one of these times he actually attack't a party, rescued a prisoner from them, and made the party submitt to him, for which the officer has been since broke as being defective in his duty for not making a good defence. All this time his partys were going down into the low countrey, pillageing and plundering the countrey people, taking from them their money, or what else they thought convenient for them; my tennents being their next neighbours had their share of this.

When I came to Scotland and was informed of these disorders, I applied to Generall Carpenter for troops, and he went very cheerfully into it. Three partys of 80 men each were ordered to march in the night from Glasgow, Stirling, and Finlayrig (a house of the Earl of Breadabine's, where a garrison now is), in order to surprise him and all his followers in their houses before break of day. It hapned most unluckily that the night apoynted for the execution was so prodigiously rainy that it was impossible for the party to come in time to the stations appoynted them. So the villains, by the favour of the daylight, had the opportunity to perceive the party's marching, and so escaped very narrowly. When they saw themselves out of danger they had the impudence to fire upon the King's troops from the rocks and precipices – killed one granadeer, and hurt some others. This resistance gave the Commandr of the party, Major Green, of Sir Charles Hotham's regiment, sufficient provocation to burn Rob Roy's house, which accordingly was done. Mr Graham, now their prisoner, being my deputy-sheriff of the countey, went along with the Major when all these things were transacted, as was likewise another Mr Graham, who has the charge of my affairs in the low countrey, whom I had directed to attend the Major with the party he had carryed from Glasgow. Rob Roy was pleased to say that now he wanted only this other gentleman to be fully revenged of the injury they had done him, and that he would make it his bussiness to find him out likewise, at least he would burn his house, which he may do, indeed, if he has a mind to it.

I can't help saying that from severall observations I have made, this rogue Rob Roy, however obnoxious he is both to the King and countrey, has his friends, but I hope the good time will come when all these dark mysterys shall come to light. In the meantime I hope I shall be able to offer a plan to His Majesty, when I shall have the honour to see him, how to bring the Highlands of Scotland immediately to be in the hands of His Majesty, that these people may be no longer a tooll in the hands of any subjects to disturb his Majesty's Government.

The letter finally sent to Lord Townshend differs from the above in two points: one quotes his money-rent for Menteith as 'above a thousand pounds sterling', and the other proposes the building of a barrack in Clan Gregor land (at Inversnaid):

I had my thoughts before of proposing to government the building of some barracks, as the only expedient for suppressing these rebels, and securing the peace of the countrie; and in that view I spoke to Genll. Carpenter, who has now a scheme of it in his hands; and I am persuaded that will be the true method for restraining them effectually; but, in the meantime, it will be necessary to lodge some of the troops in these places, upon which I intend to write to the Generall.

At no time did Montrose express any intention of ransoming Grahame. He expressed concern to Townshend, but drew the line at parting with money:

Mr Grahame, of Killearn, being my deputy-sheriff in that countrie, went along with the party that marched from Stirling; and, doubtless, will now meet with the worse treatment from that barbarous people on that account. Besides that he is my relation, and that they know how active he has been in the service of the government – all which, your Lordship may believe, puts me under very great concern for the gentleman, while, at the same time, I can forsee no manner of way how to relieve him, other than to leave him to chance and his own management.

Montrose was fully aware that any note delivered to Clan Gregor would reach Rob Roy fast. He left his kinsman not to chance, but cold-bloodedly to Rob Roy's mercy. And that murderous barbarian was inferred to have none.

After a few days' waiting on Loch Katrine, while Montrose's horsemen were galloping with expresses in every direction except the Trossachs, Rob Roy deduced what was happening and moved Grahame daily to new hideouts. At the end of a week, he realized that Grahame had no money-value to Montrose, and accordingly had him taken to Kirkintilloch, where he was given back his books and accounts (Rob had no meanness in him), and released on a Sunday night. He had twelve miles to walk to Killearn, and apparently walked with a thankful heart. When he turned up in Glasgow at the duke's Drygate house on Monday night, bathed and reclothed, he had no word of complaint of his treatment to offer his master, who might have wanted that for ammunition.

Manhunt

General Carpenter replied to Montrose next day. Although he commanded all government troops in Scotland, he was extremely reluctant to send any units into the winter hills, where Highland guerillas could run rings round them. He had his dignity, and no wish to be made to look a fool. He sent Montrose a diplomatic letter of vague assurance, but could not restrain a satirical aside on his Grace's concern for Grahame:

Montrose, November 26, 1716

My Lord, – I rec'd here the honour of your Grace's letter of the 21st, and am truly concern'd for the misfortune Mr Graham is fallen into, and also for your Grace's loss; but believe Mr Graham's condition gives you much more trouble. I hope to wait of your Grace att your house before I returne to Edinburgh; and if I can contribute in any manner to serve you in this affair will do itt with pleasure. I think some method should be contrived, if possible, to take or clear the country of such a notorious robber and his gang. 'Twill be difficult to gett him any way but by bribing one of his followers to betray him to a Party, otherwise he will always be too cunning and nimble for soldiers under armes.

While I have the honour to command his Majestys Troops
in this Country, they shall be putt in every proper place for
his service, and the security of the Country from rebells, and
robbers, in which I will have great regard to your Grace's
opinion and recommendation, of which when I have the
honour to see you
> I am, my Lord
>> Your Grace's most humble and obedient servant,
>>> Geo. Carpenter

But Carpenter was writing to a minister of the Crown, himself
experienced in the suavities used to put off unwelcome applicants
for aid. Montrose was not to be fobbed off thus like any
commoner. Knowing too that Carpenter had been recalled to
London, and could have no intention of meeting him as promised
he felt the more exasperated at his slippery wriggle. He determined
to pin down Carpenter's acting commander, Brigadier Preston,
by sending Mungo Graham of Gorthie to meet him face to face.
Gorthie was the ideal emissary. He had been forced to flee his
own home out of fear for his safety. Rob Roy was loose with God
knew how many armed men, had sworn to burn down his house,
and might well kidnap him into the bargain. Gorthie was now in
Glasgow, fuming at government inaction. Montrose briefed him
for the mission to Edinburgh, and wrote again to Townshend:

28 November 1716

My Lord, – [Here follow three paragraphs recapitulating
Killearn's capture and release, then:–]
  Tho' this affair has ended much better than I could have
expected, yet your lordship will easily judge that their's
ane absolute to have some of the King's troops lodged in
convenient places near the mountains, for the security of
the countrey below, which must otherwise lye exposed to
all the insults that may be reasonably expected from the
neighbourhood of that lawless race of people. For this
purpose I'm resolved to send a gentleman to Edinburgh to
discourse with Brigadier Preston, who now commands in the
absence of Lietenant-Generall Carpenter, and to consider of
the most proper methods to be taken for that service.

Gorthie's mission bore little fruit. Preston confirmed that the
plan for a barracks at Inversnaid had been taken up. The Board
of Ordnance would be responsible for choosing the site, which

they were now surveying, together with sites for three others at
Kilwhimen (Fort Augustus), Bernera in Glenelg, and Ruthven in
Strath Spey. He promised that Inversnaid would have priority.4
Preston, however, managed to avoid committing his regular troops
to the hills.

Montrose at this deadlock had glad news of the king's support.
Lord Townshend wrote:

Whitehall, December 1, 1716

My Lord, – Tho' I have been hitherto hindered from
acknowledging the honour of your Grace's letter of the
21 past, which came to my hands by a flying pacquett, yet
I did not faill to lay it before HRH, who hes the utmost
resentment of that insolent attempt of Rob Roy's of which
your Grace gives account and I have HRH's Directions to
assure your Grace that he will very heartily goe into anie
Measure that shall be judged effectual to suppress that
Robber and those who follow him, and to restore the
Peace and quiet of those parts which have been infested
and disturb'd by him, and I have by order of HRH writt to
Lieutenant-General Carpenter that he should lose no time
in concerting with your Grace, and putting into Execution
what may be most proper for this end, which I hope will
have its desired effect to the satisfaction of HRH, and of
all his Majestie's Servants.
 I am, with greatest respect, My Lord,
  Your Grace's most obedient humble servant,
   Townshend.

Carpenter arrived back in Scotland to be faced with Gorthie's plea
and the king's command. He searched his mind how to simulate
action yet leave a way of escape. Rob Roy would defeat any
hunting parties; of that he was sure. He must shift responsibility
away from the army. Why not to the volunteers, and to Montrose
himself? He had found the answer, and wrote to Montrose from
Perth on 9 December: ' ... No method can be so effective as
ordering the three Independent Companies to such place and on
such parties as your Grace shall think proper for that purpose,
and if the parties from the Regiments can be assisted to intercept
him and his gang, they shall be posted wherever your Grace shall
judge convenient; but for scouring the Highlands, I think none so
nimble and hopeful of succeeding as those independent companies
who know the countries, and are used to such expeditions. If your

Grace approves of this, I request that your Grace will be pleased
to send me a Scheme . . . if in the meantime your Grace would
have any companies or parties of the Regiments quartered in any
Towns or Villages, I wish to have your Grace's Commands, and
if near the hills it should be either a place tenable, or a number
sufficient to secure themselves from any insult or surprise, with
a provision made for fuel, candle, and other necessaries in that
cold season.'

He added a postscript: 'The most likely method to take Rob
Roy, and I think sure, would be to issue a proclamation with a
Pardon and Reward for any one or more who should deliver him
up, with a little care to have severall of those proclamations sent
to the places he frequents.'

Montrose had grown more and more incensed as the days
passed, and this ignorant effusion from Carpenter roused him
to fury. No man would betray Rob Roy, as he had learned from
Killearn. His own people liked him, God help them, and though
there were plenty of broken men around the south Highlands, not
one dared say a word, lest he die by the dirk. The Independent
Companies were no better, in Montrose's experience. There was
Campbell of Fonab, one of the best soldiers of the kingdom,
a commander as resolute as any general could wish, and yet
he too turned a friendly eye on Rob Roy, and gave what
protection he could. Montrose told Carpenter that, and more.
Rob Roy was active again over all Montrose's lands, pillaging the
girnels and taking all else he needed from Montrose's neighbours.
Montrose dared no longer occupy Buchanan House for fear of
molestation. Killearn and Gorthie had both come into Glasgow
with their families, and now even the Lord Justice Clerk, Sir
Adam Cockburne of Ormiston, had been reduced to writing to
him on 15 December 1716, confessing that he was 'frightened to
come by the Stirling Road on account of Rob Roy's kidnapping
way'. That this should be happening on Montrose's own lands,
while Argyll laughed at him from the other side of the Firth of
Clyde, goaded him more than anything else. He made complaint
of Argyll's harbouring rebels to the Privy Council and damned
Fonab to Carpenter.

General Carpenter requested Campbell of Fonab (who was no
longer a regular army officer) to come to Edinburgh Castle for
consultation.5 In some stern, straight talk he told him that Argyll's
best interest, as well as his own, would be served by withdrawing
protection from Rob Roy. He then wrote somewhat smugly of this
interview to Montrose on 15 December, assuring him that Fonab

'will exert either to take him or drive him out of the country'. He followed this with another on Christmas Day, adding, 'I was this day told, tho' not from sure hands, that Rob Roy was gone away. Finab went hence, seeming very earnest to take him; so I am of opinion he is, or will soon be, catch't or oblig'd to go of. I promis'd to pay £50 if he could be taken.'

Montrose must have wondered whether Carpenter was assuming this confidence just to placate him, or was really as naïve as a country girl. Probably both. This came of employing a general from south of the Border. Carpenter knew too little of the country or its people. Montrose had only himself to blame, having ousted Argyll. Fonab was Campbell's man; he had not the slightest intention of troubling Rob Roy, who would now be forewarned. If Rob had indeed 'gone away', it was cause for alarm rather than congratulation. He would be up to some more mischief.

Montrose was learning. Rob Roy had gone to ground – under Fonab's wing in Glen Shira. But not for long. He was soon back at Portnellan, from which he renewed his raids on Menteith, granting as before receipts in Montrose's name for grain taken from girnels. He never lodged long in any one place, rarely occupied a house, and kept constant patrol over the hills.

Montrose was beside himself at the ill news. He determined to organize and send out a posse of his own men, for his name was being brought into ridicule. Rob Roy and he had for some time become the talk of the Court. Ministers of the Crown, publicly indignant, had expended what sympathy they had for himself, and were privately beginning to enjoy the stories, always at his expense. There seemed never a lack of something new to amuse them. He sent his chamberlain, Graham of Gorthie, to Dumbarton Castle to raise arms for his tenantry. If he sent a big party into the Trossachs and managed to capture Rob Roy where the army had turned tail, his honour would be vindicated, Carpenter abashed, and Argyll humbled. The thought warmed his resolve.

Mungo Graham arrived at Buchanan House in March 1717 with all the muskets and ammunition required. Montrose fixed a date for the expedition, pending which Killearn called in the posse and distributed the arms. This last move was a cardinal error. Rob Roy had instant news of the distribution from scouts. He saw that his best defence was attack, chose a company of his best men, and made a lightning raid. Using proven tactics, he surprised each steading in turn, seized the arms, and made so rapid a move to the next that tenants were unable to warn neighbours and unite. The plan had been made with careful regard to topography, allowing Rob to strike as far south as the Endrick before retiring rapidly to the caves of Loch Katrine.

When the news spread around the country that Rob Roy had heavily restocked his armoury at the king's expense, Montrose had no choice but to take the field himself. He obtained Letters of Fire and Sword, by which he was commissioned to raise a body of foot and horse 'against robbers and seize their persons'. No need was seen to specify the target. Parliament had newly passed an Act of Pardon for those involved in the 'Fifteen rising, 'excepting all persons of the name of Clan Gregor'. The commission named no names, not even Rob Roy's, so that Montrose could be free to attack any clan who gave harbour.

The two contemporary stories of what happened next were oral, and concur in broad outline with the version given to Sir Walter Scott by the grandson of James Stewart, one of Montrose's tenants, who played an important role.

The first encounter came of a chance foray by a troop of horse and foot, who stumbled on Rob Roy's band in the Trossachs woodlands. Alasdair Roy had barely time to prime his gun when Rob gave the word to scatter, but one dragoon picked Rob out and rode at him, backsword swinging. He struck him a blow on the head that should have cleft him to the chin. The steel plate in Rob's bonnet deflected the blade, but the impact struck him to the ground. The dragoon jumped down for the *coup de grâce*. Rob cried out to Alasdair, who swung round and fired. The ball hit the dragoon on the heart.[6]

Montrose led his expedition from Buchanan in April. He had heard rumours of Rob Roy's lurking in Glen Ogle, and headed for Lochearnhead. He chose the hill-route from Aberfoyle to the Trossachs, where he made an excursion up Loch Katrine lest Rob had returned to Portnellan. The houses were empty save for women and children, who stood with angry eyes and refused information. Their impudence incensed Montrose, who ordered the principal house to be fired. Mungo Graham stopped him from fear of reprisals in Menteith. They turned east to Callander, and were moving north by Loch Lubnaig when fortune favoured them. They chanced on a traveller coming south who reported Rob Roy in the clachan of Balquhidder.

Rob had been well aware of Montrose's commission, but his too easy victory in Buchanan had caused him to forget that Montrose, powered by new anger, should no longer be underestimated. Montrose marched through rain and dark to

Balquhidder, discovered the house, and at dawn surprised Rob wrapped in his plaid. Ironically, it was the first time he had slept in a house since leaving Glen Shira four months ago. His arms were bound with a leather belt; he was placed on a horse flanked by dragoons. Montrose's cup was full. The cavalcade set off for Stirling.

Twenty miles south, they had to cross the Forth at Fords of Frew to reach the Stirling road. Night was falling, and the main body of horse went across first to seek some accommodation. The river was swollen, the water icy. Rob's arms were released for his own safety, and he was then remounted behind the strong man of the party, one of Montrose's tenants named James Stewart, to whom he was secured by a leather thong. Unknown to Montrose, Stewart had once received some benefit from the prisoner. At this point there are two versions of the incident, one as likely as the other. The first is that no one had discovered Rob's *sgian ockle* (armpit knife), with which he cut the thong; the other, that he persuaded Stewart by whisper to release it The certain fact is that he suddenly dropped off the horse at midstream, dived, and releasing his plaid swam clear under water. In gathering dark, the plaid drew all the fire and swordcut, while Rob landed well downstream on the north shore and escaped.

Montrose rode up to Stewart when he came ashore, demanded angrily where his prisoner was, and drawing a steel pistol struck him with the butt such a heavy blow to the head that he suffered permanent brain-damage.[8]

From this time onward, Rob Roy became in the public mind a legendary character, whom neither kings, generals, dukes, sheriffs, nor their armies, were able to capture for the gallows, who repaid enemies intent on his death with forbearance, at least in regard to their own lives, who gave to the poor the food and justice their masters withheld, and managed all this with an easy insouciance, which people envied him. The insouciance was far away from the truth – a heavy toll was being taken of Rob's superb constitution and spirit – but the rest was too near the truth for Montrose's liking. He confessed himself beaten and gave up the pursuit.

CHAPTER NINETEEN

THE DUEL WITH ATHOLL
1717–18

*'If your Grace would pleas think of some
sortt of stratagem . . .'*

THE DEFEAT and withdrawal of Montrose brought Rob
unexpected troubles. The king's and the country's interest
in the contest aroused ambitions for his capture in other men,
who had no personal quarrel with him. They were of low and
high degree: men who sought the money on his head, such as
Hanoverian soldiers, or broken men wanting better fortune; and
others who aspired more loftily – to success by ingenuity where
a man as powerful as Montrose had failed, to the challenge to
manly resource felt by the young or unsure, who might earlier
have challenged Rob's swordsmanship, or to lay claim to a fame
that would certainly be theirs, or to gain advantage at Court. In
the latter category, the principal opponent to enter the lists was
John Murray, Duke of Atholl.

The lesser men posed little real threat to Rob Roy in his own
country. They were either fools or ignorant, having no conception
of Rob's complete mastery of his environment. Yet they became by
their number an intolerable nuisance, putting him to great physical
distress. He had as before to abandon houses and townships and
keep shifting from place to place, and therefore had to split
his band into smaller detachments under leaders who operated
independently in winning their sustenance. The tales of his near
captures, narrow escapes, and clever outwitting of manhunters,
abound at this period. They are related with a wealth of detail
bearing the stamp of fiction, yet they also bear witness to the
general truth, which Rob Roy confirmed to Atholl, that he was
sorely harassed and had to accept extremes of hardship.[1] The
pressures were too great to allow him even to spend a night with
Mary at Monachyle Tuarach. An hour or two were the most he
could manage, and then he had to be off. At the Fords of Frew
he had got away on a cold April night, probably in his shirt-tails
unless he was wearing trews. Soaked to the skin, empty of belly,
and with ten miles to cover in dark across Flanders Moss and

the windy Menteith Hills, he had reached Loch Achray chilled to danger-level. The daily repetitions of exposure to cold and wet, the nightly denial of heat or dry bedding for normal recuperation, the meagre, irregular food too often inadequate to generate energy for hard action by day and bodily warmth in sleep, might all be tolerable for short periods, as in droving, or the occasional exigencies of a military campaign, but when prolonged as now for twelve months and more, the toll on body and spirit was too severe. The first sure sign of it was soon to be a lowered resistance to illness. He might have retired to Glen Shira for respite, but declined to let anyone drive him off his own country.

He had open to him one other way to be rid of manhunters. Their death by ball and blade could have been easily managed. Yet despite the pressures he rejected terrorism as a deterrent. All his life long, he had this gaiety of humour, which made it impossible for him to be too intense. He chose instead to play with them as a cat with a mouse, and deter by ridicule or fright. A notorious example was the incursion into Balquhidder by a troop of volunteers from Stirling Castle, apparently with the governor's approval.[2] As soon as they were seen to leave Callander for Strathyre, Rob had the men, women, and children of the clachans warned. The soldiers were met by eager informers, who sent them from one remote glen to another, misdirected them over difficult ground, fed them with alarms and excursions, and kept them so busy marching and counter-marching that after several days of this wild-goose chasing they had had enough. They went out by Loch Earn, sleeping the first night on heather, which Rob Roy's men set alight. In the panic of this rude awakening, one man was killed by the accidental discharge of a musket, and the rest fled, leaving behind their arms, which Rob Roy collected.

While the lesser adventurers could thus be routed, Rob had seemingly no chance against his latest and surely final opponent, the duke of Atholl. In the central and east Highlands, Atholl was as powerful as Argyll in the west. His landholding of two hundred thousand acres was reinforced by equally vast family ramifications that included Stewarts, Robertsons, Ramsays, Moncreiffes, and many other clans. His Jacobite sons, William, Charles, and George, were his Achilles Heel. William his eldest, the Marquis of Tullibardine, had raised much of the clan for the 1715 rising (and would do so again for the '45). His youngest, (by his first wife), Lord George Murray, fought also on all campaigns. John the duke none the less stood by the Whig government both in

1708 and 1715, when he might have toppled them. This political discretion had brought him no power of office. He had received his dukedom four years before Montrose, yet had to watch Montrose's preferment. He had tried to re-establish government trust in 1715 by divulging to Montrose his family's Jacobite confidences, but not surprisingly without result. A man who would betray family trust could hardly be given the Crown's.

Thought had recently been given to the duke's affairs by John Douglas, his law agent in Edinburgh. The duke's domain included Balquhidder, for which he held a viscountcy. The national furore caused by Rob Roy's skirmishings with Montrose, and the king's interest in them, brought Douglas an assurance from Cockburne of Ormiston that his master's capture of Rob Roy would bring the king's favour. He wrote on 16 April 1717, to pass on Ormiston's counsel, with a rider that treachery might serve:[3]

> May it pleas yr Gr, – I send this express by order of my Ld Justice Clerk, earnestly Intreating of yr Gr that you would be pleased to think upon some method whereby Rob Roy McGrigour might be brought to surrender to the Govermtt. If yr Gr could gett fitt people of his own Kidney to make proposals to him so as he might surrender to yr Gr, He sayes It would prove of singular use to yr Gr's Intrest & service, more as he can express att this time.
>
> Yr Gr att the same time will pleas to manadge it cautiously, and tell that you can give noe other assurances, as yt was given to Glengarie.
>
> If this will nott doe wt him, If yr Gr would pleas think of some sortt of stratagem, whereby he might be ceised att any oyr rate.
>
> I would presume to advise yr Gr to engadge in this Interprise, because yt I know to my certain knowledge, It would very much advance yr Gr Intrest above, & doe you more service as I shall express till meeting, and the rather I would engadge in it, becaus that fellow hes so often affronted D: Montrose in the like Interprise . . .
>
> Yr Gr's most obt faithfull humble servt
Jo Douglas.

Atholl promptly acted. He was short of funds, and apart from political advancement wanted repayment by the Treasury of £2464, which he had spent on arming and feeding troops in 1715, and £1000 in compensation for the plunder of Tullibardine by

Mar. Above all he wanted a pardon for his son Lord Charles, who had crossed the Forth with Borlum, been captured at Preston, and been sentenced to be shot (like his brothers William and George he had held King George's commission). Atholl had expressed his concern on these matters time and again in correspondence with his son James,[4] and now to the duke of Roxburghe, who last December had become Secretary of State on Townshend's dismissal. He had yet another reason to act. Ormiston's veiled hint that his taking Rob Roy could be more to his interest than 'he can express att this time' referred, he had soon learned from Douglas, to a new need to clip the wings of that phoenix of the west, Red John of Argyll. He accordingly wrote to Rob Roy, proposing a meeting to discuss his submission.

The idea of a token surrender to Atholl had no small appeal to Rob. His hopes were buoyed by recollection of his submission 22 years earlier. He had kept his bond to spare Atholl's lands ever since. And if Atholl was no Jacobite, at least he had strongly opposed the Treaty of Union. Rob was run down physically and badly needed rest, or at least a settled life with food and shelter and the care of his wife. Mary had become virtually a widow. Their two elder boys had become men; their three younger were suffering from the lack of a proper home life and father, which all five needed; none had enjoyed the social and clan life with the careful parental training that once had been his and Mary's. If only Atholl would let the family settle in Balquhidder, where his nephew Donald and cousin Malcolm held the duke's land, and give them the kind of protection that Argyll had allowed in Glen Shira, some happiness might be theirs at last.

Rob replied requiring a safe conduct. The duke responded by sending it through the hand of his brother Lord Edward.[5] With that assurance, Rob agreed to the meeting, and with six men for bodyguard arrived at Dunkeld House on Monday, 3 June 1717.[6]

The house was superbly sited on the banks of the Tay, opposite the inflow of the river Bran. Close by stood the cathedral, unrepaired since the battle of Dunkeld in 1689. Steeply wooded hills rose above the town and river. The beauty of the place on that June morning, with wood-pigeon cooing and blackbirds singing along the river-banks, was enough to lull suspicion. Leaving his men by the Tay, Rob went in alone.

He offered submission, which Atholl accepted not at all in the spirit in which it was made. Rob's own evidence is that Atholl, like Montrose and Ormiston before him, disclosed a plan for charging Argyll with treason, to which he required Rob's witness.[7] The historian of Clan Gregor, a lady writing in Victorian times, believed the nobility to be all honourable men; she commented, 'Rob Roy possessed many good qualities, but it is impossible to believe his Declaration.' Perhaps she had not read the letter from John Douglas, or else failed to bear in mind, as Atholl did, his agent's advice: 'think of some sortt of stratagem, whereby he might be ceised . . .' or was unaware of the activities of the *Squadrone*, an inner council of Whigs plotting political advantage, one aim of which was to contrive a charge of treason against the man they feared more than any other in Scotland, Red John of the Battles.[8]

Atholl's proposal made sense. Argyll had been re-establishing himself in London, and seemed likely to be given office soon. Walpole was his friend, and though presently in opposition would regain power. Atholl, like Cockburne and other members of the *Squadrone*, had reason to wish Campbell quickly disgraced in the king's eyes. There was no time to lose. Should Argyll win office Atholl's hope of it would be gone. Their two houses had been at feud for generations, each fearful of the other, and ill-will nurtured. Argyll's father had tried to ruin Atholl by fabrication of false evidence. Atholl was unlikely to scruple at hitting back with the same weapon, and since Rob Roy had given him aid at that time, why not now?

Atholl, then, had motive, justification (in his own eyes), and opportunity if Rob Roy would co-operate. And if Rob would not do so voluntarily, he might be screwed to it by threat of the gallows, or if that failed, be made to talk when Cockburne had him lodged in a cellar of Edinburgh Castle. It may be allowed to Atholl that the long torture of anxiety for his son, a brave and handsome lad, who always led his men on foot rather than ride a horse while they had none,[9] had quite unseated his conscience. He had thus far no more understood the man in front of him than Montrose or Cockburne. Rob refused. Atholl felt that he had to spell out the alternatives. Rob was rejecting not only land for the rehabilitation of his family and person, but sacrificing life itself. Rob heard but would not listen. That an outlaw notorious all over the kingdom should not have his price, may have caused the cynical duke a moment's surprise, especially if he had heard from the *Squadrone* of Rob Roy's spying for Argyll in 1715 without knowing it a pretence. He at least knew better than Montrose what personal integrity could mean to a clansman of good family. He regretted that Rob Roy was such a man, but knew in himself none of the anguish that was now Rob Roy's. He had armed men at call, and Rob Roy as prisoner would fetch him the gratitude of the king, £3464 sterling, and the pardon of Lord Charles. So he gave the signal and Rob Roy was seized and bound.

That Rob Roy's arrest was premeditated despite the safe-conduct given appears beyond dispute. A man so expert with his weapons, quick-witted and strong in body, could hardly have been prevented from escaping at least out of the house, unless by preconcerted force and disposal of men. Rob with all his experience of the world's duplicity would never have set foot in Dunkeld House without the duke's parole. That this was given is confirmed in a letter of July by the Reverend H. Murray of Comrie, who states that there were 'several embassies between His Grace and Rob, who at length upon promise of protection came to wait upon the Duke'.[10] The conclusion is that Rob Roy's testimony is true throughout, and Atholl's (that Rob Roy surrendered) false. Rob had come to discuss submission, which is a very different thing.

The Castle of Logierait

Atholl sent Rob under a heavy escort to Logierait, nine miles north of Dunkeld. Logierait had been the duke's Regality Court and was Perthshire's strongest prison. It stood on the hill of Tom na Croich between the confluence of the Tay and Tummel. Under it spread a panorama of wooded meadowland between hills and broad rivers. The splendid scene was not for Rob's enjoyment; he was lodged in the ground-floor guard-room, where although unbound he was without remission under the guards' eyes.

The duke that day rode south to his castle of Huntingtower near Perth (formerly called Ruthven Castle, where James VI had been kidnapped). His elation at Rob's capture was so great, after he had slept on it, that he rode north to Logierait early on Tuesday morning to view his captive, and while there, feeling like a cock on its midden, wrote a series of letters crowing his success to the world, or at least to the world that mattered: the king's principal Secretary of State, the duke of Roxburghe; the duke of Montrose; the Lord Justice Clerk at Edinburgh; and General Carpenter. These and others went off by horse, some direct to Cockburne for onward despatch by flying pacquet (fast mail-boat to London). These few days' delay in awaiting a reply from the king were Atholl's undoing. Rob Roy's men, whom he had left by the Tay, had been faster off their marks than the duke's, and were more efficient in exploiting smaller means.

Neither they nor any others were naïve enough to think for a moment that Rob Roy had surrendered. A letter to the Reverend Robert Wodrow from Edinburgh on 4 June, reports a meeting with Atholl's messenger on the Forth ferry:[11] 'He is come to town just to tell the Justice Clerk that Rob Roy has surrendered himself to the Duke, who has secured him in a castle 6 miles from Dunkeld; he had six men with him but put them off when he surrendered. 'Tis to be feared there is some sad mischief lurking under it. – D. Erskine.' Atholl would at no time admit the obvious truth. The essential letters read thus:[12]

Atholl to Carpenter   Logyraite, June 4th, 1717

Yesterday, Robert Campbell, commonly called Rob Roy, surrendered himself to me, who I sent prisoner to this place, where he is keep't in custody. He says he has not lain three nights together in a house these twelve months. I have wrote to Court that he is now my prisoner.

Lord Justice Clerk to Atholl   Edinburgh, 5th June 1717

My Lord – I cannot express the joye I was in upon Receipt of your Grace's and hopes it shall be luckie that this man has fallen in your Gr/s hands. I dispatcht your Grace's letters by a flying pacquet within less yn ane hour after they came to my hand, and I'm confident it will be most agreeable news at Court.

Yr Gr/ will excuse me to plead that Rob Roy may be brought over hither to the Castle; the prison at Logerait is at too great a distance from the troops, & I have procured a order from Mr Carpenter to the co-manding officer at Perth to send a strong detachment to bring him over. The officer is ordered to concert with your Gr/ the time your Gr/ shall cause delyver the person of Rob Roy to him. He's to use him civilly, meantime to keep a good guard upon him.

I must be allowed to say 'tis fitt Rob Roy be in good keeping for he's in no small danger if his old friends cane possibly be masters of him, and I'm perswaded they will lay all irons in the fire to Rescue him, yrfore I hope yr will be no difficulty proposed agst him coming hither, &

he shall be putt in the castle which is the best prison the King has . . .

Ad: Cockburne

John Douglas wrote to his master that same day, warning him that Cockburne had heard of a possible attempt by Argyll's Campbells to engineer Rob's escape, and so had ordered troops to give escort to Edinburgh, not from mistrust of the duke's arrangements but to aid them.

Somehow or other, both of these letters missed Atholl, who had spend the night of Wednesday 5th at Dunkeld. There is good reason to think that the men now working for Rob's release were not Campbells but Murrays, of the duke's household or his own Jacobite family. All knew of his breach of faith and would not, for the honour of their clan, accept it. The speed and precision with which they acted rules out all else. The instant close watch they placed on the Perth barracks makes clear that Cockburne's letter must have been read by them long before it reached the duke's eyes. The post from Edinburgh (horse-post had started that year for the first time) did not deliver mail en route, but carried only to a town's post-office, where letters were not delivered but collected.[13] The promptness with which they passed messages to Rob Roy, apprising him of the Perth troop-movement before it could be known to the duke of Atholl, and prescribing a method of escape, could not have been contrived unless by someone of quick mind, able to uplift the Dunkeld post, command a fast horseman, and gain immediate access to Logierait. One must look for the answer far above the heads of Atholl's servants. His sons William and George were in France, refusing pardon since Sheriffmuir, James was a Whig and in London, and Charles had been jailed. That left only his brother Edward without an alibi. He may well have been stung by Atholl's broken word. The truth will never now be known.

The bare facts are that the day after his imprisonment, Rob began to cultivate his guards, was allowed to receive a considerable quantity of whisky – a normal custom while a prisoner awaited sentence and had friends outside –[14] and on the morning of Thursday, 6 June, received word that troops had left Perth at 5 a.m. to escort him to Edinburgh. They had 22 miles to march so could reach Logierait by one o'clock, allowing for an hour's delay at Dunkeld ferry. The simple escape plan was immediately put in operation.

The guards had been flattered by the courtesy of their celebrated prisoner. He made excellent company, able to lighten the tedious hours with good talk, tales, song, and music on the chanter. This morning the whisky circulated more freely than before.[15] Around ten o'clock, a guard reported the arrival of Rob Roy's gillie, pleading for a message from the prisoner to reassure his wife and children. The gillie led a horse, and no one observed if it were a light cavalry horse rather than Rob's Highland garron. The head jailer and his men were sober enough to outward appearance, but less careful and observant than duty required. He readily gave Rob permission to scribble a note to Mary, perhaps read it if he could, and allowed Rob to go with it to the door, accompanied by a jailer. Rob spoke a few confidential words to his gillie, pacing back and forth as if searching his mind for more, while moving out of his guard's grasp. He stepped outside to pass the note, when the gillie threw him the reins and Rob sprang to the saddle. He struck in his heels and was off, galloping down to the Aberfeldy road, heading for Loch Tay and home. He had 35 miles to cover, but no pursuit was made. Logierait was, strangely, destitute of horses.

Atholl left Dunkeld at noon that day for Huntingtower. At the ferry over the Tay he was surprised to meet troops on the march, and spoke to their captain. He was astonished to hear that they had come from Perth for Rob Roy, and annoyed that General Carpenter should have taken this step without prior word to himself. The captain showed his orders, signed by Carpenter. Atholl made him turn his company right around and march back to Perth. He went on to Huntingtower and put Carpenter in his place:

Huntingtower, June 6 1717

Sr, – As I was coming from Dunkeld to this place, about two hours since, I mette Captain Lloyd with a party, who showed me his orders from you, but had no letter to me, In which orders he is appointed to receive Robert Campbell alia 'Roy', who is my prisoner att Logerate. Butt since I have wrote to the Duke of Roxburgh principall Secretary of State, to acquaint his majtie that 'Rob Roy' had surrendered himself to me, and that I expected his Majties commands about him, I hope you will excuse my not delivering him untill I have a return with his Majtie's pleasure about him which I doubt not will be in a few days, since I desired my Lord Justice Clerk to send my letter by a flying pacquett to Court.

I am &c. Atholl.

Just one hour after the despatch of that letter, a messenger came
hotfoot from Logierait. Never before had Atholl been so mortified.
Rob's escape was bad enough in itself, but that he should suffer
such humiliation in the eyes of the king – he could imagine the
comtemptuous shrug of the royal shoulders as Roxburghe told
him – be obliged to excuse himself to Carpenter immediately on
top of his snub, try to justify himself to Cockburne and Montrose
– he could see the wintry smile on Graham's face – and explain
away the escape to all others to whom he had so jubilantly written,
roused him to a wrath of ducal dimensions. He rode at once to
Dunkeld to be nearer the scene of inaction. The missing letter
from the Lord Justice Clerk awaited him there, adding fuel to
the flames. That same evening he set up a court of inquiry. As a
first step, he had the quaking head-jailer of Logierait imprisoned
in his own dungeon. He elicited the fact that Rob Roy had received
early news of the troop-movement from Perth. He summoned sixty
armed clansmen and despatched them under the leadership of his
chamberlain, Donald Stewart, with orders to bring in Rob Roy
wherever he might be. Finally, and in secrecy, he sent for Alasdair
Stewart of Innerslanie, his most expert tracker, and sent him on
a lone mission to discover Rob Roy's hiding place. News of his
task was withheld from all Atholl's servants and from the man's
own family.[16]

Next day, Atholl returned to Huntingtower and sat down to
the painful duty of telling the world what had happened. He
tried to shift some of the blame on to the army, as his letter to
Carpenter shows:

Huntingtower, June 7th 1717

Sir, – About an hour after I writ to you yesterday I had the
misfortune to accompt that 'Rob Roy' had made his escape
from the prison he was in at Logyraite yesterday, betwixt
ten and eleven in the forenoon, which was two hours after
I met Captain Lloyd with his party, so that they could have
been of no use, tho' they had marched on, for no doubt he
has had intelligence of their march whenever they came
out of Perth, which I understand was about five o'clock in
the morning, and it was betwixt 12 and one o'clock before
the party reached the boat at Dunkeld where I mett them.
I cannot express how vexed I am for this unlucky affaire,
but I assure you I shall leave no method untryed that can
be done to catch him, & I have already given orders to sixty

of my Highlanders to follow him wherever he can be found, and those that command them, have undertaken to me to bring him in if he keeps to Scotland . . . I send you a copy of the orders I left for guarding him at Logyraite, which I did think was sufficient for one that had surrendered, for I think there can hardly be an instance of any that had done so that made his escape immediately after. I have made the Jailer prisoner, but nothing can retrive this misfortune butt apprehending him, which I am very hopefull may be done, and then I shal acquaint the garrisone of Perth to receive him.

I am &c. Atholl.

His letter to Roxburghe must have been especially galling. Roxburghe on getting his first letter replied (11 June) that he had shown it to the king, who was 'mighty well pleased with his Grace's care and diligence on this occasion, and that His Majesty commanded him to say that he would have written to his Grace himself to thank him for so good a service if it had not been so late.' Atholl followed up his letters by an order of 8 June, publicly displayed throughout Perthshire, requiring 'the apprehension of Robert Campbell, Commonly called Rob Roy, who, having surrendered himself on the 3rd June as prisoner at Dunkeld, was imprisoned at Logyrate . . .'
Carpenter replied defensively to Atholl:

Edenr. June 9th 1717

My Lord, – Yesterday I sent an order for Captn Loyd to come hither, that if he has been to blame he may have his just reward. I have look't over the coppy of my order for the party to march from Perth and find it very exact with a paragraph to lett none know where or on what occasion the Party march't. 't was also sent hence with secrecy and all dispatch possible . . .

Atholl's sons were united in sympathy with Rob Roy. Even his favourite second son, Lord James, a Whig who would succeed to the title since his elder brother William was attainted, wrote from London on 11 June, 'Mr Murray has likewise told me that Rob Roy has surrendered to yr Gr. I wish it may not be fatal to him for by what I can understand he has little reason to expect any mercy.'[17] He had cause for concern. George I had been implacable in executing prisoners taken in England after the rising.

The son's sympathy was shared by so many of Atholl's tenants and followers, that long as the duke's arm might be, the claws refused to unsheath on the quarry. Rob was aided by the respect of all living in Balquhidder and the Trossachs. They were proud of him, and none would betray his whereabouts to Donald Stewart, whose sixty Highlanders searched in vain. Atholl's wisdom in sending Alasdair Stewart on a strictly secret mission was soon proven. Within five days he discovered Rob Roy's hideout, and learned too that he had 'a rose in his thigh, swelled so big that he is unable to walk',[18] but although he sent immediate word to Donald Stewart, two of the Atholl band warned the MacGregors, who had Rob Roy moved in time. He was laid low with 'St Anthony's Fire' (erysipelas), which would be accompanied by very high temperature, headache, and possibly delirium at night. He had to be carried. He was entirely dependent on the goodwill of his own people, and Clan Murray's Jacobites. None failed him.

John Douglas, meantime, had written to Hamilton of Bardowie, whose daughter was married to Gregor Ghlun Dhubh, asking him to persuade Rob Roy to surrender again 'on certain conditions'. Bardowie responded and the two sought a meeting to come to terms and agreement. But Rob Roy would not trust Atholl a second time.[19]

Atholl wrote still hopefully to Lord James:

Dunkeld, June 18 1717

Dear Son   I am so fatigued that I have scarce time to writ to you . . . I acquainted you with his unlucky escape & that I had taken all means to get him again. I have to that end employed ye person you recommended to me in Glen Tilt (Alasdair Stewart) and hope his diligence in the affair will give me a handle to do for him, but he is to go about it in ye most private manner & not to be known that he is gone from me, not even to his own family since this stratagem may perhaps do better than ye others.

. . . I am more and more convinced that if ye troops had not been sent before I had been some time acquainted with itt to have kept ye knowledge of itt from Rob Roy all had done well enough, but ye surprise of itt so soon made him goe off, as I am informed there was intelligence sent him from Perth that morning tho' ye officer did it secretly yet they were all suspecting it even before that march.

It does seem strange that Atholl could still be so blind to the truth that his Jacobite clan were opposed to him, and would not sacrifice Rob Roy to the Whigs. But his eyes must surely have been opened by a blunt letter, dated 19 June, from John Douglas: 'On the 12th, two of your Grace's men sent intelligence to Rob Roy, otherwise Donald Stewart would have seized him the next morning . . . but where he is I know not.'

The Declaration

Rob Roy was on the duke's own land of Balquhidder, where he had been nursing not only his thigh but his wrath. He was now well informed, either by his own intelligence or by Jacobite and Campbell friends, of the new motive behind the Whigs' anxiety to lay hands on him. Atholl may not have been of their inner party or *Squadrone*, and have acted as their willing tool for urgent family reasons. But even his own people were aware of the underlying political motive. On 2 July, the Reverend H. Murray of Comrie wrote to the Reverend Colin Campbell of Ardchattan describing in detail Rob's method of escape from Logierait, adding at the end, 'There is no small mortification to the squad because of the delay it gave to their hopes of a considerable charge against John Roy [Argyll].'[20]

More bluntly, since torture had been prohibited in 1708, they had to have Rob for that down at Edinburgh, where the Lord Justice Clerk could manage a secret interrogation. Rob saw the way to end their hope and stop pursuit – in the political arena, the light of publicity kills dirty tricks. Just one week after Douglas's report to Atholl, Rob, ill as he was, summoned the energy to write and distribute a declaration indicting Montrose, Cockburne, and Atholl:[21]

> *Declaration Rob Roy to all true Lovers of Honour and honesty*
>
> Honour and conscience urges me to detect the assassins of our Countrey and Countreymen, whose unbounded malice prest me to be the instrument of matchless villany

by endeavouring to make me a false evidence against a person of distinction, whose greatest crime known to me was that he broke the party I was unfortunately of. This proposal was handed me first by Graham of Killerne, from his Master, the Duke of Montrose, with the valuable offers of life and fortune, &c., which I could not entertain but with the utmost horrour. Lord Ormiston, who trysted me to the bridge of Cramond, was no less solicitous on the same subject, which I modestly shifted till I gott out of his clutches, fearing his Justice would be no check on his tyranny. To make up the Triumvirate in this bloody Conspiracy, His Grace the Duke of Atholl resolved to outstrip the other two, if possible, who, having coy-duk'd me into his conversation, immediately committed me to prison, which was contrary to the Parole of Honour given to me by my Lord Edward in the Duke's name and his own who was privy to all that pass'd btwixt us. The reason why the promise was broke to me was because I boldly refused to bear false witness against the Duke of Argyle. It must be owned, if just providence had not helped me to escape the barbarity of the monstrous proposals, my fate had certainly been deplorable, for I would be undoubtedly committed to some stinking dungeon, where I must choose either to rot, dye, or be damn'd. But since I cannot purchase the sweet offers of Life, Liberty, and Treasure at their high price, I advise the Triumvirate to send out one of their own kidney, who I'le engadge will be a fitt tooll for any cruell or cowardly interprise. To narrate all particulars made towards this foull plot, and the persecution I suffered by the Duke of Montrose's means, before and after I submitted to the Government, would take up too much time. Were the Duke of Montrose and I left alone to debate our own private quarrell, which in my opinion ought to be done, I would shew the world how little he would signify to serve either King or Countrey. And I hereby solemnly Declare what I have said in this is positive truth and that these were the only persons deterr'd me many times since my first submission to throw myself over again in the King's mercy; and I can prove most of it by witnesses.

Rob Roy McGrigor

Bawhidder, June 25 1717

Fresh copies were made dated 18 July. His gillies delivered them to Buchanan House, Blair Castle, Inveraray Castle, and to many other clan chiefs; copies were sent to Glasgow, Edinburgh, and London. If Rob had then lain low for a couple of months at Glen Shira, Atholl would have accepted defeat and retired from the field like Montrose. But for all his sagacity in trade, and planning a guerilla war, his patience in raiding, his cool calculation in side-stepping fights that offered no profit – and that without feeling his honour had suffered, for his personal bravery was not called in question – yet the fierier side of his nature took control when injustice or certain aspects of his honour were involved. There was certainly no profit beyond short-term plunder in fighting two dukes who between them controlled three counties. In the long term, they could shatter his life. But he fought on regardless of what seemed his best interest and dearest wish – a life at home on his land with his own family.

Atholl and Montrose had impugned his honour in the one, unacceptable way: an offer to trade home and land for betrayal of another man. Rob's extreme revulsion was the measure of his need not to yield. He was a trader himself, not above selling old cows as younger beasts, not too scrupulous in driving a hard bargain if his buyer had means, able to lift a whole herd with the best of his countrymen, and finding no qualm to conscience in passing bubble reports of the Jacobites to Red John. The dukes' proffered deal led to a plunge down that same path, the thing to be sold this time not cattle but a man. The temptation no doubt found ways to present itself in the best possible light, for Rob had a quick mind. A man could set himself up again if he had land – his friend Alasdair Og had done that in Glen Coe. The need was land, and Rob an outlaw. He could no longer have land unless the king or a great landowner allowed. The temptation was more severe than Rob Roy ever admitted to himself. He had to fight it to the death.

This dichotomy of mind – the need to conserve and the over-riding drive to fight – gave Rob's acts in the summer of 1717 their inconsistencies. The issue of the Declaration was a wise move to cool off his enemies; but new raids on their lands in July and August fanned dying embers, from which instruments for Rob's recapture were forged.

The first effects of the Declaration on Atholl and Montrose had been the dissolution of their mutual distrust in a salty mix of mutual sympathies; and then, when Rob was sufficiently recovered to raid their lands, their union for action. Rob, like all who determinedly vex superior forces, had to pay the penalty. Atholl was suffering most and took the first step. His failure to find Rob in Balquhidder convinced him that he must be on Montrose's land. He wrote from Dunkeld on 6 August to Montrose, confessing that his sixty men had had no joy, since Rob was 'skulking with only two or three companions', and requested Montrose to 'depute a trusted person to concert measures with himself for his capture'.[22] Montrose in reply offered to send Gorthie or Killearn, but since neither cared to risk travelling to Atholl for fear that Rob would waylay them, suggested that one of them meet Atholl in Edinburgh. He proposed too that Atholl send his chamberlain to Balquhidder, to meet whichever of his own men had not gone to Edinburgh, and so concert a plan to suppress Rob's raids pending more effective action.

Atholl issued the necessary orders, and wrote to Montrose on Monday, 9 September, to say that Donald Stewart was now on his way to Balquhidder, and asking that Gorthie or Killearn should meet him in Edinburgh on Thursday or Friday. His intention was to demand cavalry from General Carpenter.

Rob knew nothing of these moves. He had gone to Loch Katrine at the very time Stewart and Killearn were meeting at Lochearnhead. By chance they heard where he was, and went as fast as they could to Portnellan, where they split forces to search along the shores. Stewart and Killearn kept together. As they might have expected, they lost valuable time following misdirections to Rob's hideouts. When wearied, they bivouacked in a cave above the loch, and there Rob Roy surprised them at night. He seized their arms, but allowed them to go uninjured, at least in body. The other half of the party retired next day to Aberfoyle, reporting to Stewart and Killearn, who met them there, that Clan Gregor were mustering, or so it appeared from the large numbers of armed men they sighted. Their morale gone, the company dispersed.[23]

Rob thereafter made his base Balquhidder rather than Loch Katrine or Craigrostan. Much land in Balquhidder was held by James Drummond, the Jacobite duke of Perth, under Atholl's superiority. Rob's cousin Malcolm still had the farms of Inverlochlarig and Invernenty, and his nephew Donald still had Monachyle Tuarach. Mary was there, and they gave him all the help they safely could. Rob's presence at once became known to Atholl, who had obtained from the reluctant Carpenter a troop of cavalry for a quick strike. With these he might reach Rob Roy faster than Rob's scouts. Gorthie was appointed guide, and as soon as news reached him, probably from Alasdair Stewart the tracker, that Rob was at Monachyle Tuarach, Gorthie rode in and surrounded the house before Rob could have warning. He was made prisoner. Gorthie wasted no time. The perils of delay with Rob had been too well demonstrated. He was not bound, but to aid speed placed on horseback in the middle of the troop, from which escape was judged impossible. They headed south for Stirling by way of Strathyre and Callander. After reaching Loch Lubnaig, they had to reduce double file to single along the track between shore and hill-flank. At the lower stretch it became awkwardly narrow for cavalry horses. The troopers had to give closer attention to their horses' footing than to Rob. The track here rose a hundred feet from the shore towards St Bride's chapel. A nervous horse behind him refused a craggy passage, while the unaware troopers in front moved on. Rob seized his chance. He jumped off, smacked the horse's rump, and dashed up the hillside into a mixed cover of birch and oak. His startled horse had gone forward to block the forward troopers, while the nervous horse behind still blocked the rear. Before the men could bite their cartridges, prime the pans, ram the balls, and take aim, Rob was under cover. Pursuit on foot was useless.[24]

Carpenter's worst fears had been realized. His advice to government was that regular troops should not henceforth be used against Rob Roy in the Highlands, where their ineffectiveness could only encourage disaffected clans. And that in fact was the last time the army acted. The capture of Rob Roy was left to Atholl, Montrose, and the Independent Companies. For their different reasons, neither Montrose nor the Companies had heart for the task, but Atholl made one more determined effort. The near success of Carpenter's troopers had confirmed his belief that the sure way to take Rob Roy was by swift descent on horseback, otherwise his popularity in his own country ensured warning and timely support. When it came to the trial, Atholl could not repeat the first success. He gathered twenty horsemen in Glen Almond and sent them by Loch Tay to Balquhidder, but Rob had already been warned, ambushed them with a smaller force at the pass of Glen Ogle, and put them to flight. So runs the oral record, embellished with fictitious detail. Daniel Defoe, when he published his *Highland Rogue* in 1723, added a final attempt at Rob's capture by Atholl himself, when he is alleged to have raided Monachyle. The tale is from internal evidence quite fallacious.[25] The certain facts are that Montrose and General Carpenter had given up the hunt in 1717, and Atholl withdrew in 1718 (his son Charles had been reprieved).

Montrose diverted his attention to the barracks at Inversnaid.

The Board of Ordnance had chosen a site at last, close to Rob Roy's original house on a flat-topped hillock at the foot of the Snaid Glen. The ground plan was ninety feet by eighty-five, with walls seventeen and a half feet high and two and a half feet thick. Towers two storeys high at two diagonal corners would give enfilading fire along all four walls. No building had yet begun.

Legal objection had been made by the landowner and his neighbours, presumably Hamilton of Bardowie (for Rob Roy) and MacGregor of Corarklet,[26] to any building. Montrose, angered by the long delays, determined to buy them out – he had tried in vain during the last five years to get title to Craigrostan. He now made sure that as first step to that end, Rob Roy's land should be taken by the Commissioners for Confiscated Estates. They displaced Hamilton by acquiring his half share, but would not be ready to sell any forfeited estates until 1719, when all would come on the market together.[27] Meanwhile, early in 1718, Montrose made them tentative offers for Inversnaid, a bargain for which was concluded in May.[28] On 7 June, he wrote from London to Gorthie, rejoicing that the agreed sale 'removes all objections against carrying on the buildings of the barracks there'.

A week later, the Board made building contracts with Gilbert Smith, mason, and with carpenters and slaters, all of whom had been engaged for building the barracks at Kiliwhimen (later named Fort Augustus). Preliminary work had already begun in the spring, and building proper now continued through the summer under James Smith as chief director of works in Scotland, and at Inversnaid under Major Thomas Gordon as overseer, with two lieutenants as clerks of works.[29] The rise of this barracks was an affront to Clan Gregor.

Gregor Ghlun Dhubh as chieftain, and Rob Roy as 'rightful owner', concerted action to vent their wrath. To avoid retribution against the clan, they had to devise an attack using only a relatively small, unidentifiable group. A reconnaissance showed that the troops could not be surprised, but the tradesmen's workforce had been quartered in a hut well away from the barracks. Its capture would stop all work. On the wet and windy night of 8 August, Rob's party gained entry by the simplest of all devices – they knocked gently on the door. When it was opened, the workforce of eight masons and others was overpowered at dirk- and pistol-point, and carried off. Neither Major Gordon, nor the workmen when released to the Lowlands, was ever able to identify the raiders, who went down in Army Records only as 'armed Highlanders'.[30]

When Montrose had news of this raid from Gorthie, he replied from London on 28 August to confess himself speechless, but none the less managed to utter terse words asking that the officer in command of the barracks (Major Gordon) be put under arrest 'for not having the workmen under protection of the troops, and at too great a distance'. At the end of October, he was writing to Gorthie complaining yet again of the very slow progress, for all work had been called off until next spring.[31] He thought it shameful, and urged that some more responsible man should be made overseer. Carpenter, as eel-like as ever, shifted blame from the army to the contractors, and dismissed his surveyor and chief director James Smith, replacing him in January 1719 with Andrews Jelfe. The further delays thus caused gave Rob Roy much pleasure, and Montrose equivalent pain. But the barracks was built by the winter of 1719, and the first of the four to be garrisoned.

All pursuit of Rob Roy had been called off during 1718. The Inversnaid barracks project helped him – it gave ministers of the Crown assurance that something was being done, however haltingly, so that Rob was able at last to live with Mary under a common roof at Monachyle Tuarach, and to enjoy a little peace. His overtaxed, emaciated body began to recuperate and to generate full energy. Either now, or sometime before 1722 when there is a first record,[32] he obtained farmland from Malcolm of Marchfield and built a house at Inverlochlarig Beag, at the head of the long Balquhidder glen where it opened out into a great bowl, deep in the hills. His house was at 450 feet on the south-east toe of Beinn Tulaichean, 3099 feet. This bare and treeless corrie was flooded with sun, for glens opened off it north, east, south, and west. Long flats of grassland, arable, and marsh, ran a mile and half east to the head of Loch Doine. It was a wet and windy place in winter, but in summer productive.

Rob brought Mary and the boys to their new home, broke the ground, and gathered in a few beasts as though he were newly married. He was 47, and felt for a space like 22. He had won. Perhaps it never dawned on his conscious mind that he had won more than a contest with two dukes and the British army, for that was astonishing enough; yet the feat win or lose had been only the outer show of the real combat, which had been not with them but himself. The one brought an outward peace, the other began to bring inward.

CHAPTER TWENTY

~

RECONCILIATION
1718–24

The Rising of 1719

THE REORIENTATION of Rob Roy's life, apparent from 1718 in the dying out of planned aggression against the lands of Montrose and Atholl, and the resumption of stock-raising and watch services, was obscured from his countrymen by his envelopment in a double smoke-screen laid in 1719, first by the Jacobites and then by Daniel Defoe.

War with Spain had broken out in July 1718, when she attacked Sicily. Admiral Byng annihilated the Spanish fleet in the Mediterranean, Cardinal Alberoni then conceived a plan for the invasion of Britain, to be led by the duke of Ormonde, whom he called to Madrid together with the Earl Marischal of Scotland, and Prince James Edward. During Anne's reign, Ormonde had been successively Viceroy of Ireland, and Commander-in-Chief of the British Army in succession to Marlborough, until dismissed by George I. Alberoni gave him command of the invasion fleet, and commissioned the Earl Marischal to bring in the powerful exiled chiefs, the Mackenzie earl of Seaforth, the marquis of Tullibardine, and Campbell of Glendaruel. Ormonde planned that the three last should land in Kintail in spring 1719 and raise the clans, while he himself landed in the south of England and marched with five thousand Spanish troops on London. The Midland and Northern counties would rise at the same time.

Tullibardine brought in his young brother, Lord George Murray, who in the course of the winter recruited Rob Roy. Bitter experience had taught Rob to look coolly on Jacobite plots, and this new venture when he was settling at last in Balquhidder was unwelcome both in its timing and possible upset of his good relations with the duke of Argyll. Overriding that was his indebtedness to Atholl Jacobites for his recent escape from Logierait, and now for acceptance of his landholding in Balquhidder. He would not let them down. Ormonde too was a credible general, having fought in Flanders and Spain. Gregor

Ghlun Dhubh would not as yet call out the clan, but assented to Rob raising fifty volunteers.

As a first necessary step, Rob directed a series of small raids on Menteith to provision his men and their families. One such raid was made in late January on Drunkie, a farm near Aberfoyle. The cattle here were too carelessly lifted, and Rob's company was followed by a posse of Montrose's men, accompanied by twenty soldiers under an officer, up the west bank of Loch Lomond to the night-stance in Glen Falloch. The posse had taken quarters at Inverarnan when they heard that Rob Roy and fifty men were close by. They posted three sentinels, but that availed them nothing. Rob Roy was at war, and attacked. The sentries were overrun. One was killed, Rob's men fired several volleys into the house, then stormed in to disarm the posse when one other man was shot. The king at St James's published a proclamation on 10 and 12 March, giving details of the incident. He offered £200 for Rob Roy's apprehension and a free pardon to any outlaw who won it.[1]

Ormonde in March sailed for England with five thousand Spaniards and arms for thirty thousand English Jacobites. The Scottish leaders with three hundred Spanish infantry sailed ten days later in two ships. On 2 April, they disembarked on the island of Lewis at Stornoway, which was Seaforth's land, to buy food and recruit men, then sailed across the Minch to his clan's lands, at Gairloch and Kintail. Tullibardine assumed command and garrisoned the castle of Eilean Donan on Loch Alsh. This thirteenth-century castle had been a MacKenzie stronghold over the last three hundred years. It stood on a rocky islet looking westward to the Cuillin of Skye, and south-eastward to the hills of Kintail and Glenelg. He stocked a magazine there and another at Strath Croe beside his main camp. A month passed waiting for men to come, and for news of Ormonde.

During April, Tullibardine was joined by Lord George Murray, Clanranald, Lochiel, MacDougall of Lorn, and finally by Rob Roy with forty MacGregors, to a total of 1100.[2] The doubting clans had been slow in rising, and they were wise. On 4 May, despatches arrived in Strath Croe from Edinburgh. Ormonde's fleet had been wrecked by prolonged storms off Cape Finisterre. Any ships surviving had limped back to Cadiz. Tullibardine was warned to disperse his army and send the Spaniards back home while they could still get away. Before he could act, three English frigates sailed up Loch Alsh, bombarded the castle, and having ruined the walls captured a small Spanish garrison. Tullibardine was trapped. The news flickered through the hills at wildfire speed. No clan would rise. Had the command been Rob Roy's he would instantly have given the orders to 'split and squander'. They could fight another day. Tullibardine chose, with stupid gallantry, to hang on for another month.

General Wightman held Inverness for the government. His force had been too small to risk earlier, but feeling emboldened by the rebels' plight, he marched out in early June with two regiments, one battalion, four dragoon companies, Dutch auxiliaries, and 146 grenadiers. As he moved west, he gathered in men from Clans Munro, Fraser, and Sutherland, whose chiefs had declared for King George. When he came down Glen Shiel, he had 1600 men. To block him, Tullibardine moved up the lower glen to Bridge of Shiel. The glen narrowed here to a huge ravine with 300-foot mountains rising close on either side. He placed Lord George Murray and two companies of Highlanders on a hill to the south of the river-gorge; the Spaniards under the Earl Marischal on a hill four hundred yards behind them on the north bank; and seven companies including Rob Roy's contingent higher up the mountain flank to the north, parallel to Murray, where they formed the left wing under MacKenzie.

Wightman opened fire at 5 p.m. by mortar-bombing Murray's position, then attacked with a regiment of foot, which was three times repulsed in two hours. Exploding grenades set the heather on fire, Murray was hit in the leg by shrapnel, and his force had to retreat under renewed onslaughts from different sides. The Spaniards' position had been attacked in vain by dragoons supported by mortar-fire, while Wightman's right-flank infantry climbed up the mountain, turned MacKenzie's upper left flank, and infiltrated the gaps between lower units, thus exposing Tullibardine's whole left wing to fire from three sides. Tullibardine sent Rob Roy to assist the MacKenzies,[3] but before he could reach them Seaforth had his arm shattered by a ball. The MacKenzies began withdrawing uphill, carrying their chief with them. The Earl Marischal directed the Spaniards to follow, and by eight o'clock the retreat up the mountain had become general.

Wightman had lost 142 dead and wounded. The Highland losses are unknown, for Tullibardine disbanded his army that night. He and Lord George and Seaforth escaped to France. The Spanish leader, Don Alonzo de Santarem, surrendered with 274 men to General Wightman next morning. Their part in that futile battle was honored by the men of Kintail, who named the

3200-foot mountain, to which Rob and all had retreated, *Sgurr nan Spainteach*, the peak of the Spaniards.

While Don Alonzo was resigning his sword to Wightman, Rob Roy was speeding down Glen Lichd on the far side of the mountain to Strath Croe, where he blew up the magazine.[4] This duty done, he most likely escaped down the coast by sea to Arisaig or Lorn. He had no means of telling if his part in the rising was known to government, but there was high risk that Atholl would hear, and a punitive order be made against his new home in Balquhidder, if he reappeared there. He took refuge in Glen Shira. Although anxious in mind for his family, and with time on his hands, he dared to be happy, and that took the kind of courage that explains his survival all these years. He amused himself by composing a gasconade addressed to the duke of Montrose. Having written it out, and enjoyed what he read, he sent a copy to Montrose, and another to his Jacobite cousin, Patrick Anderson at Haig,[5] accompanied by a letter about the Spaniards, now held prisoner in Edinburgh.

> Sir, Receive the enclosed paper, Qn you are taking your botle; it will divert yourself and comrades. I got noe news since I saw you, only qt we had before about the Spanyards is like to continue. If I get any account about them I'll be sure to let you hear of it, and till then I will not write any more, till I have more account, I am, Sir, your affec Cn and most humble servant,
>
> Rob Roy
>
> Argyll, 1719.

The enclosed gasconade was composed as a challenge:

> Rob Roy to ain hie and mighty Prince, James, Duke of Montrose.
>
> In charity to your Grace's couradge and conduct, please know, the only way to retrive both is to treat Rob Roy like himself, in appointing your place and choice of arms, that at once you may extirpate your inveterate enemy, or put a period to your punny life in falling gloriously by his hands. That impertinent criticks or flatterers may not brand me for challenging a man that's repute of a poor dastardly soul, let such know that I admit of the two great supporters of his character and the captains of his bands to joyne with him in the combate. Then sure your Grace wont have the inpudence to clamour att court for multitudes to hunt me like a fox,

under pretence that I am not to be found above ground. This saves your Grace and the troops any further trouble of searching; that is if your ambition of glory press you to embrace this unequalled venture offerd of Rob's head. But if your Grace's piety, prudence, and cowardice, forbids hazarding this gentlemanly expedient, then let your design of peace restore what you have robed from me by the tyranny of your present cituation, otherwise your overthrow as a man is determined; and advertise your friends never more to look for the frequent civility payed them, of sending them home without their arms only. Even their former cravings wont purchase that favour; so your Grace by this has peace in your offer, if the sound of war be frightful, and chuse you whilk, your good friend or mortal enemy.

Although no more than a jest, the issue of the challenge exasperated Montrose, who wrote to Argyll demanding that he withdraw his protection of Rob Roy. Argyll replied to this, 'You feed him, but all he gets from me is wood and water.'[6]

Montrose appealed against Argyll to members of the Privy Council, but the day for that was too late. Walpole was in high favour at Court after defeating a Commons measure to limit royal prerogatives. Argyll was secure. He was that year made duke of Greenwich. Montrose's friends could give him no comfort, but he did after all have the last laugh. In October 1719, Rob heard that his old Craigrostan lands had at last been sold by the Commissioners. not directly to Montrose but to the York Buildings Company, who were exploiting the forfeited estates. They had paid £946, of which £150 had been the value of the standing timber.[7] That was the highest price paid for properties then being sold, including Mar's. The Company resold almost immediately to Mungo Graham of Gorthie as Montrose's chamberlain.[8]

Early in 1720, when Rob could see that no government action was to be taken against him, he moved back to rejoin his family in Balquhidder for the last time. This was a happier homecoming than ever before. His house at Inverlochlarig was intact, warmed up by family and kinsfolk, and ready for the new life.

The legend

Rob Roy resumed all his normal occupations. A great part of his time necessarily went to his farm: the seasonal life of ploughing and sowing, peat-cutting and gathering, the summer grazing of stock, the autumn harvest and droving, the Crieff sales, the Martinmas preparations for winter, and the training of his younger sons. He augmented his income as before by lifting stock with discretion, so that no trace could be found, and in so doing rebuilt his clientele for a Watch on payment of black mail. In Balquhidder he ruled as unofficial chieftain by force of name and character.

The latter point was promptly made plain when Mr James Robertson, the parish minister at the Kirkton,[9] demanded of his people an increase of stipend, which was normally paid in kind, and when they, feeling it excessive, tried to evade, threatened to pursue them in court. Rob Roy called Robertson to account and told him to withdraw the claim. The confrontation was more than Robertson could bear and he yielded. Every Michaelmas thereafter he received from Rob Roy the gift of a fatted cow and sheep, and had the good sense not to ask where raised.[10] Rob held this strong position even although much land around Strathyre was held by the Maclarens, who had lived here for five hundred years, with their principal farmlands at Achtow and Achleskine, in the wide strath below the Kirkton. Rob's land lay seven miles west at the farther end of the glen, where the principal landholders and nearest neighbours were Malcolm of Marchfield, his aunt's son, who held Inverlochlarig and the neighbouring glen of Invernenty, and Iain Og of Glencarnaig, whose land included a clachan of MacIntyres. But Rob it was who dominated the whole for another decade. He was able to raise a hundred and fifty men when Patrick Grant of Rothiemurchus called on him for help against an attack by clan Macintosh – a mission he concluded successfully, contriving his arrival in Strath Spey in such a way that the Macintoshes had time to withdraw without losing face, so that no blood had to be shed.[11]

His sons were of great help to him. James, a tall dark, and handsome lad of 25, was rarely at home and soon married (he later had fourteen children); Coll, aged 22, was courting Margaret, the daughter of Rob's cousin John MacGregor of Coilleitir in upper Glen Falloch (Malcolm's elder brother), and would soon be begging his stock; but Duncan and Ranald were now sixteen and fourteen respectively and able to work hard.

Robin was just four. There were six mouths to feed, not counting guests by the score.

Rob made no more heavy raids on Montrose. The toll he took was modest, even though Montrose's influence at Court and Council had waned to vanishing point. Power lay again with the Campbells, for Argyll's brother, Archibald, was in 1721 appointed minister in charge of Scottish affairs, and his influence such that his sobriquet was 'King of Scotland'. Rob's restraint suggests that his anger had been worked out.

He raided Atholl just once more. During a visit to his kinsman, Malcolm MacGregor of Coignachan in Glenalmond, he noted that Atholl was grazing great flocks of sheep on part of his Almond estate. One night a flock of 350 wethers, which had been herded off from the ewes and rams, disappeared without trace. Atholl shortly after met John Menzies of Shian at Crieff and asked his advice.[12] Menzies was foolish enough to reply in public that 'Sheep Robbie wad ken o' them', and word of the sneer went straight to Rob Roy. In consequence, every cow that Menzies grazed on the five-mile stretch of Glen Quaich, between Amulree and Shian, vanished overnight. There was no proof that Rob Roy took them, since no clue had been left. The *spreidh* must somewhere have crossed the valleys of the Tay or Earn en route to Glen Shira, but their thirty-mile lengths and ground between were scoured by Menzies' trackers in vain. The skill with which both herds had been spirited off, and the total absence of any further sight or sound of them, were held to be marvels of planning and movement disclosing Rob's masterhand. No action could be taken against him.

That same year of 1721, Coll, now 23, married Margaret MacGregor at Coilleitir. She came to him from Glen Falloch with a dowry of two thousand merks.[13] Rob had no land to give them, but he had a good friend in James Drummond, duke of Perth, who had fought at Sheriffmuir and held Strathyre. His trustees gave Coll a tack of the Kirkton of Balquhidder, which was farmed by several families.[14] After his marriage, Coll became highly regarded as a man of character. Rob felt such gratitude to the Drummond family, who were Catholics, that his wish to honour them was catalytic in his later change to their faith.

The Watch that Rob had set up in Menteith and the Lennox did not, like the later Watch of his chieftain, Gregor Ghlun Dhubh, have the blessing of the law. When he called around this time at Westerton in Bridge of Allan to collect his black mail, the too innocent laird, Mr Henderson, declined to continue the contract, placed trust in the law, and refused payment. Rob directed a band of young MacGregors to bring him in for ransom. They seized him one day from the front of his house, and carried him off through Callander en route to Balquhidder. At Kilmahog, a mile short of the Pass of Leny, they bivouacked in a barn at nightfall. The lads were very good-natured, whisky passed round, and Henderson enjoyed a merry night of music, dancing, and song. He recorded a verse improvised in the Scots for his benefit:

> Noo we've come to Kilmahog,
> Noo we've come to Kilmahog,
> We'll tak' a pint aff the carle,
> We'll tak' a pint, tak's pint aff the carle.

At last they wrapped themselves in their plaids, placing Henderson on straw between two men who lay dirk in hand. Everyone save Henderson fell so deeply asleep that he was able to recover his shoes, which had been taken off him, and slip out of the door unheard. He ran and walked some ten miles to safety. A message to Stirling Castle procured a guard for his home, but Rob left him alone.[15] He had probably a fellow-feeling for escapers.

Rob Roy still maintained a considerable band for his Watch, and when the need arose could call up a large body of his clan. An instance arose in August 1722, when the MacIntyres, who occupied a township at Invercarnaig (also called Easter Inverlochlarig, since it lay at the head of Loch Doine), were dunned for arrears of rent by Iain Og of Glencarnaig.[16] The MacIntyres had had a bad year in 1721 to 1722, and had been unable to meet the rent due in kind or money. Iain Og had won the court's adjudication of property, and was now about to descend, bearing letters of horning and caption, with messengers-at-arms, sheriff's officers, and a body of armed men, to evict the MacIntyres and seize their stock and furnishings. In such dire straits, Donald MacIntyre called to see Rob. He appealed for help.

Rob listened to the tale. If he acted, that would mean yet another open clash with the law, and perhaps with Atholl. He had no longer wish for this – furthermore, if he took up the lease of MacIntyre's land himself, it would make provision for his son Duncan, or Ranald. But the appeal was not one he could refuse. He knew too well the physical and mental hurt to a family of eviction and loss of stock. When he heard that eviction had been timed for next Wednesday, he called for his gillies, and summoned a hundred men for Tuesday afternoon. His force must be overwhelming to avoid bloodshed.

On Tuesday night, Rob laid an ambush on the shores of Loch Voil, positioned his men, bivouacked, and put out scouts. Iain Og walked straight into the trap next morning. He had 35 men strung out on the track when Rob Roy jumped them at gun- and sword-point. The law officers surrendered and were taken hostage, together with three of Iain Og's men. The main body was turned back. Rob released his prisoners next day, after they had sworn on oath not to return.[17]

Atholl's baillie, Robert Stewart in Balquhidder, reported direct to the duke:

'Ballqwidder, 11 August 1722. May it please yr Gr. These are signifying that upon Wednesday last, being the 8th instant, John Campbell of Glencharnek did come to the lands of Easter Innerlochlareg shoon in ye morning with thirty armed men, two messengers, and two other sub officers, for to uplift the whole goods of the said town, & Robert Roy McGregor having a kindnesse and favour for the MacIntyres of Innercharnek, notwithstanding of the favour he had to his own kindred, those of Innerlochlareg, did lie a night before John Campbell came with his men, in ambush with his lads, and seeing John Campbell come with his men, went out to meet them, & apprehended ye two messengers and two sub officers, with other three of the partie, and disarmed them & took them prisoners & kept a guard upon them 24 hours and at last kept their arms & did let them go, taking a promisory oath of them that they would never come againe upon that occasione.

Atholl chose to take no action. Perhaps he too thought the law unjust in this instance. He was ageing – he had only two years to live – and must have thought twice of another, unrewarding encounter. The Justiciary at Parliament House in Edinburgh were helpless to act without Atholl or the army. Enforcement lapsed. Rob reigned supreme in his glen.

Apart from this incident, life was peaceful in Balquhidder. As so often happens, when a man's most hectic days are over, or his most remarkable work is done, the world discovers him and thinks him still what he was. This time-lag between Rob's days of achievement and national awareness of it ended in 1723, when Daniel Defoe published in London his *Highland Rogue*, a fictional tale of Rob Roy. Defoe was a prolific writer, his name already famous for three great books – *Robinson Crusoe* in 1719, and *Moll Flanders* and *Journal of the Plague Year* in 1722. His

Highland Rogue was a pot-boiler, but still displaying something of his talent – an imaginative power to create circumstantial detail that rang true. In the years 1706 and 1707, when he had been Godolphin's secret agent in Scotland, he would not have known of Rob Roy, and must certainly have heard the story on his last visit of 1718. He wrote it up as the first of a trilogy on outstanding villains of his time (*Jack Shepherd* and *Jonathan Wild* followed). All were in pamphlet-form. He created Rob to accord with the pamphlet's title, gave him a foot-long beard, and launched him into amazing adventures with a substratum of truth, embellished for the readers' entrancement. The romance was read by men of all ranks. King George was enraptured. He had found the classics of English literature quite beyond him, while contemporary authors like Swift, Pope, and Steele left him cold; but Daniel Defoe he could enjoy. Rob Roy's name was thoroughly well-known to him. He could even, like most of his subjects, credit the tale, for the Highlands were a far-distant blank on the map, where anything might be allowed to happen. The work became a topic at Court and coffee-house, especially since London's literary taste had moved away from an appreciation of high moral characters to those of lesser virtue. This paper Rob Roy became a celebrity, greatly inferior in quality to the Rob Roy of Glengyle, Craigrostan, and Balquhidder, but with heroic powers that once credited by the public made life for Rob easier. His lowland clients paid black mail with greater alacrity; panic invaded the breasts of men who thought to cross him. And Argyll, amused by all this nonsense, yet appreciating that Rob was indeed a national 'character', decided that the time had come to reconcile Rob with his ducal neighbours.

The king is said to have asked Argyll to arrange a meeting with Rob at St James's.[18] If so, Rob declined to risk the king's safe conduct. Argyll instead persuaded Rob to meet Montrose and himself in 1724 on neutral ground. According to early writers, the meeting was called in London – an unlikely site when they could meet with less trouble to Rob in Edinburgh, or at Montrose's new house in the Drygate of Glasgow. There is no written record of where they met; that they did appears to have been common knowledge. Rob might well have accepted London, which he had never seen. He could trust Red John. Each had known the cathartic effect of self-abandonment in action. Rob felt that he understood him ever since Sheriffmuir, when hopelessly outnumbered he had gone out and swung that battle as could no other soldier in Scotland, and then been merciful. So

Rob agreed to meet, as always wanting peace if he could have it. Montrose would accept readily: since Walpole's return to power on the bursting of the South Sea Bubble in 1721, Argyll was a man to be propitiated. Their three-cornered feud had lasted long enough for all to be tired of it; all were middle-aged, and the mutual gains from conciliation were obvious. Rob Roy had given ground for the two dukes' last quarrel, and his presence now gave both a focus for amicable settlement of family differences.

Their business with Rob Roy explored the mutual benefits that each might confer. Gorthie and Killearn had already been proposing to Montrose that estate management would be made easier throughout the Lennox by a gentler treatment of Clan Gregor, with grants of leases and charters to more of their people, and they could point with effect to the good rule of Gregor Ghlun Dhubh, which had lasted ever since Rob Roy had bought the land. Rob Roy's new and extraordinary status in the country undermined the authority of his own chieftain, for the very mention of Rob's concern in a cause, and the chance of his presence in support, was enough to intimidate opposition.

There was this further consideration. In July that year, General George Wade had been given command of the army in Scotland, with the task of pacifying the Highlands, disarming the clans, receiving submission of disaffected chiefs, and building military roads. It was becoming anomalous that Argyll should stand high in the king's favour, have a brother responsible to the king for Scotland's good government, and at the same time befriend the nation's most celebrated outlaw. Montrose too felt concern that Rob should now join fellow outlaws in making submission through Wade to the king. It appears certain, in light of later events, that they strongly advised Rob Roy to submit, that he was reluctant to do so, but finally agreed as part of their three-cornered bargain.

The meeting was successful. They talked, and they parted, if not friends at least with better understanding of each other and forbearance in future relations. There was no further record of raids. An apocryphal tale is told that Rob on his way home from London was stopped at Carlisle by recruiting officers, who offered him the king's bounty for enlistment. Meaning to put them off, he demanded treble payment. Greatly taken by his formidable bearing, they agreed, whereupon he lifted King George's money in defrayment of his high travel expenses (not to mention the Crown's seizure of Craigrostan), and rode off into Scotland. Whether true or not, the tale squares with his code of equity.

CHAPTER TWENTY ONE

THE END OF THE RACE
1724–34

The petition to General Wade

A THOLL DIED in November 1724. Rob's peace in Balquhidder seemed assured. But he had not yet brought himself to petition Wade. He remained firmly Jacobite. On the other hand, the true king's tide of fortune was at full ebb, and his elder son Charles Edward was only four years old. It would be sensible to come to terms with realities for the years that were left to him. A submission by Rob presented difficulties. His pardon had been expressly excluded by Act of Parliament, and while the king's pardon brooked no such exclusions, none the less it must depend on good cause shown. The truth is that there was no good cause. Rob preferred to wait to see how other attainted men might fare – and they fared well.

General Wade in his first year enjoyed great success in winning over the chiefs. He ascribed this in large part to the power given him to receive petitions for pardon and to the king's new clemency in granting them. He wrote in his report to the king;[1] 'It was no sooner known that Your Majesty had empowered me to receive Submissions of those who had repented of their crimes and were willing and desirous for the future to live peaceably under your Mild and moderate government, but applications were made to me from several of them . . . As soon as the respective clans had delivered up their arms, several of these attainted persons came to me at different times and places to render their submissions . . . they afterwards sent me their several letters of submission, copies of which I transmitted to Your Majesty's Principal Secretary of State.'

Among the later petitions received, there at last appeared one from Rob Roy, dated September 15, 1725.[2] Wade records that on all such petitions the king's pardon followed. The one thing that can be said with certainly of Rob Roy's letter is that it was not composed by him:

Sir, – The great humanity with which you have constantly acted in the discharge of the trust reposed in you, and your ever having made use of the great powers with which you were vested, as the means of doing good and charitable offices to such as ye found proper objects of compassion, will, I hope, excuse my importunity in endeavoring to approve myself not absolutely unworthy of that mercy and favour which your Excellency has so generously procured from His Majesty for others in my unfortunate circumstances. I am very sensible nothing can be alledged sufficient to excuse so great a crime as I have been guilty of, that of rebellion. But I humbly beg leave to lay before your Excellency some particulars in the circumstances of my guilt, which, I hope, will extenuate it in some measure. It was my misfortune, at the time the Rebellion broke out, to be liable to legal diligence and caption, at the Duke of Montrose's instance, for debt alledged due to him. To avoid being flung into prison, as I must certainly have been had I followed my real inclinations in joining the King's troops at Stirling, I was forced to take part with the adherents of the Pretender; for the country being all in arms it was neither safe nor indeed possible for me to stand neuter. I shall not, however, plead my being forced into that unnatural Rebellion against His Majesty, King George, if I could not, at the same time, assure your Excellency that I not only avoided acting offensively against his Majesty's forces upon all occasions, but, on the contrary, sent His Grace the Duke of Argyll all the intelligence I could from time to time, of the strength and situation of the Rebels; which I hope his Grace will do me the justice to acknowledge. As to the debt to the Duke of Montrose, I have discharged it to the utmost farthing. I beg your Excellency would be persuaded that, had it been in my power, as it was in my inclination, I should always have acted for the service of His Majesty King George, and that one reason of my begging the favour of your intercession with his Majesty for the pardon of my life, is the earnest desire I have to employ it in his service, whose goodness, justice and humanity, are so conspicious to all mankind.

I am, with all duty and respect,
Your Excellency's most, &c.
Robert Campbell.

This letter is a fascinating essay in duplicity. Taken together with his letter of 1715 to Argyll, it weaves a tangled web. First, was the letter from Rob Roy's hand? The style, syntax, and false sentiment, while in close accord with those in previous petitions from chiefs or their lawyers, were not his. The answer may well have been that Argyll, finding Rob dilatory in putting pen to paper, advised him to leave the wording to the Campbell lawyers in Edinburgh. Since the law (his specific attainder) required circumvention, the job might be better entrusted to them. If that was how it happened, the result could hardly have been worse for Rob Roy's reputation. Cause for pardon seeming thin, if not entirely absent, they manufactured it with scant regard to his credit. That Rob knowingly put his name to the creeping letter does seem surprising at first sight: it argues that he had not only become an inveterate cynic in matters politic, which is most likely, but – most unlikely – no longer had any regard for his good name or his sons', or the gross offence to his family, clan, and Jacobite friends like the Drummonds, Murrays and MacDonalds, to whom he was deeply bound: and had no care what he said if the lawyers were satisfied that this was what Wade needed.

The letter after its preamble speaks few words of truth and these doctored. Far from 'not acting offensively against His Majesty's forces', he had enraged Cadogan by effective attack, and he alone among the western clans south of the Great Glen had raised a fighting force for the 1719 rising. His further claim to have 'sent intelligence' is true so far as it goes, yet highly suspect as meant for Argyll's deception. An intended betrayal of Jacobites is too far out of character, for this was the man who had rejected the Lovat-Argyll plot to bring down Atholl, and then thrice rejected the like plots by Montrose, Cockburne, and Atholl against Argyll. His bitter fight against the 'triumvirate', at such great cost to himself and his hopes of Craigrostan, and his repeatedly raising men for the Jacobite cause when others were scared, are in no accord with betrayals. His 1717 declaration had the ring of truth, uttered in dire straits when prudence counselled silence; his submission to Wade snuffled untruths. What crushing event had so broken his spirit that character changed?

There was no such event. The leopard had not changed his spots. He presumably signed this letter not of his drafting (the original has disappeared), and gave assent to its despatch, because the subject was not one he took as seriously as later critics. He signed without care, reckoning that since all submissions now made were false to the core, he need have no scruples about a formal letter meant for Wade's eyes only.

Confirmation that the letter's representations were indeed false appeared in a meeting between Rob Roy and Abercromby of Tullibody around 1726. Abercromby was barely twenty when he settled near Stirling. Rob Roy repeatedly lifted his cattle until he asked for a safe conduct and visited Rob in the Trossachs.[3] He was led to a cavern, where his host dined him on steaks cut from a cow that hung by its heels from the wall. In exchange for 'a surprisingly modest sum' Rob agreed to spare his herds in future, and to replace any lifted by others. He did so only on the distinct (but mistaken) understanding that Abercromby was a friend to the Jacobites and an enemy of the union. Abercromby did not disillusion him. Rob Roy's allegiance had no more swerved from the Jacobite party than the clans' chiefs.

The last excursions

Rob kept as active as ever in travelling the country from 1725 to 1730, but much of the farm work must have been left to his sons. He was still enjoying his Lowland Watch, based on the Trossachs. His services were in demand as far away as Strathspey, where he was engaged in the early spring of 1726, by Grant of Ballindalloch, to recover stolen horses, and to trace a riever who had reset his cattle in Breadalbane.[4] When he was so much away from home, Mary if needing money and provisions would make the black mail collection herself. She had been long used to foraging on her own. One of Wade's officers, Captain Crossley, wrote from Elgin to Charles de la Foy on 8 May 1725:[5] 'Not long before I left Stirling the famous Rob Roy's wife went through the whole town and country thereabouts to those who held any land, acquainted them who she was and that she wanted such sums which they were obliged to comply with; but this Rob Roy is a man of so much honour that, where he steals himself, those he protects from the insults of others, so that he is one of the most genteel rogues amongst them . . .'

A first-hand account of Rob Roy at work in the late 1720s was given by a man of the Lennox, who when he was fifteen worked with his father as herd for a Lennox heritor.[6] One fine October morning, they awoke to find that ten or twelve head of cattle had been lifted overnight. Since the owner paid mail to Rob Roy, he called him in to fulfil his contract. Rob promptly appeared with seven or eight men, heard all that could be told, and gave assurance that the *spreidh* would be recovered. He required only that the two herdsmen come with his party, for his own gentlemen could not be expected to drive the cattle back.

They tracked the herd north into the hills behind Callander. Rob followed signs on the heath invisible to the Lennoxmen. They slept overnight in a bothy, and next morning continued in the direction of Ben Vorlich until noon, when Rob in front signed to the party to halt. They crouched in the heather. Rob came back and told the herdsmen to cross the ridge. Below they would find a herd grazing. They must gather their own beasts, drive them out, and if any man threatened, say that Rob Roy was here with twenty men. The herdsmen felt uneasy, and asked what they should do if attacked. Rob seemed not to take the question seriously – rievers did not attack Rob Roy – but answered: 'You can say I will not forgive them.' The herdsmen crossed the hill. The herd was a big one. They had picked out and gathered their own when a woman came flyting at them in the Gaelic, but was silenced by Rob's message. Rob when he heard expressed satisfaction that no confrontation had been needed. He liked to let rievers save face and not force the token blood-spilling.

When recalling his story, the herdsmen added that Rob Roy's men gave them escort as far as a wide moor south of the Teith, where they slept in a bitter wind. Frost quickly covered their plaids. Having no plaid of his own, the lad had crept under that of a bearded Highlander, who was Rob Roy's lieutenant, Alasdair Roy, and during the night appropriated more than his share of covering, so that Alasdair's head, neck and shoulders were by dawn covered thick in hoar. The lad rose in dread of a hammering, but the big Highlander just shook himself, rubbed the hoar off his beard with his plaid, and muttered 'a cauld nicht'.

In 1727, an odd item of news appeared in the *Edinburgh Weekly Journal* of 24 January, reporting that Rob Roy had been imprisoned in Newgate with Lord James Ogilvy, that the pair had been handcuffed and carried to Gravesend for transportation to the Barbadoes, and now had been pardoned at the last minute before sailing. The story was wholly untrue. In *Highland Constable*, Howlett notes that Lord Ogilvy, formerly in exile, had already been pardoned and came home from France in 1725. Rob Roy had been pardoned in 1726 and was no longer an outlaw. Since then, no rebels had been tried or sentenced.

Rob's cattle trade continued quietly over the last ten years. The minister at Logierait recalled that one Sunday morning in summer when he was preaching in his kirkyard, he noticed Rob Roy in the congregation, and took the chance to damn robbery, directing his eye to Rob. At the close of the service, Rob asked for an explanation. The minister answered that one of his flock was a widow at Tayside, from whom Rob last week had bought a cow for half its real value. Rob claimed indignantly that she had seemed glad of the price. The minister told him that she had sold her cow to keep body and soul together, and been glad of the money only because she was starving. Rob Roy said he would see to it. Next day he returned the woman her cow and would take no money back. The incident became known, because the minister on the following Sabbath spoke of the happy result from the pulpit, commending it as 'worthy of imitation by the hard-hearted gentry of my parish'.[7]

The last lap

Rob's appearance at Logierait must have been one of his last in a Protestant church. In 1729, he and his son Coll are mentioned in the records of Balquhidder Kirk,[8] but next year he transferred to the Roman faith. He made confession to Father Alexander Drummond at Drummond Castle, the seat of the teenage duke of Perth, three miles south of Crieff.

There has been much conjecture on Rob's reasons. He was nearing the end of his life by 1730, and would have premonitions; he lived too close to nature not to have instinct for the end. His conversion had not been as sudden as it seemed to the world, but a slow germination from seed sown at the gathering of the clans before Killiecrankie, when he had first met and found comradeship with the Highlands' Catholic youth. He was no theologian. His Protestantism had been as shallow rooting as his father's, their devotion being neither to a form of church government nor its doctrine, but simply to Christ. Rob's 'conversion' owed initial growth to friendship with the Catholic fraternity, until (by report of his words to Walter Scott)[9] it was brought to flower by the kindness of the Drummond family. He wanted to respond (a lifelong trait) and could see no way to please them more. He had been little accustomed to disinterested kindness from great men. There was this further point, that with the end in sight he was feeling his loneliness, which no man can escape if he lives long, and for the first time was having peace to reflect on it. For almost fifty years events had held him captive, and their tumult taken all his attention. His feelings of patriotism, and of comradeship with men all marching to win self-advantageous goals, had seemed vital ingredients of life, until now. They were not enough. Balquhidder now had a Presbyterian minister,[10] and Calvin's doctrine that God has destined certain souls to damnation, others to salvation, may have left Rob wondering where he stood, and fearing the worst. The Presbyterian ministry of his time was hard-eyed, the Catholic forgiving, and Rob had begun to feel need of forgiveness. He had been accustomed all his life to look to the future and to make provision. That is what he did now. He was not a man to look back overlong in regret. After confession he quickly recovered his sense of humour, observing that Father Alasdair had groaned and crossed himself many times.[11]

His sons Ranald and James were giving him concern. Ranald was a wild lad of 24, and with his spirited elder brother was following a career of black mail with violence that their father would never have tolerated. They co-operated with a band of outlaws, not local men, brought in and led by Walter Buchanan of Auchmar.[12] They used a ruined castle sited on a little peninsula at the east end of Loch Voil, where they gave shelter and hospitality to benighted or storm-bound travellers. In 1731, they sheltered a Jacobite party en route to Skye, bearing in custody the notorious Lady Grange, wife of the Lord Justice Clerk, James Erskine of Grange (the earl of Mar's brother). He had housed a Jacobite meeting in Edinburgh, where his lady, who was a fervent Whig and bad-tempered, chose to eavesdrop. She had foolishly burst out with a threat to denounce them, and Lord George had judged her capable of doing just that. The lives of many men of great family being at stake, he had her abducted and held in various remote parts of the Hebrides by MacLeod of Dunvegan and MacDonald of Sleat, until she died in 1745.[13]

Before 1730, a rival band operating in Rob Roy's home ground would have been unthinkable. But he let them be. They were young, driven by need of release in shared action, experience, and effort. They were escaping the loneliness that he was now learning to meet in another way. He had this strange need of peace. He had even taken gladly the olive-branch held out by Montrose, who was granting leases at low rent to many of the Clan Gregor.[14] He had given up cattle-lifting, and now too those wearisome journeys required to collect black mail – a job taken over by Gregor of Glengyle, who commanded a Watch lawfully commissioned by government.[15]

In 1732, Ranald was at last courting Jean, the sixteen-year-old daughter of his chieftain, Gregor of Glengyle, and begging his stock. Rob and Gregor read the pair a stern lesson, and concluded that Ranald would settle down if given the chance. Rob asked and obtained from the young Drummond duke the tack of that part of the Kirkton not held by Coll, but for safeguard took the tack jointly in his own name and Ranald's. The pair were married next year, and Ranald justified the trust put in him. He limed the land, built a two-storey house, and held the tack for the next 54 years.[16]

Rob held more closely to his farm at Inverlochlarig Beag. He would find recurring to him at intervals during the next two years a whole succession of incidents that he had long forgotten or perhaps suppressed. They would come to mind with an odd sharpness and colour, as they do to all men towards the end. His recollection of past days, and a wish to appease Mary's wrath, may have caused him to respond to a last call for action in 1734.

A mile below Inverlochlarig, on the far side of Stob Breac, the Invernenty burn coursed down a grassy glen from a pass above Loch Katrine. The flat farmlands of Wester Invernenty had long been tenanted from Atholl by Rob's cousin Malcolm, but Malcolm had died impoverished and his children were now in Glengyle's guardianship. The elder boy was in need of land. The family's resumption of Invernenty, where rent had no doubt been long in arrears, was refused by Appin, who had bought and given the farm to one John MacLaren.[17] Clan Gregor were emphatic that by right of ancient occupation the land should be theirs. Rob served notice on MacLaren that he would reject his tenancy, and the MacLarens appealed for armed help to the Stewarts of Appin, who were descended from a lady of their own stock. Appin mustered two hundred men that summer and came down to Balquhidder. Rob Roy called out his men and confronted him. When the two parties met near the kirk, the MacGregors were outnumbered. A battle's toll in dead and wounded would by Rob's calculation, be out of proportion to the worth of the clan's cause. He talked to Appin, and declared that the two clans should not fight. Each was Jacobite, both had fought for a Stewart king at Killiecrankie and Sheriffmuir, and might do so again despite the forced submission to Wade. They should not spill blood on a minor domestic issue. The MacGregors would forego their claim to Invernenty. Then, that no one might think he had shirked a fight he offered himself for a trial at arms. Appin consulted with his gentlemen. Several were eager to try conclusions with one of the best swordsmen of the day, for a duel of honour would not be pressed to the death. Appin chose his brother-in-law, Alasdair of Invernahyle. He was a young, athletic man, short but well-made, and an excellent fencer. They fought with targe and broadsword until Rob's arm was cut. He dropped his point and congratulated Stewart as the first man ever to draw his blood with the sword. Alasdair Stewart responded, declaring that only youth and suppleness had allowed him to score.[18]

Rob never drew his broadsword again. The last duel was salutary, revealing that his reflexes were slowing down and his eyesight failing. By the autumn, Rob felt unable to get about and kept to his house. His sons ran the farm. They cut down the stock, as was usual after Michaelmas, leaving only 62 beasts at Inverlochlarig Beag: 13 cows, 21 sheep, 23 goats, and 5 horses.[19] When winter came, he took to his bed.

The Drummond priest had said absolution could be his if he truly repented, and whether he truly had may have worried him, for one or more of his young neighbours, who had ready access to the house – Rob like everyone kept an open door – said in later life to Walter Scott that when he expressed repentance for certain acts of his life, Mary laughed at his scruples, and that he rebuked her violence of passion, declaring that 'her counsels had put strife between him and the best men of the country, and now would divide him and his God'. That sounds much like a domestic tiff over Invernenty, in course of which some nonsense had come out in the heat of the moment. If the report had any substratum of truth, it most likely referred to the confrontation with Appin. His heart had not been in that, and he had fallen out with no other 'best men'. The men Rob respected, like Alexander Campbell of Fonab and Red John were not at strife with him although Whigs. The reports of his clansmen who liked and admired Mary were that she at no time tried to direct his political acts.[20]

While Rob was waiting through December for his God to call him away, perhaps he thought less of his deep despairs, or the long-drawn hardship that shortened life, and his memory brought him images of the land he loved so well that the power of the great men around had not sufficed to break his will to live on it, or his grasp on happiness. No man could have maintained his ground as he did for twenty years, however disciplined his body and quick his mind in the skills of living off the land like a wild animal, unless the energy fountained from deep levels of love. His land and people were a well from which his generosity of mind drew life. This had been displayed long before his misfortune, when his first big purchase of land had been not for himself but his nephew; and after it in concern for the poor and disabled throughout years of adversity; in forebearance to enemies seeking his life and abstention from killing them; in his scruple, unusual in time and place, to spill any man's blood unless in war or the defence of life and home; and above all in loyalty, for while he did dissimulate with Argyll, he never broke his pledged word or betrayed a man. On this point the gods chose to test him. The virtue he most honoured drew the most fierce assay.

Men are not left without weapons of defence in such trial. Rob had been allowed a bold spirit, a perfectly functioning body, a bright mind, and a long hard training in wildland survival. His parents had bred him through boyhood with brothers, sisters, and friends working in home and community. The life had given him both his love of country and his code of right and wrong. Anomalous as this code might be in the Highlands, where revenge was not crime but duty, and stock-lifting not theft but a form of life assurance, it asserted human rights robustly against injustices rife at his time, while holding him to a concept of human trust as inviolable. And so, he had broken the laws freely as need arose, and perhaps more often than need required, but this fact and loose play with his enemies' property fell within his Highland code. His life's trial came on another plane, on a more basic ideal of integrity. In the run up to it, he was himself betrayed, made destitute, racked by deprivations that finally broke his body, and in course of this harrowing thrice tempted to win all back. All he need do was betray a man whose ancestors had betrayed his. In the end, his fundamental integrity had stayed unbreached. A man can hardly win a greater victory.

To the world he had failed in life, and the Devil's Advocates sprang to attack. Graham of Gartmore accused him of 'having abandoned himself to all licentiousness' (black mail and cattle-lifting), but feeling obliged to admit that 'this man was a person of sagacity and neither wanted stratagem nor address', he could find no charge of cruelty or wanton bloodshed. Some Gregarach of the Ladasach line accused Rob of bullying Iain Og, keeping him five years out of Glen Carnaig, and trying to keep John MacLaren out of Invernenty; but Iain Og was believed to be posing a threat to Clan Dughaill Ciar, and MacLaren had Appin at his back. He was accused by Cockburne of acting double agent for Argyll and the Jacobites, but Cockburne had not understood the use he made of Argyll, whom he played as he would a big fish for winter mart; and by others of cowardice or worse at Sheriffmuir, which is now disproven. The main charges fall. The minor remain. No man could plunder on his scale without much ill – the very speed and secrecy that made his tactics seem infallible subsume injustices by the way. He could be arrogant to fools, cowards, and men he thought decadent. He seems not to have shared the racial characteristic of touchy pride, and never even sought occasion for swordsmanship, superb though his skill was.

It is improbable that Rob would indulge in too much introspection at the end, apart from the involuntary survey that memory offered. Most likely it offered the simple things he loved. The chase after white garrons in March below the crags of Meall Mor; Loch Katrine shining green and yellow at the April and May leafings, the Craigrostan woodlands lit by primrose clumps then spread through by a haze of bluebells; the sound of the spade in May slicing through black wet peat; the carefree days at June shielings, watching green corries speckled with black cattle; Atholl glens between cloud-dappled hills, heavy with July heat, scented with bog-myrtle; the whisper of August barley rippling before mild winds; the long slow cattle droves from the west coast in September, when the wrack-strewn shores of the sea-lochs gave a tang to the air, and the heather-pollen puffed up from the cows' hooves; still mornings in October, when every bank and bush by Loch Lomond was wrapped in silver-grey cobwebs, beaded with dew and shining in low sun; then the big winds of winter, the roar of the hill burns, the blizzards down over the mountains, the glens blanketed, white and silent, the frost that fattened the stars, then home to the peat fire and whisky, the pipes and the ceilidh.

On 28 December, Mary told Rob Roy that MacLaren of Invernenty had asked permission to visit him.[21] It was a gesture of peace and courtesy in hope of better relations for the coming year. Rob consented, but weak though he felt would not have MacLaren find him helpless in bed. He asked to be dressed in his plaid and belted with dirk and pistol, and set in his chair. This done, he received MacLaren somewhat formally and the pair talked for a while together, coolly courteous. When his visitor had gone, Rob fell back exhausted. All accounts agree on his last words. 'It is all over. Put me to bed. Call the piper. Let him play *Cha till me tuille.*'[22] He was obeyed. While the piper played the lament *I shall return no more*, Rob Roy died.

The funeral on New Year's Day 1735 was attended by a host of mourners of all ranks and most clans, from the south, central, and west Highlands. It was a great occasion in Balquhidder's history,[23] but no bell tolled for him that day. The bronze bell that he had lifted from the kirk's belfry for the benefit of Acharn School at Loch Tay had still not been recovered (nor was it till 1930).[24] Even that heinous crime was forgiven him now; the clan's pipers heralded the advance of his coffin down Loch Voil – the last time that they played at a Perthshire funeral. Reports by men present convey the universal grief.[25] They all knew that one of the last men of the old Highland stock had gone, that his like would never again be seen in the southern Highlands. The wheel of change was turning, breaking the Gaelic society apart. Most fittingly, they had chosen for his gravestone an ancient Celtic slab, carved nearly four hundred years earlier. Its crude decoration, now worn by weather to become barely decipherable, shows at centre a two-handed claymore and a warrior wearing a surcoat, with zoomorphic figures below and a Celtic knot above.

Everyone understood that Rob's driving purpose had been to uphold the life and independence of his Highland race. Since he was prepared to subordinate to that everything except personal integrity as he conceived it, that would appear after all to have been the mainspring.

Whatever his flaws and faults, they were dismissed. He had personified for them all a man stripped to nakedness defeating an immeasurably superior power and privilege by strength of will and force of character. While no one could covet the life he had lived, some could long for its immediacy and awareness. He had not lived it passively, as he might if he had taken sober counsel, but fought to keep its flame alight. People remembering how he had stood his ground, felt in his stand an elevation of their own spirits. As he was valiant they honoured him, and Roman Catholic or not, buried him where he belonged, in the graveyard of the auld kirk at Balquhidder.

Postscript

On 9 January 1735, a notice appeared in the *Caledonian Mercury:* 'On Saturday was se'nnight [28 December 1734] died at Balquidder, in Perthshire, the famous Highland partisan, Rob Roy.'

Mary had a heavy reckoning to meet after the funeral. The feeding of the multitude had cost above £400 Scots. The Inventory of Rob's estate, 'faithfully made up and given up by Mary McGrigor alias Campbell the Defuncts Spouse only Executive Dative', gives this account: 'Due to her for money expended on his funeral, rents, servants' fees, and medicines and other necessaries during his sickness, £436.10/4 Scots'. Rob Roy possessed:

1.	Two Tydie Cows at £8 Scots	£16
2.	Two Yeald Kine at £6	£12
3.	Two old Kine with a stirk at £6.13/4	£13.6.8
4.	Two Farrow Kine with a Stirk at £7.6/8	£14.13.4
5.	Two six quarters old queys [heifers] at £2.13/4	£ 5.6.8
6.	One ten quarter year old quey	£ 3
7.	Thirteen ews and one Ram	14
8.	Seven hoggs	3.10
9.	Fourteen goats with a Buck	20
10.	Eight Minchaks [young goats]	£ 4
11.	Ane old Mair with a filly	8
12.	Two horses	30
13.	A Blind horse	10
14.	Two bolls of gray corn with the straw	10
15.	The hey [the value of the stacked corn and straw]	12
16.	Saddle and arms and bridle	24
17.	Clothes and whole house plenishing	84.6.8
		£284.3.4

Debt

The said Defunct has justly addebted and resting to him the

time foresaid of his decease By Alexander McFarlane in Corectlet the sum of £100 Scots and whole annual rents thereof as part 600 merks principal specified in a Bond granted by him to Robert Campbell of Innersnait d/d 28 Nov 1707.[1]

Mary continued to live at Inverlochlarig, cared for by her sons Coll and Ranald and the people of Clan Gregor. The clan's records are that she was honoured and loved. The date of her death is unknown, but she was buried at Rob's right-hand side. To their left-hand side lie their sons Coll and Robin.

Robin, their youngest, was the black sheep of the family. He murdered John MacLaren of Invernenty in 1736. In 1745 he fought under the duke of Cumberland at the battle of Fontenoy, obtained his discharge, and married a sister of Graham of Drunkie. She died three years later. In 1750 he kidnapped Jean Key, aged twenty, from her home near Balfron and married her by force at Rowardennan – he found a priest to read the service in face of her protests. Robin was caught and hanged for this crime four years later, when he was thirty-eight.[2]

James, their eldest, ranked as major in the rising of 1745, when with twelve Gregarach he surprised and burned the barracks of Inversnaid. His valour at Prestonpans, where Prince Charles defeated Sir John Cope, was extraordinary. It brought honour to his name. He fought at Culloden, and escaped with the MacGregor battalion. He was imprisoned in Edinburgh Castle for giving aid to his brother Robin Og, but escaped through the help of his daughter. He died in Paris in great poverty, aged 59.[3]

Coll prospered, and died at Kirkton in 1745. His grandson and great-great-grandson were both major-generals. Duncan lived in Strathyre under the name of Drummond. He was tried at the High Court of Edinburgh in 1753 for helping Robin Og, and was found not guilty. He left no family and few details of his life are known. Ranald died at the Kirkton in 1786, aged eighty.[4]

The ironies of time and chance tend to be either comic or tragic. On 1 November 1975 the Provost of Stirling unveiled, close to the castle, a bronze statue of Rob Roy by Benno Schotz, the Queen's Sculptor in Ordinary for Scotland. Tears and laughter might together have brightened the eyes of Rob and Mary had they been gifted, and second sight allowed them a preview of that Stirling ceremony. In his lifetime, his name had been anathema no less in Stirling than St James's Palace. The sculpture of Rob is no likeness of the man, but the words on the plaque are well chosen – by his great-grandson five times removed – they sum up his life's assertion, from which no power moved him:

> *My foot is on my native heath,*
> *and my name is Rob Roy MacGregor.*

Text References

Abbreviations

History of Clan Gregor	HCG
Public Record Office	PRO
Register of the Privy Council	RPC
Statistical Account of Scotland	SAS
Scottish Record Office	SRO

Further details of entries given in Bibliography

CHAPTER 1 THE HOMELAND
(page 1–page 14)

1 1826: Sinclair, *Analysis of SAS.*
2 1866: Scott, *Fasti.*
3 1898: MacGregor, *HCG.*
4 1855: Campbell, *Lairds of Glenlyon.*
5 1898: MacGregor, *HCG.*
6 1963: Royal Commission on the Ancient and Historic Monuments of Scotland. The *Inventory* gives 70′ × 15′ as the size of Gregor's house at Comer *c* 1670. His chief's would be larger for use as a meeting place.
7 Published 1685 and exhibited at Balquhidder Church.
   1866: Scott, *Fasti.*
8 1966: Lamb, *Changing Climate.*
9 1747: Graham of Gartmore MS.
10 1831: Logan, *The Scottish Gael.*
11 1928: Carmichael, *Carmina Gadelica.*
12 1943: McClintock, *Old Irish and Highland Dress.*
13 1796: SAS.
14 1899: Graham, *Social Life of Scotland in 18th C.*

15 1898: MacGregor, *HCG.*
16 Ibid.
17 1930: Nicolson, *History of Skye.*
18 1730: Burt, *Letters from the North of Scotland.*
19 1899: Graham, *Social Life of Scotland in 18th C.*
   1730: Burt, *Letters from the North of Scotland.*
20 1921: MacKenzie, *A Hundred Years in the Highlands.*
21 1695: Martin, *Description of the Western Islands.*
22 1884: Rogers, *Social Life in Scotland.*
   1882: Hamilton, *Cottagers of Glenburne.*
23 1976: Fenton, *Scottish Country Life.*
24 1924: Grant, *Everyday Life on an Old Highland Farm, 1769.*
   1793: SAS.
   1807: Hall, *Travels in Scotland.*
25 1825: *Moral Statistics of the Highlands and Islands.*
26 *Regulations for Chiefs, 1616.*
27 1800: Garnett, *Observations on a Tour through the Highlands.*
28 1883: Millar, *History of Rob Roy.*

CHAPTER 2   CHILDREN OF THE
MIST (page 15–page 26).

1   1978:   MacDonald, *Clan
    Donald.*
2   1877:   Skene, *Celtic Scotland.*
    1831:   Logan, *The Scottish
    Gael.*
3   1462:   Agreement between
    Walter Stewart, brother to Sir
    John, and Campbell of Argyll.
    Register House,
    Edinburgh.
4   1598:   *The Black Book of
    Taymouth.*
5   1898:   MacGregor, *HCG.*
6   1855:   Campell, *Lairds of
    Glenyon.*
7   Menzies of Weem Papers.
    Letter d/d Drymen, 31 August
    1566, to Laird of Weem, signed
    Marie R.
8   1898:   MacGregor, *HCG.*
    (Walter Scott and other writers
    wrongly give Colquhoun's name
    as Sir Humphrey).
9   1869:   Fraser, *The Chiefs of
    Colquhoun.*
10 1898:   MacGregor, *HCG.*
11 Ibid.
12 1833:   Pitcairne, *Ancient
    Criminal Trials.*
    1812:   Arnot, *Celebrated
    Trials.*
13 1898:   MacGregor, *HCG*
    (quotes letter in full).
14 1855:   Campbell, *Lairds of
    Glenlyon.*

CHAPTER 3   THE BAREFOOT
YEARS (page 27–page 43).

1   1730:   Burt, *Letters from the
    North of Scotland.*
2   1969:   Smout, *History of the
    Scottish People.*
    1899:   Graham, *Social Life of
    Scotland in 18th C.*
3   1898:   MacGregor, *HCG.*
4   1730:   Burt, *Letters from the
    North of Scotland.*

5   Ibid.
6   1899:   Graham, *Social Life of
    Scotland in 18th C.*
    1822:   Stewart of Garth,
    Sketches.
7   1724:   Wade, *Report of the
    State of the Highlands.*
    1699–1750:   *Historical MSS.*
8   1966:   Lamb, *Changing
    Climate.*
9   1952:   Haldane, *The Drove
    Roads of Scotland.*
10 1796:   *SAS,* Buchanan Parish.
    1831:   Logan, *The Scottish
    Gael.*
    1883:   Murray, *The York
    Buildings Company.*
11 1831:   Logan, *The Scottish
    Gael.*
12 1549:   Monro, *Description of
    the Western Islands.*
    1831:   Logan, *The Scottish
    Gael.*
    1876:   Skene, *Celtic Scotland.*
    1938:   MacLeod, *The Book of
    Dunvegan.*
    1957;   Jirlow, *The Plough in
    Scotland.*
13 Ibid. (all five records).
14 Ibid. (all five records).
15 1949:   Dwelly, *Gaelic
    Dictionary.*
    1796:   *SAS,* Parish of
    Callander.
    1695:   Martin, *Description of
    the Western Islands.*
    1930:   Nicolson, *History
    of Skye.*
    1899:   Graham, *Social Life of
    Scotland in the 18th C.*
16 MacGregor of Edinchip Papers.
    1898:   MacGregor, *HCG.*
    1689–1704:   *Miscellaneous
    Tracts* (Nat. Lib.) for 1703,
    Report of Commission into the
    Massacre of Glencoe. The *HCG*
    mistakenly has Rob's sister
    marry Alasdair Og of Glencoe,
    on evidence given by him to the
    Commission, 'That Glenlyon

being his Wive's Uncle came
almost every Day and took his
Morning Drink at this House.'
This it was thought made her
the daughter of Glengyle.
In fact, as Prebble notes in
Glencoe (1966), Alasdair Og's
wife Sarah was the child of
Glenlyon's step-sister, whose
mother had taken for third
husband Duncan Stewart of
Appin, by whom she had one
daughter, who bore Sarah
by marriage to Campbell of
Loch Nell.

17 1822: Stewart of Garth.
Sketches.
1831: Logan, *The Scottish
Gael.*
18 1730: Burt, *Letters from the
North of Scotland.*
19 Ibid.
20 1876: Skene, *Celtic Scotland.*
21 1962: Kok, *Early Scottish
Highland Dyes.*
1898: Maclagan, *On
Highland Dyeing.*
1890: Campbell, *Children of
the Mist.*
22 1962: Dunbar, *History of
Highland Dress.*
23 1824: MacCulloch, *The
Highlands and Western Isles.*
24 1800: Garnett, *Observations
on a Tour.*
25 1730: Burt, *Letters from the
North of Scotland.*
26 1831: Logan, *The Scottish
Gael.*
27 1730: Burt, *Letters from the
North of Scotland.*
28 1952: Plant, *Domestic Life of
Scotland in 18th C.*
29 1800: Garnett, *Observations
on a Tour.*
1824: MacCulloch, *The
Highlands and Western Isles.*
1952: Plant, *Domestic
Life of Scotland in the
18th C.*

30 1885: Campbell, *Records
of Argyll.*
31 1582: Buchanan, *Rerum
Scoticorum Historia.*
1831: Logan, *The Scottish
Gael.*
1962: Dunbar, *History of
Highland Dress.*
32 Ibid.
1885: Campbell, *Records
of Argyll.*
33 1893: Wishart, *Memoirs of
James, Marquis of Montrose.*
34 1796: *SAS*, Parish of
Aberfoyle.
35 1899: Graham, *Social Life of
Scotland in 18th C.*
1969: Smout, *History of the
Scottish People.*
1920: Johnston, *History of the
Working Classes.*
36 1938: MacLeod, *The Book of
Dunvegan.*
37 1899: Graham, *Social Life of
Scotland in 18th C.*
38 1817: Scott, *Rob Roy.*

CHAPTER 4 PREPARATION
(page 44–page 52).

1 1831: Logan, *The Scottish
Gael.*
1907: Stalin, *Pistolet Ecossais.*
1923: Whitelaw, Treatise on
Scottish Hand Firearms.
1962: Dunbar, *History of
Highland Dress.*
2 1831: Logan, *The Scottish
Gael.*
3 His claymore was exhibited in
the Library Hall of Long Island
Historical Society, New York,
in 1890. Its whereabouts is now
unknown.
4 1896: Drummond-Norie, *The
Highland Sword.*
1962: *History of Highland
Dress.*
5 1831: Logan, *The Scottish
Gael.*
1805: Matthewson,

Fencing – Art of the Scotch Broadsword.

6   1899: Graham, *Social Life of Scotland in the 18th C.*
    1730: Burt, *Letters from the North of Scotland.*
7   1771: Pennant, *A Tour in Scotland.*
    1831: Logan, *The Scottish Gael.*
    1793: *SAS.*
8   1976: Fenton, *Scottish Country Life.*
9   1817: Nimmo, *History of Stirlingshire.*
    1898: MacGregor, *HCG.*
10 Ibid.
11 1727: Defoe, *A Tour through Great Britain.*
    1730: Burt, *Letters from the North of Scotland.*
    1817: Scott, *Rob Roy.*
    1800: Garnett, *Observations on a Tour.*
12 Ibid.
13 Ibid.

CHAPTER 5   YOUTH 1685–87
(page 53–page 64).

1   1695: Martin, *Description of the Western Islands.*
2   Translation of a simile from Per Hallström.
3   1855: Campbell, *Lairds of Glenlyon.*
    1908: *Chronicles of Atholl and Tullibardine.*
    Breadalbane Muniments.
4   1834: Maidment, *Argyll Papers 1640–1723.*
5   1816: Kincaid, *Depredations on Clan Campbell 1685–6.*
    1908: *Chronicles of Atholl and Tullibardine.*
    1890: Campbell, *Children of the Mist.*
6   1908: *Chronicles of Atholl and Tullibardine.*
7   1898: MacGregor, *HCG.*

8   1909: Brown, *History of Scotland.*
    1899: Graham, *Social Life of Scotland in 18th C.*
9   1831: Logan, *The Scottish Gael.*
10 1730: Burt, *Letters from the North of Scotland.*
    1831: Logan, *The Scottish Gael.*
11 1796: *SAS*, Strathblane.
    1898: MacGregor, *HCG.*
    Record of Stirling Quarter Sessions, 3 Feb 1658.
12 1964: *Dewar MSS.*
13 1730: Burt, *Letters from the North of Scotland*

CHAPTER 6   YOUTH 1688–89
(page 65–page 74).

1   1952: Plant, *Domestic Life of Scotland in 18th C.*
2   1952: Haldane, *The Drove Roads of Scotland.*
3   1899: Graham, *The Social Life of Scotland in 18th C.*
4   1817: Scott, *Rob Roy.*
5   1952: Haldane, *The Drove Roads of Scotland.*
    1723: Macky, *Journey Through Scotland.*
6   1932: Plant, *Domestic Life of Scotland in 18th C.*
7   1730: Burt, *Letters from the North of Scotland.*
8   1899: Graham, *Social Life of Scotland in 18th C.*
9   1874: Cockburn, *Lord Cockburn. Memorials.*
    1899: Graham, *Social Life of Scotland in 18th C.*
    1952: Plant, *Domestic Life of Scotland in 18th C.*

CHAPTER 7   THE RISING OF THE CLANS (page 75-page 84).

1   1905: Terry, *Graham of Claverhouse, Viscount Dundee.*
2   1898: MacGregor, *HCG.*

3 1831: Logan, *The Scottish Gael*.
1793: *SAS*.
1695: Martin, *Description of the Western Islands*.
1976: Fenton, *Scottish Country Life*.

4 1905: Terry, *Graham of Claverhouse, Viscount Dundee*.

5 1747–87: Roy, *Map of the Highlands*.

6 1822–33: *Chartulary of Clan Gregor*.

7 1898: MacGregor, *HCG* quoting RPC.

8 1586: Camden, *Britannia*.

9 1798: Douglas, *Baronage of Scotland*.

10 1691: Philip of Almerieclose, *The Grameid*.

11 1716: Cameron, John, Young Lochiel, Letter of June 24.

12 1965: MacDonald, *Slaughter Under Trust*.

13 1714: *Memoirs of Viscount Dundee*.

CHAPTER 8 KILLIECRANKIE
(page 85–page 93).

1 1908: Tullibardine, *Military History of Perthshire*.

2 1905: Terry, *Graham of Claverhouse, Viscount Dundee*.
1714: *Memoirs of Viscount Dundee* (supplemented by 1691: Philip, *Grameid*).

3 1714: *Memoirs of Viscount Dundee*.

4 1905: Terry: *Graham of Claverhouse, Viscount Dundee*. (Site of battle is wrongly marked on O.S. maps).

5 1689: *Proceedings of the Estates of Parliament*, No. 56, p 129.
1905: Terry, *Graham of Claverhouse, Viscount Dundee*.
Gen. Mackay, who saw Dundee's body at Old Blair on

7 Sept., reports that Dundee had been shot in the eye.
1908: *Chronicles of Atholl and Tullibardine*. A hole in Dundee's body-armour, later believed made by the fatal ball, is recorded as made by a carpenter for the fourth duke of Atholl 'to improve its warlike appearance', hence error in later histories.

6 1909: Brown, *History of Scotland*.

7 1962: Dunbar, *History of Highland Dress*.

8 1714: *Memoirs of Viscount Dundee*.

9 1898: MacGregor, *HCG*.

10 Ibid.

11 1817: Nimmo, *History of Stirlingshire*.

12 1689: *Proceedings of the Estates of Parliament*.

13 1855: Campbell, *Lairds of Glenlyon*.

14 1690: RPC.

15 Leven and Melville Papers.
1898: MacGregor, *HCG*.

16 1899: Graham, *Social Life of Scotland in 18th C.*

17 1690: RPC.

18 1898: MacGregor, *HCG*.

CHAPTER 9 KIPPEN
(page 94–page 104).

1 1969: Smout, *History of the Scottish People*.

2 1817: Nimmo, *History of Stirlingshire*.

3 1691: RPC, *Acta*, 12 Feb.

4 1898: MacGregor, *HCG*.
1908: *Chronicles of Atholl and Tullibardine*.

5 1834: Maidment, *Argyll Papers*.

6 Malcolm was his sister's son, not his brother's.

7 1779: Arnot, *History of Edinburgh*.
1898: MacGregor, *HCG*.

8   1932: Mackenzie, *Prince Charlie*.
    1811 Grant, *Essay on the Superstitions of the Highlands*.
9   1883: Millar, *History of Rob Roy*.
10 Bitterns became extinct in Scotland in the 18th century.
11 1976: Fenton, *Scottish Country Life* – scythes were not in general use until early in the 19th century.
12 1898: MacGregor, *HCG*.
13 1796: *SAS*, Vol. 18, p 332.
    1817: Nimmo, *History of Stirlingshire*.

CHAPTER 10   MACGREGOR OF INVERSNAID
(page 105–page 122).

1   1883: Millar, *History of Rob Roy*.
2   1889: Graham, *Social Life of Scotland in 18th C*.
3   1898: MacGregor, *HCG*.
4   Letter by Capt Crossley, 8 May 1725, in State Papers, Bundle 16, No. 17, SRO.
5   1898: MacGregor, *HCG*.
6   1866: Scott, *Fasti*.
    1796: *SAS*, Buchanan Parish.
7   1836: Penny, *Traditions of Perth*.
8   1952: Plant, *Domestic life of Scotland in 18th C*.
    1831: Logan, *The Scottish Gael*.
    1791–99: *SAS*.
    1889: Graham, *Social Life of Scotland in 18th C*.
    1730: Burt, *Letters from the North of Scotland*.
9   The ceremony is known from record of its Highland form: see 1828: Scott, *The Fair Maid of Perth*.
10 Buchanan of Leny Papers.

11 'Myln lands multure' – this conveyed right to charge multure at mills (usually 1/12th to 1/30th of the grain brought in for milling: *see* 1831: Logan, *The Scottish Gael*). There were several mills in Craigroston, e.g. at Stucnaroy and Inversnaid.
12 1898: MacGregory, *HCG*.
13 Ibid.
14 1952: Haldane, *The Drove Roads of Scotland*.
15 1908: *Chronicles of Atholl and Tullibardine*.
16 1856: Scott, *Highlanders of Scotland*.
17 Atholl Papers.
18 1967: Moncreiffe, *The Highland Clans*.
    1908: Mackenzie, *Simon Fraser, Lord Lovat*.
19 1730: Burt, *Letters from the North of Scotland*.
20 1899: Graham, *Social Life of Scotland in 18th C*.
21 1969: Smout, *History of the Scottish People*.
22 1826: Sinclair, *Analysis of the SAS*.
23 1899: Graham, *Social Life of Scotland in 18th C*.
24 1976: Fenton, *Scottish Country Life*.
25 1899: Graham, *Social Life of Scotland in the 18th C*.
26 Ibid.
    1969: Smout, *History of the Scottish People*.
27 1730: Burt, *Letters from the North of Scotland*.
28 1909: Brown, *History of Scotland*.
29 1920: Johnston, *History of the Working Classes*.
30 Buchanan of Leny Papers – copy of deeds.
31 1898: MacGregor, *HCG*.
32 1747: Graham of Gartmore MS.

33 1898: MacGregory, *HCG*.
34 1817: Scott, *Rob Roy* – a report made to Scott.

CHAPTER 11 THE TUTOR OF GLENGYLE (page 123–page 134).

1   Opinion of the Scottish National Portrait Gallery.
2   1810: Mackintosh, *Historical Notes*.
    1822: Stewart of Garth, *Sketches*.
    Small stature was a consequence of low diet. Scott, while a young lawyer, visited Balquhidder in 1788. The descriptions he had of Rob Roy were from men who had known him.
3   1747: Graham of Gartmore MS.
    1818 Anon., *The Trials of James, Duncan, and Robert MacGregor.*
4   Daniel Defoe reported of Rob Roy, 'He gained the love of all that knew him; for he had good natural parts, was obliging to every body, and a very diverting pleasant fellow in conversation.'
5   1817: Scott, *Rob Roy.*
    1819: Macleay, *Historical Memoirs of Rob Roy.*
6   Binning, Lord, *Collections of Original Poems by Scotch Gentlemen*, Vol. 11 p 125.
7   Date inferred from Rob's assumption of Tutorship.
8   1898: MacGregor, *HCG.*
9   1952: Plant, *Domestic Life of Scotland in 18th C.*
10 Ibid.
11 1952: Haldane, *Drove Roads of Scotland.*
12 Ibid.
13 1813: Douglas, *Peerage of Scotland.*
14 Montrose Papers.
    1908: *Chronicles of Atholl and Tullibardine.*

1712: *Edinburgh Evening Courant*, June 12.
15 Montrose Papers.
    1898: MacGregor, *HCG.*
16 Montrose Papers. Letter from Rob Roy to James Grahame, 1712.
17 Ibid.
18 1898: MacGregor, *HCG.*
19 1834: Maidment, *Argyll Papers.*
20 Atholl Papers.
21 1908: *Chronicles of Atholl and Tullibardine.*
22 1817: Scott, *Rob Roy.*

CHAPTER 12 THE TREATY OF UNION (page 135–page 143).

1   Montrose Papers.
2   1952: Haldane, *Drove Roads of Scotland.*
3   1808: Walker, *Economic History of the Hebrides and Highlands.*
4   Abercromby's personal report to Scott, 1829, in *Waverley*, Notes.
5   Buchanan of Leny Papers.
    1898: MacGregor, *HCG.*
6   1668: Dryden, *Essay on Dramatic Poesie.*
7   1712: *Edinburgh Evening Courant*, 18–21 June.
8   1709: Defoe, *History of the Union.*
9   1909: Brown, *History of Scotland.*
10 1977: Dickson, *Red John of the Battles.*
11 1909: Brown, *History of Scotland.*
12 1817: Nimmo, *History of Stirlingshire.*
13 1880: Fraser, *The Red Book of Menteith*. One of four letters from Rob Roy copied from Breadalbane Muniments.
14 Montrose Papers.
15 1898: MacGregor, *HCG.*
16 Ibid.

1817: Nimmo, *History of Stirlingshire.*

17 1909: Brown, *History of Scotland.*

18 1714: Lockhart, *Memoirs.*

CHAPTER 13 TIME AND CHANCE
(page 144–page 157).

1 Montrose Papers. Rob Roy undertook payment of Stewart's outstanding debts.

2 Atholl Papers.

3 1817: Nimmo, *History of Stirlingshire.*
1898: MacGregor, *HCG.*

4 Montrose Papers.

5 Ibid.
Historical MSS Commission, Third Report.
1883: Murray, *York Buildings Company.*

6 Montrose Papers.

7 1817: Nimmo, *History of Stirlingshire.*

8 1723: Defoe, *Highland Rogue.* Defoe reports the general opinion of Rob's character at this time. 'He kept good company and regarded his word with the greatest strictness imaginable.'

9 Montrose Papers.

10 1899: Graham, *Social Life of Scotland in 18th C.*

11 1717: Rob Roy's *Declaration* in MacGregor of Edinchip Papers.
1883: Millar, *History of Rob Roy.* Prof. Millar says that the offer was in writing, but that is hard to believe; he quotes no source, and no evidence has since been found.

12 Ibid. Prof. Millar says that Argyll laid the case before the Court in England and accused Montrose of stirring up strife in Scotland. No confirmation appears in the Argyll Papers. He perhaps confused Argyll in

1713 with Atholl in 1703.

13 1898: MacGregor, *HCG.*
1822–33: *Chartulary of Clan Gregor.*

14 1817: Nimmo, *History of Stirlingshire.* Editor's note in Latin.

15 1819: Macleay, *Historical Memoirs of Rob Roy.*
1883: Millar, *History of Rob Roy.*

CHAPTER 14 PRELUDE TO WAR
(page 158–page 170).

1 Montrose Papers.

2 The gable-end of a ruined house still stands on the terrace, with remains of a byre to its west side. A board on the wall has the words, almost obliterated in 1982: *Rob Roy's House. Please do not damage or remove anything.* The ground plan is 40′ × 21′ externally. The gable wall, about 2′ thick, has a chimney stack. The chimney hole is well-built and mortared, and given a sharp bend left and right. The corner stones have been cut square and the gable-top has normal pitch. These features mean that the house is a nineteeth-century replacement of Rob Roy's. Gable fireplaces began to develop sporadically in smaller buildings only towards the end of the eighteenth century, and only in districts where coal was readily available directly from pits or sea-ports. The site is confirmed as correct from recorded topographical detail of the 1716 ambuscade.

3 1826: Sinclair, *Analysis of the SAS.*

4 Montrose Papers.

5 Ibid.

6 1819: Macleay, *Historical Memoirs of Rob Roy.*
1883: Millar, *History of Rob*

Roy. (Scott in *Rob Roy* names him Macanaleister).

7   1883: Millar, *History of Rob Roy*, reporting the common knowledge of the people.
    Montrose Papers.

8   1730: Burt, *Letters from the North of Scotland*.

9   Ibid.

10 1883: Millar, *History of Rob Roy*.

11 1834: Maidment, *Analectica Scotica*. Letter of 20 Feb.

12 1798: Douglas, *The Baronage of Scotland*.

13 1898: MacGregor, *HCG*.

14 1813: Douglas, *Peerage of Scotland*.

15 Montrose Papers.

16 Ibid.

17 1855: Campbell, *Lairds of Glenlyon*.

18 1898: MacGregor, *HCG*.

19 Argyll Papers. Letter dated 21 Nov. 1715 from Rob Roy to Argyll, exhibited Inveraray Castle.

CHAPTER 15 THE 'FIFTEEN
(page 171–page 181).

1   1898: MacGregor, *HCG*.
    1817: Scott, *Rob Roy*.

2   1745: Campbell, *Life of John, Duke of Argyll*.

3   1746: Rae, *History of the Rebellion*.
    1717: Patten, *History of the late Rebellion*.

4   1970: Baynes, *Jacobite Rising of 1715*.

5   1746: Rae, *History of the Rebellion*.

6   1855: Campbell, *Lairds of Glenlyon*.

7   1746: Rae, *History of the Rebellion*.

8   1715: Wodrow, *Letters*.

9   1855: Campbell, *Lairds of Glenlyon*.

10 1715: Mar's Campaign Orders.

11 1898: MacGregor, *HCG*.

12 1715: Wodrow, *Letters*.

13 1883: Millar, *History of Rob Roy*.

14 1715: Mar's Campaign Orders.

15 1817: Scott, *Rob Roy*, quoting records of State Paper Office.

16 1715: Mar's Campaign Orders.

17 Historical MSS Commission, Third Report.

18 1746: Rae, *History of the Rebellion*.

19 1898: MacGregor, *HCG*. Letter from Balhaldie to Mar, 1715.

20 MacGregor of Edinchip Papers.
    1746: Rae, *History of the Rebellion*.

21 1715: *Loch Lomond Expedition*.

22 1746: Rae, *History of the Rebellion*.

23 1715: Report by Finlayson, eye-witness, 15 Oct., in Wodrow's *Letters*.

24 1715: *Loch Lomond Expedition*.

25 1715: Report by Finlayson, eye-witness, 15 Oct., in Wodrow's *Letters*.

26 1715: Wodrow's *Letters*. Report d/d 23 Oct. from Inveraray.

27 Ibid.

28 1831: Logan, *The Scottish Gael*.

29 1813: Douglas, *Peerage of Scotland*.

30 Montrose Papers: Atholl's letter of 26 July 1715.

CHAPTER 16 SHERIFFMUIR
(page 182–page 194).

1   Inferred from John Cameron's letter of 24 June 1716 (see

Bibliography, 1904: Mackay),
and from Mar's Campaign
Orders.

2   1746:   Rae, *History of the
Rebellion*
1898:   Society of Antiquaries,
Battle of Sheriffmuir.
1717:   Patten, *History of
the late Rebellion*. Report by
General Wightman.

3   1716:   John Cameron,
Young Lochiel – inference
from his letter of 24 June (see
Bibliography, 1904: Mackay).

4   Ibid.

5   Ibid.
1717:   Patten, *History of the
late Rebellion*.
1746:   Rae, *History of the
Rebellion*.
1855:   Campbell, *Lairds of
Glenlyon*.
1898:   Society of Antiquaries,
Battle of Sheriffmuir.
1908:   Tullibardine, *Military
History of Perthshire*.

6   Letter from Mar to Governor
of Perth, Nov. 1715, in
Patten's *History of the late
Rebellion*. 1717.

7   1855:   Campbell, *Lairds of
Glenlyon*.

8   1898:   Society of Antiquaries,
Battle of Sheriffmuir.

9   1717:   Patten, *History of the
late Rebellion* – Report by
General Wightman.

10   1898:   Society of Antiquaries,
Battle of Sheriffmuir.

11   1717:   Patten, *History of the
late Rebellion*. Mar's Report on
the battle.

12   1908:   Tullibardine, *Military
History of Perthshire*.

13   1717:   Patten, *History of
the late Rebellion*. General
Wightman's report on
the battle.

14   1745:   Campbell, *Life of John,
Duke of Argyll*.

15   1835:   Monteath, *Dunblane
Traditions*.

16   John Cameron, Young Lochiel,
letter of 24 June 1716.
1904:   Mackay, *The Camerons
in the Rising of 1715*.

17   1908:   Tullibardine, *Military
History of Perthshire*.

18   1819:   Hogg, *Jacobite Relics*.

19   1746:   Rae, *History of the
Rebellion*.

20   1898:   Society of Antiquaries,
Battle of Sheriffmuir.

21   1717:   Patten, *History of
the late Rebellion*. General
Wightman's despatches.

22   1908:   Tullibardine, *Military
History of Perthshire*.

23   Ibid.

24   Ibid.

25   Argyll Papers. Original letter at
Inveraray Castle.

CHAPTER 17   TEMPTATION IN
THE WILDERNESS (page 195–
page 208)

1   1747:   Graham of Gartmore's
report of Rob Roy.

2   1715–17:   Wodrow, *Letters*.
1834:   Maidment, *Analectica
Scotica*.

3   1717:   Rob Roy's *Declaration*,
in MacGregor of Edinchip
Papers.

4   1715–17:   Wodrow, *Letters*.
1896:   Smith, *Strathendrick*.
A printing error gives
MacLachlan's capture as 1710,
which should be 1716.

5   1715–17:   Wodrow, *Letters*.

6   1883:   Millar, *History of Rob
Roy*. No source or date given.

7   1715–17:   Wodrow, *Letters*.

8   Ibid.

9   Ibid.

10   Ibid.

11   Historical MSS Commission,
Third Report.

12   1883:   Millar, *History of
Rob Roy*.

13 1977: Dickson, *Red John of the Battles*.

14 1715: Mar's Campaign Orders.
1898: MacGregor, *HCG*.

15 1715–17: Wodrow, *Letters*.

16 Montrose Papers.

17 MacGregor of Edinchip Papers.

18 1745: Campbell, *Life of John, Duke of Argyll*.

19 1717: Rob Roy, *Declaration*. In MacGregor and Montrose Papers.

20 Ibid.

21 This report on Highlanders' character is thoroughly attested. See (among many others):
1695: Martin, *Description of the Western Islands*.
1702: Sacheverall, *An Account of the Isle of Man with a Voyage to I-Columb-kill*.
1730: Burt, *Letters from the North of Scotland*.
1771: Dalrymple, *Memoirs of Great Britain*.
1810: Mackintosh, *Historical Notes*.
1810: Simond, *Journal of a Tour and Residence in Great Britain*.
1822: Stewart of Garth, *Sketches*.
1924: Grant, *Life on an Old Highland Farm, 1769–82*.

22 1842: Franks, *Mines and Collieries*.

23 Montrose Papers.

24 Ibid.

25 1883: Millar, *History of Rob Roy*.

26 Montrose Papers.

27 Ibid.
1715–17: Wodrow, *Letters*.

28 1716: *Flying Post*, 18 Oct.

29 1885: Campbell, *Records of Argyll*.

30 1890: Campbell, *Children of the Mist*.

31 1800: Garnett, *Observations on a Tour*.

32 1885: Campbell, *Records of Argyll*.

33 Balquhidder Kirk Records – no date given for bell's removal. Date of return, 1930.

34 1885: Campbell, *Records of Argyll*.

CHAPTER 18 THE DUEL WITH MONTROSE (page 209–page 221).

1 1964: Domhnull Gruamach, *Foundations of Islay*.

2 Montrose Papers.

3 Ibid.

4 Historical Records of the War Office, 1718.
1963: Royal Commission on Ancient and Historical Monuments, *Inventory of Stirlingshire*.

5 Montrose Papers.

6 1817: Scott, *Rob Roy*, Introduction.

7 1908: *Chronicles of Atholl and Tullibardine*.

8 1817: Scott, *Rob Roy*, Introduction.
1883: Millar, *History of Rob Roy*.

CHAPTER 19 THE DUEL WITH ATHOLL (page 222–page 240).

1 Atholl Papers.
1908: *Chronicles of Atholl and Tullibardine*.

2 1883: Millar, *History of Rob Roy*.

3 1908: *Chronicles of Atholl and Tullibardine*.

4 Atholl Papers.

5 1908: *Chronicles of Atholl and Tullibardine*. Letter from Rev. H. Murray, July 1717. Atholl, MacGregor, and Montrose Papers: Rob Roy's *Declaration*, 1717.

6 1717: Wodrow, *Letters*, reporting Rob at Dunkeld.

7   MacGregor and Montrose
    Papers.
8   Gregorson of Ardtornish
    Papers.
9   1813: Douglas, *Peerage of
    Scotland.*
10 1908: *Chronicles of Atholl
    and Tullibardine.*
11 1715: Wodrow, *Letters.*
    1834: Maidment, *Analectica
    Scotica.*
12 1908: *Chronicles of Atholl
    and Tullibardine.*
13 1899: Graham, *Social Life of
    Scotland in 18th C.*
14 Ibid.
15 Letter from Rev. H. Murray of
    Comrie to Rev. Colin Campbell
    of Ardchattan, 2 July 1717, in
    HCG 1898. Murray had been
    treasurer at Dunkeld Cathedral
    in 1689.
16 Letter from Atholl to Lord
    James Murray, 18 June 1717,
    in *Chronicles of Atholl and
    Tullibardine,* 1908.
17 1908: *Chronicles of Atholl
    and Tullibardine.*
18 Ibid.
19 Atholl Papers.
20 Gregorson of Ardtornish
    Papers.
21 MacGregor of Edinchip Papers.
    Montrose Papers.
22 Ibid.
23 1883: Millar, *History of
    Rob Roy.*
24 Ibid.
25 Ibid.
    1723: Defoe, *Highland
    Rogue.*
26 Montrose Papers, 1718.
27 1883: Murray, *York Buildings
    Company.*
28 Montrose Papers, 1718.
29 Historical Records of the War
    Office at PRO, Kew, ref. WO
    47/31, p 57.
    1963: Royal Commission
    on Ancient and Historical

Monuments, *Inventory of
Stirlingshire.*
30 Ibid.
    Prof. Millar's account in
    History of Rob Roy of Rob's
    capturing the barracks in 1713
    (sic) and expelling 'Nasmyth' in
    a blizzard, thus causing his ruin
    and death, is wholly fictional.
31 Historical Records of the War
    Office at PRO Kew, ref. WO
    47, 31, p 57.
    Montrose Papers, Oct.1718.
32 1908: *Chronicles of Atholl
    and Tullibardine.*

CHAPTER 20
RECONCILIATION
(page 241–page 251).

1   Royal Proclamation of
    12 March 1719. Copy in
    MacGregor of Edinchip Papers,
    No. 687.
2   1908: Tullibardine, *Military
    History of Perthshire.*
3   Oliphant of Gask Papers.
    1871: Oliphant, *Jacobite
    Lairds of Gask*: Report from
    Tullibardine to Mar.
4   1908: Tullibardine, *Military
    History of Perthshire.*
5   1817: Scott, *Rob Roy* – copy
    of letter in Scott's hands.
6   1885: Campbell, *Records
    of Argyll.*
7   1883: Murray, *York Buildings
    Company.*
8   Ibid. – Report to Parliament by
    Commissioners of Inquiry.
9   1866: Scott, *Fasti.*
10 1817: Scott, *Rob Roy,*
    Introduction.
11 1898: Grant, *Memoirs of a
    Highland Lady.*
12 1883: Millar, *History of
    Rob Roy.*
13 1898: MacGregor, *HCG.*
14 Parish Records, Balquhidder.
15 1883: Millar, *History of Rob
    Roy,* quoting family records

of Sir James Alexander of
Westerton.

16 1908: *Chronicles of Atholl
    and Tullibardine.*

17 Ibid.

18 1883: Millar, *History of
    Rob Roy.*

CHAPTER 21 THE END OF THE
RACE (page 252–page 263).

1 1895: Spalding Club,
   Historical Papers, 1699-1750.

2 MacGregor of Edinchip Papers
   – copy of letter.

3 Report by Abercromby to
   Sir Walter Scott *c* 1792, in
   Waverley, Notes.

4 1898: Grant, *Memoirs of a
   Highland Lady* – letter from
   Rob Roy d/d Inverlochlarig, 26
   March 1726.

5 State Papers, Scotland, bundle
   16, No. 17.

6 First-hand report made to
   Sir Walter Scott, *Rob Roy*,
   Introduction.

7 1819: Macleay, *Historical
   Memoirs of Rob Roy.*

8 Kirk Session Records
   Balquhidder.

9 1817: Scott, *Rob Roy.*

10 1866: Scott, *Fasti.*

11 1883: Millar, *History of
    Rob Roy.*

12 1819: Macleay, *Historical
    Memoirs of Rob Roy.*

13 1845: New *SAS*, Skye.

14 1817: Scott, *Rob Roy*,
    Introduction.

15 1898: MacGregor, *HCG.*

16 Ibid.

17 Ibid.
    1817: Scott, *Rob Roy*,
    Introduction.

18 Personal account given by
    Invernahyle to Sir Walter Scott
    – *Rob Roy*, Introduction.

19 1735: Books of Commissariat
    of Dunblane, *Inventory*,
    Vol. 19.

20 1898: MacGregor, *HCG.*

21 1817: Scott, *Rob Roy*,
    Introduction.
    1819: Macleay, *Historical
    Memoirs of Rob Roy.*
    1883: Millar, *History of
    Rob Roy.*
    1898: MacGregor, *HCG.*

22 This tune became the basis
    of the famous pibroch.
    MacCrimmon's Lament.

23 1822: Stewart of Garth,
    Sketches.

24 Balquhidder Kirk Records.

25 1819: Macleay, *Historical
    Memoirs of Rob Roy.*
    1890: Campbell, *Children of
    the Mist.*

POSTSCRIPT
(page 264–page 266).

1 1735: Books of the
   Commissariat of Dunblane,
   Vol. 19, *Inventory.* Also in
   1880: Fraser, *The Red Book
   of Menteith.*

2 1817: Scott, *Rob Roy*,
   Introduction.
   1818: Anon., *The Trials of
   James, Duncan, and Robert
   MacGregor.*
   1926: Millar, *Gregarach*
   – trials of Rob Roy's sons.
   (Erroneous in much detail apart
   from the trials).

3 Ibid. (all three records).

4 1898: MacGregor, *HCG.*

5 Inscription on plaque. Rob's
   descendant was then alive.

Bibliography

1549   MONRO, DONALD, *A Description of the Western Islands.*

1582   BUCHANAN, GEORGE, *Rerum Scoticorum Historia.* Trans. James Aikman, 1827.

1598–   BOWIE, WILLIAM, *The Black Book of Taymouth.* The MS of the family notary from the Breadalbane Charter Room. Edited Cosmo Innes for Bannatyne Club, Edinburgh, 1855.

1622   Records of the Baron Court of Breadalbane, January 11 (In 1938: Gillies, *In Famed Breadalbane*).

1689–96   Highland Papers. Political condition of the Highlands. Maitland Club, Glasgow, 1945. (Vol LV, 198: Campbells of Glenorchy).

1691   PHILIP, JAMES of Almerieclose, *The Grameid.* Narrative verse on Dundee's campaign of 1689. Latin with English translation. Scottish Historical Society, 1887–8.

1693   SLEZER, J., *Theatrum Scotiae.* Prints of Glasgow.

1695   MARTIN, MARTIN, *Description of the Western Islands.*

1699   SIBBALD, ROBERT, *Provision for the Poor in time of Dearth and Scarcity.*

1699–   *Historical Papers.*
1750   General Wade's Report on Scotland, 1724. Spalding Club, 1895, Vol.I.

1705   TAYLOR, JOSEPH, *A Journey to Edinborough.*

1709   DEFOE, DANIEL, *History of the Union of Great Britain.*

1712   SACHEVERELL, W., *An Account of the Isle of Man with a Voyage to I-Columb-kill.*

1714   An officer of the Army, *Memoirs of the Lord Viscount Dundee.* Edited Henry Jenner, 1903.

1714   LOCKHART, GEORGE, *Memoirs of the Affairs of Scotland.*

1715   Mar's *Campaign Orders* (in 1746: Rae, *History of the Rebellion*, second edition).

1715   The *Loch Lomond Expedition.* An account by eye-witnesses dated 15 October 1715, two days after the expedition. Original papers in Library of Faculty of Advocates, pub. 1834.

1715–17   WODROW, Rev. ROBERT, *Letters.* In *Loch Lomond Expedition*, printed 1834.

1716   *Journal of the Earl of Mar.*

1716   CAMERON, JOHN, Young Lochiel, *Letter*

of 24 June from South Uist. In Transactions of the Gaelic Society of Inverness, 1904, Vol. XXVI.

1717 PATTEN, Rev. R., *History of the late Rebellion.*

1723 DEFOE, DANIEL, *The Highland Rogue.*

1723 MACKY, JOHN, *Journey Through Scotland.*

1724 WADE, General GEORGE, *First Report on the State of the Highlands.*

1727 DEFOE, DANIEL, *A Tour through Great Britain in 1724.*

1730 Collection of Original Letters and Papers relating to the Rebellion, 1715. Edinburgh.

1730 BURT, EDWARD, *Letters from a Gentleman in the North of Scotland.*

1733 MACKY, JOHN, *Memoirs of Secret Services.*

1735 Books of the Commissariat of Dunblane. Inventory of Rob Roy's personal estate in Vol. 19.

1736 DUNBAR, JAMES, *Smegmatalogia* (The art of making soap and potashes and bleaching linen).

1742 MACKINTOSH, WILLIAM, *A Short Scheme to stop Depredations.*

1745 CAMPBELL, ROBERT, *Life of John, Duke of Argyll.*

1746 RAE, Rev. PETER, *History of the Rebellion Raised against His Majesty King George I.* Second edition with Mar's Campaign Orders.

1747 GRAHAM OF GARTMORE MS, *An inquiry into Causes of Disturbances in the Highlands.* Printed as an appendix to Burt's Letters, 5th edn, 1822.

1752 CAMPBELL, JOHN, *A Full and Particular Description of the Highlands of Scotland.*

1771–73 DALRYMPLE, Sir JOHN, *Memoirs of Gt Britain and Ireland.*

1771–75 PENNANT, THOMAS, *A Tour in Scotland and the Western Isles.*

1779 ARNOT, HUGO, *History of Edinburgh.*

1787 KNOX, JOHN, *A Tour through the Highlands of Scotland in 1776.*

1791–99 SINCLAIR, Sir JOHN, Editor, *The Statistical Account of Scotland,* 21 vols.

1793 HERON, ROBERT, *Observations made in a Journey through the Western Counties of Scotland.*

1796 The *Statistical Account of Scotland,* Vol. 9, Buchanan; Vol. 10, Aberfoyle; Vol. 11, Callander; Vol. 18, Kippen, Strathblane.

1798 DOUGLAS, Sir ROBERT, *The Baronage of Scotland.*

1800 GARNETT, T., *Observations on a Tour through the Highlands.*

1805 MATTHEWSON, THOMAS, *Fencing Familiarised – a new Treatise of the Art of the Scotch Broadsword.*

1807 HALL, JAMES, *Travels in Scotland by an Unusual Route.*

1808 WALKER, J., *An Economic History of the Hebrides and Highlands.*

1810 MACKINTOSH, ANEAS, *Historical Notes.*

1810–11 SIMOND, LOUIS, *Journal of a Tour and Residence in Great Britain.*

1811 GRANT, ANNE of Laggan, *Essay on Superstitions of the Highlands.*

1812 ARNOT, HUGO, *Criminal Trials.*

1813 DOUGLAS, Sir ROBERT, *The Peerage of Scotland.*

1814 SCOTT, WALTER, *Waverley.*

1816 KINCAID, ALEXANDER, Editor, *Account of the Depredations committed on Clan Campbell, 1685 and 1686.* Losses of the Atholl Raid presented as a financial account by Ewing of Bernice, 1690. (In Scottish National Library.)

1817 NIMMO, WILLIAM, *History of Stirlingshire.*

1817 SCOTT, WALTER, *Rob Roy.*

1818 Anonymous, *The Trials of James, Duncan, and Robert McGregor.*

1819 HOGG, JAMES, *Jacobite Relics.*

1819 MACLEAY, K., *Historical Memoirs of Rob Roy.*

c 1820 STEWART, D., *The Life and Surprising Exploits of Rob Roy.* 31 pp. Newcastle.

c 1820 Anonymous, *The Life, Exploits and Daring Adventures of Rob Roy, the Scottish Outlaw.* 16 pp.

1822 STEWART of Garth, General Sir DAVID. *Sketches of the Character, Manners, and Present State of the Highlands.*

1822–33 STIRLING, WILLIAM MACGREGOR, *The Chartulary of Clan Gregor,* 3 vols. Compiled from the Register of the Privy Council of Scotland and other records. Analysed and revised by Sir Evan MacGregor.

1824 MACCULLOCH, JOHN, *The Highlands and Western Islands.*

1825 *The Moral Statistics of the Highlands and Islands.*

1826 SINCLAIR, Sir JOHN, *Analysis of the Statistical Account of Scotland.*

1827 SCOTT, WALTER, *The Two Drovers.*

1831 LOGAN, JAMES, *The Scottish Gael.*

1833 PITCAIRNE, R., *Ancient Criminal Trials in Scotland.*

1834 MAIDMENT, JAMES, *Analectica Scotica.*

1834 MAIDMENT, JAMES, Editor, *The Argyll Papers, 1640–1723.*

1835 MONTEATH, JOHN, *Dunblane Traditions.*

1836 PENNY, GEORGE, *Traditions of Perth.*

1842 BROWNE, JAMES, *History of the Highlands.*

1842 FRANKS, R. H., *Mines and Collieries.* Report of the Children's Employment Commission.

1843 *Leven and Melville Papers.* Bannatyne Club, Edinburgh.

1843 KEITH, GEORGE, Earl Marischal of Scotland, *Memoirs of Mareshal Keith.*

1849 BURTON, J., *Darien Papers.*

1855–58   CAMPBELL, DUNCAN,
The Lairds of Glenlyon.
Family records of
Glenlyon House.
Pub. for Sir Donald
Guthrie of Garth and
Glenlyon, 1886.

1856   SCOTT, WALTER,
The Highlanders of
Scotland.

1866   SCOTT, HEW, Fasti
Ecclesiae Scoticanae
(succession of ministers
of the Church of
Scotland).

1869   FRASER, Sir WILLIAM, The
Chiefs of Colquhoun and
their Country.

1871   OLIPHANT, T. L. K., The
Jacobite Lairds of Gask.
Appendix: Report by
Tullibardine to Mar
on the Rising of 1719
(original in Gask Papers).

1874   COCKBURN, HENRY T.,
Lord Cockburn.
Memorials of his Time.

1875   KELTIE, J. S., A History of
the Scottish Highlands,
Highland Clans, and
Highland Regiments.

1876–80   SKENE, W.F., Celtic
Scotland.

1879   HENDERSON, E., Annals
of Dunfermline,
1069–1878.

1880   GARNETT, T.,
The Highlands of
Scotland.

1880   FRASER, WILLIAM, The
Red Book of Menteith, 2
vols. Family Papers.

1881   ANDERSON, JOSEPH,
Ancient Scottish
Weapons.

1882   MICHEL, F., A Critical
Inquiry into the Scottish
language.

1882   HAMILTON, E., Cottagers
of Glenburnie.

1883   MILLAR, A. H., History of
Rob Roy.

1883   MURRAY, DAVID,
The York Buildings
Company (for the sale
and purchase of forfeited
estates after the Rising
of 1715).

1884   ROGERS, CHARLES, Social
Life in Scotland from
Early to Recent Times.

1885   CAMPBELL, Lord
ARCHIBALD, Records
of Argyll.

1890   CAMPBELL, Lord
ARCHIBALD, The
Children of the Mist or
the Scottish Clansmen in
Peace and War.

1893   WISHART, GEORGE
Memoirs of James,
Marquis of Monotrose.

1895   Historical Papers,
1699–1750, Vol. I. New
Spalding Club (2 vols.)

1896   DRUMMOND-NORIE, W.,
The Highland Sword. In
Celtic Monthly, June to
October.

1896   MACDONALD, A., Clan
Donald. 3 vols.

1896   SMITH, J. GUTHRIE,
Strathendrick.

1897   SMALL, J. W., Old
Stirling.

1898   MACGREGOR, A.G.M.,
History of Clan
Gregor, 2 vols.

1898   GRANT of
Rothiemurchus,
ELIZABETH, Memoirs of a
Highland Lady.

1898   The Battle of
Sheriffmuir. Compiled
by the Society of
Antiquaries in Scotland
from original sources.

1898   MACLAGAN, R.C., On
Highland Dyeing
and Colourings of

Native-made Tartans. In Transactions of Royal Scottish Society of Arts, Vol. XIV.

1889 GRAHAM, HENRY GREY, *Social Life of Scotland in the Eighteenth Century*.

1901 RAIT, R.S., *The Scottish Parliament*.

1902 MACLEAN, MAGNUS, *The Literature of the Celts*.

1902-9 TERRY, C.S., *The Scottish Parliament*.

1904 MACLEAN, MAGNUS, *The Literature of the Highlands*.

1904 MACKAY, WILLIAM, *The Camerons in the Rising of 1715*. In Transactions of the Gaelic Society of Inverness, Vol. XXVI, 1904-7. Letter of 6000 words from John Cameron, Young Lochiel, d/d June 24, 1716 from South Uist to gentlemen of his clan, describing the Camerons' part in the Risings of 1689 and 1715, and his meeting Rob Roy at Sheriffmuir. (Mackay's own account of the battle is remote from the known facts.)

1905 TERRY, C.S., *John Graham of Claverhouse, Viscount Dundee*.

1907 MACKENZIE, JOHN, *The Beauties of Gaelic Poetry*.

1907 BARBOUR, J., *W. Paterson and the Darien Company*.

1907 STALIN, M. GEORGES, *Pistolet Ecossais*.

1908 MACKENZIE, W.C., *Simon Fraser, Lord Lovat*.

1908 *The Chronicles of the Atholl and Tullibardine Families*. From the Atholl Papers. Privately printed (National Library of Scotland, Gen. 8A. Also in Scottish Record Office, Historical Room.)

1908 TULLIBARDINE, Marchioness of, *Military History of Perthshire, 1660-1902*. Vol. I gives battles of Killiecrankie, Sheriffmuir, and Glen Shiel.

1909 BROWN, P. HUME, *History of Scotland*. 3 vols.

1909 DALTON, C., *The Scots Army, 1661-88*.

1909 MACGILL, W., *Old Rosshire*.

1911 FLOOD, W. H. GRATTAN, *The Bagpipe*.

1914 ELDER, JOHN R., *The Highland Host of 1678*.

1916 MACKENZIE, W. C., *Races of Ireland and Scotland*.

1920 JOHNSTON, THOMAS, *The History of the Working Classes in Scotland*.

1921 MACKENZIE, OSGOOD, *A Hundred Years in the Highlands*.

1923 WHITELAW, C.E., *Treatise on Scottish Hand Firearms of the 16th, 17th, and 18th Centuries*.

1924 GRANT, I.F., *Everyday Life on an Old Highland Farm* From account books of Mackintosh of Balnespick, 1769-82.

1926 MILLAR, A.H., *Gregarach—The Strange Adventures of Rob Roy's sons*. (Largely fictitious, in part accurate.)

1927 MACGREGOR, A.A., *Wild Drumalbine*.

1928-54 CARMICHAEL,

ALEXANDER, *Carmina Gadelica.*

1930 NICHOLSON, A., *History of Skye.*

1932 MACKENZIE, COMPTON, *Prince Charlie.*

1934 SALMOND, JAMES, *Wade in Scotland.*

1935 MACGREGOR, A.A., *Somewhere in Scotland.*

1938 MACLEOD, *The Book of Dunvegan*, from Macleod Papers.

1938 GILLIES, Rev. W. A., *In Famed Breadalbane.*

1943 MCCLINTOCK, H.F., *Old Irish and Higland Dress.*

1947 MILLER, A.E. HASWELL, *The Truth about the Tartan*. Scotland's Magazine, November.

1949 DWELLY, EDWARD, *Illustrated Gaelic Dictionary.*

1950 HOWLETT, HAMILTON, *Highland Constable.*

1952 HALDANE, A.R.B., *The Drove Roads of Scotland.*

1952 PLANT, MARJORIE, *Domestic Life in Scotland in the 18th Century.*

1953 FRASER, CHARLES IAN, *The Clan Cameron.*

1956 MILLER, A.E. HASWELL, *Common Errors in Scottish History.*

1957 JIRLOW, R., and IAN WHITTAKER, *The Plough in Scotland.* Scottish Studies, Vol. 1, University of Edinburgh.

1961 GRANT, I.F., *Highland Folk Ways.*

1962 DUNBAR, JOHN TELFER, *History of Highland Dress*. A definitive study of custom and tartan, civil and military, including weapons.

1962 KOK, ANNETTE, *Early Scottish Highland Dyes*. In History of Highland Dress.

1963 ROYAL COMMISSION ON THE ANCIENT AND HISTORICAL MONUMENTS OF SCOTLAND, *Inventory of Stirlingshire*, 2 vols. Detail of Inversnaid Barracks in Vol.2.

1963 SMOUT, T.C., *Scottish Trade on the Eve of the Union.*

1964 DEWAR, JOHN, *The Dewar MSS*. West Highland Folk Tales, collected 19th century. Translated from the Gaelic by Hector Maclean. Edited John MacKechnie.

1964–70 DOMHNULL GRUAMACH, *The Foundations of Islay*, 2 vols. Privately printed: Graham Donald, Islay.

1965 MACDONALD, DONALD J., *Slaughter Under Trust.*

1965 SMOUT, T.C. and A FENTON, *Scottish Agriculture Before the Improvers.* In Agricultural History Review, Vol. XIII.

1966 COLLINSON, FRANCIS, *The Traditional and National Music of Scotland.*

1966 LAMB, H.H., *Changing Climate.*

1966 PREBBLE, JOHN, *Glencoe*

1967 MONCREIFFE of that Ilk, *The Highland Clans.*

1967 MILLER, R., *Land Use by Summer Shielings*, in Scottish Studies, Vol. II, University of Edinburgh

1968 FERGUSON, W., *Scotland 1689 to the Present.*

1968 PREBBLE, JOHN, *The Darien Disaster.*

1969 SMOUT T.C., *A History of the Scottish People, 1560– 1830.*

1970 BAYNES, JOHN, *The Jacobite Rising of 1715.*

1976 FENTON, ALEXANDER, *Scottish Country Life.*

1977 DICKSON, PATRICIA, *Red John of the Battles.* Biography of John, second Duke of Argyll.

1978 MACDONALD, DONALD J., *Clan Donald.*

ESTATE PAPERS

Argyll Papers: Inveraray Castle and Scottish Record Office.

Atholl Papers: Blair Castle and National Register of Archives, West Register House, Edinburgh.

Breadalbane Muniments: Scottish Record Office.

Buchanan of Leny Papers: Scottish Record Office.

Gregorson of Ardtornish Papers: Scottish Record Office.

Leven and Melville Papers: Scottish Record Office.

MacGregor of Edinchip Papers: Glasgow University Archives.

Montrose Papers: Scottish Record Office.

Oliphant of Gask Papers: National Library of Scotland, Keeper of MSS.

HISTORICAL MSS

1603 Register of the Privy Council of Scotland. First series VI, 534–5: Clan Gregor's proscription.

1681–95 Register of the Privy Council: Scottish Record Office.

1689 Proceedings of the Estates of Parliament: No.56, p. 129 – Dundee's death.

1689–90 Proceedings of the Estates in Scotland, edited E.W.M. Balfour-Melville for Scottish History Society, Edinburgh, 1954–5.

1689–96 The Highland Papers: Maitland Club, Glasgow, 1945.

1703 Report of the Commision of Enquiry into the Massacre of Glencoe: Scottish National Library, Miscellaneous Tracts 1689–1704 (original at Public Record Office, London).

1718 War Office Historical Records, Public Record Office, Kew: *Inversnaid Barrack*, ref. WO 47/30, 288–9; plans in National Library, Edinburgh, ref. MS1648, Z311 and Z3 16–18.

1719 Report on the battle of Glen Shiel by the marquis of Tullibardine to the earl of Mar. Original in Mar's handwriting: Gask Papers.

1721 Parish Records, Balquhidder.

1729 Records of Kirk Session, Balquhidder.

1775 Original Papers on 'Secret History of Great Britain from Restoration to the Accession of George I,' edited James Macpherson. Historical MS Commission, *Third Report*: Scottish National Library.

NEWSPAPERS

1710–15   *The Scots Courant*:
Edinburgh Central
Library.

1712   *The Edinburgh Evening
Courant*, June 18–21.

1716   *Flying Post*, October
18 (the Army's raid on
Inversnaid).

1727   *Edinburgh Weekly
Journal*, 24 January.

1735   *Caledonian Mercury*,
January 9.

MAPS

1650   Glasgow
1700   Edinburgh
1747–87   Loch Lomond and
Trossachs, from *The
Highlands*, surveyed by
General William Roy.

Index

Clan names are listed alphabetically, but chiefs' christian names within each family are listed where possible in order of precedence.